The
MONETARY
ECONOMICS
of EUROPE

The contributions in this volume were commissioned by the Association for the Monetary Union of Europe in connection with its report to the European Parliament on Economic and Monetary Union. The report is published as two related volumes: *Europe's Monetary Future* and *The Monetary Economics of Europe: Causes of the EMS Crisis*.

The MONETARY ECONOMICS *of* EUROPE

CAUSES *of the* EMS CRISIS

Edited by
CHRISTOPHER JOHNSON
and STEFAN COLLIGNON

FAIRLEIGH DICKINSON UNIVERSITY PRESS
Rutherford • Madison • Teaneck

© 1994 by the European Parliament

All rights reserved. Authorization to photocopy items for internal or personal use, or the internal or personal use of specific cirents, is granted by the copyright owner, provided that a base fee of $10.00, plus eight cents per page, per copy is paid directly to the Copyright Clearance Center, 222 Rosewood Drive, Danvers, Massachusetts 01923. [0–8386–3607–1/94 $10.00 + 8¢ pp, pc.]

Associated University Presses
440 Forsgate Drive
Cranbury, NJ 08512

Library of Congress Cataloging-in-Publication Data

A record of this title is available from the Library of Congress

ISBN 0-8386-3607-1

Printed in Great Britain

CONTENTS

List of contributors   vii

INTRODUCTION   1
Christopher Johnson

Part I
COUNTRY CASE STUDIES OF EXCHANGE RATE INSTABILITY   9

1 The EMS Crisis and the French Franc   11
  Christian de Boissieu

2 Spain and the Real Exchange Rate Problem   18
  Philippe Bacchetta

3 What Coherent Strategy is there for the Escudo?   33
  Teodora Cardoso

4 The Irish Pound and the ERM: Lessons from the September Crisis and its Aftermath   39
  Brendan Walsh

5 Italy in the EMS: After Crisis, Salvation?   61
  Stefano Micossi and *Pier Carlo Padoan*

6 The UK and the Exchange Rate Mechanism   84
  Christopher Johnson

7 On Widening the EMS to Central and Eastern Europe   103
  Stefan Collignon

Part II
GENERAL ANALYSES   111

8 The Determinants of Realignment Expectations under the EMS   113
  Zhaohui Chen and *Alberto Giovannini*

9	Towards Monetary Union in Europe – Reforms of the EMS in the Perspective of Monetary Union *Niels Thygesen*	141
10	How to Save the EMS *Barry Eichengreen* and *Charles Wyplosz*	166
11	A Rethink for the Ecu? *Lord Cobbold*	184
12	Determinants of Long-term Interest Rates in Selected Countries: Towards a European Central Bank Policy Design *Wolfgang Gebauer and others*	189
13	Is There an 'EMS effect' in European Labour Markets? *Michael Artis* and *Paul Ormerod*	227
14	The Implications of Different Labour Market Regimes in Europe and the Lessons from the German Unification for the EMS and EMU *Heiner Flassbeck*	250
15	The Need for Real Convergence in a Monetary Union *Paul de Grauwe*	269

Appendix 1   Money Markets and Foreign Exchange Instruments in the Trading Room   281
Florence Sirel

Appendix 2   The Ecu Markets and the EMS Crisis   300
Taoufik Kharroubi

Index   305

CONTRIBUTORS

Michael Artis is Professor of Economics at the University of Manchester.

Philippe Bacchetta is at the Institut d'Analisi Economica, Barcelona.

Christian de Boissieu is Professor of Economics at the University of Paris and a member of the G7 Council.

Teodora Cardoso is Consultant at Banco Portuguès de Investimentò.

Zhaohui Chen is at the London School of Economics and Political Science.

Lord Cobbold is Chairman of Gaia Corporation.

Stefan Collignon is Research Director of the Association for the Monetary Union of Europe.

Barry Eichengreen is Professor of Economics at the University of California at Berkeley.

Heiner Flassbeck is at the Deutsche Institut für Wirtschaft, Berlin.

Wolfgang Gebauer is Professor of Economics at the Goethe University, Frankfurt am Main.

Alberto Giovannini is at the Graduate School of Business, Columbia University.

Paul de Grauwe is Professor of Economics at the Catholic University of Leuven.

Christopher Johnson is UK Adviser of the Association for the Monetary Union of Europe.

Taoufik Kharroubi is at Matif, Paris.

Stefano Micossi is Chief Economic Adviser to Confindustria, Rome.

Paul Ormerod is Director of the Henley Centre for Forecasting.

Pier Carlo Padoan is at the University of Rome.

Florence Sirel is a financial consultant.

Niels Thygesen is Professor of Economics at the University of Copenhagen.

Brendan Walsh is Professor of Economics at the University College of Dublin.

Charles Wyplosz is at INSEAD, Fontainebleau.

INTRODUCTION

Christopher Johnson

The economics profession has in recent years made enormous contributions to published literature on Economic and Monetary Union (EMU). Yet economics has been more the servant than the master of rapidly changing national and international policies in the field of economic and monetary integration. When the European Monetary System (EMS) was set up in 1978, few economists had a good word for it. It was regarded as a political move, with insecure economic and financial foundations. The success of the EMS saw a remarkable U-turn by many leading economists, encouraged by the EC Commission's path-breaking study *One Market, One Money*. The basis of the economic argument gradually changed from a survey of the economic conditions of an optimum currency area to a search for the foundations of credibility for a free market exchange rate system. After the two crises of September 1992 and July 1993 in the Exchange Rate Mechanism (ERM), many economists suddenly began to give convincing proofs of why it had been doomed all along – they had just not liked to say so out loud for fear of being accused of sabotage!

Economists' explanations of what went wrong are nevertheless helpful as diagnosis, leading to prognosis and to prescription for a healthy convalescence and eventual return to a long and happy working life for the ailing EMU. The contributions in this volume fell naturally into two halves: reports on individual countries and general analyses. (The more technical chapters by Sirel and Kharroubi appear as appendices.)

The countries chosen are those particularly affected by the ERM crisis of September 1992, in the sense that there was doubt about whether they would be able to maintain their central exchange rate parities. They fall into three categories: France successfully resisted the attacks on the franc; Ireland, Portugal and Spain devalued (more than once in each case) but remained within the ERM; Italy (after a short-lived devaluation) and the UK left the ERM altogether. Germany, the three Benelux countries and Denmark were not affected in the same way, although Belgium and Denmark have had problems more recently. Collignon's chapter on the EMS in Central and Eastern Europe is of interest for what it may offer as the monetary dimension of EU enlargement.

Seven countries thus did not change their central parities, and five either did so, left the ERM, or never joined it (Greece). The argument about whether ERM has been a success or a failure is like that about whether the glass is half full or half empty. At least there is no doubt that, as the Maastricht Treaty comes into operation, the ERM on which its monetary provisions are based still exists, if in a somewhat battered and depleted state. Glib talk of collapse should not mislead us into overlooking the fact that the foundations and the main building are still there, even if some of the outworks are in ruins.

As de Boissieu points out, the French franc's problems have been more of political than economic making. The closeness of the French referendum in September 1992, and the run-up to the April 1993 general election, caused high risk premia on French short-term interest rates, which were quickly reversed. In the case of the general election, it was not the result which was in doubt, but the policy of the Gaullist wing of the new government coalition, which turned out to be fully supportive of the ERM. The no-devaluation pledge of the new Prime Minister, M. Balladur, was observed by the brilliant and unexpected device of widening the ERM bands to 15 per cent in August 1993. France has nevertheless felt constrained not to cut short-term interest rates faster than Germany. Such a policy has been justified, not only by the desire to prevent further falls in the exchange rate, but by the hearteningly low long-term interest rate, even if fewer French than German borrowers have access to long-term finance.

Spain, to judge by Bacchetta's disillusioned survey, is a good example of how the ERM is only a framework, and cannot in itself deal with structural defects in the economy, which also require tough domestic policies. This is particularly true of late entrants, whose domestic policies before entry had been run on quite different lines from those required after membership. It is hard to quarrel with his conclusion that Spain entered at too high an exchange rate, and badly needed to devalue its currency after a few years. This was all the more true because the high exchange rate was surprisingly ineffective in bringing down inflation, particularly during the boom at the end of the 1980s.

The high interest rates which were the price of Spain's continued membership were an important factor in the economic slowdown which, more than ERM membership, reduced the inflation rate close to convergence levels. This success was achieved only at the price of an unemployment rate of over 20 per cent. Even though three devaluations have restored competitiveness, a weak Spanish government still had to combine an incomes pact to restrain pay rises with labour market reforms designed to reduce unemployment. Spain thus encapsulates in its most extreme form a policy problem which the EU countries as a whole have recognized rather late in the day as a potentially fatal obstacle to EMU – high and in many countries rising unemployment. EMU is not in itself responsible for unemployment, since its members would have had to raise interest rates to defend their currencies even outside the ERM. However, EMU runs the risk of being blamed for whatever economic problems governments have not been able to deal with themselves.

Portugal has shared with Spain the defects of an overvalued exchange rate leading, as Cardoso points out, to inflationary capital inflows. Devaluation was equally necessary, all the more so in view of the greater integration of the Iberian economy brought about by the two countries' simultaneous entry into the EU. Portugal's late entry into the ERM in April 1992 was even worse timed than Spain's, since the exchange rate could be maintained only for a matter of months. Portugal has performed far better than Spain in labour market flexibility, with one of the lowest unemployment rates in Europe, but has not done much better in controlling pay increases, and may thus find it difficult to avoid further realignments of the exchange rate.

Ireland, as Walsh argues, has had a remarkable record in convergence on economic fundamentals, and yet was no more able to avoid devaluation than Spain and Portugal, in spite of its much lower inflation rate. The unemployment level of over 20 per cent, about the same as Spain's, made it difficult, and not credible, to keep Irish interest rates at high nominal levels – and amazingly high real levels, in view of the low inflation rate – for very long, particularly in a British-type financial system dominated by variable short-term rates. The high degree of integration of the Irish and British economies also made it hard for Ireland to stay up with the DM as the pound fell in late 1992. However, the Irish case has demonstrated that devaluation need not impair subsequent credibility of the new exchange rate as long as the fundamentals are sound.

Italy, although it had been in the ERM from the outset, did not succeed in adapting domestic policies to the new framework any better than the latecomers. During the early years, Italy was able to avoid becoming uncompetitive thanks to periodic realignments and the good export performance of manufacturing industry. After 1987, the lira quickly became uncompetitive because of the lack of realignments (apart from the small 1990 change) and excessive pay increases, as Micossi and Padoan point out. Italy, like Spain, allowed public sector wages to rise too rapidly – thus worsening the already divergent public deficit – and failed to make the high exchange rate bite on domestic inflation. Only by high nominal interest rates was Italy able to claw back some part of its failing credibility, and strenuous attempts to reduce the large fiscal deficit were overshadowed by a series of crises along the bumpy road of political reform.

Italy, like the UK, has found life easier outside the ERM, but, unlike the UK, wants to return when possible because of its political commitment to EMU. The period of exile is at least being used to good effect both to reform the corrupt political system and to improve domestic economic policies in a way that ERM membership never did. Italy has de-indexed wages, but needs to curb public expenditure, before it can regain credibility as a reformed character back inside the ERM. The 15 per cent bands might, however, make it easier for Italy to re-enter earlier than otherwise. At least Italy has shared with Spain and the UK the 'free lunch' following devaluation, of enhanced export competitiveness without inflation through higher import prices.

The UK is a special case in more ways than one. Both political ambivalence and the desire to retain control over national monetary policy kept the UK out of the ERM until October 1990, and then contributed to its undignified exit less than two years later. The debate about whether to join the ERM cast its shadow over British domestic policy right from the 1978 negotiations – which did result in the UK joining the EMS though not the ERM – through the 1980s. The Thatcher and Lawson memoirs show how this debate split the government on numerous occasions, with the Prime Minister's economic adviser, Professor Sir Alan Walters, at least remaining consistent in his opposition to British entry.

As Johnson argues, the pound went into the ERM at an exchange rate suited to bringing inflation down, but needed a downwards realignment once the result was achieved, and competitiveness reasserted itself as the long-run requirement for the credibility of the currency in the ERM and the viability of manufacturing industry in the Single European Market. Although the brief period of membership was quite successful in helping to bring down both inflation and nominal interest rates, the accumulated past inflation differential could not be ignored. The chances of a real devaluation by means of lower than average wage and price rises always seemed unlikely in the free-for-all British pay bargaining system. Nominal devaluation, accompanied by lower interest rates, allowed unemployment to fall and recovery to be shifted forward in time.

One of the paradoxes of the ERM is that the British government failed to retrieve its popularity in spite of breaking loose from the ERM shackles, while the new centre-right French government achieved popularity, in its early months at least, in spite of continuing to bind itself to the Bundesbank. The wider 15 per cent bands would have made it possible for the UK to rejoin the ERM, but this has been excluded because of right-wing backbench political opposition until after the next general election. The UK is also a prime example of how quickly healthy budgetary positions can diverge outside the 3 per cent of GDP limit set by the Maastricht Treaty. It remains to be seen whether the UK will not find it more difficult to achieve the convergence targets – which it accepts on domestic grounds – outside the ERM framework, and without the spur of wishing to opt into Stage III of EMU in 1996 or 1998.

The more general contributions themselves are of two types. One sets out detailed analyses and policy reforms of the ERM itself, while the other addresses the wider economic setting within which the ERM succeeds or fails. Chen and Giovannini give a convincing account of ERM realignments. In the first eight years, he gets the intuitively appealing result that staying close to the central parity, and lengthening the time since the last realignment, make the next realignment less probable. Nothing succeeds like success. However, this analysis breaks down, as he points out, after 1987, because after some years of no realignments, the time since the last realignment ceases to be a significant factor in predicting the next one. Some have even gone so far as to say that the next realignment came to seem more likely rather than less so with the passage of time, once the spell of the pseudo-monetary union had been broken.

Thygesen suggests ways of reforming the ERM to make it more like a monetary union for those that can stand the pace. Although the move to wider bands seems to contradict such ideas, the arguments for closer cooperation within a hard core of strong currencies, broadening the DM anchor, remain valid. It is consistent with Chen's findings to point out that wider bands are of little help in making central parities more credible. Thygesen is sceptical, however, about some of the current ideas for closer monetary integration, on the grounds that they lack political support. His proposals for a monitoring procedure for the degree of sterilization, and for greater central bank independence, point the way to how the new European Monetary Institute may develop in a politically uncontroversial manner.

A frequently expressed reform proposal is that toyed with by M. Delors, the EU Commission President, to reintroduce capital controls. This is put forward by Wyplosz and Eichengreen, but does not appear in the main AMUE report. Although their suggested measures would be indirect, by requiring non-interest bearing deposits on foreign exchange exposure, they would have the same effect as capital controls. They would be unlikely to work, because foreign exchange business would shift to unregulated financial centres. They would also be difficult to apply because banks' foreign exchange positions vary enormously from one minute to the next, and any snapshot measure of exposure would be subject to window-dressing. It would be even harder to police the increasingly important activities of non-banks in the market. Such measures could not save the EMS, but they would destroy the freedom of capital movements finally achieved as part of the Single European Market by mid-1990.

The Ecu itself receives attention from Cobbold. Although his proposals run counter to the EU Commissions' interpretation of the Maastricht Treaty, they provide a useful focus for discussion. They combine the twin merits of making the Ecu both stronger and more user-friendly by linking it in a simple 1:2 relationship with the DM, and fixing the percentages rather than the amounts of the basket constituents. As he points out, the difficulties of 'selling' the new currency to public opinion could be unnecessarily compounded by outlandish conversion factors running to several places of decimals. This idea of hardening the existing Ecu should not, however, be confused with the UK 'hard Ecu' project, see Johnson, which would have confusingly set up another Ecu beside the basket Ecu, thus giving not 13 but 14 competing currencies!

Gebauer's analysis of the relationship between short and long-term interest rates is of importance not only in understanding what went wrong, but in planning the single monetary policy which EMU will require. It is a timely warning against leaving too much of the fight against inflation to central banks using short-term interest rate instruments. While long-term rates fluctuate less from week to week than short-term, they cannot lead a life of their own in a universe of Platonic fundamentals.

The econometrics show that long-term are influenced by short-term rates, though with an elasticity more like a half than one, and after variable time-lags – with the notable exception of the UK, where there appears to be no link between short and long-term rates. If it is long-term rates that mainly affect economic activity – and this varies across countries – then short-term rates must to some extent affect it too, both directly and through long-term rates. Gebauer and his colleagues also point to the importance of the term structure of interest rates, and see it as a better monetary target than broad money.

The remaining three contributors focus on the labour market, which policy makers have also rediscovered as the key to the success of EMU. It is short-sighted to think of convergence as to do only with price inflation, without taking into account wages as one of the main determinants of prices. Artis points to the importance of non-wage labour costs, which diverge even more than wage costs, in determining levels of employment and competitiveness in a monetary union. (These divergences are well documented in Table 5.6 of Micossi and Padoan.) He is not entirely convinced that there has been an EMS effect in labour markets, although the explanatory power of German wages over those in other ERM members suggests that there has.

The behaviour of UK wages during the two years of membership also indicates some marginal improvement over previous experience. It will be interesting to see whether the gains are thrown away with the UK again outside the ERM, although deregulation might be thought to have brought about some permanent structural change for the better. Wage behaviour should be more sharply influenced by a regime in which exchange rates are assumed not to change than by one in which devaluations are taken to be possible. Yet pay increases in 1987–1992 were influenced more by the peak of the business cycle than by the supposed fixity of ERM exchange rates. The moral may be that no fixed exchange rate regime is ever totally credible compared with a single currency area; conversely even under flexible exchange rates suitable domestic arrangements can deliver pay restraint.

The importance of different national pay bargaining arrangements, and the way in which wage differentials are handled, is stressed in a notable contribution by Flassbeck, which has something in common with the Layard school of analysis at the London School of Economics. Any German economist must be dismayed by the speed with which wages in East Germany have been dragged upwards by the level prevailing in West Germany. Yet a monetary union based on political union – the German case – is different in kind from one based on different nation-states – the EMU case. There is no reason why workers in lower-income members of the EMU should expect soon to equalize wages with those in high-income countries, although they may legitimately hope to narrow the gap gradually thanks to greater potential for increasing total factor productivity from a lower base.

While de Grauwe argues in favour of real convergence, he interprets this more as being between regions of one country than between countries which may have very divergent starting points in GDP per head. He points out that there is more labour market flexibility in terms of wages and mobility within than between countries, and points out that such flexibility will also be needed over the whole EU area if EMU is to work without unacceptably high unemployment costs. He is in favour of incomes policy of the 'backstop' kind used in Belgium, and against fiscal transfers from rich to poor regions, on the grounds that, once instituted, they become irreversible. (Will the transfers from West to East Germany or from the EU core countries to the Mediterranean countries become like those from northern to southern Italy? One can only hope not.)

Labour market flexibility is clearly a high priority if the EMU show is to get back on the road and reach its destination. While countries can learn from each other's best practice, and EU social policy has a role (exemplified by the Social Chapter), in the last resort there must be a good deal of subsidiarity. Labour markets have different histories and structures across countries, and cannot easily or quickly be harmonized. Some countries may find national incomes policy still has a part to play, while others may prefer to rely on deregulated firm and plant bargaining to achieve similar results. The wide variety of employer social security tax rates needs to be harmonized downwards, but competition may well ensure that countries with the highest rates bring them down without waiting to be told. Regulations on minimum pay levels, working hours, compensation for dismissal, and closed shops need to be reduced, while minimum standards of health, safety and workplace rights are maintained.

It has sometimes been suggested that a minimum unemployment percentage should be added to the EMU convergence criteria. If this were to be, say, 7 per cent, as being the non-accelerating inflation rate of unemployment (NAIRU) for many countries, it would give a convergence target within which a number of recession-affected countries need to come. (Some smaller countries with unusually high unemployment rates might need to aim at a specified reduction rather than an absolute level in the unemployment percentage.) The wide differences in national unemployment definitions would first need to be harmonized, and based on labour force surveys rather than benefit entitlements.

The low interest rates which EMU was originally supposed to deliver would themselves help to reduce unemployment by stimulating economic activity, but structural labour market reforms are also needed. While monetary policy can thus play some part in reducing unemployment, labour market policy can also contribute to the achievement of monetary union. The economic and the monetary sides of EMU are closely linked, and it would be unwise to give one priority over the other. Until 1992, the monetary side had moved too far ahead of the economic. After 1992, there is the opposite danger that the economic side will move too far ahead of the monetary. The central banks working together in the European Monetary Institute from the beginning of 1994 will no doubt seek to avert this danger as they settle down to their Treaty responsibility for developing monetary cooperation, promoting the use of the private Ecu, and overseeing the Exchange Rate Mechanism.

Part I

COUNTRY CASE STUDIES OF
EXCHANGE RATE INSTABILITY

1

THE EMS CRISIS AND THE FRENCH FRANC

Christian de Boissieu

The purpose of this chapter is to present some reflections on the crisis of the EMS and the recent evolution of the French franc. The two topics are interrelated: the turmoil in the overall EMS since the Danish 'no' (June 1992) and particularly since September 1992 spilled over into many EC currencies, including the French franc which, by standard calculations, was not (and is not) overvalued vis-à-vis the DM. Conversely, speculative attacks against the French currency jeopardized, at one point, the very existence of the EMS and its Exchange Rate Mechanism.

SOME LESSONS FROM THE CRISIS OF THE EMS

The crisis of the EMS, initiated by the Danish 'no', the narrow 'yes' in France and the dramatic turmoil in European foreign exchange markets in September 1992, is not over. But after the French elections, and the successive interest rate drops in Germany and other EMS countries, the pressure has receded. Several lessons could be drawn from the events since the summer of 1992.

(1) The crisis of the EMS was not coincidental. It was generated by several factors, one of them being the confusion between phase 1 (opened since July 1990) and phase 3 (which will begin as of January 1997 or January 1999) of the transition to EMU. It was a mistake not to adjust the parities of the exchange rate mechanism (ERM) between January 1987 and September 1992, and to create such an overvaluation of the pound, the lira, the peseta, the escudo, etc. Instead of being an exception to the interplay of fundamentals (inflation rates, unit wage costs, etc.) the crisis was an exact expression of it. One direct implication: we must not forget that the ERM corresponds to a system of 'fixed but adjustable' exchange rates. During phases 1 and 2, parities

will have to be adjusted, since they must share the burden of the adjustment to persistent divergences. The present set of parities is not that on which to base the transition to a single currency.

(2) The crisis of the EMS has jeopardized the credibility of the entire monetary integration process in Europe. Urgent initiatives have to be taken in order to restore this credibility. Given the position of the UK and Italy, they must come from deeper Franco-German monetary cooperation. From the extensively cited 'inconsistency triangle', we know that perfect capital mobility, fixed exchange rates and autonomous national monetary policies are incompatible. One way or another, monetary cooperation is required to reconcile financial liberalization with stable exchange rates.

(3) The role of the DM as the anchor of the EMS and the ERM has been strengthened by the crisis, despite the lasting fragility of the German economy created by the unification process. Several proxies illustrate monetary asymmetry, such as market shares (for invoicing imports and exports, for holding official reserves, etc.) and risk premia vis-à-vis German interest rates. Whereas market shares vary slowly (e.g., the share of the DM for invoicing world exports fluctuated between 10 and 13 per cent in the 1980s), risk premia are exposed to short-run movements and, for several EMS currencies, they widened markedly during the second half of 1992 (see below).

(4) The management of the crisis has been based on interest rate policy, affirmation of monetary cooperation between France and Germany and activation of the facilities organized by the Basle-Nyborg accord (1987) as regards intra-marginal interventions. In this respect, the implication of the Bundesbank was very effective for the defence of the French franc.

(5) The scenario of a two-speed (or rather multi-speed) Europe, de facto accepted by the Maastricht Treaty and its convergence criteria, now prevails. The turmoil in the EMS speeded up an unavoidable development, the split between the 'hard core' (Germany, France, Benelux, with a big question mark concerning countries such as Denmark and Ireland) and the 'periphery'. As far as the precise pattern of the multi-speed Europe is concerned, the concrete implementation of convergence criteria will be the crux. The loosening of fiscal policy in several EC member countries is going to raise a huge difficulty for compliance with Maastricht criteria. According to a recent EC commission forecast, the average budget deficit of EC countries will reach 5.75 per cent of EC gross domestic product, much above the 3 per cent limit set by the Maastricht Treaty (for public sector deficits). European monetary integration will be valuable, according to most cost–benefit analyses, only if a certain number of countries are, in due course, eligible for phase 3. Given the economic outlook for Europe and the timetable adopted in the Treaty, this would require a more pragmatic approach to convergence criteria concerning public deficits and debts. Pragmatism does not mean laxity, and the search for more flexibility has to be contained within certain limits.

THE FRENCH FRANC IN THE LIGHT OF THE EMS CRISIS

The situation before the general elections (March 1993)

During the period June 1992 to March 1993, a dramatic increase in risk premia via-à-vis German rates took place (Figures 1.1 and 1.2). For short-term rates, they passed from 20 basis points in May 1992 to 400 basis points in February 1993. Regarding long-term rates, fluctuations were more moderate but still significant: risk premia increased from 40 to 100 basis points during the same reference period. How to explain the dynamics of risk premia, in the light of the French macroeconomic record? Was there a 'French puzzle'?

Several French fundamentals were and still are very competitive by European standards: inflation and growth of unit wage costs have been much lower than the German figures for a couple of years; French trade was significantly positive in 1992, after an extended sequence of trade deficits, and remained in surplus in 1993; during the period 1991–1992, French real growth was higher than the European average; the budget deficit as a proportion of GDP was low by international standards. But market operators care not only about inflation, wage costs, trade balance and budget imbalances; they also monitor other fundamentals. In the case of France, three of them played an important role:

1. The risk of a devaluation of the French franc vis-à-vis the DM. Until the general elections, a devaluation of the franc was probable, whereas the probability of devaluing the DM was and still is nil. This is another aspect of the monetary asymmetry within the ERM.
2. Since mid-1992, many market operators have been worrying about the social and political consequences of the dramatic rise in unemployment figures. The overall rate of unemployment is around 10.5 per cent, continuously increasing and showing specific features (high youth unemployment, size of long-term unemployment). According to convergent simulations, 3 per cent real growth would be necessary in order to stabilize the unemployment situation. In 1992, real growth was just above 1 per cent, and for 1993 only 0.5 per cent. The social risk derived from the labour market situation is partially embedded in the risk premia vis-à-vis German rates.
3. The dependence of the Banque de France on the government has generated some doubt concerning the continuity of French monetary policy.

It is quite impossible to assess the respective weights of the three factors presented above. Nevertheless, their interplay was crucial and overwhelming when compared to the role of more traditional fundamentals. The French experience is not a puzzle provided that fundamentals are not limited to inflation and the trade balance, etc., and that they include social and institutional risks.

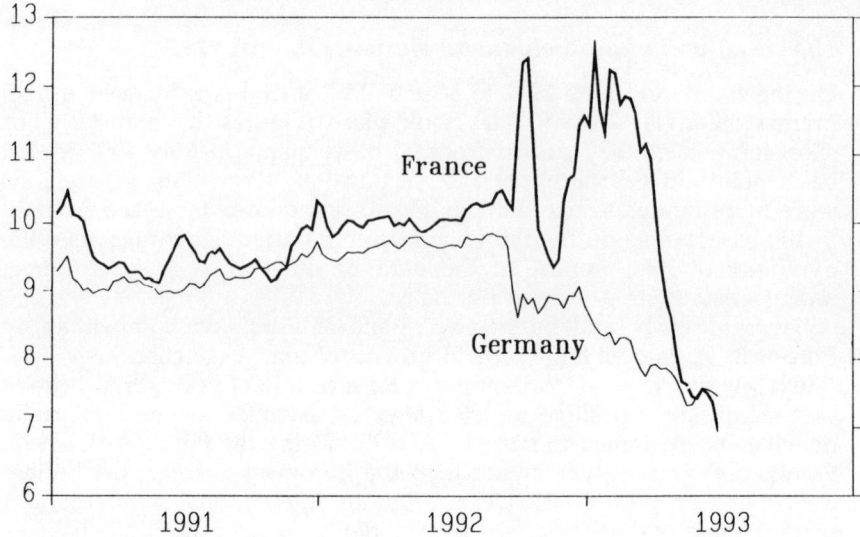

Figure 1.1 Short-term interest rates: France and Germany (three-month Euro rate, %) Last observation 25 June 1993

Source: WEFA.

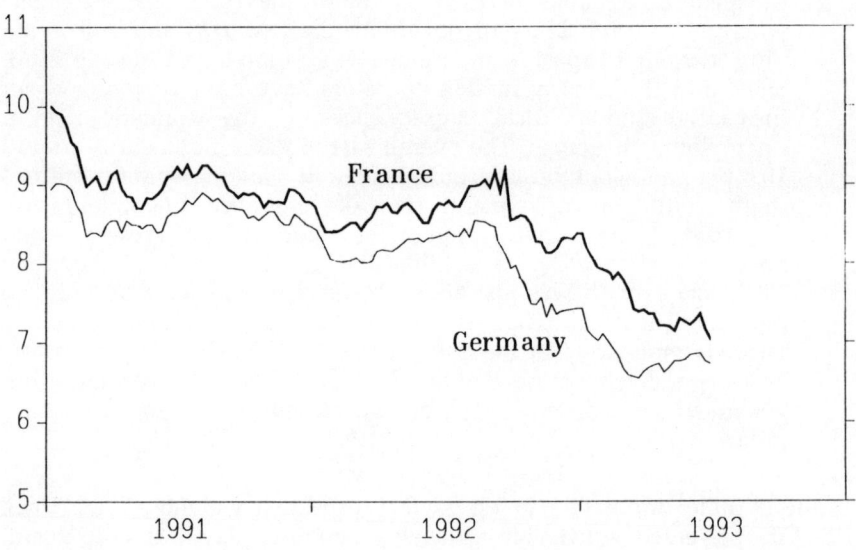

Figure 1.2 Long-term interest rates: France and Germany (%) Last observation 25 June 1993

Source: WEFA.

After the elections

In April 1993, risk premia dropped markedly and returned to 100 basis points for short-term rates and 50 basis points for long term rates. This dramatic reduction could be explained by the credibility of the new government, its firm commitment to FFr–DM parity and its first policy measures. A law giving independence to the Banque de France will be voted by the new National Assembly and the Senate. Despite some possible discussion within the Gaullist Party, it will be supported by a large majority. This law borrows some of its features from the Maastricht Treaty (and the rules concerning the European System of Central Banks and the European Central Bank), the functioning of the Bundesbank, and the Board of Governors of the Federal Reserve System. Nevertheless, it is not a pure aggregation (or combination) of those references, since the new government is keen to promote a 'French model' of an independent central bank. According to the new law, decisions concerning interest rates and credit policy will be taken by a council of monetary policy, chaired by the governor (appointed for a fixed term and irrevocably) and composed of nine independent members. The government will stay in charge of exchange rate policy, the Banque de France being responsible for its implementation (this is a standard formulation, introduced in the Maastricht Treaty, in the law giving its independence to the Bank of Spain (Article 6), etc.). A controversial topic is the supervision of banks. In France, the Banking Commission (Commission Bancaire) is closely linked to the Banque de France, whereas the equivalent body in Germany is attached to the Ministry of Finance, but works in close cooperation with the specialized department of the Bundesbank. Several experts advocated the implementation of the German solution in France. My own view is that, during the transition to EMU (namely, until January 1997 or 1999), the status quo is preferable. The new law does not change the organization of prudential control in France. In the new financial environment, monetary policy and prudential control are more and more interwoven. Moreover, the Banque de France has developed a deep expertise in banking supervision and control. Given the vagueness of the Maastricht Treaty on this aspect, the relevant issue is the organization of prudential policy in phase 3, with the European Central Bank and the single currency. It is likely that the management of banking crises will remain, in phase 3, decentralized and subject to the subsidiarity rule. Nevertheless, given the overlapping of domestic banking systems in Europe, harmonization of regulations and coordination of prudential policies must be rather ambitious.

Granting independence to the Banque de France will enlarge the continuity and credibility of French monetary policy. What could be the impact of this institutional change on risk premia vis-à-vis German rates? Many market operators have already included the autonomy of the Banque de France into their expectations and behaviour.

Nevertheless, some residual influence could be expected (between 10 and 30 basis points?).

Risk premia in French short-term rates have reverted to negative figures since June 1993, whilst they stay close to zero for long-term rates. Could the figures obtained for Belgium and the Netherlands (around 40 basis points vis-à-vis short-term German rates) be considered as a benchmark? Could we expect France to go beyond that and to gain more autonomy vis-à-vis German rates? On the one hand, the public debt ratio is much lower in France than in Belgium. On the other hand, France, unlike the Netherlands, does not belong to the DM zone (with a narrow band of fluctuation). And social risks generated by the development of unemployment are likely to put a floor under the level of negative risk premia vis-à-vis German rates. In early July 1993, German short-term rates were above French rates by a gap close to 30–40 basis points.

SCENARIOS FOR THE EMS

Coming back to the EMS as a whole, three basic scenarios could be envisaged from now.

1. To return to the first phase of the ERM (that of the early 1980s), with frequent parity realignments to cope with persistent macroeconomic divergences. An extreme version of this scenario corresponds to the generalization of the British and Italian attitudes and the transition to floating exchange rates in Europe (i.e. to the end of the ERM). We must consider an important caveat: what could (perhaps) be good for the UK and Italy, whilst other European countries stay in the ERM, would not be the same with the extension of floating exchange rates and the risk of competitive devaluations.
2. To consolidate the EMS and ERM and comply with the timetable of Maastricht as regards the transition to EMU. Consolidation means further drops in European nominal and real interest rates, new activations of the Basle-Nyborg accord in case of a crisis, closer monetary cooperation through existing bodies (the committee of governors etc.), and a reflection concerning the desirable bands of fluctuation during phase 2. At some point, during phase 2, it could be desirable for the French franc to enter the DM zone, and to have a 1 per cent margin vis-à-vis the German currency. But it would be also risky and potentially counter-productive to speed up this transition, as long as the EMS remains fragile. Market operators would be keen to test the new bands, with possible adverse effects on the DM–FFr parity.
3. To speed up the transition to EMU, given the risks generated by a gradual approach. This scenario means that the length of phase 2

would be reduced. Shortening the transition could only apply to 'hard core' countries, even if some convergence criteria were loosened somewhat.

Before the French elections and the 22 April 1993 drop in German leading rates, the probability of the first scenario was fairly high. Since then, the second scenario is more likely. But the major challenges are still ahead. Phase 2 is both too short to allow European adjustment (e.g., adjustment of public deficits and debts), and too long compared with its institutional content, which is rather modest (the creation of the European Monetary Institute (EMI), endowed with limited monetary power). In order to face the challenges of phase 2, the EMS and the ERM have to be greatly strengthened. Besides consolidation measures referred to above, a reflection on convergence criteria and multilateral surveillance procedures in Europe and concrete steps to favour the regeneration of the private Ecu market seem urgent. The EMI will not be a true central bank. But it will have to be active in its fields of intervention (harmonization of monetary and financial statistics, closer monetary cooperation, promotion of the Ecu market) and also to be ambitious on more optional aspects, such as the pooling of a significant proportion of official reserves of EC central banks and possible interventions on foreign exchange markets.

2
SPAIN AND THE REAL EXCHANGE RATE PROBLEM

Philippe Bacchetta

INTRODUCTION

One of the main features of the Spanish economy in the 1980s has been the gradual decline in inflation. Figure 2.1 shows that inflation went down from about 15 per cent in 1982 to less than 5 per cent in 1988. With the hope of enhancing the credibility of its monetary policy and further reducing inflation, Spain joined the Exchange Rate Mechanism (ERM) of the European Monetary System (EMS) in June 1989 with a ±6 per cent band of fluctuation. Inflationary discipline, however, did not materialize and the inflation rate actually increased to more than 6 per cent on average in the period 1989–1992. This rate was almost 2 per cent higher than the average of other ERM countries. As the nominal value of the peseta remained stable until September 1992, its real value increased.

Figure 2.2 shows the evolution of the trade-weighted real exchange rate index of the peseta with respect to industrial countries and based on the consumer price index (CPI). The appreciation has been practically continuous from mid-1983 to August 1992 (the total appreciation was 44 per cent over this period). The two devaluations in the autumn of 1992 have corrected the situation, but the value of the index is still higher than in previous years. For example, the value of the index in March 1993 was 24 per cent higher than its average over the period 1970–1979. At the same time, a significant current account deficit has developed. From a surplus of 1.8 per cent of GDP in 1986, the current account reached a deficit of 3.2 per cent in 1992.

There are two basic questions related to the above developments. The first is whether the present level of the peseta in the ERM is sustainable. The second is why did ERM membership not help reduce

SPAIN

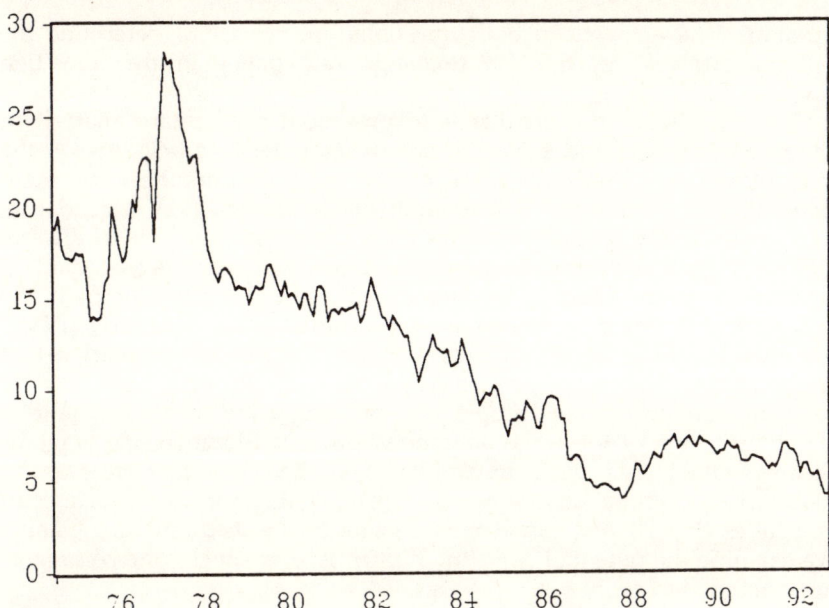

Figure 2.1 Spanish inflation (consumer price index, Jan. 1975–March 1993)

Source: Instituto Nacional de Estadistica.

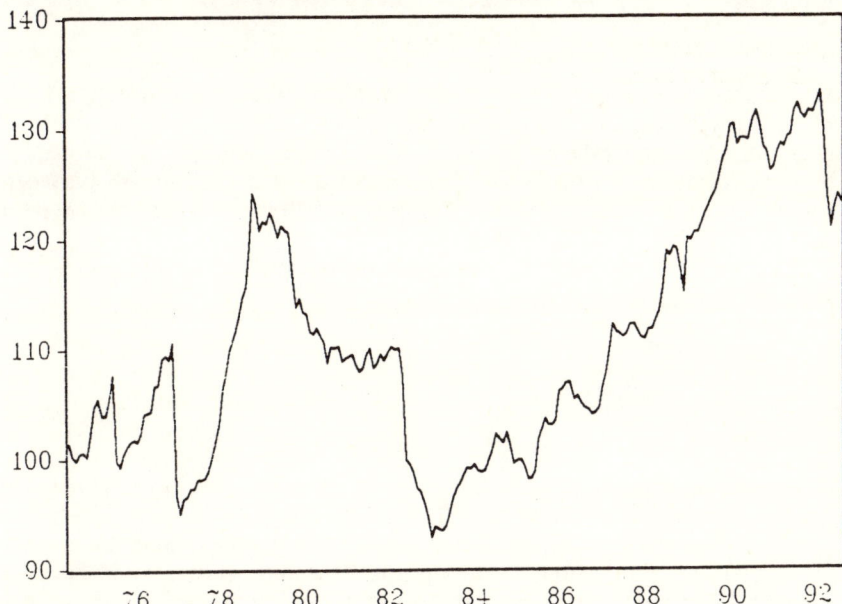

Figure 2.2 Real effective peseta exchange rate vis-à-vis developed countries. Based on CPI indices

Source: Banco de España.

inflation. The answers to both questions are crucial to determine the optimal strategy for Spanish exchange rate policy in the transition towards EMU.

The objective of this chapter is to provide a preliminary analysis of the recent inflation and exchange rate developments to help answer the two questions posed above. The next section examines the main determinants of the real appreciation of the peseta. It is argued that strong demand and capital inflows played an important role in the late 1980s, while wage increases were the most significant determinant in most recent years. These factors are added to a higher price inertia in the non-tradeable sector combined with a disinflationary monetary policy. We then examine the developments in the Spanish labour market that might explain the recent growth in wages. Two elements appear to be relevant: an increasing proportion of temporary contracts and a decentralization of the wage bargaining process. Moreover, no wage or income policy has been implemented in the last few years. The penultimate section discusses the sustainability of the peseta and concludes that its real value must decline in the medium run. Finally, we examine the potential adjustment process, and concluding comments are offered.

EXPLAINING THE REAL APPRECIATION OF THE PESETA

The previous section has shown the strong appreciation of the peseta in real terms in the late 1980s and early 1990s. To determine the optimal nominal exchange rate policy, it is crucial to understand the causes of this appreciation. To organize ideas, it is useful to distinguish between traded and non-traded goods.[1] Assume that there is a proportion α of non-traded and $(1-\alpha)$ of traded goods.

If P_N and P_T represent the prices of non-traded and traded goods, the aggregate price level P is:

$$P = \alpha\, P_N + (1-\alpha) P_T. \tag{1}$$

We can assume a similar relationship in other countries where we denote foreign variables by α^*, P_N^*, P_T^*, and P^*.

What distinguishes traded from non-traded goods is that the former are subject to international competition. This means that there exists a direct relationship between domestic and foreign traded goods of the following type:

$$\tau \cdot P_T = E \cdot P_T^*, \tag{2}$$

where E is the nominal exchange rate (e.g. Ptas/DM) and τ represents deviations from purchasing power parity (PPP) in traded goods. As the nominal exchange rate E is more flexible than prices, these deviations will appear in the short run with fluctuations in E. These deviations, however, are short-lived and should disappear over time. Over a longer horizon, a major factor determining τ is the presence of tariffs, as they impede the arbitrage between Spanish and foreign goods. For example, if there are tariffs in Spain but not in other countries, τ will be less than 1.

Defining the real exchange rate, R, to be equal to EP^*/P,[2] we can use equations (1) and (2) to write:

$$R = \tau \cdot \frac{\alpha^*(P_N^*/P_T^*) + (1-\alpha^*)}{\alpha(P_N/P_T) + (1-\alpha)}. \tag{3}$$

Hence, the real exchange rate appreciates (R decreases) when the relative price of non-tradeables to tradeables increases more in Spain than in other countries. There will also be an appreciation when τ decreases or α increases (assuming $P_N/P_T > 1$).

An explanation of the real appreciation of the peseta can therefore be provided in terms of the ratios of traded to non-traded goods prices. Changes in these ratios are likely to explain most changes in the real exchange rate, at least in the medium run. The parameters α and α^*, i.e. the proportion of traded to non-traded goods consumed, can only move slowly. There might be more significant movements in τ, i.e. in the deviations from PPP for traded goods.

As the exact price ratio of non-tradeables to tradeables is in general not known, a proxy is typically taken. Figure 2.3 shows the monthly development of the ratio of the price of services with respect to the price of industrial goods (as components of the CPI) between 1976 and 1992. Although a rise in this ratio can be observed in other European countries,[3] the increase experienced by Spain since 1986 has been dramatic, and much larger than the average of European countries.

It is often argued that the higher inflation in the non-traded goods sector is explained by lack of competition and other structural problems. While these features can explain why prices move differently in the two sectors, they cannot explain the inflation differential itself. Such a differential must be explained by exogenous changes in other economic variables.

Most determinants of the ratio P_N/P_T can be derived by using the so-called dependent economy model.[4] The predictions of the simplest version of the model are intuitive. First, the ratio P_N/P_T is affected by relative changes in productivity. If productivity in the tradeable sector increases faster than in the non-tradeable sector, P_N/P_T increases.

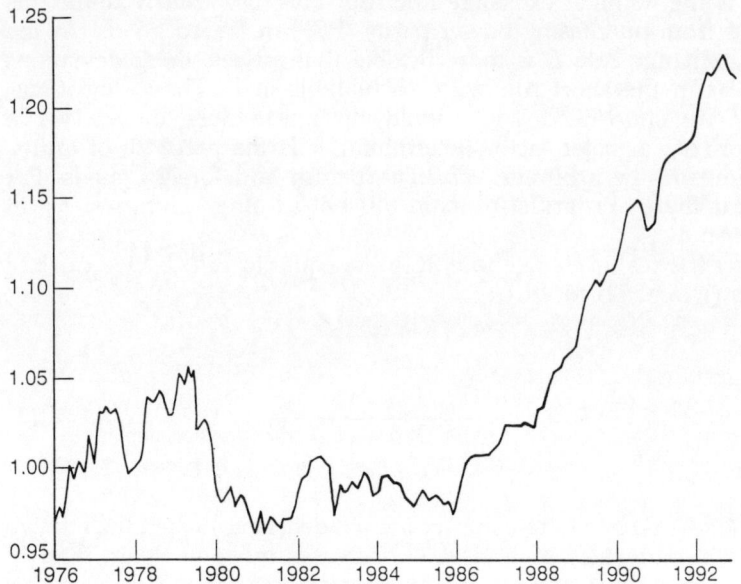

Figure 2.3 Price of services relative to price of industrial goods in Spain, 1976–1992 (components of the CPI index)

Source: Banco de España.

Second, a general increase in demand increases P_N/P_T: as P_T depends on foreign competition, any inflationary pressure has more effect on P_N. Third, a capital inflow generally increases P_N/P_T by increasing demand.[5] Finally, the model can be extended to include a non-competitive labour market, for example by introducing trade union bargaining over wages.[6] In this case, there can be an exogenous wage increase, for example through an increase in union bargaining power or real wage target. This wage increase can be shown to increase P_N/P_T: the higher labour costs can be transmitted to prices in the non-traded goods sector, but not in the traded goods sector due to foreign competition. A corollary of the increase in wages is a reduction in employment in the traded goods sector. Finally, it should be noted that except in the case of productivity change, an appreciation of the real exchange rate is associated with a current account deficit. To summarize, the determinants of the price ratio are: productivity gains in the tradeable sector, increase in demand, capital inflows, and a wage increase.

The impact of changes in these variables depends on the structure of the economy. An important change in the Spanish economy is its opening up. While the ratio of imports to GDP was less than 20 per cent in 1975, it was larger than 35 per cent in 1991. This phenomenon means that the tradeable sector is much more sensitive to foreign competition and the price of traded goods is more closely linked to foreign prices. As there is no such pressure for non-traded goods, the differences between the two sectors, and the distortions in the non-tradeables sector, become more apparent. Consequently, the factors examined have a much larger impact on relative prices today than before the 1980s.

The relative significance of the four determinants mentioned is examined below. There is, however, an additional potential explanation that cannot be easily represented in the dependent economy model. In the presence of a disinflationary process, like that experienced by Spain, there might be a significant inflation inertia for several reasons.[7] Because the tradeable sector is likely to be more competitive, this inertia will be stronger in the non-tradeable sector. Hence inflation will decline faster in the tradeable than in the non-tradeable sector and the relative price will increase. While this explanation is certainly part of the story, it cannot explain why total inflation increased in both sectors in 1988/89.

What are the other sources of the increase in the price of non-traded to traded goods in Spain in the late 1980s and early 1990s? The first determinant mentioned above, productivity, is not a good candidate. It is often argued that the potential for productivity gains is much higher in the tradeable than in the non-tradeable sector, in particular given the large share of services in the latter. Hence, when the economy grows the tradeable sector should become more productive and the currency appreciate in real terms. This is the so-called Balassa–Samuelson effect. In the late 1980s, however, productivity growth in Spain was lower than in other European countries.[8] Figure 2.4 shows the development of total labour productivity between 1975 and 1992 and shows a clear decline between 1985 and 1991. This period coincides precisely with the period of real exchange rate appreciation. Nevertheless, at a disaggregated level, productivity in services was lower than for industrial goods. Between 1987 and 1991, productivity increased on average by 0.2 per cent in services and by 1.2 per cent in industrial goods excluding construction (*Annual Report*, Bank of Spain). However, this increase in the productivity of tradeables is small compared to the real appreciation. Moreover, it cannot explain the increase in the current account deficit. Hence, the change in productivity cannot be a significant explanation.

Domestic demand was particularly strong in the late 1980s. For example, its average growth between 1986 and 1989 had been 7.5 per cent in real terms. The main source of increase was investment (13.9 per cent), even though the other components (government consumption, 7 per cent, and private consumption, 5.4 per cent) grew at a relatively strong rate.[9] An important factor if the spectacular growth in investment was probably a perceived increase in the marginal efficiency of capital due to European integration (Spain joined the EC in 1986). In 1991–1992,

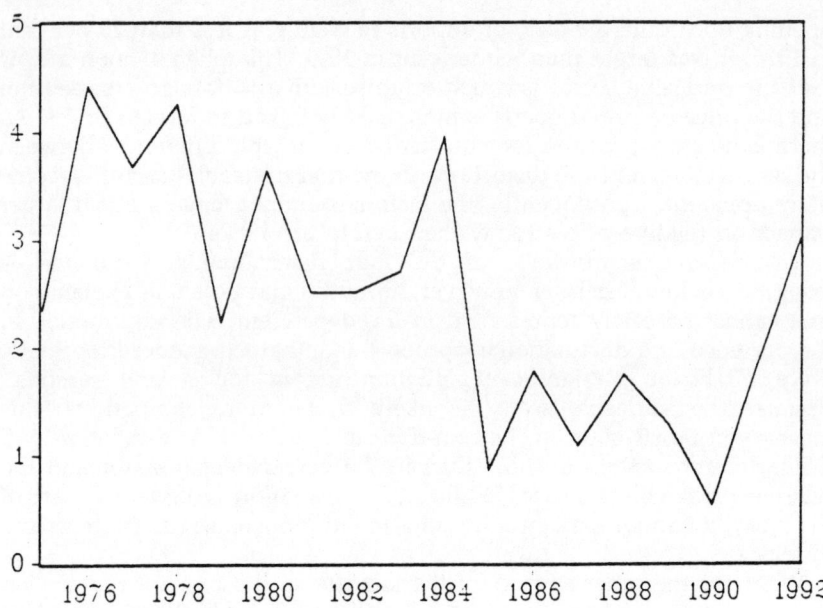

Figure 2.4 Labour productivity in Spain (annual increase, 1976–1992)
Source: Instituto Nacional de Estadistica.

however, demand growth slowed down significantly (to around 2 per cent), especially investment (negative growth). Only government consumption growth remained at high levels (around 4 per cent in real terms). Because it falls heavily on non-traded goods and it is a policy variable, the role of public consumption has traditionally attracted particular attention.[10] While it is true that public consumption in Spain has increased its share of GDP substantially since 1975, most of this increase occurred before 1985 and the real exchange rate did not appreciate correspondingly.[11]

An interesting issue is the role the EMS has had on demand. Some authors argue that ERM membership has allowed a decrease in interest rates due to a gain in credibility.[12] In the case of Spain, however, no significant decline in interest rates could be observed after entering the ERM. Moreover, the strong increase in demand preceded ERM membership. Nevertheless, this issue is difficult to evaluate. First, ERM membership was anticipated by at least one or two years and could have had an effect before 1989. Second, credibility in the exchange rate regime usually takes time to be established.[13]

Capital inflows also increased substantially in the late 1980s. This phenomenon is closely related to the increase in demand as the inflows are basically used to finance its components.[14] Three basic factors explain the surge in capital inflows. First, inflows increased for the same

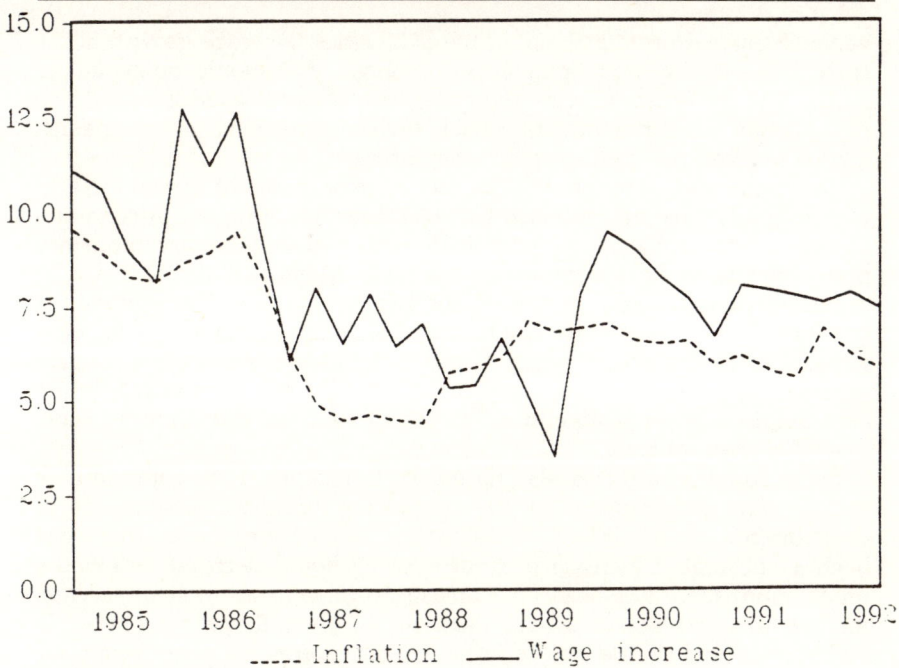

Figure 2.5 Inflation and wages in Spain (annual increase, 1985–1992)

Source: Banco de España.

reason as investment did, i.e. due to an increase in the perceived returns to investment. Second, there has been a process of financial liberalization, including a liberalization of capital movements.[15] Third, the macroeconomic policy mix of a restrictive monetary policy and expansionary fiscal policy has implied very high interest rates. On the other hand, private capital inflows decreased substantially in 1992 and could no longer finance the current account deficit. In 1992, most of the deficit was financed by a decrease in foreign exchange reserves held at the Bank of Spain.

Finally, an element that might explain the rise in the relative price of non-tradeables to tradeables is a wage increase. This explanation is a strong candidate. Figure 2.5 shows the development of average wages between 1985 and 1992. A moderation in wage growth can be observed in 1987 and 1988, which might explain the success in the disinflation process during this period. Since 1989, however, wages have risen in real terms. While similar increases could be observed in 1989 and 1990 in other countries, nominal wage growth declined in 1991 and 1992 in most countries except Spain. For example, in 1990 compensation per employee rose by 7.9 per cent in Spain compared to an EC average of 7.5 per cent (Eurostat). In 1992, the increase was 9 per cent in Spain versus 5.8 per cent on average in the EC. Hence the wage growth in the early 1990s is a specific Spanish phenomenon that should be explained and is a likely cause of increase in the price of non-traded goods.[16] The next section examines in some detail the developments in the Spanish labour market that could explain this increase.

To summarize, the growth in the relative price of non-traded to traded goods must be explained by several factors. A higher price inertia in the non-tradeable sector combined with a disinflationary monetary policy seems to be an important element. Moreover, the increase in domestic demand and in capital inflows in the late 1980s played a significant role. In the early 1990s, however, the main source of increase appears to be the rise in wages. These factors have had a larger impact on relative prices than in the past as the Spanish economy is more exposed to foreign competition. Productivity does not seem to have played a relevant role.

From equation (3), it is also necessary to examine the evolution of τ and α. The development of the proportion of non-traded goods in consumption, α, is difficult to determine. On the one hand, there has been a substantial increase in trade which should decrease α. On the other hand, there has been an increase in the consumption of services relative to other goods, which increases α. Overall the net impact is ambiguous, and should not be large. Distinct forces are also in play for the determination of τ. On the one hand there has been a decline in tariffs between 1986 and 1993. With respect to other EC countries, an average tariff of 14 per cent has been eliminated during this period.[17] This would increase τ. On the other hand, the appreciation of the nominal exchange rate tends to decrease τ temporarily. Such an appreciation occurred especially between 1987 and 1989 and might have dominated the impact of tariff reductions. The nominal devaluations in the autumn of 1992, however, have practically offset this appreciation and increased τ.[18]

RECENT DEVELOPMENTS IN THE SPANISH LABOUR MARKET

In 1993, Spain had the highest unemployment rate in the EC, which is an indication of the inefficiencies of the Spanish labour market.[19] While the objective of this chapter is not a detailed analysis of this market, it is interesting to examine two significant changes which occurred in the last few years and which might explain the rise in nominal wages.

The first element of change in the Spanish labour market is the introduction, in 1984, of six-month temporary contracts (renewable up to three years). As these contracts bear low firing costs, they have been used extensively. In 1992, workers with temporary contracts represented 34 per cent of total employees. The Spanish labour market can therefore be characterized as a two-tier market with temporary and permanent contracts. The evidence also shows that wages tend to be lower for temporary workers. The presence of temporary contracts has two effects on wages.[20] First, as the average wage is lower, an increase in these contracts decreases average wages in the economy. This is the composition effect (see Dolado and Bentolila, 1992). Second, as trade unions tend to feel less concern about temporary workers, it will affect their bargaining behaviour. If we take the insider–outsider approach to wage determination, temporary workers can be considered as outsiders. In this case, trade unions can push for higher wages for the insiders (permanent contracts), as the temporary workers will suffer most from a decline in employment. Dolado and Bentolila find that this bargaining effect is significant. While the composition effect might dominate initially when the share of temporary workers increases, the bargaining effect will take over when this share stabilizes. As this share increased mostly in the 1980s (it was 30 per cent in 1990), it appears that this phenomenon can explain part of the wage increase in the early 1990s.

The other significant change in the Spanish labour market has been the decentralization of the wage bargaining process. Until 1986, wages were decided nationwide between the government, firms and trade unions. In 1987, unions moved out of this process and since then bargain with firms at various levels: firm, industry and nationwide. This mixed process is therefore between a centralized and decentralized one. It is well known that such a bargaining process is worse than a centralized one, as unions do not internalize the impact of wage increases.[21] Jimeno (1992) provides empirical evidence that this change in the bargaining process has indeed led to more wage pressure.

By being left out of the direct bargaining process, the government has obviously lost influence in the process of wage setting. It has tried repeatedly to propose a social pact with the unions, especially in 1991 with the 'pacto de competitividad', but it has been rejected by the unions. Trade unions seem actually to have gained in both power and aggression in recent years. For example, while the number of working days lost declined sharply in other European countries, it increased in Spain.[22]

The other mechanism through which the government can influence wages is by setting low wage increases in the public sector. Such a strategy was not pursued before 1992 and public wages actually rose significantly in the late 1980s. In early 1993, bargained wage increases in the central administration were on average 1.8 per cent. It is not clear whether this policy can greatly influence private wages.[23] For example, the state railways company (RENFE) has agreed on an average increase of 4.4 per cent and other public sector entities have agreed on even higher increases.

In conclusion, there is no income or wage policy to speak of at present in Spain. Moreover, the only policy that is being considered (by various political parties) is a return to social consensus. At this stage, however, trade unions are strongly opposed to it. Some people argue in favour of a tax on wage increases (e.g. Alvaro Espina, 1992), but this is not taken seriously at the political level.

ON THE SUSTAINABILITY OF THE PESETA[24]

The real appreciation of the peseta would not represent a significant problem if the currency were floating freely. Other countries (e.g. the USA) have experienced even larger appreciations that were corrected through a nominal depreciation. The value of the peseta, however, is in principle locked in through the commitment to the ERM. It is therefore important to know whether the value of the peseta in the ERM, set on 21 November 1992 after the second devaluation, is sustainable.[25]

It is difficult to evaluate the adequate level of a currency. A naive approach is the simple rule of thumb that 'what goes up must come down'. More sophisticated methods would examine sustainability either in terms of an 'equilibrium' exchange rate or in terms of balance-of-payments developments. Starting with the naive approach, one could just use the real exchange rate index presented in Figure 2.1 to see that the peseta must depreciate significantly even after the two devaluations in 1992. The necessary adjustment will depend on the base year, but also on the index that is used. Indices based on unit labour costs or the GDP deflator give a picture similar to the CPI index. On the other hand, if one considers only ERM countries in the index, the real appreciation is smaller and the level in 1993 is similar to 1989. Moreover, if the industrial price index is used instead of the CPI, the level in 1993 is lower than in 1989 (with respect to ERM countries). Considering only a subset of goods or of countries in the index, however, might not be very helpful in this context. For example, a stable real exchange rate for industrial goods, that are mainly traded goods, only means that equation (2) holds. Overall, the naive approach indicates that the peseta should depreciate in real terms, but the necessary adjustment is unknown.

The main problem with the naive approach is that even though the base year and the adequate index could be determined, the real exchange rate does not necessarily need to go back to its 'initial' value. In other words, its long-term 'equilibrium' value might fluctuate over time. Therefore, if the long-run equilibrium real exchange rate has appreciated, an adjustment might not be necessary. Based on the discussion on pp. 20–23, three major factors might explain a long-run appreciation. First, if the relative increase in productivity in the tradeable sector is larger than in other countries, the real exchange rate naturally appreciates. This productivity increase was small, at least in recent years, and cannot have had a large effect. The second factor is a permanent increase in demand towards non-traded goods. This is caused by the increase in government expenditure, that falls mainly on non-traded goods, and an increase in the private consumption of services. The third factor is the financial liberalization that has attracted large capital inflows. This change might mean that international investors now include Spain in their portfolios, which might therefore be considered as a permanent change. What matters, however, are net capital flows and it is not obvious that net inflows would be maintained.[26]

Against these factors, there are a few elements going in the other direction, i.e. towards a long-run depreciation. The main element is the reduction in tariffs between 1986 and 1993. As mentioned above, these tariffs were estimated at 14 per cent on average in 1986. They have been practically eliminated with respect to EC countries and were reduced to around 5 per cent with respect to other countries (see Viñals et al., 1990). As no such tariff reduction occurred on Spanish exports, the long-run value of τ in equation (3) increases, which means a long-run depreciation. In addition, two other factors, related to the balance of payments, lead to a similar movement. First, the accumulation of current account deficits implies increased debt service for the country. Second, there might be a problem of trade hysteresis, in the sense that it is difficult to recover lost market shares caused by a previous overvaluation. Both factors mean that the equilibrium real exchange rate should depreciate compared to its initial value.

Therefore, there are factors leading to both a real appreciation and depreciation of the long-term equilibrium value of the peseta and the net effect is difficult to determine. Consequently, the more sophisticated analysis based on 'equilibrium' exchange rate does not provide more information than the naive rule of thumb.

Finally, the sustainability of the real exchange rate can be evaluated by examining the balance of payments. It has been argued that large current account deficits in Spain were created by an investment boom. Although this was true in the late eighties, this is no longer the case in the early nineties as the ratio of total investment to GDP has declined since 1990. This decline was especially marked in 1992, as investment decreased in real terms due to the recession. For 1993, despite the two 1992 devaluations and the recession, the current account deficit is forecast at around 3 per cent of GDP. This deficit does not appear to be sustainable. Until 1992, current account deficits were financed by private capital inflows. Since the autumn of 1992, however, the main source of financing has been the decline in foreign exchange reserves at the Bank of Spain. It should be obvious then, that the only way to reduce this deficit in the medium term is a depreciation of the real exchange rate. Nevertheless, the extent of the necessary adjustment is difficult to evaluate. Econometric analyses indicate that the price elasticity of net merchandise trade is low by international standards.[27] Given the drastic changes in the Spanish economy, however, such analyses may not provide good predictions of the sensitivity of trade flows to exchange rate movements.

CONCLUSIONS

The examination of the real exchange rate and of the current account indicates that the May 1993 real value of the peseta is not sustainable. The conclusion from this analysis is that the real exchange rate should decline in the medium run. The important question is how to reach this lower value. There are basically two, possibly complementary, solutions: either the exchange rate depreciates in nominal terms or non-traded goods prices increase less than in partner countries.

If the nominal exchange rate were totally fixed, the adjustment would have to be through prices only. Given the existing inflation inertia, this adjustment would probably require a recession.[28] A change in the nominal value of the currency could avoid this recession to the extent that it can affect the *real* exchange rate.[29]. There is in effect a risk that a nominal depreciation implies a similar adjustment in the price of non-traded goods leaving the real exchange rate practically unchanged. Hence, a nominal depreciation can only be considered as an instrument if at the same time price pressure, and especially wage pressure, in the non-tradeable sector can be kept under control.

Developments in the labour market therefore turn out to be crucial. If wage moderation could be combined with a nominal exchange rate adjustment (as in Italy in 1992/3), the adjustment in the real exchange rate might be done at a low cost. On the other hand, if wage pressures are maintained and wages are highly indexed, a nominal depreciation might not be very useful and the nominal exchange rate might as well remained fixed. The problem with the latter is that the value of the peseta in the ERM is not credibly fixed and the cost of maintaining the parity is particularly high. Moreover, a devaluation might be forced by the markets. This is obviously the worst scenario where, on the one hand, the real exchange rate adjustment is done through a recession and, on the other hand, the country enters an inflation–devaluation spiral.

The choice of the optimal exchange rate policy for Spain in the next few years is a difficult one. It will depend, first, on the extent of wage moderation and, second, on the speed of progress towards indefinitely fixed exchange rates. Failure on either of these two fronts is likely to make the presence of the peseta in the ERM untenable.

NOTES

1 Several authors use a similar approach to analyse the recent real exchange rate developments in EMS countries. See, for example, Danthine et al. (1991), Froot and Rogoff (1991), or de Gregorio et al. (1993).
2 An alternative definition of the real exchange rate, not considered here, is simply P_N/P_T.
3 For example, Italy has experienced a significant increase in this ratio in the last two decades, but the increase seems to have been smaller in the last five years (see De Gregorio et al., 1993).
4 The description of the basic model can be found in works such as Dornbusch (1980), Burda and Wyplosz (1993) and Sachs and Larrain (1993).
5 The exact impact of a capital inflow depends on the use of the extra capital.
6 See, for example, De Gregorio et al. (1993) for such an extension.
7 Dornbusch (1991) favours such an interpretation.

8   Part of the low productivity is explained by cyclical factors, as it was a period of employment growth.
9   Government consumption has traditionally been procyclical in Spain. See Dolado et al. (1993).
10 For example, Froot and Rogoff (1991) attribute an important role to government expenditure in the real appreciation of the lira, while Viñals (1992) and OECD (1993) do so in the case of the peseta.
11 See Bacchetta (1993) and the references therein for a description of the Spanish public sector. De Gregorio et al. (1993) finds that the impact of government consumption on the real exchange rate is small.
12 See, for example, Giavazzi and Spaventa (1990).
13 See Ayuso et al. (1993) for an analysis of the credibility of the peseta in the ERM.
14 Capital outflows have been very small. See Bacchetta (1992b) for a description of the Spanish capital account.
15 Danthine et al. (1991) analyse this issue in the dependent economy model.
16 De Gregorio et al. (1993) and García Perea (1992) take a similar view.
17 See Viñals et al. (1990).
18 The devaluation will also lower the relative price of non-traded to traded goods. Since P_T will increase over time the impact of the devaluation on τ decreases.
19 For a description of the Spanish labour market, see for example Bentolila and Blanchard (1990), Viñals et al. (1990) or Dolado and Bentolila (1992).
20 See Dolado and Bentolila (1992) for a careful analysis of this issue.
21 See, for example, Bruno and Sachs (1985). The intermediate process is also worse than a totally decentralized one.
22 In the period 1982–1986, the number of lost working days per 1,000 workers was 610 in Spain against 705 in Italy and 419 in the UK. In the period 1987–1991, the numbers were 677 for Spain versus 275 and 126 for Italy and the UK (Eurostat).
23 At the time of writing private wage increases were not yet determined.
24 This section is partially based on Bacchetta (1992c).
25 The peseta was devalued by 8 per cent in May 1993.
26 For example, Bacchetta (1992a) shows that a financial liberalization might lead to an initial period of capital inflows followed by a period of outflows.
27 See for example Sebastián (1991).
28 See Drifill and Miller (1992) for a discussion of these issues.
29 In the past, empirical evidence indicates that changes in the nominal value had real effects. See, for example, Gardeazabal and Regúlez (1993).

REFERENCES

Ayuso, J., Pérez Jurado, M. and Restoy, F. (1993), 'Indicadores de credibilidad de un régimen cambiario: el casa de la peseta en el SME', *Cuadernos Económicos del ICE*, forthcoming.

Bacchetta, P. (1993), 'The lessons from fiscal reform in democratic Spain', ESADE Paper no. 100.

Bacchetta, P. (1992a), 'Liberalization of capital movements and of the domestic financial sector', *Economica*, 59, 465–74.

Bacchetta, P. (1992b), 'Abolishing capital controls in Spain: a challenge for the 90s', in H. Gibson and E. Tsakalotos (eds), *Economic Integration and Financial Liberalization: Prospects for Southern Europe*, London, Macmillan.

Bacchetta, P. (1992c), 'Por que es necesaria una devaluación de la peseta', in J. Pérez-Campanero (ed.), *El tipo de cambio de la peseta ante el Mercado Unico y la Unión Monetaria Europea*, Madrid, FEDEA and Ediciones Mundi-Prensa.

Bentolila, S. and Blanchard, O. (1990), 'Spanish unemployment', *Economic Policy*, 10(5), 233–81.

Bruno, M. and Sachs, J. (1985), *Economics of Worldwide Stagflation*, Princeton, NJ, Harvard University Press.

Burda, N. and Wyplosz, C. (1993), *Macroeconomics - A European Text*, Oxford, Oxford University Press.

Danthine, J.P., de Grauwe, P., Katseli, L. and Thygesen, N. (1991), 'North/South in the EMS – convergence and divergence in inflation and real exchange rates', CEPS Paper no. 50.

De Gregorio, J., Giovannini, A. and Kreuger, T. (1993), 'The boom of nontradeable goods prices in Europe: evidence and interpretation', *Moneda y Crédito*, forthcoming.

Dolado, J.J. and Bentolila, S. (1992), 'Who are the insiders? Wage setting in Spanish manufacturing firms', mimeo.

Dolado, J.J., Sebastian, M. and Vallés, J. (1993), 'Cyclical patterns of the Spanish economy', mimeo.

Dornbusch, R. (1980), *Open Economy Macroeconomics*, New York, Basic Books.

Dornbusch, R. (1991), 'Comment on Froot and Rogoff', *NBER Macroeconomics Annual*, 317–22.

Driffill, J. and Miller, M. (1992), 'Is the road to Monetary Union paved with recession?', Centre for International Economics, University of Aarhus, working paper 1993-10.

Espina, A. (1992), *Recursos humanos y política industrial: España ante el Unión Europea*, Madrid, Fundesco.

Froot, K. and Rogoff, K. (1991), 'The EMS, the EMU, and the transition to a common currency', *NBER Macroeconomics Annual*, 269–317.

García Perea, P. (1992), 'El proceso de convergencia de precios y costes en las principales economías europeas', *Boletín Económico*, Banco de España, 49–68.

Gardeazabal, J. and Regúlez, M. (1993), 'Los efectos de una depreciación nominal de la peseta sobre la balanza comercial real española', *Cuadernos Económicos del ICE*, forthcoming.

Giavazzi, F. and Spaventa, L. (1990), 'The "New" EMS', in P. De Grauwe and L. Papademos (eds), *The European Monetary System in the 1990's*, London, Longman.

Jimeno, J.F. (1992), 'Las implicaciones macroeconómicas de la negociación colectiva: el caso español', FEDEA working paper no. 92-08.

OECD (1993), *Economic Survey on Spain*, Paris, OECD.

Sachs, J. and Larrain, F. (1993), *Macroeconomics In The Global Economy*, Brighton, Harvester Wheatsheaf.

Sebastián, M. (1991), 'Un análisis estructural de las exportaciones e importaciones españolas', *Información Comercial Española*, 699, 9–23.

Viñals, J. et al. (1990), 'Spain and the EEC cum 1992 shock', in C. Bliss and J.B. de Macedo (eds), *Union with Diversity in the European Economy*, Cambridge, Cambridge University Press.

Viñals, J. (ed.) (1992), *La economía española ante el Mercado Unico europeo*, Madrid, Alianza Editorial.

3

WHAT COHERENT STRATEGY IS THERE FOR THE ESCUDO?*

Teodora Cardoso

When Portugal joined the EC at the beginning of 1986 the economy was coming out of a deep recession, the latest episode in a history of instability that started in the mid-seventies. The strict stabilization policy implemented from mid-1983 through 1985 had set the scene for the subsequent recovery. Together with the oil price decline of 1986 and the effect of Community transfers, this helped make a success of the first years of integration and led to a period of political stability and accelerated economic growth. Led by very buoyant domestic demand, GDP increased by 4.6 per cent between 1986 and 1990, and the rate of unemployment declined from 8.6 to 4.7 per cent. The current account remained nearly balanced and a large amount of capital inflows removed the constraint that its financing had almost continually presented in the past.

The economy's degree of openness increased, mainly as a result of the boost to trade with Spain, which rapidly became one of the most important trade partners (first supplier, second customer in 1992) from a modest position before both countries joined the EC. Trade became more concentrated in the Community and, with around 75 per cent of exports going to and 72 per cent of imports coming from EC countries in 1991, Portugal is one of the countries whose trade is heavily reliant on the Community market.

Although some diversification of exports took place, partly brought about by foreign investment, the proportion of small-scale, labour-intensive export firms is still very high. This is partly the result of the crawling-peg exchange rate policy maintained until 1990, though the pre-announced monthly rate of depreciation gradually declined after

---

* In a context of accelerated development – a brief characterization of the Portuguese economy after the EC accession.

1986, allowing for a small real appreciation of the escudo. The crawling peg was a legacy from the instability period and was a key element in a system of informal indexation put in place in 1977. Although under this system all nominal variables tended to be adjusted roughly in line with inflation, this was not done automatically and in practice it helped to bring about important real changes.

The system proved effective as a means of rapidly correcting excessive real wage increases but was powerless to avoid unwarranted growth of nominal variables. Real wage flexibility is a confirmed characteristic of the Portuguese economy, but one that used to be achieved through a succession of expansionary and recessionary phases that left little room for structural adjustment and the rationalization of long-term investment.

The phasing out of this system became a clear necessity once the country joined the Community, but has proved a difficult task. A gradual approach was used from 1986 to 1990. The real income rise generated by the gain in terms-of-trade in 1986 and the increase in EC transfers at first allowed real wages and profits to grow, even as a relatively tight fiscal stance was adopted.[1] However, little structural adjustment took place in the period. The increase in exports continued to be supported by the depreciation of the exchange rate. It remained largely concentrated in labour- and resource-intensive industries and for the most part crucially dependent on the low wage level, the natural counterpart to low productivity. In the domestic market, the boost in demand[2] temporarily made room for large increases in both imports and domestic production, with the depreciation of the exchange rate continuing to provide shelter for the less-competitive firms.

Apart from a few more dynamic firms and those where foreign investment gained relevance, most of the economy continued to function in much the same way as before. In particular, firms continued to expect that domestic prices fully reflect cost increases, with no real concern for productivity gains or the improvement of marketing techniques. Such behaviour obviously also implied that the exchange rate should continue to depreciate in order to maintain competitiveness in the traded goods sector.

The persistence of these expectations made it impossible for the financial system to develop fixed rate medium- and long-term instruments and practically all interest rates remained indexed. In the meantime, progressive deregulation made the system more competitive and effective at circumventing the existing credit restrictions, thus annulling the effectiveness of domestic monetary policy, which relied heavily on the interplay between interest rates and credit ceilings, given the current procedure of passing costs (including financial charges) through to prices.

In 1989 the CPI increase re-accelerated to 12.2 per cent after reaching a low of 9.2 per cent in mid-1988, and was followed by strong wage growth (over 17.5 per cent) in both 1990 and 1991. The high level of activity and low unemployment rate had created tensions in the labour market which the existing economic policy had no means of checking. On the contrary, it helped fuel wage rises and domestic demand as public sector pay and the fiscal deficit expanded significantly in 1990/91.

An inevitable conclusion from the developments of 1986-1990 was that Portuguese economic decision-makers and workers had to be made aware of the new competitive background in which the economy was operating. This became all the more important as the opening up of trade with Eastern Europe, as well as the increasing competitiveness of developing countries, presented a new challenge and made it essential that Portuguese manufacturing become better integrated in the European industrial structure and less reliant on low wages and high labour content.

The instrument chosen by the authorities to bring about this outcome was the exchange rate, which was allowed to float in October 1990, giving rise to a cumulative effective appreciation of the escudo by 7 per cent until the end of 1992. Taking into account the inflation differential accumulated in the same period, the real appreciation amounted to 18 per cent. The emphasis on the exchange rate was justified by the fact that the existing incomes policy based the guidelines for wage increases in prospective rather than past inflation, which should allow them to reflect the more moderate expectations concerning price increases. In April 1992 the escudo formally joined the ERM with a fluctuation band of 6 per cent.

Concerned with the need to check domestic inflation, monetary policy maintained interest rates at a high level (real short-term lending rates in the domestic banking system typically reached 10 per cent in 1991/92) and tried to restrict capital inflows. These, however, remained very substantial and, in the absence of credit ceilings, the high interest rates proved insufficient to check the surge in demand for credit.

Fiscal policy also became more expansionary. Government consumption rose from 16.1 per cent of GDP in 1989 to an estimated 18.2 per cent in 1992, leading to a parallel increase in the government borrowing requirement, from 3.2 to 5.1 per cent of GDP.

Fiscal and monetary expansion combined with the nominal appreciation of the exchange rate led to an increase of nearly 30 per cent in relative unit labour costs until the end of 1992. This did not imply an equivalent loss in competitiveness as the relative price of exported manufactures hardly changed in the same period, allowing the current account to remain surprisingly strong. Though partly cushioned by cheaper imported inputs, these developments induced a strong profit squeeze that became clear during 1992 and produced a slowdown in activity and employment. This finally led to two successive realignments of the escudo and a nominal effective depreciation of 4.2 per cent in the first five months of 1993.

PRESENT OUTLOOK AND ELEMENTS OF A COHERENT GROWTH STRATEGY

Notwithstanding its effects on profitability and the level of activity, the real appreciation of the currency had two important positive consequences. It brought inflation down, despite the adverse effects of other policies, and made entrepreneurs aware of the need to restructure their productive, pricing and marketing processes if they are to remain competitive in the single market environment. The currency realignments created new breathing space which, together with the decline in interest rates that followed the May realignment of the escudo and the peseta[3] and the more moderate wage increases expected in 1993, should bring about a slight recovery of the levels of activity and investment.

The positive signs do not, however, warrant an over-optimistic assessment of the present state of the economy. On the one hand, the expected increase in wages, of 8–10 per cent on average in 1993, though moderate compared to previous years, is still high given the current rate of inflation (5.7 per cent in May, on a year-on-year basis) and the accumulated loss of competitiveness. On the other hand, there are disquieting signs of a further deterioration of the budget deficit. Public sector borrowing has been increasing fast since the beginning of 1993, despite the initially projected fall of the overall budget deficit by 1 per cent of GDP. Revenue shortfalls have been very significant in the first months of 1993 and the desired improvement now seems difficult to achieve.

The low level of income in Portugal compared to other EC countries not only makes it desirable that the economy should secure a high rate of growth in order to bring about a better balanced social and economic situation in Europe this has also become a credibility requirement for domestic policy. Apart from periods of recognized balance of payments crisis, governments find it very hard to establish credibility for policies that do not provide for visible short-term welfare improvements along with long-term stability.

A high rate of growth is therefore a crucial goal of economic policy in Portugal. If it is to be achieved, the economy must remain competitive and be able to sustain a significant level of public investment in infrastructure and education. Moreover, there will be a need to continue creating a large number of new jobs in order to absorb workers shed by agriculture and traditional industries, where restructuring and competition from Eastern European and developing countries is bound to reduce the level of employment significantly.

It is also clear that competitiveness in the new environment cannot be achieved by means of the traditional policy which amounted to using the depreciation of the exchange rate to depress real wages. An increase in real wages over and above productivity growth would also mean disaster. To avoid that outcome, in a context of growth with restructuring and diversification of production, one key element of economic policy strategy must consist in making the most of the wage flexibility that characterizes the Portuguese labour market, both at the national level and across sectors. The fact that unemployment will become a very real threat should give new impetus to this well-proven mechanism.

Improving public finances is the other priority. The government will face increased expenditures in investment and education as well as the social areas, including unemployment benefits. Increasing the efficiency of expenditures and tax collection procedures will be essential, as Community transfers cannot be expected to take the full burden of adjustment. The need to increase the discipline exerted by fiscal policy also arises from the fact that, together with incomes policy, it will have to take up the restraining macroeconomic role that monetary policy played in the past.

Given the level achieved by financial integration, monetary policy cannot be expected to maintain a level of interest rates that is out of line with the adopted exchange rate policy, although a small amount of insulation, along the lines proposed by Eichengreen and Wyplosz, see Chapter 10, would be welcome in order to avoid unnecessary instability in the money and exchange markets. Neither can it be expected to make successful use of credit ceilings other than for very short-term purposes. Besides more general considerations, a de facto monetary integration with Spain is about to be realized and its appropriate management within the European context will be the main task of Portuguese monetary policy. Contributing to the stable development of the financial system by means of suitable regulations and supervision will be the other.

As to the exchange rate, it seems inevitable that the escudo cannot aim at full stability in the short to medium run. No matter how efficiently fiscal and incomes policies are managed, the Portuguese situation will not bear the wage freeze and/or the fiscal tightness that would be consistent with a fully fixed exchange rate under present conditions. That being said, economic policy will also need to take full advantage of the newly acquired awareness to the exchange constraint. This means that firms must not be allowed to continue taking it for granted that currency depreciation will take care of all cost increases and general problems of competitiveness. The part left for exchange rate adjustments must become smaller and be eventually phased out. Together with domestic policy efforts, this also requires that the ERM discipline remains operative. Again, a system like that proposed by Eichengreen and Wyplosz seems advisable for this purpose and easier to manage than any attempt at pre-defining a path for exchange rate adjustments.

One aspect of this strategy that must be underlined in the case of Portugal is that in a certain way it will redefine the meaning of economic performance and shift most of the responsibility for the quality of that performance to the private sector. Given the imbalances of the seventies and early eighties too much emphasis still tends to be placed on strictly *macroeconomic* performance, especially short-term growth and balance of payments equilibrium, and too little on ensuring the capacity for structural adjustment needed to keep the country on a growth path, with increased levels of wages and productivity. The choice of a more stable exchange rate is more demanding in terms of productivity adjustment, and this cannot be the outcome of a simple government decision as is the case with a currency devaluation. Experience shows that such a change in attitudes can be as hard to bring about as any change in macroeconomic policy strategy.

NOTES

1 According to OECD estimates, the general government borrowing requirement declined from 7.5 per cent of GDP in 1985 to 3.2 per cent in 1989. In the same period and as a percentage of GDP, current revenue increased from 35.9 to 38.7, while current expenditure declined from 39.5 to 37.8.
2 Private consumption and total domestic demand increased by 5.2 and 7.1 per cent between 1986 and 1990.
3 Short-term money market rates declined by 6 percentage points since April.

4

THE IRISH POUND AND THE ERM: LESSONS FROM THE SEPTEMBER CRISIS AND ITS AFTERMATH*

Brendan Walsh

HISTORICAL BACKGROUND[1]

The financial provisions of the Act of Union between Great Britain and Ireland, which came into force in 1826, suppressed the Irish currency and replaced it with sterling. Following the foundation of a Free State in 1922 a separate Irish currency was introduced in 1927, but the new currency was fully backed by sterling reserves and freely convertible at a 1:1 no-margins exchange rate. A central bank was not established until 1942, and did not acquire the full range of powers until the legislation of 1971, which among other provisions made it possible to change the exchange rate by government order.

The costs and benefits for the newly independent state of the sterling link were debated in the 1920s and 1930s, when there was some support for floating the currency and establishing financial independence from sterling. More cautious views prevailed, however. The issue received renewed attention when sterling was devalued in 1949 and 1967, but

---

* This chapter examines the effects of the EMS crisis of September 1992 on the Irish pound. A review of the Irish experience in the exchange rate mechanism is presented, including an assessment of the extent to which the hard-currency peg pursued after the devaluation of 1986 could be said to have gained credibility for the Irish pound. The behaviour of Irish interest rates in the aftermath of sterling's departure from the ERM and the reasons for the protracted attempt to avert a devaluation of the Irish pound are studied. Some implications for progress towards a monetary union in Europe are drawn.

despite some unease at having to share sterling's decline against the dollar, no change was made in the exchange rate regime.

Ireland's adherence to the European (Economic) Community in 1973 and the instability of foreign exchanges caused by the return to generalized floating led to renewed interest in alternative exchange rate arrangements. The merits of the sterling link were once again debated against the backdrop of Britain's failure to remain in the Snake. However, no realistic alternative to the sterling link was available until the plans to create a 'zone of monetary stability' in Europe began to crystallize in the second half of the 1970s. As the prospect of the formation of the European Monetary System (EMS) materialized, when it seemed that the UK would participate in the Exchange Rate Mechanism (ERM), the Irish authorities were eager to join. Over two-thirds of Ireland's external trade was with this larger EMS and a fixed exchange rate with it would have been a logical extension of the well-established sterling link. But as it became clear that Britain was unlikely to participate in ERM, the Irish authorities were faced with an issue that has been at the centre of exchange rate policy ever since: would the benefits of participating in the ERM outweigh the costs of breaking the exchange rate link with its main trading partner? The arguments in favour of Ireland joining even at the cost of breaking the sterling link were rehearsed. These may be summarized as follows:

* The belief that the sterling link condemned Ireland to importing high British inflation and interest rates, whereas a switch to a DM peg would result in lower inflation and interest rates.
* The fact that over the years Irish trade had become increasingly diversified geographically and less dependent on the UK. This increased the benefits from exchange rate stability with Continental Europe relative to the costs of introducing instability vis-à-vis sterling.
* The desire to take a *communautaire* stance in relation to a major EC initiative.
* The belief that the transfer of resources offered by Ireland's EC partners would be adequate to assist the country to adjust to any deflationary pressures that the new exchange rate regime might entail.

The risks of entry into the ERM were acknowledged. The White Paper published in December 1978 stated that

In the initial period of operation of the EMS, the parity of our currency might be higher than it would otherwise be. This could impose severe strain on Ireland's competitiveness, leading to a possible loss of output and employment.

However, the belief was expressed by the Irish central bank that 'given sensible domestic policies, the adjustment problems will be manageable and of relatively short duration' (*Annual Report*, 1979).

The sharp appreciation of sterling during the first two weeks of the operation of the EMS forced the Irish authorities to choose almost immediately between the commitment to the narrow band of the ERM and retaining the sterling link. It was decided to hold the Irish pound in its permissible range in the narrow band with the result that, for the first time since the early nineteenth century, it diverged from sterling at the end of March 1979. Paradoxically the creation of the new zone of monetary stability had the result of breaking up the oldest monetary union in Europe and Ireland's quest for greater exchange rate stability resulted in a floating exchange rate with its main trading partner.

THE EXPERIENCE IN THE ERM

It is logical to distinguish between the early years of the ERM's operation, when realignments were frequent, and the second half of the 1980s, which was a period of exchange rate stability and convergence of inflation and interest rates.

The first phase: 1979–1986

NOMINAL EXCHANGE RATES

During the first seven years of the existence of the EMS the Irish pound was the most stable currency in the ERM. It was devalued only once, by 3.5 per cent in March 1983, and its central Ecu rate fell by only 7.6 per cent. However, by 'going through the middle' at most of the realignments the Irish pound depreciated markedly relative to the German mark and Dutch guilder, while appreciating relative to the French and Belgian francs, the Danish krone and the Italian lira. As may be seen from Figure 4.1, between 1979 and mid-1986 the Irish pound/DM exchange rate fell by almost a third. Thus the Irish authorities' declared intention of maintaining a fixed exchange rate with the hard-currency core of the ERM was not in fact achieved during the first seven years of the EMS's operation.

Of even greater significance in the light of subsequent events was the depreciation of the Irish pound relative to sterling over these years, which facilitated Ireland's continued participation in the ERM during Britain's absence from it. In fact from March 1979 to September 1993 the nominal Stg£/Ir£ exchange rate remained below the old 1:1 parity (see Figure 4.2). Contrary to expectations, membership of the ERM proved to be the soft option vis-à-vis sterling. By participating in it, Ireland was spared the sudden sharp real appreciation that would have occurred had the sterling link been maintained.

INFLATION AND REAL EXCHANGE RATES

Hopes of a quick disinflation following entry to the ERM were not realized. In fact Ireland's wage and price inflation accelerated in 1980

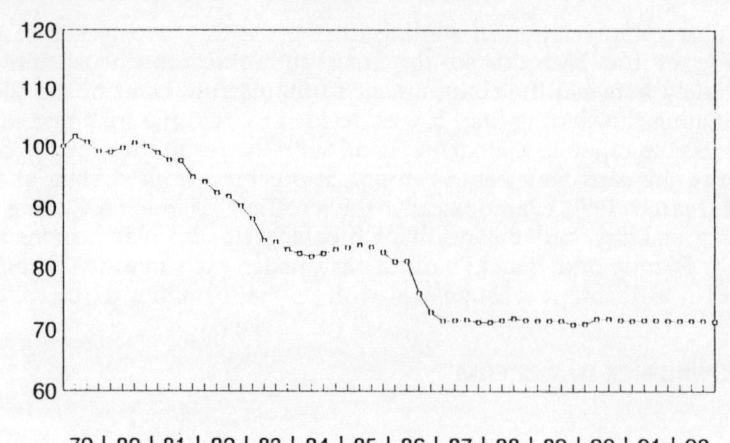

Figure 4.1 DM/Irish pound nominal exchange rate, 1979–1992 (1979Q1 = 100)

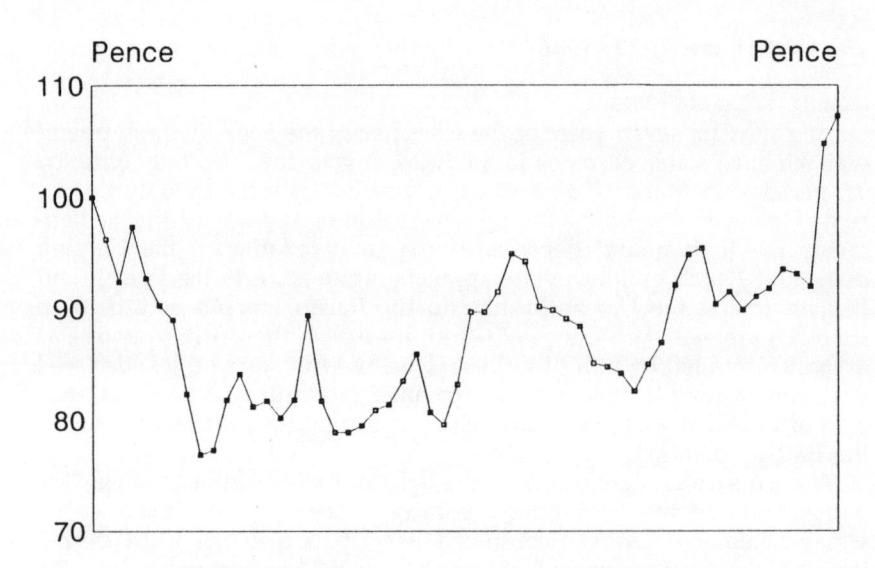

Figure 4.2 Sterling/Irish pound nominal exchange rate, 1979–1992 (1979Q1 = 100)

and remained over 10 per cent for the next two years. The fall in the nominal DM/Irish pound exchange rate was not sufficient to offset the persistence of excess inflation in Ireland, and there was a marked rise in Ireland's real exchange rate relative to the DM (Figure 4.3) and other narrow-band currencies. However, the sharp rise in sterling in the early 1980s, combined with the continued close association between Irish and British inflation rates, resulted in a significant real depreciation of the Irish pound relative to sterling. This gain was, however, quickly eroded as inflation in Britain fell and sterling weakened towards the end of 1982, while inflation in Ireland remained high (Figure 4.4). These trends generated the pressures that led to the decision to devalue in March 1983.

THE REAL ECONOMY

The decision to join the ERM did not alter either the wage setting process or the stance of fiscal and monetary policy in Ireland. During the initial years of membership the economy was clearly on an unsustainable trajectory, having tried to avert the impact of the global recession through expansionary domestic policies. The primary budget deficit rose to 8.9 per cent of GDP in 1981, total and external public debt was rising rapidly, both absolutely and relative to GDP.

The process of fiscal adjustment was begun in 1982. The rise in the debt/GDP ratio was halted in 1985 and by 1987 the primary budget deficit had been eliminated. However, unemployment, which had risen from 7.1 per cent in 1979 to 11.4 per cent in 1982 continued to rise until it peaked at 17.6 per cent of the labour force in 1987.

The rise in unemployment has been attributed to several factors, including

- the fiscal correction initiated in 1982;
- the increase in the supply of labour in Ireland due to the fall in net external migration as UK unemployment rose;
- the impact of the global recession on Irish net exports;
- the rise in the real exchange rate relative to the narrow-band ERM currencies;
- the rise in the real interest rate.

It is not possible, on the basis of available research, to allocate the overall rise in unemployment among these factors. However, the Dornbusch (1989) version of the events, in which adherence to the ERM resulted in an overvalued currency which had to be defended by high real interest rates, does not appear accurate as a description of this period. The rise in the real exchange rate was confined to the narrow-band ERM currencies, which accounted for less than one-third of Ireland's trade. For most of the period, there was competitive gain relative to sterling, which offset the real appreciation relative to the narrow-band currencies. While it is true that real interest rates rose from −8 per cent to +8 per cent between 1981 and 1986, this reflected a similar

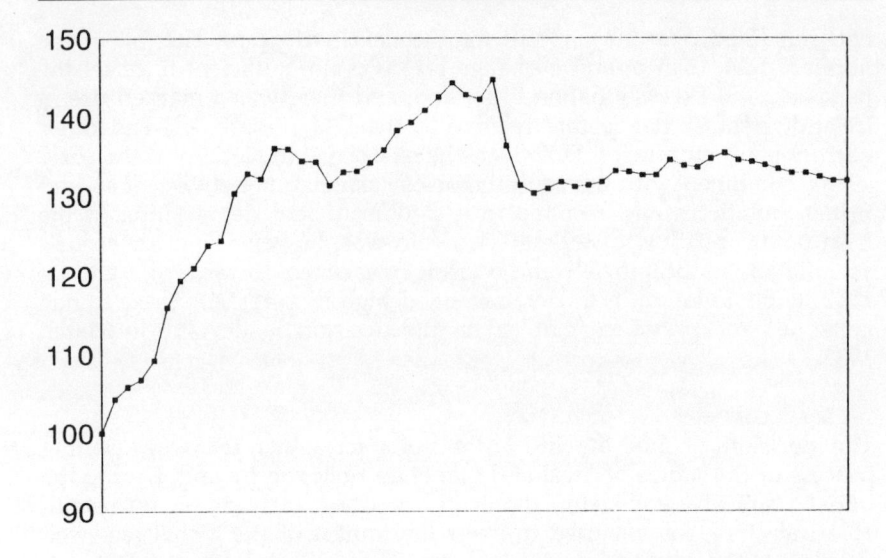

Figure 4.3 DM/Irish pound real exchange rate, 1979–1992 (1979Q1 = 100)

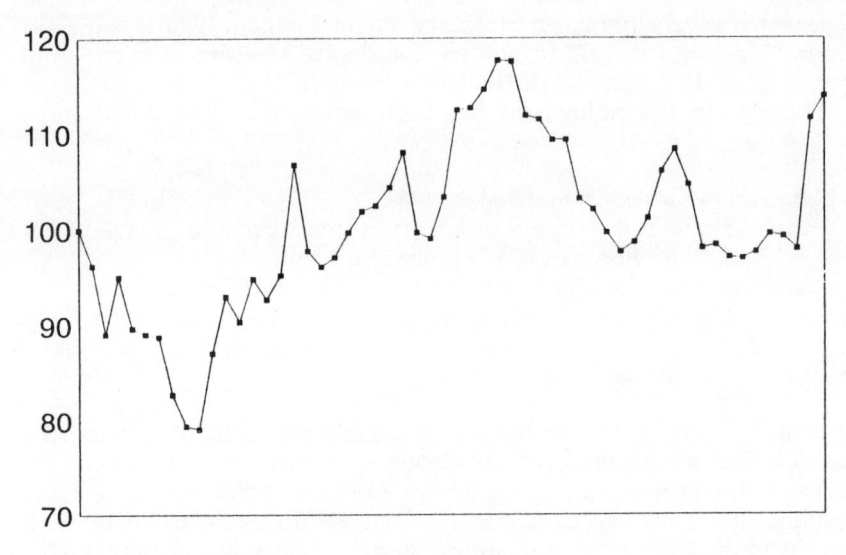

Figure 4.4 Sterling/Irish pound real exchange rate, 1979–1992 (1979Q1 = 100)

trend in other countries. The evidence, which is discussed in greater detail below, suggests that despite the persistence of relatively high inflation in Ireland, the differential between Irish and German nominal interest rates narrowed steadily after 1979 *provided the sterling/Irish pound exchange rate was at a sustainable level.*

The second phase: 1986-1992

These years were marked by increasing stability in the ERM. There were no significant realignments between 1987 and 1992, inflation rates fell and nominal convergence was apparent. The ERM was enlarged to include Spain, UK and Portugal, and Italy entered the narrow band. The schedule for progressing to full-scale monetary union by the end of the decade proposed in the Maastricht Treaty in January 1992 seemed realistic. Ireland looked forward to satisfying the Maastricht criteria and participating in EMU from the start.

Irish exchange rate policy

At the ERM realignment of March 1986, the Irish pound was held unchanged. During the following three months, however, sterling and the dollar fell sharply on the foreign exchanges. By July the Irish pound's effective exchange rate index was 11 per cent higher than it had been a year previously. These pressures led to the unilateral 8 per cent devaluation at the beginning of August.[2]

The August 1986 devaluation ushered in a period of exchange rate stability. As may be seen from Figure 4.1, there is a marked contrast between the steady depreciation of the Irish pound relative to the DM over the period 1979-1986 and the stability of its value over the period from August 1986 to August 1992.[3] When the crisis broke in 1992, the governor of the Irish central bank referred to the change of policy that occurred in 1986 and indicated that it would not be altered by the departure of sterling from the ERM:

Since 1987, exchange-rate policy has been expressed clearly in terms of the ERM commitment and the Government remains committed to a policy similar to the *franc fort* policy pursued in France. Over this period, financial markets in Ireland have become more closely integrated with continental markets ... because of the greater credibility of domestic policies, continental investors have become major investors in Irish Government securities. Generally speaking, developments in Irish financial markets – particularly movements in interest rates – strongly mirror developments in our narrow band partners.[4]

The perceived benefits of the stability of the Irish pound in the ERM – credibility in the eyes of foreign investors and a narrowing of interest rate differentials with Germany – played an important role in the resistance to devaluation by the Irish authorities over the period from September 1992 to January 1993.

INTEREST RATES

Early in 1986 markets became convinced that a devaluation of the Irish pound was likely at the next realignment. The Irish–German short-term interest rate differential widened by 500 basis points. Since Irish long-term rates fell, the yield curve rose sharply. However, there was no change in the value of the Irish pound at the April realignment, but nonetheless interest rates subsided and remained stable throughout the summer, even as the real exchange rate appreciated sharply. There was little increase in interest rates ahead of the August devaluation. By resisting devaluation in April and deciding on a quick devaluation in August the authorities took the market by surprise.

Both short-term and long-term interest rates rose in October. Sterling had weakened further, so that the breathing space that had been bought by the devaluation was lost. Added to this was the unsettling effect of unexpectedly adverse quarterly exchequer returns. Another devaluation was expected, but did not materialize. A penalty in the form of high short-term interest rates was borne until the second quarter of 1987 when a strengthening of sterling took the pressure off and short-term rates fell back.

For the rest of 1987 and the following four years there was a marked narrowing of interest rate differentials between Ireland and the UK and Ireland and Germany. During 1988 Irish rates did not rise in sympathy with UK rates, and a significant negative differential opened up between the two countries and persisted for some time (Figure 4.5). At the same time, the differential between Irish and German rate narrowed steadily, until by mid-1992 the gap was only 50 basis points. For over three years after mid-1989 the yield gap was negative. This was the first time since Ireland joined the ERM that the markets expected interest rates to fall (apart from brief episodes associated with surges in short-term rates in anticipation of a devaluation). These developments combined with lower inflation in Ireland than in either Britain or Germany, generated considerable optimism and it was widely believed that the long-hoped-for benefits of the ERM were finally within Ireland's grasp.

The econometric evidence shows that Irish interest rates did indeed come increasingly under the influence of German rates, and less under that of the UK, but that this process was not complete by 1992 (Walsh, 1993). The weights shifted as follows between the first and second half of the six years 1986–1992:

	86m8–89m7	89m8–92m8
i^{DM}	0.438	0.683
i^{STG}	0.680	0.315

Although its influence was more than halved in the second period, the sterling interest rate nonetheless remained a highly significant influence on Irish money markets.

However, the econometric evidence also shows that the sterling/Irish

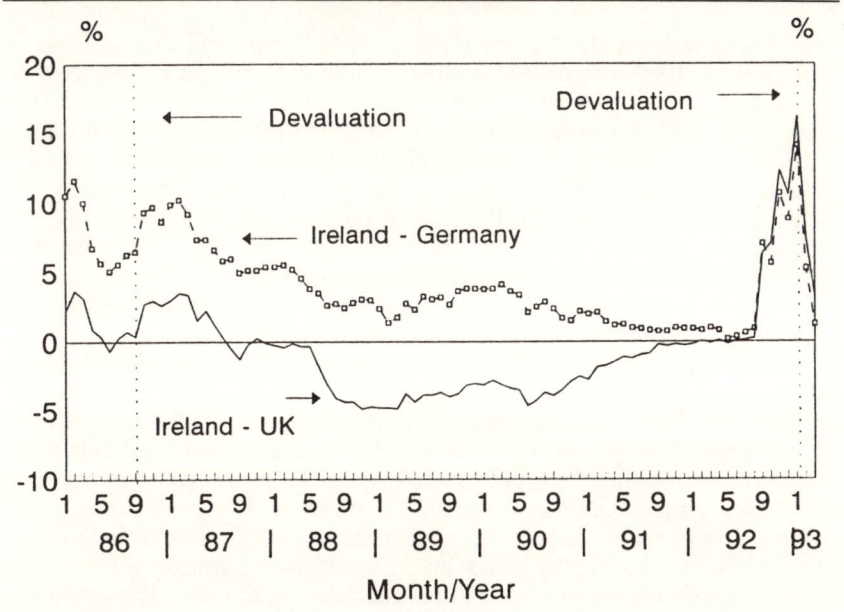

Figure 4.5 Interest rate differentials: Ireland/Germany, Ireland/UK (three-month rates)

pound exchange rate exercised an important, and persistent, influence on Irish interest rates. Using quarterly data for 1979–1992 Honohan and Conroy (1993) estimated that a rise of Stg£0.10 in the nominal exchange rate was associated with a 200–300 basis point increase in Irish interest rates. Using monthly data for the period 1986–1992 Walsh estimated that a 10 per cent increase in the real exchange rate raised interest rates by about 350 basis points. This effect persisted even as the time from the 1986 devaluation increased, although its magnitude diminished from 400 basis points in the first three years to 157 in the second three-year period. This finding is readily understood in terms of uncovered interest parity theory: as the Irish pound strengthens relative to sterling, a devaluation is regarded as increasingly likely and hence an interest rate premium is demanded for holding the currency.

These issues may also be addressed in terms of the target zone literature. Both inflation and short-term interest rate differentials, Ireland relative to Germany, show that the narrow-band target zone viz-à-vis the DM lacked credibility from 1979 until the end of 1987. Moreover, the long bond yield lay well outside the limits implied by the DM target zone until 1990, when it approached, but never actually entered, the range (Hughes and Hurley, 1993).

THE REAL ECONOMY

The fiscal correction initiated in 1982 was consolidated in the following years. From a peak of 8.9 per cent of GDP in 1981, the primary budget deficit was reduced to 2.1 per cent in 1984. It was still at this level in 1986, but by 1989 it had been converted into a *surplus* of 7.3 per cent of GDP. Since unemployment continued to rise over this period, the adjustment in the underlying, structural deficit was even more impressive. The debt/GDP ratio peaked (albeit at 129 per cent of GNP) in 1987 and declined significantly in the following years, and the external debt/GNP ratio declined even more rapidly.[5]

The Irish economy expanded by over 25 per cent between 1986 and 1990. The rate of unemployment declined from a peak of 17.6 per cent of the labour force in 1986 to 13.7 per cent in 1990, the lowest level since 1981. It is true that increased emigration, in response to the rapid growth of employment in Britain, accounted for some of this reduction, but there was also an impressive growth in private sector employment, which more than offset the contraction in public sector jobs and led to a net increase of 4¼ per cent in total employment between 1987 and 1990. The current account of the balance of payments improved from a deficit of 3.6 per cent of GNP in 1986 to a surplus of 3.75 per cent in 1991, rising to an extraordinary 6.5 per cent in 1992. These favourable developments allowed the government to begin to lighten the burden of taxation while continuing to reduce the debt/GDP ratio. The economy appeared to have escaped from the trap described in Sargent and Wallace's unpleasant monetarist arithmetic.

There was initial concern that the transformation in the public finances was being achieved mainly by tax increases rather than reductions in public expenditure, but the feared deflationary effects of the fiscal contraction did not materialize. Private sector consumption and investment spending increased sharply over the period 1986–1989. This prompted a debate as to whether Ireland was experiencing an 'expansionary fiscal contraction' à la Giavazzi and Pagano (1990).[6] While other factors have to be included in the explanation of Ireland's favourable performance in the second half of the 1980s – the 1986 devaluation, the strength of sterling and overheating of the British economy, the exceptionally large impact of the collapse of oil price on the Irish economy – it is plausible to argue, as have Bertola and Drazen (1993), that the Irish experience after 1986 is an illustration of a successful fiscal stabilization based on cuts in government consumption that changed the private sector's expectations about future deficits and tax burdens and led to a compensating increase in private spending. However, the contrast between what happened in 1982 and 1986 has been exaggerated. True, after 1986 there were cuts in government spending, including current consumption, whereas the 1982 reduction was achieved mainly by raising taxes and choking off capital spending, but the dramatic fall in the deficit in 1987/88 also owed a good deal to increased tax payments. Whatever the mix of factors that should be credited with the transformation of the Irish economy in the late 1980s, Dornbusch's verdict that Ireland's stabilization failed appears untenable.

THE SEPTEMBER 1992 CRISIS

Chronology of events

When the crisis in the ERM began to develop in the aftermath of the Danish 'no' vote in June 1992 there were grounds for hoping that the Irish pound would have gained sufficient reputation to have insulated it from the problems faced by sterling, whose commitment to the ERM was more recent and less firm. This hope was confounded in September. Sterling's departure from the ERM and sharp depreciation pushed the sterling/Irish pound exchange rate to unprecedented heights. From a level of Stg£0.91 in May it touched Stg£1.10 in November and again in January. The markets regarded these levels as unsustainable, speculative attacks drained liquidity out of the banking system and short-term interest rates rose to astronomical levels (Figure 4.6). The Irish central bank suspended its short-term facility towards the end of November, raising the cost of funds to 100 per cent on occasions.[7] The one-month rate peaked at 44 per cent. Despite efforts by the bank to insulate the retail markets from these developments, the cost of borrowing to businesses rose sharply as debt was rolled over and variable mortgage rates were adjusted to reflect the rising cost of money to the lenders. Official reserves of foreign exchange had begun to fall during the summer as tensions increased in the ERM; by the end of the year net reserves were virtually expended.

Towards the end of December the pressure on the Irish pound eased, and the short-term interest rate differential relative to Germany fell to 'only' 6 per cent (compared with over 9 per cent at end-November), but as sterling weakened again towards the end of January interest rates rose to new heights and the Irish pound fell below the floor of its band in the ERM. On 27 January the central bank announced that its overnight rate would again be raised to 100 per cent. The level of wholesale rates warranted further increases in retail rates, including mortgage rates, a prospect that was particularly unpalatable to the government. On Saturday 30 January the Irish pound central rate in the ERM was lowered by 10 per cent. The devaluation brought the trade-weighted index of the Irish pound back to its mid-1992 level (Figure 4.7).

After the devaluation Irish interest rates fell from the crisis levels of January, but remained high relative to German rates as sterling weakened further. However, once sterling passed the low point of Stg£1=DM2.33 at the end of February, Irish rates fell rapidly. By April the Irish–German differential in short-term interest rates was lower than it had been before the crisis of mid-1992 and the Irish pound was close to the top of the permissible range in its new band in the ERM. Equally impressive has been the rapid replenishment of the central bank's reserves, albeit at considerable cost to the Irish taxpayer.[8] The outcome has been more favourable than even advocates of devaluation expected in January.

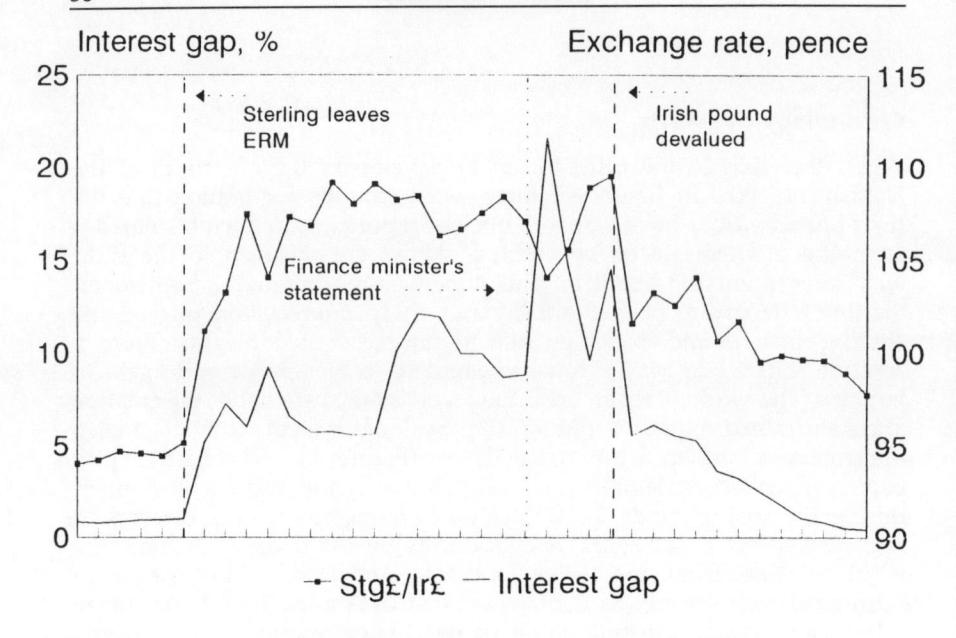

Figure 4.6 Irish–German interest rate differential and sterling exchange rate, 7 August 1992 to 23 April 1993

It could be argued that the favourable evolution of events since the devaluation reflects the strength of the resistance to devaluation and the resources devoted to the defence of the old central rate. A more plausible explanation, supported by the econometric evidence, is that since September the dominant influences on Irish interest rates have been the Stg£/Ir£ exchange rate and the level of UK interest rates, with the influence of German interest rates receding. The fall in UK interest rates following sterling's departure from the ERM exerted a strong influence on Irish interest rates, and once the Stg£/Ir£ exchange rate was lowered to a sustainable level Irish interest rates fell to a lower level, relative to German rates, than had been achieved after six years of stability in the DM/Ir£ exchange rate.

Interpretation of the events

Inevitably, accounts differ as to why the decision to devalue was resisted for so long and why it was finally taken when it was. In its commentary in its Spring 1993 *Bulletin* the Central Bank of Ireland attributes an important role to political factors. Having described the improvement that occurred towards the end of December, it goes on to state that 'during January, however, market sentiment deteriorated as perceptions changed regarding the national consensus to defend the

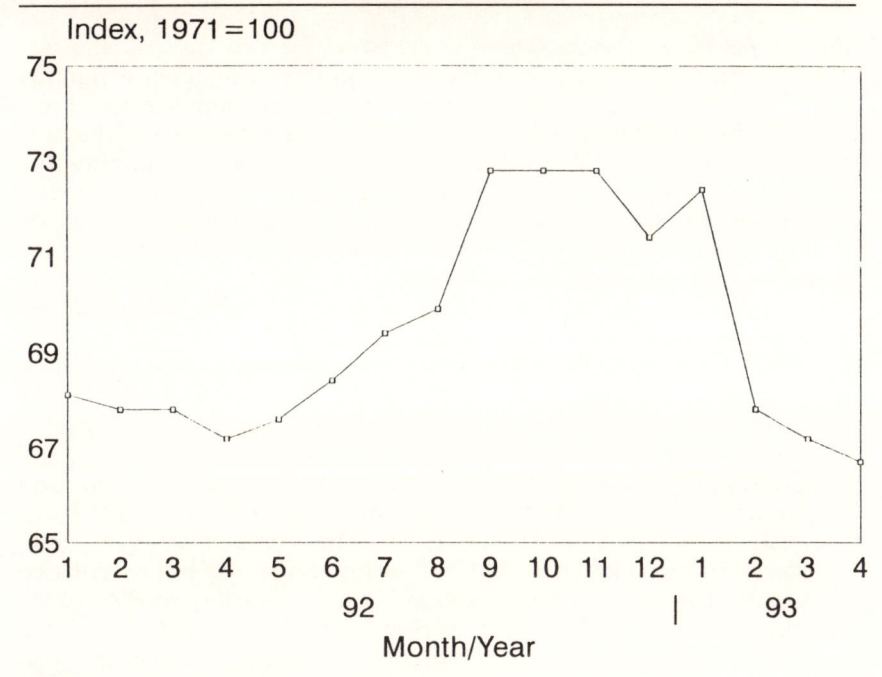

Figure 4.7 Trade-weighted index of Irish pound

currency' (p.17). The background is that when the crisis broke in September the government was adamant that it would not devalue. However, the government was dissolved on 5 November 1992 and the election held on 26 November was inconclusive. A period of negotiations followed before a new government was formed 12 January 1993. Fianna Fáil, which had formed the outgoing government on its own, entered into a partnership with the Labour Party and the outgoing prime minister and finance minister were retained. No difference of opinion emerged between the two government parties on the question of exchange rate policy: they agreed that a devaluation would be harmful and had to be resisted. However, they also insisted that their first priority was to tackle the problem of unemployment by creating sustainable employment. Pronouncements on exchange rate policy were divorced from those relating to employment policy.

Whether a consensus to defend the currency ever existed may be questioned.[9] A substantial section of business sentiment favoured a devaluation from end-November onwards. Even the political commitment to defending the pound was at times equivocal, with hints that the pound might be devalued should an opportunity present itself at a multilateral realignment or should sterling fall beyond some level. The specific event which the bank probably had in mind in its reference to the weakening of the consensus occurred as the new government was being formed during the first week of January. The finance minister stated that although he was opposed to devaluation we could not 'stagger on indefinitely' and that the new government would have to review the situation. This caused a temporary surge in interest rates. But at the end of the day it was the fact that the Irish economy was seriously threatened by the persistence of the high exchange rate relative to sterling and its concomitant, extraordinarily high real interest rates, that made devaluation inevitable.

It is revealing that even as evidence was becoming available that the devaluation was more successful than even its proponents had predicted, the Central Bank appears to have continued to believe that it could have been, and presumably should have been, avoided. The reasons advanced for not devaluing may be summarized:[10]

- **Sterling overshooting.** It was claimed that sterling had overshot and would soon return to its equilibrium value, relative to which the Irish pound was not misaligned. The competitive gain from sterling's devaluation would be quickly eroded as British inflation accelerated. Temporary subsidies would enable smaller firms vulnerable to competition from British firms to survive.
- **The structure of trade.** While the trade-weighted index of the Irish pound increased by about 8 per cent between the middle and end of 1992, its value in terms of sterling rose by more than 18 per cent. It was argued, however, that the diminished importance of sterling to the Irish economy insulated it from the impact of the sudden real appreciation. This was based on data on the geographical pattern of commodity trade which did not reflect the relative contribution of trade to employment or the effects of the depreciation of sterling on Irish firms in the domestic market and third countries.
- **The burden of external debt service.** It was argued that the real burden of servicing the country's large overhang of foreign currency borrowing, which had been concentrated in narrow-band ERM currencies in recent years, would increase as a consequence of a devaluation. Account was not taken of the countervailing effect of a devaluation on the Irish pound value of export receipts and transfers from the EC.
- **Credibility.** A devaluation would undermine the credibility that had been gained through the stability of the Irish pound/DM exchange rate over the preceding six years. It was in the country's long-term interest to maintain stability vis-à-vis the narrow-band ERM currencies rather than to return to a de facto sterling peg. Furthermore, it was claimed that the evidence from the aftermath of the 1986 devaluation showed that Irish interest rates would carry a risk premium relative to German rates for a long time after a devaluation. The fact that Spanish interest rates had risen after the peseta was devalued in September was cited as further evidence of this.

Table 4.1 Economic indicators: Ireland, UK and EC

	1987	1988	1989	1990	1991	1992
Inflation rate						
Irl	3.2	2.1	0.4	3.4	3.2	3.0
UK	4.2	4.9	7.8	9.5	5.9	3.8
EC	3.3	3.6	5.1	5.7	5.0	4.3
General govt. balance (% GDP)						
Irl	−9.7	−4.8	−1.8	−2.5	−2.5	−2.5
UK	−1.3	1.0	0.9	−1.3	−2.7	−0.6
EC	−4.1	−3.6	−2.9	−4.1	−4.6	−5.4
BoP current a/c (% GDP)						
Irl[a]	−0.3	0.3	−1.6	1.6	3.8	6.5
UK	−2.0	−4.5	−5.1	−3.5	−1.8	−1.8
EC	0.8	0.1	−0.1	−0.2	−0.6	−0.4
Debt/GDP ratio (%)						
Irl	122.0	120.4	110.1	103.0	103.0	100.4
UK	55.7	50.3	45.1	42.8	43.8	45.8
EC	51.5	81.0	50.3	60.3	61.8	63.4
Hourly earnings (% change)						
Irl	4.9	4.3	4.1	4.5	4.5	4.5
UK	8.0	8.5	8.7	9.4	8.2	6.0
EC	5.3	5.4	5.7	6.5	6.6	5.6
Hourly earnings[b]						
Irl	114	111	107	113	110	114
Unit wage costs[b]						
Irl	83	77	71	74	71	68

Notes: [a] The Irish figures for recent years are the revised ones published in March 1993.
[b] In common currency, 1980 = 100.

Sources: Government statement of 25 January 1993 and Central Bank of Ireland, *Quarterly Bulletin*.

- **'Our fundamentals are sound.'** The five indicators which the government repeatedly invoked to buttress this claim were inflation, the fiscal deficit, the current account,[11] the debt/GDP ratio and the rate of increase in hourly earnings. On four of these five indicators the Irish performance in 1992 was superior to the EC average (see Table 4.1). The exception was the debt/GDP ratio, but this had fallen from 122 to 100 per cent since 1987, whereas the EC average had risen from 51.5 to 63.4 per cent. Ireland was, and is, more likely to conform to the Maastricht criteria for admission to the EMU than all but a few other EC countries. The Irish authorities were anxious that the Irish pound be taken seriously as a candidate for membership of an inner circle or fast track within the ERM. It was argued that this prospect would be jeopardized by a devaluation.[12] The trend in labour unit costs could have been added to the list of favourable indicators: both the level and trend of wages in manufacturing industry adjusted for labour productivity compared favourably with those of other EC countries expressed in a common currency.

Missing from these arguments is an awareness of the effects of the sudden appreciation against sterling on the real economy, and in particular the level of employment and unemployment. The rate of growth of real GDP fell from 8.3 per cent in 1990 to 2.5 per cent in 1991 and 2 per cent in 1992. While these growth rates were the highest recorded in the EC, they were not high enough to generate any net increase in employment. The already-rapid growth of the labour force was augmented by a net inflow of population as conditions deteriorated in Britain. The numbers registered as unemployed increased by a third between early 1990 and the beginning of 1993. Ireland vied with Spain for the unenviable distinction of having the highest rate of unemployment in the EC. Against this background, the sudden real exchange rate appreciation caused by sterling's depreciation was particularly threatening due to the importance of Britain as a competitor in many labour-intensive markets such as clothing, food processing, electrical engineering, tourism and other services, as well as a rival location for transnational investment.[13]

Several Irish economic indicators – notably, the balance of trade, the composition of trade, unit labour costs – are heavily influenced by the performance of a relatively small number of transnational companies whose output is measured at prices designed to maximize the advantages of the favourable corporate tax regime. For example, three industrial sectors (pharmaceutical, office and data processing machinery and 'other foods') account for 28 per cent of the net output of Irish industry but only 7 per cent of industrial employment. These sectors are dominated by branches of foreign-owned companies and almost all their output is exported, but relatively little of it goes to the UK.[14] At the other extreme is the labour-intensive clothing industry, 63 per cent of whose exports go to Britain. During the debate on exchange rate policy after September 1992 it became clear that the traditional trade-weighted index of the geographical pattern of trade was a poor guide to the importance to the real economy of movements in bilateral exchange rates, the sterling/Irish pound rate in particular.

The second crucial consideration, omitted from the anti-devaluation arguments, was the effect of high interest rates on the economy. Most

Irish debt is short-term or at variable rates. Despite attempts by the Irish central bank to insulate retail credit markets from the effects of the loss of liquidity due to heavy selling of the pound on the foreign exchanges, by the end of 1992 businesses were faced with massive increases in the cost of borrowing and mortgage holders with up to 30 per cent increases in repayment.[15] The allocation of savings was affected as depositors moved money to higher paying accounts. Returns of over 15 per cent were offered at the retail level to attract funds. Cash was syphoned from businesses into these high-yielding deposits.

Finally, it may be asked whether the reaction of the markets to the rise in the sterling/Irish pound exchange rate was rational or were the authorities right to believe that markets could be persuaded that there was no need to devalue? Would it have been possible or desirable to have continued to try to convince the markets that the formal target zone vis-à-vis the DM should prevail over the informal one vis-à-vis sterling?

To answer these questions account should be taken of the econometric evidence, summarized above, which showed that the gain in credibility from Ireland's hard-currency policy after 1987 was incomplete and continued to be conditional on the level of the sterling/Irish pound exchange rate. The influence of the sterling exchange rate on Irish interest rates was an established phenomenon throughout the period of Ireland's adherence to the ERM and had not disappeared in the months before the September 1992 crisis. The relationship estimated over the preceding years suggested that an 18 per cent revaluation of the Irish pound relative to sterling would have led to an increase of between 3 and 8 per cent in the level of Irish short-term interest rates relative to an average of British and German rates. Moreover this response could be readily rationalized in terms of a model in which markets form a view as to the equilibrium sterling/Irish pound exchange rate and believe that positive deviations from this increase the probability of a depreciation. Thus the market reaction to the implications of the depreciation of sterling for the Irish pound was predictable.

In the Appendix to this chapter it is shown that it is possible to model the behaviour of Irish interest rates satisfactorily even during this turbulent period. The key influences were the sterling exchange rate and British interest rates. There was a structural break with the past reflected in the enhanced importance of the British variables (the interest rate and the exchange rate) and the diminished role of German interest rates.

THE LESSONS TO BE LEARNED

A number of lessons should be learned from the Irish experience during and after the 1992 crisis in the EMS. These include:

- Reversing a sudden and unwarranted real exchange rate appreciation by lowering a currency's central rate in the ERM does not undermine credibility. This is borne out by the rapid falls in Irish interest rates since the January 1993 devaluation and by the resumption of the long-run trend reduction in the Irish–German interest rate differential after the 1986 devaluation.
- Holding on to an overvalued exchange rate in the face of market sentiment is costly and misguided. Markets had a clear view of the importance of the (real) sterling exchange rate to the Irish economy. It was futile for the authorities to try to shake the conviction that the pound was overvalued or to argue that this did not matter for the real economy. *Real* fundamentals, especially the prospects for employment and unemployment, cannot be ignored in deciding on exchange rate policy.
- Increased national cooperation, taking the form of large-scale intervention to support the Irish pound, would not have resolved the problem. Even if the market's expectations that the Irish pound was going to be devalued could have been broken, this would only have eliminated the interest rate premium. The misalignment against sterling would have remained and continued to damage the real economy.

The Irish case is unique in the EMS because of the importance of sterling and its volatility outside the ERM. The Irish road to monetary union remains very uncertain in the face of this problem. This uncertainty cannot be resolved by proposals for increased cooperation between central banks to support currencies that come under pressure due to well-founded beliefs about their sustainable levels. A move to the wider band in the ERM might prove helpful, but if sterling continues to be as volatile in the future as it has in the past, such a measure would be relatively ineffective. However, a recognition by both the Irish and EC authorities that a realignment of the Irish pound in response to a loss of competitiveness due to the depreciation of sterling does not mean a devaluation 'on its own initiative' would be both realistic and helpful.

APPENDIX: MODELLING THE BEHAVIOUR OF IRISH INTEREST RATES

Ireland's situation as a member of the ERM when its main trading partner, Britain, was not provides an interesting opportunity for modelling the influences on interest rates in a small open economy. Table 4.2 contains the results of estimating an error-correction model based on the two considerations: (i) that Irish interest rates are influenced by both German and British rates and (ii) that the level of the (real) Irish pound/sterling exchange rate affects expectations about the probability of a devaluation of the Irish pound in the ERM. (The model was originally applied to the pre-crisis period in Walsh, 1993.

Table 4.2 Regression of Irish short term interest rates (i) on German interest rates (i^{DM}), British interest rates (i^{STG}) amd the Stg£/Ir£ real exchange rate (ε^{STG}) (dependent variable = Δi)

Period	86m8–92m8	86m8–89m7	89m8–92m8	92w32–93w16	92w32–93w16
Intercept	−6.96 (3.33)	−10.14 (3.13)	−10.69 (3.45)	−45.97 (4.25)	−43.87 (4.06)
Δi^{DM}	0.1875 (1.11)	0.0983 (0.40)	0.4750 (2.04)	−0.166 (0.13)	
Δi^{STG}	0.1848 (1.65)	0.2022 (1.25)	0.2589 (1.76)	−0.266 (0.12)	1.298 (0.89)
$\Delta \varepsilon^{STG}$	0.1445 (4.00)	0.1464 (2.76)	0.1517 (3.72)	0.502 (3.25)	0.421 (2.94)
i^{DM}_{-1}	0.1845 (3.49)	0.1296 (0.60)	0.6110 (3.89)	2.161 (1.13)	
i^{STG}_{-1}	0.0703 (2.68)	0.2013 (1.53)	0.2819 (4.29)	−0.362 (0.40)	0.662 (2.71)
ε^{STG}_{-1}	0.0907 (3.36)	0.1181 (3.02)	0.1405 (3.56)	0.359 (2.68)	0.451 (4.38)
i_{-1}	−0.265 (3.99)	−0.2961 (3.37)	−0.8946 (4.75)	−0.524 (5.96)	−0.531 (5.99)
D1[a]	2.2940 (4.69)	2.2940 (4.61)			
D2[b]				14.45 (7.02)	13.79 (7.16)
$\bar{R}^2$	0.60	0.66	0.67	0.72	0.71
SE	0.389	0.446	0.254	1.78	1.80
Prob (F)[c] (serial correlation)	0.568	0.582	0.607	0.271	0.246

Notes: [a] D1 is a dummy variable for October 1986 to reflect exceptional fiscal developments.
[b] D2 is a dummy variable for week ending 8 January 1993, to reflect effect of finance minister's statement.
[c] The F-statistic is for the Lagrange multiplier test of residual serial correlation.
t-statistics are in parentheses.

Source: Weekly data supplied by Davy's Stockbrokers.

For the period between the 1986 devaluation and the September 1992 crisis, the model works well and, as has been summarized in the body of the chapter, indicates that the weights of German and British interest rates shifted as the time from the devaluation lengthened, with the weight of the German rate increasing and that of the British rate diminishing. The sterling exchange rate was a significant influence throughout, indicating that an appreciation against sterling increased expectations of a devaluation and led to higher interest rates in Dublin.

When re-estimated for the period August 1992 to April 1993 (on weekly, as distinct from monthly, data) the model continues to perform well, but the magnitude of the coefficients changes dramatically, indicating a clear structural break. The declining influence of sterling interest rates is reversed and German interest rates can be deleted from the equation without significant loss of explanatory power. When this is done, the hypothesis that the coefficients of the (lagged) Irish and British interest rate variables are equal and opposite in sign cannot be rejected, suggesting that over this period Irish interest rates came fully back under the influence of UK rates. The influence of the sterling exchange rate is also enhanced, and indicates that during the crisis a 10 pence rise in the value of the Irish pound relative to sterling, *ceteris paribus*, added 849 basis points to short-term Irish interest rates. The major, if transitory, impact of the hint by the finance minister, early in January, that there might be a change in policy is also striking.

While the switch from German to British dominance in Irish financial markets following the events of September 1992 was beneficial in the short run, as sterling's float outside the ERM resulted in much lower rates in Britain than in Germany, the longer-run implication is that the Irish policy of gaining credibility as a member of the inner core of the ERM was undermined, if not destroyed. The prospects for rebuilding this credibility depend ultimately on British policy relating to the ERM.

NOTES

1 This summary draws on Leddin and Walsh (1992), Chapters 11 and 13.
2 This was the largest unilateral devaluation in the history of the ERM, but it was surpassed by Belgium's 8.5 per cent devaluation in 1982, when Denmark also devalued.
3 The Irish pound participated in the general 3 per cent devaluation against the DM in January 1987, but this had relatively little impact on the market rate.
4 'From EMS to EMU: the case of Ireland', Central Bank of Ireland, *Quarterly Bulletin*, Winter 1992, p.45.
5 There was also a switch from government borrowing in foreign currencies to selling Irish government securities to non-residents.
6 The meeting of the Irish Economic Association in September 1991 was devoted to this topic and the papers published in *The Economic and Social Review*, April 1992.

7   The remaining exchange controls allowed the central bank to prevent Irish banks lending to non-residents wishing to sell the Irish pound short.
8   It is estimated that the fall in reserves plus the total of increased external borrowing and intervention amounted to about £4bn. Repaying this at a premium of about 8 per cent represents a cost of £320m or just over 1 per cent of GNP.
9   However, in some circles the position of the Irish pound in the ERM became a symbol of national independence (from Britain?). In an editorial published 9 January 1993 *The Irish Times* stated that 'It is the duty of a sovereign government to defend its currency as it would its national territory.' After the devaluation, the same newspaper proclaimed its 'grief' at the decision.
10 A summary of these was contained in a government statement issued just days before the devaluation.
11 It is not without significance for the debate on the soundness of Ireland's fundamentals that at the time of the currency crisis the surplus for 1992 was estimated as equalling 8 per cent of GNP. In March 1993 the Central Statistics Office published revised figures that substantially reduced the size of the surplus. A disturbing feature of the Irish balance of payments data is that, even after the recent revision the estimated net residual (that is, the sum of the current and capital accounts) amounts to 5.8 per cent of GNP in 1990.
12 There was no discussion of whether an Irish devaluation in the circumstances of January 1993 would constitute a devaluation 'on the country's own initiative', which is what the Treaty refers to in Article 109j and the relevant Protocol.
13 During the currency crisis Digital announced that it was moving most of its Galway plant to Scotland as part of a worldwide rationalization. While this particular move may not have been directly affected by the exchange rate, an overvalued currency would in the long run encourage more such decisions.
14 Data are for 1988. 'Other foods' includes plants that produce and export well-known soft-drink concentrates.
15 Due to recent changes in the tax system, the typical taxpayer enjoyed little relief on the increased interest payments.

REFERENCES

Bertola, Giuseppe and Drazen, Allan (1993), 'Trigger points and budget cuts: explaining the effects of fiscal austerity', *American Economic Review*, 83 (1), March, 11–26.

Dornbusch, Rudiger (1989), 'Credibility, debt and unemployment: Ireland's failed stabilization', *Economic Policy*, 8, March, 174–209.

Giavazzi, Francesco and Pagano, Marco (1990), 'Can severe fiscal contraction be expansionary? Tales of two small European countries', in Olivier Blanchard and Stanley Fischer (eds), *NBER Macroeconomic Annual 1990*, Cambridge, MA, MIT Press, pp.75–110.

Honohan, Patrick and Conroy, Charlie (1993), 'Sterling movements and Irish pound interest rates', The Economic and Social Research Institute, Dublin, mimeo, January.

Hughes, Jenny and Hurley, Margaret (1993), 'Simple tests of target zones: the Irish case', Centre for Economic Research, University College, Dublin, Working Paper 1993-4.

Leddin, Anthony and Walsh, Brendan (1992), *The Macroeconomy of Ireland* (2nd edn), Dublin, Gill and Macmillan.

Walsh, Brendan (1993), 'Credibility, interest rates and the ERM: the Irish experience 1986-92', *Oxford Bulletin of Economics and Statistics*, forthcoming.

5

ITALY IN THE EMS: AFTER CRISIS, SALVATION?

Stefano Micossi and Pier Carlo Padoan

MACROECONOMIC DEVELOPMENTS IN THE EIGHTIES

In 1980, after the second oil shock, the rate of (consumer price) inflation was above 20 per cent, some 16 points higher than in Germany; by the end of 1986 it had come down to below 6 per cent (Table 5.1).

The initial impulse to disinflation came from very severe monetary and exchange rate policies. Interest rates on government paper went up from 12–13 per cent in late 1978 to 20–21 per cent at the end of 1981, those on bank loans to 22–24 per cent. Between 1979 and 1982 the lira appreciated in real terms by 7 per cent (Visco, 1990).

Firms in the manufacturing sector reacted by seeking productivity increases through labour shedding; 1 million workers were displaced from industry between 1980 and 1985, with labour productivity increases totalling almost 25 per cent. Economy-wide productivity, however, only went up by about 5 per cent, owing to the decline observed for services and construction not involved in the restructuring process and also saw an increase in the number of jobs (+1.7million) that more than compensated the reduction in industry. Some one-third of this increased employment was in the public sector.

The restructuring of industry was supported by government subsidies for investment, and by unemployment compensation mechanisms (Cassa Integrazione Guadagni, or CIG) that preserved almost entirely replaced workers' wages, but also worked to reduce the impact of unemployment on the labour market. Nominal wages and labour costs per worker decelerated considerably, but still showed nominal increases well above those of competitors; over 1981–1985 real wage increases averaged 2.1 per cent per year, albeit that there was a slowdown in 1984/85. However, firms were still enjoying the benefits of the reduction

Table 5.1 Italy: basic data (% changes unless otherwise specified)

	1980−85	1986−89	1990−91	1992
GDP	1.9	3.3	1.7	0.9
Consumption	2.3	3.9	2.4	1.8
Investment	0.7	4.6	2.2	−1.4
Exports	1.6	5.3	3.6	5.0
Imports	2.6	6.6	5.5	4.6
GDP deflator	15.2	6.7	7.5	4.7
CPI deflator	15.2	5.9	6.5	5.4
Wages				
manufacturing	16.6	7.5	9.0	6.3
services	15.3	7.4	9.4	5.7
public sector	18.9	9.8	12.2	2.7
Unit labour cost				
manufacturing	11.3	3.5	7.2	3.3
services	15.7	5.4	8.7	4.1
Trade balance[a]	−2.5	−0.3	−0.4	−0.2
Current account balance[a]	−1.1	−0.4	−1.6	−2.1
Public sector				
total spending	21.7	10.4	11.7	8.7
'primary' spending	20.9	9.9	10.6	6.5
total revenues	21.4	12.3	11.8	11.2
total balance[a]	−11.0	−10.8	−10.6	−9.5
'primary' balance[a]	−4.0	−2.4	−0.7	1.9
outstanding debt stock[a]	70.0	93.4	102.3	110.5

Note: [a] Percentage ratios to GDP.

of social security contributions (equivalent to some 4 per cent of the wage bill; cf. Giavazzi and Spaventa, 1989 and Micossi and Traù, 1989) introduced in the late seventies.

Meanwhile, the public sector deficit was increasing rapidly, to a peak of 12.6 per cent of GDP in 1985, owing to the various measures decided in support of industry and the unemployed, to generous improvements in the pension system and, more broadly, to an acceleration in all components of current spending that was incompletely offset by rising revenues; between 1980 and 1985 total public sector spending, as a ratio to GDP, went up by some 9.1 percentage points, largely as a result of increased 'primary' (i.e. non-interest) spending.

The period 1984–1986 saw an attempt to strengthen disinflation through income policies and some correction of fiscal imbalances. Wage indexation was effectively reduced to under 50 per cent (with the 1986 reform; cf. Visco, 1990); in 1984 the government forced the unions to accept 'predeterminated' cost of living adjustments based on planned rather than actual price developments. By the end of 1984 the rate of inflation and unit labour cost increases were down to around 8 per cent.

After increasing rapidly up to 1985, public spending was (more or less) stabilized as a share of GDP, and the deficit started to come down slowly. In that year the dollar began to depreciate and in 1986 the price of oil fell sharply, leading to a terms-of-trade gain close to 16 per cent and pushing domestic inflation (for a short while) below 5 per cent.

In 1986–1989 growth picked up to a buoyant 3.3 per cent rate but the decline in inflation first came to a halt and then was reversed; in 1990/91 the rate of consumer price increase was 6.5 per cent, above the average for 1987–1989. Inflation would have been even higher were it not for a new sizeable external bonus stemming from renewed depreciation in the dollar.

The apparent immediate source of this return of inflation was the acceleration in wages in 1987–1989: compensation per worker in manufacturing went up by 8.1 per cent, 2.7 per cent in real terms. Even higher was the increase in non-market services (public sector) wages (10.4 per cent, 4.8 per cent in real terms), bringing the economy's average up to 8.7 per cent (3.2 per cent in real terms). Higher still was the increase in labour cost per worker, notably in manufacturing, due to the phasing out of social security contribution exemptions that had been granted in the late seventies (Figure 5.1).

Two factors combined to hide for some time the price pressures that were building up. First, developments in international prices and exchange rate of the dollar remained fairly favourable; after the large bonus of 1986, smaller but still appreciable gains were made in the ensuing three years (0.8 per cent per year). As a result, in 1987–1989 the foreign component on the whole added very little to price changes. Second, the acceleration of activity brought about large gains in productivity (3 per cent per year for the total economy, 4.7 per cent for manufacturing) that kept the increase in labour cost per unit of output below 6 per cent for the total economy and just above 4 per cent in manufacturing.

Thus, the full impact of rising domestic costs was only felt in 1990, when industrial production peaked and then started to decline; GDP growth fell to around 1 per cent in 1991/92.

Up until 1987/88, the exchange rate policy did not accommodate inflation differentials, thus representing a disciplining factor on domestic cost pressures, and yet was careful to avoid the emergence of major imbalances in Italy's competitive position, with timely recourse to realignments of the lira central rates. After 1987, however, the exchange rate policy became more rigid, and in 1990 Italy decided to adopt the narrow fluctuation band for the lira. As can be seen (Figure 5.2), the real exchange rate started to appreciate sharply in 1988, leading to an overall worsening of Italy's competitive position, since the inception of the ERM, of some 10 to 15 per cent, depending on the measure adopted.

The real appreciation of the lira in the eighties showed up, over the years, in the deterioration of the real trade balance vis-à-vis the rest of

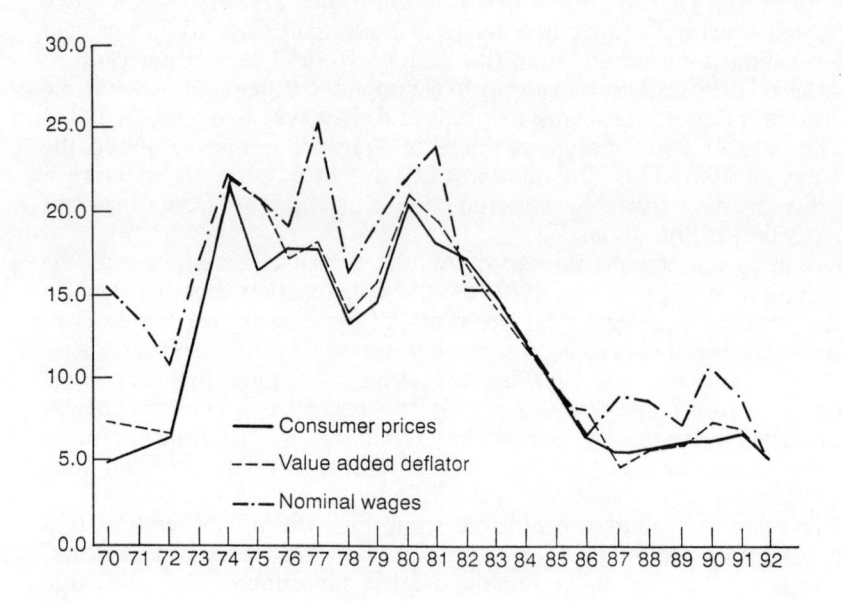

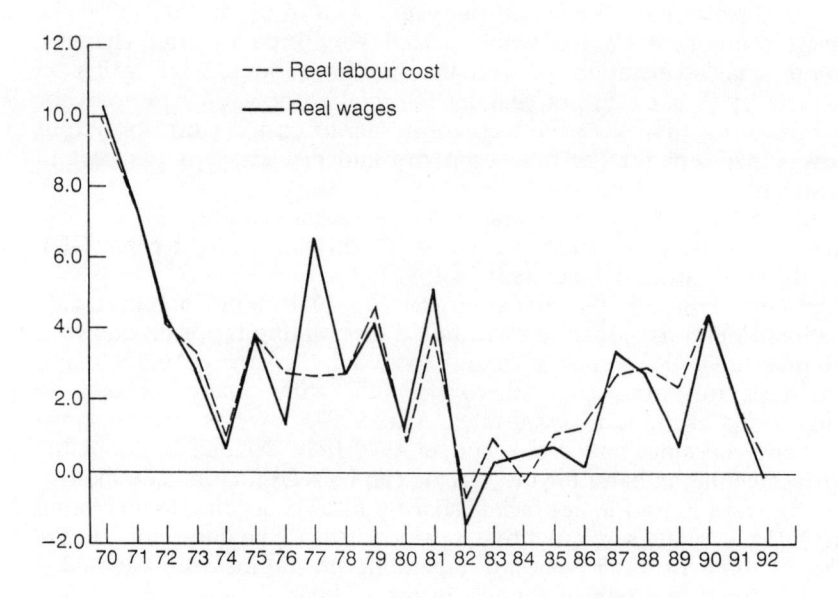

Figure 5.1 Prices and wages in Italy, 1970–1992 (percentage changes)

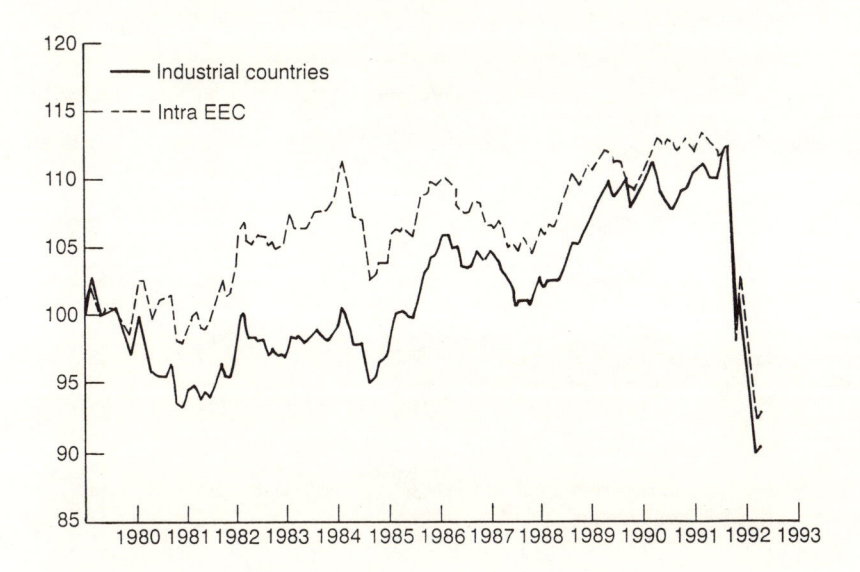

Figure 5.2 Italy: real exchange rates (1980 = 100) Based on producer prices in manufacturing. Increase = real appreciation, decrease = real depreciation

Source: CSC estimates based on OECD, ISTAT data.

Europe (partly hidden in nominal figures by the steady improvement in terms of trade) and a sharp increase in import penetration. The share of manufacturing in total output (at current prices) shrank from some 30 to 25 per cent: in the late eighties deindustrialization started to become an issue.

The exchange rate discipline hit hard on industry, where remarkable productivity increases were recorded, but much less so on the rest of the economy; productivity in the public sector actually declined in the first half of the eighties, partly as a result of employment increasing to absorb labour shed by industry, and showed modest increases in most of the private service sector (Pellegrini, 1992).

Consumption was always rising more rapidly than GDP, and more rapidly than in the rest of the EC (Table 5.2); exports and investment showed lower-than-GDP growth rates and below-average performance in Europe; imports grew more than GDP (with a strong rise in import penetration), more or less in line with the rest of Europe. The real appreciation of the lira also contributed to shifting relative prices and resources in favour of domestic absorption, notably consumption and services, and away from exports and investment in industry.

In sum, the picture of a country with a systematic excess of demand

Table 5.2 GDP growth and main demand components in Italy and the EEC in the 1980s[a]

	Italy		EEC[b]	
	1980–91	1987–91	1980–91	1987–91
GDP growth (yearly average)	2.3	2.8	2.3	2.9
Consumption				
(yearly average) percentage change	2.9	3.5	2.1	3.0
% share of GDP: beginning of period	61.9	63.8	60.6	61.5
: end of period	65.5	65.5	61.1	61.1
Investment				
(yearly average) percentage change	2.2	4.1	2.2	5.1
% share of GDP: beginning of period	23.2	20.9	20.7	19.4
: end of period	21.9	21.9	21.1	21.1
Exports				
(yearly average) percentage change	3.1	5.1	4.5	6.0
% share of GDP: beginning of period	18.5	21.1	28.8	32.5
: end of period	23.3	23.3	37.3	37.3
Imports				
(yearly average) percentage change	4.4	6.8	4.3	7.0
% share of GDP: beginning of period	21.5	24.1	30.1	33.1
: end of period	27.6	27.6	38.7	38.7

Notes: [a] Growth rates on data at constant prices (geometric means); shares of GDP on data at current prices.
[b] EC-12 excluding Italy.
Source: ISTAT and EUROSTAT, National Accounts.

over domestic output, mainly related to rapid consumption growth and a significant increase in the propensity to consume, is fairly clear. At the same time, historical experience shows that the eighties are the only period in postwar history when Italy was growing less rapidly than the rest of Europe; the exchange-rate constraint can explain this only in the presence of extensive rigidities and non-neutralities.

When financial markets started to have doubts on the solidity of the European construction, in the spring of 1992, Italy found itself with high costs and low competitiveness, a very high public-debt to GDP ratio (over 100 per cent), and high unemployment (above 10 per cent). It obviously offered an excellent target for speculators: high unemployment and the risk of debt explosion made it clear that interest rates could not be raised for very long to the heights required to fend off speculation. Failure by European bodies to agree on a broader realignment, early in September 1992, and delays in enacting much-needed corrective measures to trim the public deficit domestically, eventually doomed the lira, and it was pushed out of the ERM on 17 September.

EMS CREDIBILITY EFFECTS

It has often been argued that many benefits from membership in the ERM stem from the 'discipline' effects on inflation of the exchange rate constraint, and from the 'credibility bonus' enjoyed by members, who can thus pay a lower price – in terms of lost output and jobs – for disinflation. To the extent that wage-earners and enterprises believe that the government 'means business' in its determination to lower inflation, inflation will go down as a result of changed expectations.

This discipline-credibility hypothesis can be, and has been, tested with wage-price and other labour market data, and with financial markets data. We will examine in turn the evidence that has been produced in these two areas.

Wages, prices and the labour market

As can be seen in Figure 5.3, unemployment was steadily rising during disinflation and did not recover much in the ensuing period of rapid expansion of activity. Real wages showed a decline only in one year (1982), then picked up again with a distinct acceleration in the second half of the decade (Figure 5.1), notably in the public sector and in manufacturing, as soon as the economy returned to buoyant expansion.

Formal econometric testing has failed to confirm any role of price expectations in helping disinflation or mitigating adjustment costs.

The role of expectations in disinflation is belittled by direct analysis of survey data on inflation expectations.[1] Visco (1984a) had shown that the generating process of these price expectations (for wholesale and consumer prices), while being consistent with the requirement of efficient use of information and absence of bias, basically is an adaptive error-learning model combined with regressive (return-to-normality) elements. Estimation of wage equations that included inflation expectations, in Visco (1984b), also showed that any effect of expectations on nominal wages is short lived; catching up for past anticipation errors plays a crucial role in ensuring neutrality and absence of inflation unemployment trade-offs in the long run. The implication of these results is that what matters most in wage determination is lagged actual inflation.

De Nardis and Micossi (1991) re-estimated the Visco equation for wages over the sample periods beginning in 1970 and ending in 1982-IQ, 1984-IIQ and 1989-IVQ: they found that in the eighties, over time, the impact of unemployment on wage changes declined after the sharp increase of the early eighties. Indeed, in the second part of the

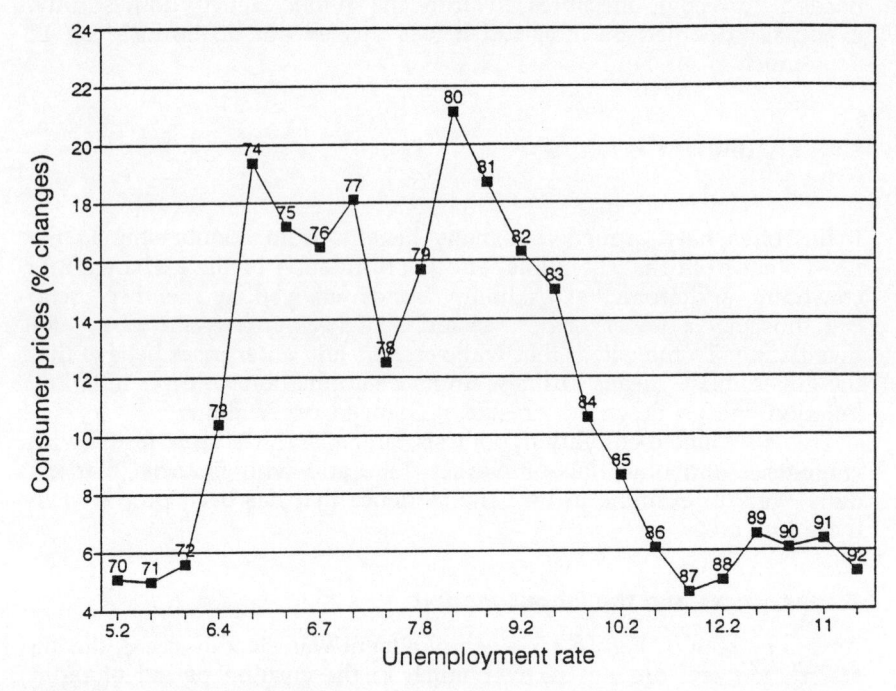

Figure 5.3 Inflation and unemployment in Italy

decade unemployment stabilized around a rather high level and seemed 'disconnected' from output growth. Altogether, the Visco equation performs remarkably well through the decade, and its basic 'learning-adaptive' features are maintained: in other words, there was little change in the expectation generating mechanism.

These results were confirmed by Egebo and Englander (1992), who found that for Italy (as well as other ERM participants) the wage relationships estimated over 1972–1986 either fit the post-1986 data reasonably well or underpredict actual real wage increases. Their evidence clearly points to the conclusion that any credibility effect stemming from ERM membership was small and slow to come about, and hence to the need to ground in other (supply side) policies successful stabilization of the exchange rate and nominal convergence.

Credibility in financial markets

Italy completed capital liberalization before the deadline requested for phase 1 of monetary unification, and the lira entered the narrow band in January 1990. This was interpreted as a sign of a strengthened commitment to a fixed parity in the ERM. The evidence for this could be

Table 5.3 Bertola–Svensson test – selected results

Data frequency	k (months)	a_1	(t-value)	Mean reversion
Daily	1	0.295	(6.47)	No
Daily	6	−0.7	(8.39)	Yes
Weekly	3	−0.38	(3.34)	Yes
Weekly	6	−0.87	(6.98)	Yes
Monthly	1	−0.605	(3.51)	No
Monthly	6	−0.542	(1.67)	No

Notes: Regression equation: $SC(t + k) - SC(t) = a_0 + a_1 SC(t) + u_t$; $k = 1, 3, 6, 12$ months; sample period: 1990–1992.
$SC(t)$ = difference between (log) current exchange rate and (log) central rate.

traced to the increasingly large capital inflows which more than compensated the – also increasing – current account deficit; the lira appreciated in nominal terms vis-à-vis the DM until the end of 1990.

Capital inflows peaked in 1990 and then started to decline while the current deficit kept on growing. In 1991 the interest rate differential with the DM started to rise again, after declining for several years, in spite of declining inflation differentials.

These facts still do not answer a very simple question: had the Italian currency ever obtained full credibility of its ERM peg on financial markets? Two pieces of evidence seem to suggest the contrary. One, reported by Eichengreen and Wyplosz (1993), is based on the behaviour of forward exchange rates: from 1987 to 1989 and again since the beginning of 1992, the forward rate remained below the bottom of the ERM band; it was within the band in 1990/91. This evidence is consistent with rising credibility starting from the end of 1988, as confirmed by massive capital inflow in 1989/90. It also suggests, however, that credibility was never solid enough to be able to conclude that the lira exchange rate was seen as 'irrevocably' fixed.

Similar evidence can be obtained from the application of the Bertola–Svensson (1990) test for credibility of a target zone applied to the EMS currencies. On this basis, Frankel and Phillips (1991) had found the lira participation in the ERM credible over the period January 1987–December 1989.[2] We have extended the exercise to 1990–1992, and have found that credibility weakens steadily, already starting in 1990 (Table 5.3).

INFLATION AND THE PUBLIC SECTOR

Now the questions that arise in trying to understand Italy's experience in the EMS stand out more clearly: how was it possible that consumer prices, notably the prices of services, and wages could continue to increase steadily above the European average despite non-accommodating monetary policy? Since the persistent shortfall of domestic supply relative to domestic demand must be an important part of the explanation, how was it possible that this disequilibrium could be sustained for so long? In sum, how was it possible that more than ten years of stringent exchange-rate policies failed to change private behaviour and expectations?

Indeed, if normal adjustment forces worked, over time the real appreciation of the exchange rate should have led to higher unemployment, slower wage growth, and reduced excess demand. Since we did get the increase in unemployment but did not get the ensuing equilibrating responses, we must look for some systematic factor that muted the effects of those equilibrating forces.

In a very interesting paper on the experience of Belgium in the late seventies and early eighties, de Grauwe (1983) had noted that expansionary fiscal policy could be an important factor impeding or retarding adjustment in a country with an overvalued exchange rate. Froot and Rogoff (1991) had also tried to show that public spending had been a main cause for the appreciation of the lira real exchange rate, basically via aggregate demand pressures. We believe that both these stories are relevant, but that the perverse role of the public sector has been more pervasive, working also through the supply side; and that the broad behaviour of the public sector can provide a good deal of the explanation of Italy's inflation problem in the eighties.

Price, wage, and productivity data leave an outside observer with little doubt that the public sector has been a direct source of inflation, simply as a result of financial laxity and inefficient management.

The non-sale services (public administration) deflator displayed in 1980–1991 an average yearly increase of 13.8 per cent; it declined from 17.5 per cent in 1980/85 to 9.2 in 1986/89, but rose again to 12.1 per cent in 1990/91. The corresponding figures for manufacturing were 8.1 per cent in 1980/91, 12.4 in 1980/85, 4.5 per cent in 1986/89, 2.9 per cent in 1990/91. Thus as may be seen, the rate of increase of the public sector deflator was a multiple of private industry's and was rising again since 1986.

The public sector also displayed the highest wage increases and the lowest increases in productivity through the eighties; in 1990/91 unit wages accelerated to a 12.2 per cent rate of increase, after growing by 8.4 per cent in 1986/89 (8 and 7.4 per cent respectively in manufacturing). As a result of higher growth over a decade, in 1991 the average compensation per employee (based on NA data) was just above 49m lire for the public administration, around 40m for the rest of the economy (41m for industry, 39m for services).[3]

Loose budget constraints, inefficiency, overmanning and generous wages also characterize many public utilities, public enterprises, and the banking system (which is also largely publicly-owned). The Mediobanca (1992) survey of 1,790 large companies, for instance, shows in 1991 average wages of 55m lire for private companies, 58m for public companies. This number rises to 63m lire for public utilities in the sample, 71.5m lire for transportation. It goes without saying that most public companies have accumulated large debts, often close to or above the value of their annual sales.

Detailed studies on public utilities were conducted by Prosperetti (1992a and 1992b; see also Centro Studi Confindustria, 1992b): they show in general higher costs and lower quality of services, relative to other industrial countries.

A recent study prepared for the EC Commission (Ernst & Young, 1992) on public procurement has provided fresh evidence on the high costs paid by the public sector for its services, supplies and equipment; important side effects of lowering technological standards and muting competitive pressure in suppliers' markets are also identified. A recent wave of judiciary inquiries, exposing extensive bribery on public works and other public contracts, has confirmed that the price eventually paid by the public sector was often a multiple of the initial contract-award price.

It is already clear from the above that direct influences on prices are only part of the story: extensive government intervention systematically altered relative prices, income distribution, and the structure of production and employment. Large increases in direct taxation and social security contributions, that had led Italy, at the end of the eighties, to an above-average tax pressure relative to the EC, added further to distortions.

Some basic facts are worth recalling in this regard. Italy's decision to become a member of the EMS, in 1979, almost exactly coincided with a sharp acceleration in public spending, that led over the ensuing decade to some 11 percentage-points increase in the ratio of spending to GDP (Table 5.4). Revenues were also growing rapidly, as a share of GDP, less rapidly than spending until 1985, more rapidly afterwards. The public sector deficit, as a result, continued to increase (to a peak of 13 per cent of GDP) until the middle of the decade, and declined afterwards; it has remained through the eighties and early nineties above 10 per cent of GDP, leading to a sharp increase in the debt-to-GDP ratio (which in 1990 surpassed 100 per cent).

The increase in spending was largely concentrated by functional category in interest payments, personnel, pensions and other welfare; by government level in decentralized spending units (local governments and USL, the health management bodies; see Franco, 1992). In the second half of the eighties there was a distinct slowdown in transfers to enterprises (that declined in real terms) and capital spending, while payments to households accelerated in real terms (Table 5.4).

Revenues grew through the decade more rapidly than GDP, with the indirect taxes and social security contributions picking up in 1987–1991. Tax burdens remained unevenly distributed, with agriculture, small handicraft, most of small distribution and liberal professions, and the Mezzogiorno de jure or de facto subject to very light burdens.

Table 5.4 Selected variables in public sector finances (yearly percentage changes and percentage ratios to GDP)

	Percentage changes				Percentage ratios to GDP		
	1980–91		1987–91		1979	1986	1991
	Nominal	Real	Nominal	Real			
Total spending	16.1	5.1	10.9	4.5	41.2	51.0	53.9
net of interest	15.4	4.4	10.3	4.0	36.2	42.5	43.7
Current spending	16.3	5.2	11.3	4.9	37.1	45.9	49.1
Interest payments	20.5	9.1	13.8	7.2	5.0	8.5	10.2
Personnel	15.1	4.2	11.5	5.1	10.8	11.7	12.7
Pensions	16.0	5.0	12.0	5.6	9.6	11.2	12.4
Transfers to enterprises	12.0	1.3	4.1	−1.9	2.8	3.1	2.4
Total revenues	16.7	5.6	12.0	5.6	31.6	39.4	43.7
Tax revenues	17.8	6.6	13.1	6.6	16.5	21.9	25.6
direct	18.8	7.5	12.3	5.9	8.4	12.9	14.5
indirect	16.7	5.6	14.2	7.7	8.0	9.1	11.1
Social security contrib.	14.9	3.9	10.8	4.5	12.8	13.9	14.7
Total balance[a]	−10.9		−10.6		−9.6	−11.6	−10.2
net of interest[a]	−2.9		−1.6		−4.6	−3.1	−0.0
Current balance[a]	−6.3		−6.0		−5.6	−6.8	−6.1
Total debt					61.6	88.2	104.0
Per memoriam							
GDP	13.6	2.8	9.7	3.4			

Note: [a] Percentage ratios to GDP.

Source: ISTAT, National Accounts.

Distortions are magnified by the complexity of legislation, the large number of special cases, and poor administration. There is evidence that forward shifting of taxation by wage-earners was significant and increasing over time (Tullio, 1986; Micossi and Tullio, 1991): the effect, of course, is that increases in direct taxation have become more inflationary. The share of taxes collected from enterprises, the self-employed, and the regions of the Centre-North increased during the decade.

On the whole, therefore, there was sizeable redistribution, through the budget, in favour of households in lower income brackets and the Mezzogiorno, against middle–high income brackets, enterprises, and the Centre-North. Moreover, since most revenues were collected centrally and an increasing share of spending was undertaken by decentralized spending units, administrators were encouraged to overlook the budget constraint, while the beneficiaries of spending programmes and citizens in general had limited perception of their costs.

Closer inspection of disaggregate data for households and enterprises can help complete the picture. As for households, it has been mentioned already that the increase in spending mainly took the form of direct job creation, pensions and other benefits; there was a large increase both in the number of people receiving benefits and in the average payment (Franco, 1992). The increase in payments well outpaced that of revenues, so that net transfers to households went up (Micossi and Papi, 1993). In the Mezzogiorno in 1988 the sum of personnel and welfare spending by the public sector had reached 49 per cent of the area's GDP, some 70 per cent of disposable income (Micossi and Tullio, 1991).

In Table 5.5 we have decomposed increases in NA disposable income by source. Again, the growing weight of payments from the public sector – interest payments, welfare, public sector wages – is striking: public sector wages and pensions 'explain' 41 per cent of disposable income growth in 1980–1991 (7.2 percentage points out of 12.9 total nominal growth), 46 per cent in 1987–1991 (5.5 per cent out of a total of 8.8); if interest payments on public debt are included these numbers become respectively 56 per cent in 1980–1991 and 63 per cent in 1987–1991. While there is no evidence on the influence of these developments in determining the rapid increase of consumption and the conditions of 'excessive absorption' that were noted above, one would guess that they must have played some role, given their distributional implications.

Turning to enterprises, three aspects should be noted. First, during the eighties there was a trend ('structural') increase in the tax wedge between labour cost and net pay: Italy's wedge ranks among the highest in the industrial world (Table 5.6). Second, for the first part of the decade the trend increase was delayed, or hidden, by discretionary exemptions of part of statutory rates; cost-reduction effects were reinforced by mechanisms for temporary unemployment compensation that made it easier for firms to shed labour and reduced labour cost. Third, transfers to enterprises were used to foster the restructuring process but also worked to an important extent to slow exit from sectors hit by declining competitiveness: this is made evident by the high share of transfers that were utilized for 'defensive' purposes and the small share that was reserved for manufacturing, exports and R&D (Ford and Suyker, 1989, Centro Studi Confindustria, 1992a).

Large increases in personal transfers must also have had important consequences on the labour market. The fact is that unemployment is largely concentrated in the South; that wages are almost the same in the North and the South, despite labour productivity differentials of the order of 20 per cent; and that in the eighties migration from the South to the North came to a virtual halt. The difference in labour costs that would have resulted from equal wages with different productivity has been made up by a special exemption from social security contributions in the South; not only was there no tendency for the productivity gap to close, but in the eighties it widened again (Svimez, 1992).

Table 5.5 Disposable income growth and its components[a]

	1980–91		1987–91		Weights in total income	
	% change and contributions	Share of total increase	% change and contributions	Share of total increase	1980	1991
Disposable income	12.9	100.0	8.8	100.0	100.0	100.0
Wages and salaries	5.8	45.0	4.2	47.7	46.2	45.4
private sector	4.1	31.8	2.9	33.0	35.7	32.8
industry	1.8	14.0	1.2	13.6	19.7	15.2
services	2.0	15.5	1.4	15.9	13.1	15.1
public sector	1.7	13.2	1.3	14.8	10.5	12.6
Social security payments[b]	3.6	27.9	2.7	30.7	18.6	25.8
Interest payments on public debt	1.9	14.7	1.5	17.0	4.7	12.3
Other incomes[c]	1.6	12.4	0.4	4.5	30.6	16.5
Per memoriam						
Real disposable income	2.1	100.0	2.6	100.0		
due to terms of trade changes[d]	0.5	23.8	0.2	7.7		

Notes: [a] Yearly geometric averages.
[b] Pensions and other welfare.
[c] Profits, other interests and dividends, net foreign income and residual item.
[d] Approximated by change in export prices (in lire) times exports at constant prices minus change in import prices.

Source: ISTAT, National Accounts and our estimates.

Table 5.6 Tax and social contribution wedge between labour cost and direct compensation for an unmarried worker (in 1989) (net compensation of a worker in manufacturing = 100)

		Italy	France	Germany	UK
1. Gross compensation	1979	125	125	146	142
	1989	138	132	155	139
	change	13	7	9	−3
2. Social contributions charged on workers	1979	11	15	23	9
	1989	12	23	27	13
	change	1	8	4	4
3. Income tax	1979	14	10	23	33
	1989	26	9	28	26
	change	12	−1	5	−7
4. Net compensation (1−2−3)	1979	100	100	100	100
	1989	100	100	100	100
5. Social contributions charged on firms	1979	58	47	23	14
	1989	67	59	27	14
	change	9	12	4	0
6. Labour cost (1+5)	1979	183	172	169	156
	1989	205	191	182	153
	change	22	19	13	−3

Source: Centro Studi Confindustria (1990).

Bodo and Sestito (1991) in their careful analysis of Italy's labour market show that in recent years there was a significant increase in 'wait' unemployment in the South, where most increased transfers concentrated, and that this can contribute to explain the declining sensitivity of wages to unemployment that has been observed. Micossi and Tullio (1991) present evidence that in the eighties welfare spending in the South was 'leading', rather than following, unemployment; Attanasio and Padoa Schioppa (1990) confirm that the decline in internal migration flows are a consequence of increased government transfers.

More generally, real wage resistance must have been encouraged by ready availability of public support for workers displaced from industry during the phase of restructuring. Moreover, since workers tended to move to the 'protected' sector during cyclical downswings, but the reverse flow was weaker during upswings, the labour market in the 'exposed' sector tended to remain close to full employment, and wage pressures were ready to develop as soon as industry accelerated its growth (De Nardis and Micossi, 1991; Bodo and Sestito, 1991).

1991/92: A CHANGE OF POLICY REGIME?

As has been recalled, the government was not able to take appropriate budgetary measures before the foreign exchange crisis; the shock of the September crisis and fear of a collapse of the Treasury paper market achieved what reason had not been able to. In the very days after the lira left the ERM, the government adopted a package of measures to increase revenues and slow down spending growth. These measures were expected to produce (in 1993) expenditure savings amounting to 42 trillion lire, and additional revenues of 51 trillion lire (out of which 7 trillion to come from the privatization programme). The total estimated improvement in the government financing requirement (93 trillion) would correspond to some 6 per cent of GDP.

These government estimates are in fact somewhat optimistic; the actual improvement in the budget will probably fall short of announcements by some 20 trillion lire (see Table 5.7, where government estimates are compared with those of Centro Studi Confindustria). And yet, there is little doubt that this was a considerable effort; moreover, for the first time in many years, public sector wages and pensions were not left untouched, and indeed suffered a severe curtailment.

A second, very important change had already taken place before the crisis. At the end of December 1991, entrepreneurs' associations and trade unions had agreed to eliminate any price indexation from wage mechanisms; the new contracts (1991–1994) also entail very low wage increases (3–4 per cent per year).

Sharp curtailment of domestic demand and wage moderation have led to a dramatic slowdown in inflation (Figure 5.4): the GDP deflator (the price of domestic output) is now increasing at a 3 per cent rate, consumer prices at a 4.2 per cent rate, and this despite the sharp increase in import prices brought about by the lira depreciation.

Italy's economic prospects and its ability to return to the ERM and maintain the goal of (eventual) monetary union with its European partners, depend on its success in restoring a sustainable balance in the public sector accounts and keeping domestic demand and inflation under control, so that the full benefits of the devaluation can be reaped.

To some extent the two issues are interlinked. High wages in the public sector and high public spending would make it very difficult to restrain inflation; hence wages in the private sector would also tend to grow too rapidly.

A private-sector specific problem could arise as soon as demand picks up for exports and investments. As was noted, in the past workers laid off by private companies were often compensated with jobs in the public sector, pensions or other subsidies, with the result that the 'functioning'

Table 5.7 Central government finances in 1993 (billion lire and percentage ratios to GDP)

	1992	1993 Target (RP&P) (1)	1993 Forecasts (CSC) (2)	Differences (2−1)
1. Total revenues	538,100	587,870	566/573,870	−14/−21,000
Current revenues	523,500	564,770	550,770	−14,000[a]
Capital revenues	14,600	23,100	16/23,100	0/−7,000
privatizations	0	7,000	0/7,000	0/−7,000
2. Total expenditures	701,200	737,870	740/743,870	3/6,000
Current expenditures	627,600	659,860	662/665,860	3/6,000
interest	171,100	200,000	195/192,000	−5/−8,000
personnel	140,720	145,600	148,100	2,500
health	81,500	82,500	85/88,500	3/6,000
pensions	70,290	68,748	70/73,748	2/5,000
goods and services	34,840	36,255	36,755	500
Capital expenditures and financing operations	73,600	78,010	78,010	0
Treasury financing requirement (1−2)	−163,100	−150,000	−167/−177,000	−17−/27,000
(in % of GDP)	(−10.7)	(−9.5)	(−10.6/−11.2)	
net of interest	8,000	50,000	28/15,000	−22/−35,000
(in % of GDP)	(0.5)	(3.2)	(1.8/0.9)	
Public sector debt in % of GDP, end of period	110.5	113.1[b]	117.2	—
Fiscal pressure in % of GDP	42.2	42.4	42.2	—

Notes: [a] Loss of tax revenue and social security contributions due to a rate of growth below government forecasts (−0.2% instead of +1.5%), an insufficient broadening of the tax base consequent to the implementation of the 'minimum tax', and the deflationary effect of the Budget Law.
[b] *Documento di programmazione economico-finanziaria per gli anni 1993–95*, July 1992.

Source: Relazione previsionale e programmatica, September 1992; *Rapporto di previsione Centro Studi Confindustria*, December 1992; *Relazione sul fabbisogno di cassa del settore pubblico per il 1993*, March 1993.

labour market continued to operate close to full employment. Geographical segmentation of the labour market and low labour mobility only added to the problem. As a result, in 1987/89, when the economy picked up, local labour 'scarcities' developed and industrial wages accelerated very early in the upswing, soon outpacing

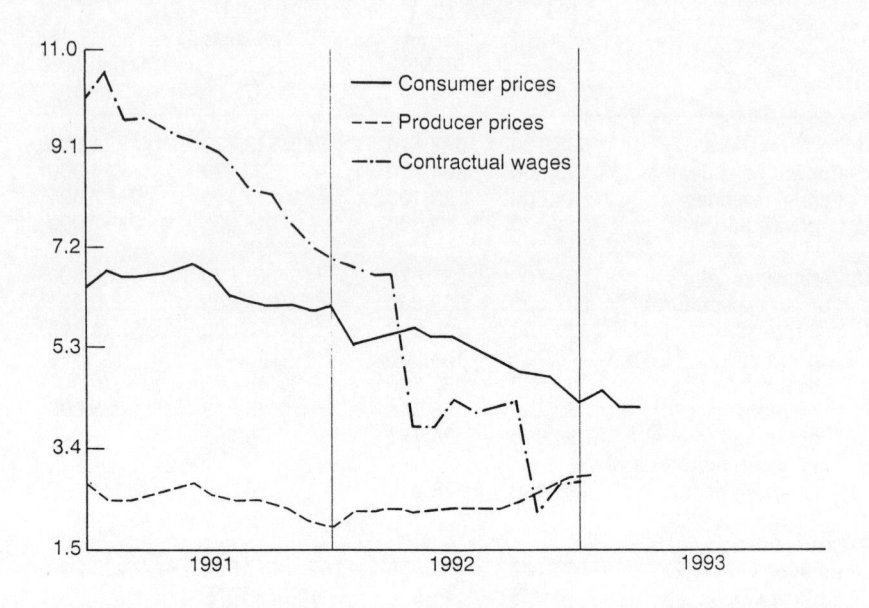

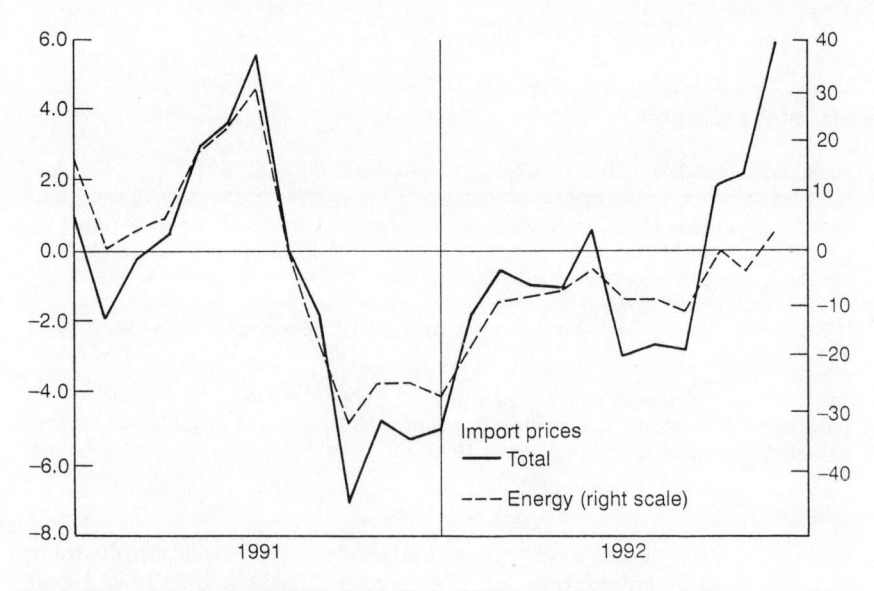

Figure 5.4 Prices and wages in Italy, 1991–1993 (percentage changes) Producer prices = manufacturing

Source: CSC estimates based in ISTAT data.

productivity increases. It also appears that in a number of cases firms either overestimated the 'permanent' component of productivity increases, or at least accommodated excessive wage demands for fear of being unable to meet rising demand for their products.

It is essential that the mistake is not repeated in the upswing expected in the near future: measures that decrease rigidity and segmentation in the labour market are required to that end. The ongoing attempts at reforming industrial relations and the structure of wage negotiations should also help: Confindustria aims at simplifying the present approach, that involves national (sectoral) and company-level wage negotiations, and that should be substituted by one single negotiating level, so that the overall increase would be determined either at national (sectoral) level or at company level.

As for public finances, the measures adopted in 1992 have brought about a slowdown of current spending, but that is not enough to stabilize the debt/GDP ratio; the room for further tax increases is limited, given that tax pressure has already surpassed the EC average, and the low quality of public services is resulting in strong resistance to any further increase in direct taxation. Therefore, most of the burden of stabilization will have to fall on the spending side of the budget; since public spending is mostly represented by personnel, pensions and interest payments on the debt, serious political difficulties can be expected.

We have presented in Table 5.8 a feasible (but not certain) macroeconomic scenario for 1993–1995: it is predicated on the hypothesis that indeed wage growth remains on its current slow path, so that inflation remains below 5.5 per cent in 1993 and declines rapidly afterwards (this entails, of course, some real wage decline in 1993: the decline should concentrate in the public sector that had enjoyed very large increases in 1987–1991).

As can be seen, growth picks up in 1994 and 1995, led by exports and investment; consumption and domestic demand grow less than GDP, and the foreign balance improves dramatically. This is the scenario of successful devaluation, with expenditure-switching and expenditure-reducing policies mutually reinforcing.

In this scenario, nominal public spending – excluding interest payments – is maintained on a 3–4 per cent *nominal* growth path, which entails already considerable restraint relative to past behaviour. It also entails that current transfers – mainly to cover losses of public or semi-public companies – be dramatically curtailed. As can be seen in Table 5.9, this is still not enough to ensure stabilization of the debt/GDP ratio. The balance will have to be made up by raising taxation (mainly, we would argue, indirect taxation), and by accelerating privatizations.

If the government manages to stick to these policies, interest rates can be expected to decline towards more reasonable levels, more in line with those observed in most other EC members. Thus stabilization of the debt/GDP ratio could be facilitated by a return of confidence in the Italian economy and Treasury creditworthiness.

Table 5.8 A macro-scenario 1993–1995 (% changes unless otherwise specified)[a]

	1992	1993	1994	1995
Gross domestic product	0.9	0.4	2.2	3.0
Total demand	1.0	−1.4	0.7	1.8
Private consumption	1.8	−0.9	0.6	1.9
Gross fixed investment	−1.4	−3.3	1.7	3.4
Net foreign demand[b]	−0.1	1.8	1.5	1.1
Exports of goods and services	5.0	8.0	8.2	7.6
Imports of goods and services	4.6	0.4	2.3	3.3
GDP deflator	4.7	3.3	3.9	2.8
Private consumption deflator	5.4	5.4	3.8	3.1
Export prices	0.7	11.0	4.1	2.0
Import prices	1.1	18.9	3.8	4.9
Compensation per employee				
Private sector	5.7	4.5	4.1	3.5
Public administration	2.7	2.3	3.5	3.0
Unit labour cost				
Private sector	3.9	3.0	2.5	1.9
Public administration	4.3	3.3	4.1	3.6
Trade balance[c]	0.2	0.3	1.4	1.7
Current account balance[c]	−2.1	−1.8	−0.6	−0.2
Terms of trade	−0.4	−6.6	0.3	−2.7
Competitiveness[d]	−1.8	−5.5	1.6	−0.1

Notes: [a] The forecast was made using the Centro Studi Confindustria econometric model.
[b] Contribution to GDP growth.
[c] Percentage ratio to GDP.
[d] Based on manufactured goods prices; calculated with respect to both foreign and domestic markets.

In sum, a feasible path of stabilization, that would make it possible for Italy to avoid a return of inflationary pressures and (possibly) a financial crisis, does exist. It entails hard choices and strong restraint of domestic incomes and demand for a number of years; it requires that macro stabilization be accompanied by micro supply-side policies designed to improve flexibility of the labour market, open up the service sector to competition, and facilitate the flow of resources to the export and investment sector.

CONCLUSIONS

We have discussed the sources of imbalances and the consequences of high public spending in the Italian economy, and have shown what are the conditions for steady growth with price stability.

Table 5.9 Public sector finances in 1992–1995 (% changes unless otherwise specified)

	1992	1993	1994	1995
Total spending	8.7	4.4	3.5	2.2
net of interest payments	6.5	2.2	4.6	3.9
out of which: personnel	4.7	3.4	4.0	3.5
: pensions	13.4	3.5	7.6	5.7
Total revenues	11.2	3.5	6.4	4.7
Net indebtedness of the public sector[a]	−9.5	−9.9	−8.5	−7.1
'primary'[a]	1.9	2.4	3.2	3.4
Treasury financing requirements[a]	−11.0	−10.7	−9.1	−7.7
'primary'[a]	0.4	1.7	2.5	2.9
Total public debt (end of period)[a]	110.5	117.2	119.4	120.5
Debt-stabilizing primary balance[a]	6.1	8.7	5.1	4.2

Note: [a] Percentage ratios to GDP.

If such a course is indeed confirmed by the new government (which appears likely), then Italy could seek re-entry into the ERM fairly soon, maybe before the end of this year. Financial market conditions abroad will probably help, to the extent that interest rates come down in Germany and the DM weakens in foreign exchange markets.

Full participation by Italy in the monetary unification process, however, can only be founded on permanent acceptance of low-wage dynamics, a reduction of the weight of the public sector in the economy, and a determined effort to open up the economy to foreign competition.

NOTES

1 The survey on inflation expectations is that produced by ISCO-Mondo Economico since 1952.
2 This test is based on decomposing (expected) exchange rate changes (ds/dt) into expected changes in central rates (realignment) and expected changes within the band:

$$E \frac{ds}{dt} = g_t + E \frac{dsc}{dt}.$$

If $g_t = 0$ (no realignments are expected), then $E(dsc/dt)$ should display mean reversion (that is the implicit relationship between current position in the band and expected exchange rate change should be negative, since the exchange rate is expected to remain within the band).
3 Nominally, the public sector displays a higher share of high-quality jobs and higher-education employees, which has been used to argue that the average compensation should indeed be higher in the public sector: the fact is that

very often upgrading of positions and employees has been used to grant wage increases, while in most cases only the worst graduates from high schools and universities would take jobs in the public sector.

REFERENCES

Attanasio O.P. and Padoa Schioppa F. (1990), 'Regional inequalities, migration and mismatch in Italy, 1960–86', in F. Padoa Schioppa (ed.), *Mismatch and labour mobility*, Cambridge, Cambridge University Press.
Bertola G. and Svensson L.E.O. (1990), 'Stochastic devaluation risk and the empirical fit of target zone models', mimeo.
Bodo G. and Sestito P. (1991), *Le vie dello sviluppo*, Bologna, Il Mulino.
Centro Studi Confindustria (1992a), 'Industria italiana e Mercato Unico Europeo', *XIV Rapporto*, Rome, SIPI, May.
Centro Studi Confindustria (1992b), 'I servizi di pubblica utilità', in *Previsioni dell'economia italiana*, Rome, SIPI, December.
CER (1991), *Le due inflazioni*, Rapporto no. 5.
de Grauwe P. (1983), 'Symptoms of an overvalued currency: the case of the Belgian Franc', in M. De Cecco (ed.), *International Economic Adjustment*, Oxford, Basil Blackwell.
De Nardis S. and Micossi S. (1991), 'Disinflation and reinflation in Italy and the implications for transition', *BNL Quarterly Review*, June.
Egebo T. and Englander A.S. (1992), 'Institutional commitments and policy credibility: a critical survey and empirical evidence from the ERM', *OECD Economic Studies*, 18, Spring.
Eichengreen B. and Wyplosz C. (1993), 'The unstable EMS', mimeo, March.
Ernst & Young (1992), *The implications of opening up public procurement in the excluded sectors in Italy*, a Report to the EC Commission Advisory Committee for Public Procurement, January.
Ford R. and Suyker W. (1989), 'Industrial subsidies in OECD economies', OECD Working Paper, December.
Franco D. (1992), 'L'espansione della spesa pubblica in Italia (1960-90)', in *Il disavanzo pubblico in Italia: natura strutturale e politiche di rientro*, vol. I., Bologna, Il Mulino.
Frankel J. and Phillips S. (1991), 'The European Monetary System: credible at last?', NBER Working Paper, no. 3819, August.
Froot K.A. and Rogoff K. (1991), 'The EMS, the EMU, and the transition to a common currency', NBER Working Paper, no. 3684, April.
Giavazzi F. and Spaventa L. (1989), 'Italy: the real effects of inflation and disinflation', *Economic Policy*, April.
Mediobanca (1992), *Dati cumulativi di 1790 società italiane*, Milan.
Micossi S. and Papi L. (1993), 'Italy's inflation problem: the role of the public sector', OCSM Working Paper, no. 31, Luiss, March.
Micossi S. and Traù F. (1989), 'Finanziamento delle imprese e trasformazioni produttive: il ruolo della politica monetaria nel processo di ristrutturazione', *Rivista di Politica Economica*, July–August.
Micossi S. and Tullio G. (1991), 'Fiscal imbalances, economic distortions, and the long run performance of the Italian economy', OCSM Working Paper, no. 9, Luiss, October.
Pellegrini G. (1992), 'La produttività nei servizi destinabili alla vendita: nuove evidenze per un vecchio problema', mimeo, Banca d'Italia, April.

Prosperetti L. (1992a), 'La regolazione delle tariffe dei servizi pubblici italiani: alcune proposte', mimeo, Politecnico di Torino, Spring.
Prosperetti L. (1992b), 'Efficienza e qualita nei principali servizi di pubblica utilità: l'Italia nel contesto internazionale', mimeo, Politecnico di Torino, Spring.
Svimez (1992), *Rapporto 1991 sull'economia del Mezzogiorno*, Bologna, Il Mulino.
Tullio G. (1986), 'Taxation and real wages: an empirical analysis of wage behaviour in 8 industrial countries: 1960–83', mimeo.
Visco I. (1984a), *Price expectations in rising inflation*, Amsterdam, North Holland.
Visco I. (1984b), 'Inflation expectations: the use of Italian survey data in the analysis of their formation and effects on wage changes', unpublished, Augus.
Visco I. (1990), 'L'economia italiana dal 1975 al 1989', mimeo (prepared for Encyclopedia Italiana), October.
Visco I. (1992), 'Caratteri strutturali dell'inflazione italiana (1986–91)', Relazione alla XXXIII Riunione Scientifica Annuale della Società degli Economisti (30–31 October), mimeo.

6

THE UK AND THE EXCHANGE RATE MECHANISM

Christopher Johnson

In this chapter we consider the UK's relationship with the EMS Exchange Rate Mechanism between 1978 and 1993. The chapter is divided into six sections. First, we consider the UK's original decision not to join the ERM in 1987. Second, we examine UK policy towards the ERM from 1979 to 1990. Third, we look at the UK's decision to join in 1990. Fourth, we review the UK's period of membership of the ERM in 1990–1992. Fifth, we show how and why the UK suspended membership in September 1992. Finally, we assess the prospects for the UK's return to the ERM. The chapter closes with our conclusions.

THE UK'S DECISION NOT TO JOIN

The British Labour government, led by James Callaghan, was taken by surprise by the success of the joint initiative in summer 1978 by President Giscard d'Estaing and Chancellor Schmidt to set up the European Monetary System (EMS). The government seriously considered joining the proposed Exchange Rate Mechanism (ERM), but retreated under pressure from the trade unions and the Parliamentary Labour Party, who were afraid that the UK would be prevented from devaluing the pound in order to maintain competitiveness and employment. Callaghan, who retained a majority in the House of Commons thanks only to the support of the small Liberal Party, compromised by joining only the EMS but not the ERM.

The ERM started some weeks late in March 1979, without the UK, which proceeded to the May general election and the replacement of Callaghan with Margaret Thatcher. One of the few points on which the new government agreed with the old was the decision to stay out of the

ERM. To join was incompatible with domestic monetarism, in which the interest rate was used to determine the quantity of money, and the exchange rate left to float – preferably up. It is ironic that the original Conservative desire for freedom to revalue was the mirror-image of the Labour wish for freedom to devalue. In the end, Thatcher made just as much use of exchange rate freedom in the downward as in the upward direction.

As Britton (1991) points out, the decision to stay out was based on matters of detail as well as principle, which were later to reassert their importance.

The British authorities wanted a system in which the obligations of surplus and deficit countries, lenders and borrowers, were symmetrical. This was not just a disinterested preference, as experience suggested that sterling would be weak most of the time against the mark, if not against the franc or the lira. They did not want to join a DM zone, in which it would have been their responsibility alone to keep sterling in line.

UK POLICY TOWARDS THE ERM 1979–1990

As early as January 1982, Thatcher called a meeting to consider whether Britain should join the ERM, as revealed by Walters (1990). As Walters rightly points out, it would not have been a good moment, since the pound had by then risen to about DM4.30, or more than 20 per cent higher than the 1978 average. It was the first of many occasions when the government decided that the time was not ripe (or right – it makes little difference). However, had the UK already been in the ERM, the rise in the sterling exchange rate in 1979/81, which was due as much to high interest rates as to North Sea oil, would have been considerably reduced, because the ERM rules would have prevented a rise in interest rates, as well as postponing the abolition of exchange controls in October 1979 which fuelled it. An upward realignment of the pound might still have been required because of the asymmetrical oil price shock. The severity of the impact of monetary policy on the economy would thus have been mitigated.

By 1984, it was clear that, in the five years of the ERM's existence, member countries had succeeded in both stabilizing their exchange rates and reducing their inflation rates, perhaps not as rapidly as the UK, but with less sacrifice of output and employment. In October 1984, the governor of the Bank of England was publicly pressing British membership of the EMS Exchange Rate Mechanism (ERM) as preferable to any of the domestic monetary targets (see Leigh-Pemberton, 1984).

Having given thumbs down to money GDP, the governor said:

A second alternative, in place of a domestic monetary target, has been the adoption of an exchange rate objective, through a pegged relationship with a foreign currency, or in earlier times with gold. For the UK with its close political and economic ties with our European neighbours, there could be a number of attractions in taking a full part in the exchange rate mechanism of the EMS.

In 1985, the Confederation of British Industry also came out, after much debate, in favour of British membership of the ERM. In the summer of that year, there was a major parliamentary enquiry into the case for joining (see Treasury and Civil Service Committee, 1985). Their report concluded that there were three strategies:

- Immediate entry with the possibility of a realignment at a later stage to bring the pound into a more competitive relationship with the ECU.
- Membership following a substantial devaluation of sterling or when the exchange rate is judged to be appropriate.
- Continued independence responding to the developing situation and retaining a greater degree of flexibility in order to manage the domestic economy in the national interest.

The Committee chose the third strategy, little knowing that, behind closed doors, the debate about membership was splitting the government. After another five years of agonizing, the government chose the second strategy, but, with hindsight after the September 1992 crisis, it should have chosen the first.

Nigel Lawson, who became Chancellor of the Exchequer in 1983, was already thought in 1985 to be 'shadowing' the DM, keeping the pound close to it in spite of being outside the ERM. He had been drawn into the heady atmosphere of international meetings of the major powers to deal with exchange rate fluctuations led by the dollar, from which the UK suffered more than most. The achievements in the battle against inflation were put at risk when the pound fell almost to a dollar in January 1985, pushing the inflation rate up briefly to 7 per cent in mid-year. This was due as much to the dollar's strength as to the pound's weakness, which also affected the DM and the EMS currencies. The Plaza Agreement of September 1985 gave the dollar a push after it had already started moving down from its February peak, and the Louvre Agreement in February 1987 attempted to stabilize the dollar close to its new, lower levels. Here, and at the annual IMF meetings, Lawson was in his element sketching out grand designs for world currency reforms.

For Britain to join the ERM seemed to Lawson to fit well into this wider picture. After a series of meetings beginning in January 1985, the final decision on his proposal to join the ERM was taken at a ministerial meeting in November, and was vetoed by Thatcher, acting on the advice of Walters, in spite of widespread support from other ministers and the Bank of England. It was a crucial moment at which to seek to stabilize the exchange rate, because the sharp fall in oil prices which had just begun was to pull the 'petropound' down. After the decision not to join the ERM, the pound fell by 18 per cent in effective rate terms between the third quarter of 1985 and the fourth quarter of 1986, which reversed much of the benefit of lower oil prices to inflation, even though it made UK manufactured exports more competitive.

Lawson, who was energy secretary from September 1981 to June 1983, had been thinking about the 're-entry' problem for the UK as oil production declined, although neither he nor anyone else could have foreseen how rapidly the oil price would fall, creating similar difficulties. He told a Cambridge energy conference in April 1984:

Once oil production is past its peak, it is reasonable to expect that there will be some return to the traditional trade pattern of a surplus in manufacturing and invisibles offsetting deficits in food, basic materials and, eventually, fuel. This will probably require a real exchange rate lower than it is today. But this does not necessarily mean that the nominal exchange rate has to fall. The real exchange rate can also adjust by better productivity performance and greater restraint on pay. Policy will need to be conducted to make it more likely that the adjustment will occur in that way.

Lawson continued his policy of shadowing the DM nonetheless, but by 1987 this came to mean preventing the pound rising above DM3.00 from the low point of DM2.80 reached in that year, rather than preventing it falling from DM3.70, as in November 1985. Shadowing the DM, far from allowing Lawson the autocratic power over interest rates to which he professed, caused him to bring them down by stages from 11 per cent at the beginning of 1987 to 9 per cent by March 1988, to prevent the pound rising above the DM3.00 barrier. He was forced by Thatcher to uncap the pound in March, with the famous words: 'There is no way in which one can buck the market'. He had lost a second major battle to stabilize the exchange rate.

Although Thatcher agreed to the principle of entry at the June 1989 Madrid summit, after a joint resignation threat by Lawson and her foreign secretary, Sir Geoffrey Howe, it was for some time afterwards not clear when she would agree that the time was ripe. Lawson resigned in October 1989 because of Thatcher's refusal to sack her economic adviser, Sir Alan Walters, whose views on the EMS she clearly preferred to his.

Lawson revealed in his post-resignation speech in the House of Commons that he had long advocated ERM entry, and that he was in favour of an independent Bank of England (see Lawson, 1992). Full UK membership, he said, 'would signally enhance the credibility of our anti-inflationary resolve in general and the role of exchange-rate discipline in particular'. He had made it clear, however, that he saw the ERM as self-sufficient, and not as a stage towards full Economic and Monetary Union (EMU), which he rejected in his January 1989 Chatham House speech as requiring a federal political union.

Walters (1990) claimed to have detected a fatal flaw in the EMS, which came to be known as the 'Walters critique'. On the assumption of fixed exchange rates, he said:

The EMS forces countries to have the same nominal interest rates. If, however, Italy is inflating at a rate of 7 per cent and Germany at a rate of 2 per cent ... then there is a problem of perversity. With the same interest rate at, say, 5 per cent, the real rate of interest for Italy is minus 2 per cent and for Germany plus 3 per cent. Thus Italy will have an expansionary monetary policy while Germany will pursue one of restraint. But this will exacerbate inflation in Italy and yet restrain further the already low inflation in Germany. This is the opposite of 'convergence', namely, it induces divergence.

Lawson comments: 'Incredibly, this assertion was greeted as a major contribution to economic policy thinking by a number of economists who should have known better ... I could not help noticing that, so far from being the same, short-term interest rates in France exceeded those in Germany ...' The Walters critique clearly does not apply at times when realignments are thought to be possible, and risk premia were required for high-inflation currencies such as the lira even when no realignment was expected in the run-up to September 1992.

In autumn 1989 the government published a proposal designed to make a positive contribution to the debate on EMU triggered off by the Delors Report published in April of that year (see Treasury, 1989). Thatcher, Howe and Lawson were all agreed on one thing, that the report of the Delors Committee, which included the governor of the Bank of England in his personal capacity, was unacceptable, and that Stage I of EMU was as far as the UK wanted to go. The proposal, in line with the free market beliefs of Thatcherism, set out a blueprint for competing currencies. If it was anything more than a delaying tactic, it was a recipe for making the EC a DM area even more explicitly than the ERM had already done, and was thus a curious way of trying to preserve British monetary independence.

The competing currencies proposal was followed by a more European-looking proposal for a 'hard Ecu' as a parallel currency, which might become an important competitor to national currencies, but without replacing them as the single currency. The idea had come from Paul Richards, a City of London merchant banker, and had been taken up by Sir Michael Butler, former UK representative to the EC, and Chairman of the European sub-committee of the British Invisible Exports Council (see British Invisible Exports Council, 1990, and, for a full discussion, House of Lords, 1990). The hard Ecu was designed as a distinctively British contribution to the Inter-Governmental Conference (IGC) starting in December 1990. The scheme was flawed, not least because it would have created a second type of Ecu alongside the existing private basket Ecu. The idea of hardening the existing Ecu was taken up by the Deutsche Bundesbank during the IGC, but was not in the end adopted in the Maastricht Treaty.

THE UK DECISION TO JOIN IN 1990

The manner and the rate at which the UK joined were later to be the subject of much criticism. At the time, the advocates of entry in both the government and the CBI were so relieved that Thatcher had dropped her opposition that they did not look the gift horse in the mouth, in case it was no longer on offer the following week. The CBI had in any case expressed the view that the important objective was exchange rate stability, rather than any particular rate. The pound had been able to coexist with a wide range of different DM rates in the previous decade, and the dollar rate was equally important to many British companies.

The UK's European partners were also so relieved at Thatcher's decision that they paid only lip-service to the idea that rates should be the subject of multilateral decision-making. They accepted both the timing of UK entry and the rate as unilateral decisions by the British government. Lawson, writing in May 1992 (see Smith, 1993), was highly critical of his successor, for taking the UK in at too high a rate, and without proper consultation with the Bundesbank. He even attributed the September 1992 crisis to this: 'Sterling joined at a rate which the Bundesbank regarded from the outset as too high and which it felt under no moral obligation to support – a fact that was later to become all too apparent to the financial markets.'

Major had surprised everybody by departing from his previous insistence that UK inflation rates would have to fall from their double-figure mid-1990 levels to German levels, and interest rates with them, before the time would be ripe for the UK to join. During the end-September IMF meeting in Washington, however, he changed the condition to convergence of 'prospective' inflation rates. For those who understood English, this clearly meant that the UK's forecasts for British and German inflation would have to be roughly the same. As the Treasury's forecast, to be published in the November 1990 Autumn Statement, showed a fall in UK Retail Price Index inflation from 10.25 per cent in the fourth quarter of 1990 to 5.5 per cent in the fourth quarter of 1991, the condition was more or less fulfilled.

Initially, the pound strengthened slightly against the DM on entry, but the main burden of criticism of the entry rate was that it was too high rather than too low. It was clear that the UK had preferred an entry rate high enough to help to reduce inflation – the main priority at the time of entry – rather than one low enough to improve the balance of payments deficit by ensuring competitiveness. Instead of cutting interest rates by one percentage point at the time of entry, the UK could have carried out one or more such cuts before announcing the intention to join, waiting until sterling fell to a rate more widely seen as competitive.

Views varied on whether the entry rate was competitive. Much depended on the base period in relation to which competitiveness was being judged. For example, the pound had been much lower in 1978, when the ERM was being launched, than in 1980, when the 'petro-pound' effect was at its height, so it was possible to show that the entry rate was uncompetitive by reference to the earlier base, and competitive by reference to the later base, since when the pound had been declining.

The UK became uncompetitive in manufactures as a result of the rise in the exchange rate and in the inflation rate between the end of 1976 and the end of 1980, with a doubling of relative unit labour costs in a common currency in those five years (see OECD, 1991, Annex 2). By 1989, the UK had regained its early 1979 competitiveness, again measured by relative unit labour costs, thanks to the gradual fall in the exchange rate, and the improvement in relative productivity, which made up for the high annual pay increases. The rise in the exchange rate in 1990, and the increase in British unit labour costs relative to other countries due to higher inflation, reduced competitiveness again, by about 10 per cent, to the less competitive level prevailing at the end of 1979.

It also made a difference whether the real exchange rate was being calculated by reference to relative consumer prices, GDP deflators, export prices, or unit labour costs, and whether these were taken as changes from a base period or absolute levels. (Purchasing power parity means an equal level of consumer prices, not an equal change over any particular period.) Unit labour cost comparisons also differed enormously according to whether they were wage costs only, or also included non-wage costs, such as social security taxation, and whether they applied only to manufacturing or to the whole economy.

The UK's competitiveness in terms of levels of unit labour costs rather than changes seemed not too unsatisfactory taking the 1980s as a whole. In 1982-1990, according to OECD (1991), the UK's level of unit labour costs in manufacturing was the same as the average in its 17 major trading partners, compared with 6 per cent below them in 1975-1981. The comparable figures for Germany were 16 per cent above average for 1982-1990, and for France 15 per cent below. However, according to the US Bureau of Labor Statistics cited by Goodhart (1993), German hourly pay levels were 25 per cent above British in 1991, which roughly corresponds to the difference in productivity, estimated to be about 20 per cent higher in Germany according to O'Mahony (1992). Higher German labour costs are explained by non-wage labour costs, which were 78 per cent of labour costs in Germany, but only 37 per cent in the UK on Goodhart's figures.

Another important difference is whether the UK is being compared with an average of 17 trading partners, some of which have as high or higher inflation rates, or with major EC trading partners, notably Germany, the anchor country, with its low inflation rates. According to figures showing wage inflation divergence in the ERM in the convergence chapter of Collignon, 1994 (Table 9), British unit labour costs rose by 188 per cent between 1978 and 1992, compared with 49 per cent in Germany, a relative rise of 93 per cent. This would have required a devaluation of 49 per cent in the pound–DM rate from a 1978 base to offset it, but the DM2.95 entry rate represented a devaluation of only 24 per cent, so that the pound's real exchange rate was 48 per cent higher against the DM than in 1978, implying a nominal rate of about DM2.00 for the same real exchange rate.

This is an analysis of changes rather than levels. Taking into account the OECD's view that UK labour cost levels were relatively low in 1975–1981, one may judge that the 1978 base for changes in UK relative to German figures is somewhat low, although clearly 1980 is too high. On the analysis of changes since 1978, the DM has become undervalued against all the 'Latin' currencies – the French franc, the lira, the peseta and the escudo, as well as the pound, because Germany was able to combine relatively low labour cost inflation due to domestic monetary policy with the exchange rate stability due to the ERM. The DM has become overvalued against the Benelux countries, which also had low labour cost inflation, but got some devaluation against the DM in the early 1980s. On a weighted average basis, the DM has become more under- than overvalued, but this was to a great extent corrected by the devaluations following the September 1992 crisis.

Another quite different way of judging the UK entry rate is by fundamental exchange rate equilibrium (FEER) analysis (see Barrell and in't Veld, 1991; Williamson, 1991). Williamson defines the FEER as 'the real exchange rate consistent with macroeconomic balance in the medium run'. He quotes findings by Barrell and in't Veld (1991) and Wren-Lewis et al. (1991) that on this analysis the pound was, soon after ERM entry, overvalued by 5–10 per cent in the ERM, but concluded that the 6 per cent margins would allow a devaluation of this order without any change in the market rate. He quotes a rate of DM2.24 as the FEER pound–DM rate for the first quarter of 1990, but says this is too low because of the undervaluation of the DM in the ERM. He gives a rate of DM2.60 on the assumption that one more downward realignment would be carried out, or DM2.40 as the final rate for entry into full EMU.

The foreign exchange markets appear to have settled on the DM2.40–2.60 range as about right for the pound now that it is floating after the September 1992 crisis. The DM2.95 rate, as Barrell pointed out, could have been sustained in the medium term only if inflation had been lower in the UK than in Germany for five years or so, as may well be happening in France. While this may be the case in the short term in the UK too, the cost of maintaining such low British inflation in the medium term might well have been too high in terms of lost output and employment.

The FEER approach, based as it is on economic models, has the merit of showing where the sterling exchange rate needs to be if the balance of payments deficit of 2–3 per cent of GDP is to be eliminated within the next few years. By this standard, the UK needs an advantage in competitiveness compared with countries close to external balance. According to the Group of Ten (1993):

The discipline imposed by the parity at which the UK entered the ERM in October 1990 facilitated the subsequent reduction of inflation in the UK, but while inflation fell below the German rate in the course of 1992 it did not fall sufficiently to improve Britain's competitive position against its partner countries. Moreover, current account deficits that have recently been running around 2 per cent of GDP, despite the domestic recession, likely reinforced the impression that sterling was overvalued, particularly against the US dollar.

The pound's real appreciation was particularly marked in the early months after entry, before inflation began to call. According to the IMF (1993), 'from the time the pound sterling joined the ERM in 1990 ... up to the recent crisis, sterling had appreciated by 10 per cent in real terms against the D-mark. Compared with its low of 1987, the pound's real appreciation against the D-mark had been close to 20 per cent.'

Given that it was difficult to determine a 'correct' rate for entry, the UK authorities would have done better to keep in reserve the possibility of a surprise realignment once inflation had come down, and before downward pressure on sterling had made the government put its reputation on the line by refusing to do any such thing. The option of realigning within the bottom half of the 6 per cent band, and at the same time moving to narrow 2.25 per cent bands had worked well for the lira in January 1990, but the UK authorities did not consider it seriously. Any damage to their credibility from such a move, however, would have been far less than that inflicted in September 1992.

THE UK'S MEMBERSHIP OF THE ERM

The UK remained in the ERM from October 1990 to September 1992, a period of nearly two years. Norman Lamont, who was Chancellor of the Exchequer for most of this period, still regarded it as a success even after the country left the mechanism in September 1992. The RPI inflation rate came down from 10.9 per cent in October 1990 to 3.6 per cent in September 1992 and 1.3 per cent in April 1993. Bank base rates came down from 15 per cent in October 1990 to 10 per cent in September 1992 and 6 per cent from January 1993 onwards. The average increase in earnings fell from 9.75 per cent in October 1990 to 5.5 per cent in September 1992. However, unemployment rose from just over 6 to just over 10 per cent in the same period, and real GDP fell by 2.5 per cent.

It is clear that the recession already underway when the UK joined would have given similar results even outside the ERM. Over such a short period, it is difficult to say how much ERM membership influenced behaviour, and either brought inflation down more rapidly, or reduced the cost of a given fall in inflation. It goes almost without saying that the exchange rate against ERM countries was more stable, in other words higher, than it would otherwise have been, and this made it possible to lower the level of interest rates more rapidly, given the desired tightness of monetary conditions. However, experience since departure has contradicted the view held during membership that interest rates would have needed to be higher rather than lower if the pound had been floating downwards instead of being in the ERM.

The government clearly hoped for a quick ERM effect on pay bargaining (see Treasury, 1991): 'Employers and employees will need to take account of wage settlements in other countries within the ERM. The quicker the growth of labour costs moderates, the sooner the UK will be able to combine low inflation with a satisfactory rate of growth of output.' The Treasury, in evidence to Treasury and Civil Service Committee (1991b) took the view the ERM was having some effect. 'The fall in pay settlements has exceeded most forecasters' earlier expectations, perhaps because of the beneficial effects of ERM entry on inflation expectations.'

The Treasury (1991) noted the required change in its own monetary policy:

Membership of the ERM sets a new framework for monetary policy. Interest rate decisions must now be set consistently with keeping sterling within its announced bands ... There may be occasions when tensions arise between domestic conditions and ERM obligations, with domestic conditions pointing to interest rate levels either higher or lower than those indicated by ERM obligations. But such occasions are expected to be the exception rather than the rule and to be relatively short lived ...

Unfortunately, this proved to be an over-optimistic view, in the light of a German monetary policy which was not predicted at the time.

Leigh-Pemberton (1991) showed a similar overoptimism on the part of the Bank of England: 'In fact membership ... appears to have had a powerful calming effect on the behaviour of the foreign exchange market, and may have allowed somewhat easier interest rates than would otherwise have been feasible.' The governor even took the view that, outside the ERM, the political uncertainties caused by Thatcher's downfall in November 1990 might have actually required interest rates to be raised above 15 per cent rather than lowered. This opens up the intriguing possibility that Thatcher's decision to join the ERM provided the Conservative Party with a safety-net allowing it to replace her without the threat of a sterling crisis.

By July 1992, Lamont (1992) was claiming an outstanding success for ERM membership in his speech to the European Policy Forum. 'The ERM is not an optional extra', he said, 'an add-on to be jettisoned at the first hint of trouble. It is and will remain at the very centre of our macroeconomic strategy.' After listing the anti-inflation achievements, he went on: 'I cannot believe we could have achieved all this outside the ERM.'

Lamont considered and rejected five alternatives:

1. *Cut interest rates immediately within the ERM.* He dismissed this possibility, arguing that markets would not believe that the pound would regain its central parity if lower interest rates sent it to the bottom of its 6 per cent bands.
2. *A German realignment.* This was rejected on the grounds that other European countries would not allow their currencies to be devalued against the DM. However, it later became clear that the Bundesbank was in favour of such a realignment. The French government was against it, but this need not have prevented the UK, Italy and Spain from proceeding. The UK could not accept that the pound was weaker than the franc, and should therefore be devalued against both it and the DM. 'The issue is simply not on the agenda', according to Lamont, but it later emerged that the Bundesbank requested the German government to put it there, but it failed to get on to the agenda in a way that has never been fully explained. In the words of the governor of the Bank of England (see Treasury and Civil Service Committee, 1992): 'It became perfectly clear that France did not – if there was a realignment – wish to realign against the D-mark and it was generally felt that a general realignment was, as a result, not appropriate.'
3. *Devaluation within the ERM.* This – meaning for the UK and not for France – was rejected on the grounds that it would have meant higher, not lower, interest rates. This later became the UK's reason for leaving the ERM rather than devaluing. Given that a devaluation as large as that obtained by leaving would not have been agreed by other ERM countries, it was probably correct to reason that a small devaluation would have led to market expectations of a further devaluation, and thus have caused interest rates to rise.
4. *Leave the ERM and cut interest rates* (the option adopted some weeks later). 'It's the cut and run option; cut interest rates and a run on the pound . . . Devaluation just does not work in Britain . . . Our initial gain in competitiveness would soon be eroded as import prices soared and pay deals rose . . . We would have given up after less than two years. [The markets] would conclude that we were back to our bad old ways; that given the chance we would always delude ourselves by thinking that with a little more inflation we could get a little more growth.'
5. *Leave the ERM and set interest rates according to domestic monetary targets.* This was dismissed on the grounds that broad money targets had proved unreliable in the 1980s, and were not a good guide to setting interest rates.

Lamont's bravura could not conceal the fact that the fall in UK inflation would have allowed interest rates to be cut from 10 per cent, thus allowing the economy to recover more rapidly from recession, had it not been for high German short-term interest rates, and the premium, albeit a shrinking one, still required by the markets on sterling interest rates.

The difficulties of the Maastricht Treaty further increased the unpopularity of the ERM, but the UK authorities clearly hoped at first to ride out the storm, thanks to lower German interest rates and the ERM defence mechanisms. Unfortunately, the one obvious defence that they could not contemplate was to raise short-term interest rates; instead, they let sterling fall towards the bottom of its band, taking comfort in the slight improvement in competitiveness thus obtained without formally realigning.

Lamont's five alternatives were seen at the time as 'straw men' being knocked down in order to reinforce the case for remaining in the ERM. However, with hindsight it might be thought that some of those in the Treasury had been contemplating some of the alternatives rather more seriously than that. The conclusion must be, however, that the UK wanted to remain within the ERM, but the September crisis made it impossible. If the UK could have continued in the ERM without having to raise interest rates, it might have settled for postponing a fall in rates. Nine months after the crisis, in June 1993, French and German short-term rates at about 7.5 per cent were only 1.5 per cent above British at 6 per cent.

THE SUSPENSION OF UK MEMBERSHIP

It will not be our task here to recount the detailed history of the September 1992 ERM crisis, which has already been told by Hutton (1992) and Norman and Barber (1992), and will doubtless be told many more times as revelations accumulate. We try to analyse some of the key factors specific to the UK, and to assess whether the outcome of the crisis was inevitable, or could have been avoided either by better luck or by better management. To a great extent the causes of the crisis were common to the ERM as a whole, and are described in Collignon, 1994. Specific UK factors are examined in Treasury and Civil Service Committee (1992), containing both the select committee's report and the oral evidence of the Chancellor of the Exchequer and the governor of the Bank of England. All quotations in the next two sections are from this source unless otherwise indicated.

The surprise result of the Danish referendum in May created turbulence in the foreign exchange markets, which was worsened by the French decision to hold a referendum on 20 September, of which the result might also have been against the Maastricht Treaty. Had the French referendum been held earlier, or not at all, the outcome might have been different. In Lamont's words it 'gave the foreign exchange markets something they had never experienced before – a fixed and definite date against which they could speculate'.

The general realignment which might with advantage have been carried out in an attempt to forestall the crisis was ruled out by the 5 September Ecofin Council meeting in Bath, in spite of the Bundesbank's obvious and long-standing advocacy. While the British government knew that a realignment was a theoretical possibility, it denied receiving any request from the German government for a meeting of the EC Monetary Committee in order to discuss the matter, and clearly the French government would not have welcomed such a meeting either, in view of its own problems in defending the franc.

The devaluation that took place on 13 September – without a meeting of the Monetary Committee – was only of the lira, by 7 per cent. It might have been better to have no realignment at all, than to deal with only one of a number of currencies widely regarded as misaligned. This devaluation was not even sufficient to stop speculation against the lira, and only encouraged tidal waves of speculation against other currencies, with the pound in the front line, having already fallen below its maximum divergence spread in August, as the Bundesbank pointed out. By the time the lira was devalued, as Lamont later admitted 'the game was up'.

The UK nevertheless tried to maintain its ERM obligations by continuing to intervene massively in the markets. The published figures show that the reserves, which had been bolstered by foreign borrowing, fell by $7bn in August and September, while foreign borrowing rose further by $22bn in September. The Bundesbank observed its obligation to extend credit under the Very Short Term Financing Facility when sterling was at the bottom of the band, but it could not be expected to give unlimited, immediate and unconditional support in defence of a parity that had become unsustainable.

Since the German credits, though drawn in DM, were denominated in Ecu, both the Bundesbank and the Bank of England lost on the deal. The Ecu, because of the devalued currencies in the basket, went down against the DM, but up against the pound. (This feature of the ERM arrangements is to be rectified by a compensation system, but only for the strong currency.)

The UK authorities weakened the impact of intervention by refusing until the last possible moment to raise interest rates in defence of the pound, after having lowered base rates from 15 to 10 per cent since joining the ERM. Lamont said: 'The more fundamental underlying cause . . . was the far reaching consequences of German reunification and the conflict that engendered between German policy needs and those of most other countries.' This was a reference to the conflicting interest rates required by Germany on the one hand, and the UK and other ERM countries on the other. The ERM, from being a framework within which interest rates could be lowered faster and more safely, had become a brake on further lowering.

Lamont rationalized his obvious reluctance to raise interest rates on political grounds by arguments about market psychology: 'I did not put up interest rates in June, July or August but . . . I would have done so had I felt it was necessary or that that would have helped us in the period I saw coming . . . Frankly, had I done so I think that most people would have judged that that was a very desperate thing to have then done, and would have been difficult to sustain, and I suspect it would have undermined rather than strengthened our position.'

This argument might have been used to rule out in advance the panic increase of base rate on 16 September, first to 12 per cent, then to 15 per cent (the following day), which were cancelled after the UK decided later that day to suspend its ERM membership. The lack of credibility of such rises was explained by Leigh-Pemberton: 'There was a sort of dilemma for us because the credibility of interest rates turned enormously on the extent to which the markets would believe we could actually raise them enough and sustain them at that level long enough to choke off the speculation without the effect of those interest rates coming through into the real economy in a way which was, quite honestly, going to be unacceptable and unrealistic.'

The authorities were unable, in deregulated financial markets, to insulate mortgage and small-firm bank lending rates from the short-term cost of marginal funds in wholesale markets. This was due to the prevalence of variable rate as against fixed rate lending, in order to reduce the risk of inflation variability. According to Barker et al. (1993) 'the Bundesbank has estimated that the level of short-term interest rates is the reference point for only 15 per cent of borrowing in Germany, compared with 33 per cent in France and 66 per cent in Britain'.

The government's dilemma on whether to raise interest rates can be summed up in the old saying: 'They were damned if they did, and damned if they didn't.' By the time 16 September was reached, it was clear that, in Lamont's words, 'we had no option but to withdraw'.

By that time, the size of sterling devaluation that could have been mutually agreed by the Monetary Committee could not have been as large as the 15 per cent or so that the markets imposed. One option that had been seriously considered while ERM entry was still under discussion was the 'congé' (see Lawson, 1992), by which sterling could have been temporarily suspended during some critical episode such as an election or a referendum. It seems from Lamont's resignation speech that he considered this possibility in the run-up to September, and it was publicly aired after the crisis by Sir Leon Brittan, Vice-President of the EC. The use of the word 'suspension' on 16 September even left open the hint of a quick return, but events were to rule it out. By the time Lamont was explaining himself to the Treasury Select Committee four weeks later 'suspension' had become 'withdrawal'.

PROSPECTS FOR THE UK'S RETURN TO THE ERM

Lamont's notorious reference to singing in the bath indicated that, in leaving the ERM, the UK was making a virtue of necessity. Inflation continued to fall, interest rates were cut to 6 per cent, the recovery got underway, and even unemployment began to fall from its January 1993 peak, a mere 8,000 short of the crucial 3 million figure which was generally expected to be surpassed. Both Britain and Italy appeared to have achieved the 'free lunch', restoring export competitiveness by devaluation while still benefiting from the after-effects of ERM inflation discipline.

The UK's policy regime changed to a direct inflation target of 1–4 per cent in the current Parliament, or 0–2 per cent in the longer term. Domestic monetary policy was dedicated essentially not to intermediate monetary targets, but directly to the inflation target. The Bank of England, without achieving the independence it sought, was given a higher profile by being given responsibility for a quarterly inflation report, which the Treasury had the right to see in advance, but not to change.

In a letter to Treasury and Civil Service Committee (1992), Lamont set out conditions for the return of sterling to the ERM, which he said were 'unlikely to be satisfied soon'. The first, 'an end to the current turbulence in the foreign exchange markets' may be considered to have been met, after the three further realignments between September 1992 and May 1993. The second, 'reflection and analysis', popularly referred to as the search for 'fault lines' in the ERM, was carried out by the Monetary Committee and the Committee of Central Bank Governors reporting to the Ecofin Council in May 1993. (The present report, comprising this volume and Collignon (1994), to the European Parliament is part of the same exercise.) In this connection, Treasury and Civil Service Committee (1992) said: 'It needs to be considered whether a high level of unemployment is a reliable indicator of lack of convergence.' The UK has also reasserted its long-standing desire for symmetrical intervention obligations by strong as well as by weak currencies.

The third, and most important, was 'the requirements of German monetary policy and those of the UK must come closer in line. The present wide differential in interest rates between Germany and the US which has contributed to strains in the ERM will need to narrow.' It should be noted that by June 1993 the short-term differential had narrowed to 1.5 percentage points in nominal terms, and about 1 percentage point in real terms, with German inflation, on a comparable basis, about 0.5 per cent higher than British. The UK exchange rate of around DM2.56 at the time of writing also looks sustainable, in the light of the analysis on pp.90–92, without calling forth protests of 'competitive devaluation'.

The British government has nevertheless discouraged suggestions that it might return soon to the ERM, and the new Chancellor of the Exchequer, Kenneth Clarke, has said that he considers it unlikely before the next election, which need not be held until May 1997, but is likely, on past showing, to be held during 1996. It became clear that the government could count on getting the Maastricht Treaty through the House of Commons only if it played down the possibility of rejoining the ERM.

The Treasury went to considerable lengths to try to refute what seemed to pro- and anti-Europeans alike a Maastricht Treaty obligation in Article 109j to try to achieve exchange rate convergence within the narrow bands during the two years leading up to the 1996 decision whether Stage III of EMU should go ahead in 1997, and whether the UK should opt in or out. Reference was also made to Article 109m of the Treaty making 'exchange rate policy a matter of common interest'. The Treasury actually raised the possibility that the Commission could take the UK to the European Court of Justice for infringing 109m, but concluded that even if the UK lost the case, it would then be free to decide how to remedy the default, and this would not necessarily be by rejoining the ERM.

The Treasury rejects the idea that the convergence provisions require ERM membership, referring not to Article 109j but to the much vaguer Article 109e, see Appendices 1 and 5 to Treasury and Civil Service Committee (1992). The criterion set out in 109j reads: 'the observance of the normal fluctuation margins provided for by the ERM of the EMS, for at least two years, without devaluing against the currency of any other member state'. This is interpreted in the convergence protocol as 'the member state shall not have devalued its currency's bilateral central rate against any other member state's currency on its own initiative', an important qualification.

It is clear from this that if the UK is either unwilling or unable to achieve exchange rate convergence as defined by the Treaty, it may be disqualified from entering Stage III, and will thus have opted out in advance. The point was well put by Leigh-Pemberton:

If the Community is going to come to stage three by the earlier date, which is 1 January 1997, then it is perfectly true those who will qualify under the present criteria have to get into the ERM during 1994 and remain in the narrow band for those two years. That is what the Treaty says. I do not regard myself as being in a position to say whether we will achieve that or not. If I may make a surmise: my view is we are unlikely to achieve the 1 January 1997 date and it is more likely to go into the later date the treaty envisages, which is 1 January 1999, and that consequently gives a much longer period in which one can both improve economic convergence and also join the ERM.

The governor made a broader point in relation to the convergence criteria, on which there appear to be mixed views within the British government: 'We have accepted, the Government has accepted, the convergence criteria as economic objectives in their own right whether we join or not and even now whether we are in the ERM or not. I agree with that, they are respectable criteria to aim at.' Francis Maude, a former treasury minister in the British government, told the Rome meeting of the Association for the Monetary Union of Europe in June 1993 that the acceptance of the convergence criteria on domestic grounds was the 'unspoken agenda' for the government.

It is a case of 'heads I win, tails you lose'. If the government wishes to opt in to Stage III, then the observance of the criteria becomes a necessary condition. If the government wishes to opt out of Stage III, the observance of the criteria will still be beneficial for purely domestic policy reasons. The observance of the criteria is thus required if the UK is to have a genuine decision in 1996 whether to opt in or out, rather than being excluded by default. The European Parliamentary elections in June 1994 would provide an appropriate moment for the UK to rejoin the ERM.

Apart from the problem of whether and when to rejoin the ERM, the British government faces two major policy tasks in relation to convergence. The first is to prevent inflation rising from its present low level to above the target range of 4 per cent under the twin impacts of devaluation feeding through to import prices and recovery allowing businesses to carry out price increases delayed by recession. The second is to reduce the structural element of the public sector financial deficit, officially forecast at 8.8 per cent of GDP in financial year 1993/94, so as to bring it down close to 3 per cent of GDP in the recovery phase of the cycle by 1996.

The government will, under Article 109e, have to present convergence programmes to the Commission, which will then be the subject of a multilateral surveillance procedure by the Council. This could be presented as similar to parallel exercises that have for many years been carried out by the IMF and the OECD, or as unwelcome intrusion into domestic economic policy. Much depends on whether the UK is thought by other EMS countries to be aiming at a genuine attempt to prepare for a decision to opt in to Stage III of EMU, even if the final decision is not to be taken until after what may be the most crucial general election for many years in 1996. The UK's experience of the ERM provides a classic example of what economists call 'time-inconsistency', the advantage to governments of announcing that they will act in one way, then later acting in another. Departure from the ERM was 'time-inconsistent', in that the UK derived short-term economic advantages by abandoning its commitments to remain a member. Return to the ERM in 1994 would also be 'time-inconsistent' in restoring exchange rate stability as a weapon against rising inflation in spite of a commitment not to rejoin for some years. After that, however, the UK's credibility would sink to zero if it continued to tack in and out of the ERM in such a way as to maximize short-term advantage.

CONCLUSIONS

1. The UK was wrong not to join the ERM in 1978.
2. Mrs Thatcher was wrong to veto UK entry in 1985.
3. The UK joined at too high an exchange rate in 1990.
4. UK membership of the ERM was initially successful.
5. The UK's exit was due to bad luck and bad management.
6. The UK should return to the ERM by 1994, at latest 1996.

REFERENCES

Barker, Kate et al. (1993), 'European pitfalls on road to recovery', *The Guardian*, 5 July.
Barrell, Ray and Veld, J.W. in't (1991), 'FEERs and the path to EMU', *National Institute Review*, 137, August.
British Invisible Exports Council (1990), *The Next Stage in an Evolutionary Approach to Economic and Monetary Union*, BIEC.
Britton, A.J.C. (1991), *Macroeconomic Policy in Britain 1974–1987*, Cambridge, Cambridge University Press.
Collignon, S. (1994) *Europe's Monetary Future*, London, Pinter.
Davies, Gavyn (1989), 'Britain and the European monetary question', Institute for Public Policy Research, Economic Study 1.
Goldstein, Morris et al. (1993), *International Capital Markets*, Part I, *Exchange Rate Management and International Capital Flows*, Washington, DC, International Monetary Fund.
Goodhart, David (1993), 'Brussels gurus raise old taboos to find mysteries of job creation', *Financial Times*, 24 June.
Group of Ten (1993), *International Capital Movements and Foreign Exchange Markets*, Rome, Banca d'Italia.
House of Lords Select Committee on the European Communities (1990), *Economic and Monetary Union and Political Union*, 2 vols, report and evidence. House of Lords papers 88-i and 88-ii. Session 1989–90, 27th report, London, HMSO.
Hutton, Will (1992), 'Inside the ERM crisis', *The Guardian*, 30 November and 1 December.
International Monetary Fund (1993), *World Economic Outlook: Interim Assessment*, January, Washington, DC, IMF.
Lamont, Norman (1992), 'Britain and the Exchange Rate Mechanism', Speech to European Policy Forum 10 July 1992, Treasury press release.
Lawson, Nigel (1992), *The View from No. 11*, London, Bantam.
Leigh-Pemberton, R. (1984), 'Some aspects of monetary policy', *Bank of England Quarterly Bulletin*, December.
Leigh-Pemberton, R. (1991), 'The economy and ERM membership', *Bank of England Quarterly Bulletin*, February.
Norman, Peter and Barber, Lionel (1992), 'Behind the ERM crisis', *Financial Times*, 11–12 December.
OECD (1991), *OECD Economic Surveys: United Kingdom 1990/91*, Paris, OECD.
O'Mahony, Mary (1992), 'Productivity levels in British and German manufacturing industry', *National Institute Economic Review*, 139, February.
Pöhl, Karl-Otto et al. (1990), *Britain and Economic and Monetary Union*, London, Centre for Economic Performance in association with Financial Markets Group, London School of Economics.
Prout, Sir Christopher (1991), *Britain and EMU. Second Brandon Rhys Williams Memorial Lecture*, London, European League for Economic Cooperation.
Smith, David (1993), 'Lawson blames Major for creating ERM fiasco', *Sunday Times Business*, 30 May.
Treasury (1989), *An Evolutionary Approach to Economic and Monetary Union*, London, HMSO.
Treasury (1991), *Financial Statement and Budget Report 1991–92*, House of Commons Paper 300, London, HMSO.

Treasury (1992), *Financial Statement and Budget Report 1992–93*, House of Commons Paper 319, London, HMSO.
Treasury and Civil Service Committee (1985), *The Financial and Economic Consequences of UK Membership of the European Communities: The European Monetary System*, Memoranda, Report and Minutes of Evidence, Thirteenth Report Session 1984–85, House of Commons papers 57-III, 57-IV and 57-V, London, HMSO.
Treasury and Civil Service Committee (1990), *The 1990 Autumn Statement*, First Report Session 1990–91, House of Commons Paper 41, London, HMSO.
Treasury and Civil Service Committee (1991a), *The 1991 Budget*, Second Report Session 1990–91, House of Commons Paper 289, London, HMSO.
Treasury and Civil Service Committee (1991b), *The 1991 Autumn Statement*, First Report Session 1991–92, House of Commons paper 58, London, HMSO.
Treasury and Civil Service Committee (1992), *The 1992 Autumn Statement and the Conduct of Economic Policy*, First Report Session 1992–93, House of Commons paper 201, 16 December 1992, London, HMSO.
Walters, Alan (1986), *Britain's Economic Renaissance*, Oxford, Oxford University Press.
Walters, Alan (1990), *Sterling in Danger*, London, Fontana/Collins.
Williamson, John (1991), 'FEERs and the ERM', *National Institute Review*, 137, August.
Wren-Lewis, Simon et al. (1991), 'Evaluating the UK's choice of entry rate into the ERM'. *The Manchester School*, 59 (supplement), June.

7

ON WIDENING THE EMS TO CENTRAL AND EASTERN EUROPE

Stefan Collignon

Economic and monetary cooperation between the newly emerging market economies in Central and Eastern Europe and the Community will gain increasing cooperation during Stages II and III of EMU. This will also be necessary in order to reduce the risks and dangers from the increasing political and economic instability in what used to be the Soviet-dominated east of Europe for the integration process within the Community and the transition to the single currency. The systemic transformation of former planned economies to a market system needs to be completed and an environment created which will allow long-term growth in the region. The European Community can obviously play an important role in this process. Particularly for countries that have proven to be committed to a rapid transition to a market economy, an institutional framework of cooperation could lay the ground for a future full integration of those economies into the European Union.

Systemic transformation and economic stabilization require external support. Joseph Schumpeter, having failed to achieve Austrian stabilization as finance minister in 1919, came to the same conclusion: 'Without external assets there cannot be a stabilization of currency and hence no order in the public finances. The reverse sequence, first to establish internal order and then to seek external credit, is a path of desperate dissipation [*Verblutung*] which has been taken all too often in financial history. The fateful vicious circle: no external credit, no internal order, but without internal order no external credit, must be solved.'[1]

Numerous governments and politicians in Central and Eastern Europe have declared their intention to solve this dilemma by joining the European Community. But such integration requires time in order to make the joining economies compatible with the delicate balance of interests that marks the Community. Full integration should therefore be the strategic long-term target, while intermediate steps help to reach this goal. A short-term response can be the strengthening of the association agreements; a medium-term support structure could be the creation of an Ecu zone.

THE CREATION OF AN ECU ZONE

In order to stimulate discussion on greater monetary cooperation between East and West, the Association for the Monetary Union of Europe has made a proposal[2] for the creation of an Ecu zone. The aim is to assist the integration of the economies of Central and Eastern Europe with those of Western Europe, on the basis of a properly functioning monetary market economy. Only if the reforming countries converge over time to the stability standards of the European Union, outlined in the Maastricht Treaty, will it be possible for them to join the Community.

In creating such an Ecu zone, the participating countries in Central and Eastern Europe would pool part of their reserves into an Eastern European stabilization fund. In exchange they would receive a supporting convertibility standby facility by the European Community and those funds together could be used for stabilizing exchange rates. The Ecu zone resembles in some ways the European Monetary System, *but several of its features are more suitable to Eastern Europe and allow far greater flexibility.*

Three instruments of cooperation form the institutional foundation of the Ecu zone: (1) the Ecu Zone Surveillance Board, (2) the Reserve Pool & Stabilization Fund and (3) the Exchange Rate Mechanism for the Ecu zone. The proposal is meant to create a legal and institutional framework which allows the coordination of policies and the improvement of free trade among the related countries. The proposal also wishes to stimulate trade not only between East and West, but also between the fast-transforming economies themselves. Finally, the creation of an Ecu zone would help to strengthen the quality of local currencies by improving the credibility commitments to greater macroeconomic stability. In this way the creation of an Ecu zone would establish a kind of *antechamber for full EMS membership* in the future. It is an instrument that would permit a managed adjustment of the economic and political convergence of Central and Eastern Europe to the standards of the European Community and would provide added security to foreign investors, so that private market forces rather than public aid would become the engine of growth.

The Ecu zone Surveillance Board (EZSB)

The purpose of such a board is to ensure that economic policies in the participating countries converge to the stability norms of the European

Community. It assures the day-to-day management of the pooled foreign exchange reserves of the participating countries and of the standby facility from the European Community. The board would also coordinate the Ecu zone Exchange Rate Mechanism and monitor the macroeconomic compatibilities of the monetary and economic policies pursued. The EZSB would also contribute to the creation of new institutions that will be adapted to future membership of the European Union. The EZSB would thereby permit a *gradual integration* of the fast-reforming economies into the European Community by providing an institutional framework of cooperation and coordination of policies. At the same time it would provide a mechanism which would allow the *controlled opening of markets* for products, services and capital, which are necessary if full membership of these countries in the European Community is ultimately intended.

The decision-making body of the Surveillance Board would consist of representatives from the participating Central and Eastern European governments and central banks (these banks should be made independent of political influences, similar to the European Central Bank), the European Community institutions as well as the IMF and EBRD.

This would ensure that recommendations and implementations of the board would be based on the broadest possible consensus. It would also give a clear signal to wage bargaining parties (trade unions, managements of firms, governments) what kind of income policies are compatible with the long-term objective of joining the exclusive club of the rich EC countries. This should increase the political and social acceptability of the measures suggested by the EZSB.

The Ecu zone Stabilization Fund

At the heart of the proposal is the Stabilization Fund, into which the participating Central and Eastern European countries would transfer a significant part of their reserves. On the other side, the European Community would establish a standby facility on which the Ecu zone Stabilization Fund could draw when necessary, within the guidelines set by the Ecu zone Surveillance Board. The standby facility would be unlimited for very short-term requirements, and subject to strong conditionality for medium and long-term borrowing.

The purpose of this fund is to strengthen convertibility of local currencies and to stabilize foreign exchange transactions on a day-to-day basis for the fast-reforming economies of Central and Eastern Europe, *without locking them into detrimental rigidities*. At the same time the fund would help to increase the credibility of monetary and economic policies in those countries so that private investors rather than governments can take the lead in creating investment and growth. The final objective of the Ecu zone Stabilization Fund is to provide the means for exchange rate interventions.

Table 7.1 Intra-industry trade with the EC: CSFR, Hungary and Poland engage in more intra-industry trade with the EC than Portugal and Norway. (100 indicates 100% of trade with EC is two-way trade in similar products)

F	UK	NL	CH	BL	D	E	S	A	I
82	77	77	77	76	75	73	70	68	63

DK	IRL	H	CS	PL	P	SF	N	GR	IS
63	59	50	46	42	42	39	36	29	4

Notes: F = France, UK = United Kingdom, NL = Netherlands, CH = Switzerland, BL = Belgium-Lux., D = Germany, E = Spain, S = Sweden, A = Austria, I = Italy, DK = Denmark, IRL = Ireland, H = Hungary, CS = Czechoslovakia, PL = Poland, P = Portugal, SF = Finland, N = Norway, GR = Greece, IS = Iceland.

Source: Baldwin (1992).

The Ecu zone Exchange Rate Mechanism

A stable currency with competitive exchange rates is a useful device in order to stimulate exports and growth. Rather than allowing savage 'beggar-thy-neighbour' policies and wild competitive devaluations, a managed exchange rate policy with respect to the European Community could be a useful stabilizing anchor for the fast-reforming economies. It is therefore suggested that the countries participating in the Ecu zone would peg their exchange rates to the Ecu but not necessarily in the same way as EMS countries do among themselves. The Ecu in its present form as a basket of EC currencies already represents the best weighted average of different interests in Western European economies. Furthermore, as the Ecu is intended to become the single European currency of the Community, using the basket Ecu today is a useful means of anticipating future relations within Stage III of EMU.

The importance of exchange rate policy is obvious from the structure of trade flows. Seventy-five per cent of East–West (OECD) trade between the former CSFR, Hungary, Poland, Bulgaria and Romania is oriented to the European Community and 13 per cent to the EFTA states.[3] Intra-industry trade between the three Central European countries and the EC is also rather important (see Table 7.1) and likely to expand rapidly without much political resistance. Within the Ecu zone Exchange Rate Mechanism *several different regimes are possible*. They need to be chosen with respect to the different stages of economic development in the respective countries. In view of the different economic comparative advantages, structural rigidities, and difficulties in reducing inflation in individual countries, a large degree of flexibility is required.

Countries beginning the economic transformation process under the constraint of sticky wages and an insufficient tax system, aiming to restructure their production potential in order to give it greater export orientation, may wish to establish at first a *crawling peg*, compensating for high rates of inflation. To the degree that stabilization policies become effective, the crawling peg may be *reduced, according to a pre-announced schedule*, and ultimately the exchange rate regime could be transformed into a *fixed, but adjustable exchange rate peg* like in the EMS. The objective of such an exchange rate mechanism is to allow gradual convergence towards the stability standards of the European Community and to tie the participating Ecu zone countries to the discipline that goes with this. However, given the structural rigidities, the nominal exchange rate has to maintain for some considerable period of time a degree of flexibility that is necessarily larger than within the European Monetary System of the European Community, or even a full Monetary Union.[4]

Qualification and participation

The institutional arrangement of the suggested Ecu zone is naturally linked to the perspective of joining the European Community at some future stage. It is also clear that only those countries that have already achieved a substantial degree of systemic reform could participate, as otherwise the instruments of policy correction of the Ecu zone would be insufficient. At present, Hungary, the Czech Republic and Poland seem the most likely candidates, although other fast-transforming economies in the Baltics, Slovakia, Slovenia, Bulgaria and Romania may qualify in due course.

As for some of the smaller emerging countries in Eastern Europe, it may be wise for them to base their monetary system on some kind of a currency board scheme and then link this arrangement to the Ecu zone. The first example of such reform was provided by Estonia in June 1992, although the kroon was pegged to the DM and not to the Ecu.[5] Linking the currency board to the Ecu zone arrangement could provide additional credibility which would allow the relaxing of capital controls.[6] It would also have the advantage of maintaining and even strengthening traditional trade links between countries which are regionally close and whose productive structures are still to a large degree interdependent. This issue will gain in urgency after the break-up of the rouble zone.

CONCLUSION

The creation of an Ecu zone for Central and Eastern Europe would allow participating countries to reap some significant benefits in the course of the transformation of their internal economies. It would permit the

Central and Eastern European economies to stabilize their macroeconomic policies less harshly, as the external support from the Community would provide greater confidence in the measures envisaged and would encourage private investors to seize the opportunities in the new markets. It would also help to make the hardships of economic transformation more acceptable for the public at large, as they would see the possibilities of full EC membership at the end of the road. The greater stability in the system would contribute to the formation of workable capital markets, which are ultimately the precondition for economic development. However, the Ecu zone would also benefit Western Europe. It would guarantee greater stability in the East and could thereby help to slow down the migration flows, not to mention military instability. It would provide new investment opportunities and last but not least, enlarge the use and credibility of the Ecu as an attractive currency, even before it has become Europe's single currency. In this way the Ecu would truly become a unifier, not only within the European Community, but also between East and West.

NOTES

1. Quoted in Dornbusch (1992), p.406.
2. For details of the suggestion see Collignon (1991) and (1992a, b and c).
3. See Baldwin (1992).
4. For the viability of such solutions for Eastern Europe see Bofinger (1991).
5. IMF (1992), p.52.
6. See Bofinger (1991) on some of the difficulties of currency boards in Eastern Europe.

REFERENCES

Baldwin, R. (1992), *An Eastern Enlargement of EFTA: Why the East Europeans should Join and the EFTANS should Want Them*, CEPR occasional paper, no. 10, London.

Bofinger, P. (1991), *Options for the Payments and Exchange Rate System in Eastern Europe*, CEPR discussion paper no. 545, London.

Collignon, S. (1991), 'Asymmetrie und Reversibilität im EWS: Bedroht die deutsche Einheit die Ankerfunktion der D-Mark?', in A. Westphal et al., *Wirtschaftspolitische Konsequenzen der deutschen Vereinigung*, Frankfurt/New York.

Collignon, S. (1992a), 'A proposal to create an Ecu zone to assist Eastern Europe's transition to a market economy', *De Pecunia*, 3(3), December. (In Italian:'Una zona Ecu per l'Europa dell'est', *Revista di Politica Economica*, March.)

Collignon, S. (1992b), 'An Ecu zone for Central and Eastern Europe: a supportive framework for convergence', in R. Barrell (ed.), *Economic Convergence and Monetary Union in Europe*, London.

Collignon, S. (1992c), 'Intégrer les pays de l'est à l'Europe: une zone Ecu', *Revue d'Économie et Financière* (special), September.
Dornbusch, R. (1992) 'Monetary problems of post-communism: lessons from the end of the Austro-Hungarian Empire', *Weltwirtschaftliches Archiv*, 128(3).
IMF (1992), *World Economic Outlook*, October, Washington, DC.

Part II

GENERAL ANALYSES

8
THE DETERMINANTS OF REALIGNMENT EXPECTATIONS UNDER THE EMS: SOME EMPIRICAL REGULARITIES*

Zhaohui Chen and Alberto Giovannini

INTRODUCTION

One of the central questions in the theory of international monetary regimes is whether fixed but adjustable exchange rates are a contradiction in terms. In other words, can a system of adjustable parities survive? Is it, in some sense, stable? This question has

---

* This chapter is an extension of the research project begun in Chen and Giovannini (1992a), presented at the Ossola Memorial Conference, and contains a modified empirical methodology and new results. We thank Bernard Delbecque, Charles Goodhart, Luigi Spaventa, Niels Thygesen, and seminar participants at IMF and Université Catholique de Louvain for comments. All errors are ours.

The stability of the EMS depends crucially on realignment expectations of the market participants. In this chapter we discuss how to measure such expectations and how to relate them to economic fundamentals, central bank reputation, and institutional arrangements of the EMS. We find the following empirical regularities for FFr/DM and IL/DM exchange rates: (1) expected devaluations are positively related to the current exchange rate deviation from the central parity; (2) expected devaluations are negatively related to the length of time since the last realignment in the short and medium run; (3) the Basle-Nyborg agreements seem to have a stabilizing effect for both currencies examined, albeit through different channels; (4) large revaluation expectations occur immediately after devaluations. (1) and (4) are not inconsistent with the hypothesis of overspeculation or market inefficiency.

dominated the policy debate on the European Monetary System (EMS), especially since the liberalization of international capital movements in the second half of the 1980s. It also characterized the debate on exchange-rate based stabilizations, started by Diaz Alejandro (1981), Dornbusch (1982) and Calvo (1983).

Recent research in international finance, in particular the work of Flood and Garber (1984) and the empirical research in the vein of Lizondo (1983), has clearly and convincingly established the linkage between the collapse of a fixed exchange rate and expectations held by actors in financial markets. In addition, the analysis of the stabilizing properties of monetary policy rules – Simons (1936), Friedman (1968) and Barro and Gordon (1983) – has shown that the crucial channel through which such rules can stabilize inflation and economic activity is the behaviour of the private sector's expectations. Hence the 'strength' or 'weakness' of an adjustable rate system is directly related to the behaviour of expectations under such a regime.

This chapter is an exploration of the determinants of expectations of the French franc/DM and lira/DM parity changes during the EMS period. Such an exploration should be, in our view, the first step of a broader analysis of the stability properties of a fixed-but-adjustable rate system. More precisely, the questions we ask are: What determines the expectations of parity changes? Are the institutional arrangements of the EMS – designed to stabilize the foreign exchange market, such as the target zone and intergovernmental coordinations – effective at all? In order to answer these questions we need to obtain reliable estimates of such expectations, and then attempt to relate them to economic and institutional variables.

The next section deals with the empirical measurement of realignment expectations, the third section discusses how to select the fundamental and institution variables, and we then discuss the estimation methodology. The penultimate section reports the results, and we end with some concluding remarks.

MEASURING EXPECTED PARITY CHANGES

The first step in studying the empirical behaviour of market expectations is to find an empirical measurement of such unobservable expectations. The measurement of expected parity changes has to take into account two problems. The first is the measurement of expected changes in exchange rates. In this study, we assume interest rate parity. That is, interest rate differentials reflect expectations of exchange rate changes and that risk premia, or other sources of differences between ex-ante returns in different currencies, are insignificant. Svensson (1990) argues that in a managed exchange rate regime with target zones, given realistic distributional assumptions about fundamentals, the exchange rate risk premium should be insignificant.

The second problem in measuring parity changes is the presence of exchange rate bands, or target zones. Since exchange rates are flexible within these target zones, in order to estimate the expected change in a central parity it is necessary to separate the expected changes within the band and the expected shift of the central parity. In this, we extend the work of Collins (1984, 1986), who first studied realignment expectations in the EMS using interest-rate differentials.

To fix ideas, decompose the log exchange rate S into the log central parity c and the log percentage deviation from the central parity x:

$$s_t = c_t + x_t. \tag{1}$$

It follows that the one-period expected change (devaluation) of the exchange rate can be decomposed into the expected central parity shift and the expected change in the percentage deviation from the central parity:

$$E[\Delta s_t | I_t] = E[\Delta c_t | I_t] + E[\Delta x_t | I_t]. \tag{2}$$

All expectations are conditional upon information available at time t, denoted by I_t. Under interest rate parity, the left hand side can be replaced by the interest rate differential between the home country and the foreign country. Denote the differential of interest of deposits of maturity j by δ^j, the expected devaluation can be written as:

$$E[c_{t+j} - c_t | I_t] = \delta_t^j - E[(x_{t+j} - x_t) | I_t]. \tag{3}$$

With δ_t^j observed in the interest rate data, the task of measuring expected devaluation is reduced to measuring expected changes in x. Notice that the expectation is a *full information* expectation in the sense that the information set I_t should contain information concerning the possibility of both a realignment and no realignment in the next j periods, in other words, the observations on x should reflect the market's assessment of future realignment possibilities.[1] It is thus essential to make sure that the sample on x contains enough realignment observations. When the data are available, we can obtain the ex-post measure of expected realignment devaluation as

$$c_{t+j} - c_t = \delta_t^j - (x_{t+j} - x_t). \tag{4}$$

We can obtain an ex-ante measure of realignment expectations by projecting the above on the current information set, as will be defined below.

CHOOSING THE VARIABLES IN THE INFORMATION SET

To determine what information variables are to be included in the projection equation, it would be ideal to have a theoretical model that links the fundamental variables to expected realignment in equilibrium. It is well known, however, that the available theoretical models do not tell us what constitute the 'fundamentals', so they are suggestive at best. A familiar brand of models, based on the Barro and Gordon (1983) framework of monetary policy games, describe the central bank's main objective as price stability, which can be achieved through exchange rate targeting as in the EMS. However, the central bank also has other objectives, and when those objectives are in crisis, the central bank may deviate from the exchange rate targeting policy. This notion of 'crisis mentality' is consistent with evidence found in the Bernanke and Mishkin (1992) case study of central bank behaviour in major industrialized countries. Giovannini (1990) contains a model of this kind, known as an 'escape-clause model'. Instead of resorting to a particular model, we rely on the projection-equation approach. The following observations serve as background to our choice of variables in the information set.

Assume that q is the probability of a large adverse shock to the economy occurring in the next period, and that the shock is so big that it warrants a realignment attempt (the escape clause). The government may choose to devalue, or to defend the parity. Suppose the public assigns a subjective probability p to the event that the government will devalue in face of the shock, then the expected devaluation $E\Delta c$ is a probability weighted average defined as follows:

$$E \Delta c = (1 - p) \times 0 + p[q\hat{c}^{e,d} + (1 - q) \times 0], \qquad (5)$$

where $\hat{c}^{e,d}$ is the expected size of devaluation if the central bank is pursuing a discretionary (devaluation) policy. Its value can be determined in the equilibrium. In general, it is positively related to the adverse shock and the weakness of the economy and the exchange rate mechanism – the stronger the economy and the better the inter-governmental coordination in defending the parity, the easier it is for the government to weather the negative shocks, and therefore the smaller the expected size of realignment. Simplifying, the above definition can be written as

$$E \Delta c = pq\hat{c}^{e,d}. \qquad (6)$$

It can be clearly seen that expected realignment depends on p, q and $\hat{c}^{e,d}$. The empirical task now is to find proxies that capture the essence of these three variables.

To measure p, the public's subjective probability that the central bank will devalue the currency under crisis, we need to specify a rule on how this probability is formed. One hypothesis, as suggested by the experience of many EMS countries, is that the longer the central bank manages to keep the exchange rate parity free of realignment, the smaller is p, since the public may gain more confidence in the central bank based on its past record of success. A simple way to capture this idea is to use the length of time since last realignment (we actually use $ln(1+t)$) as a proxy for this behaviour of p. The hypothesis suggests that we should expect to find a negative correlation between p and this measure of time. An alternative hypothesis is the so called 'honeymoon' effect commonly seen in the post-election popularity of a winning political party: the popularity surges after the election, and gradually dies out, exhibiting a hump-shaped pattern.[2] In the case of the public's perception of the central bank after a realignment, one can imagine a similar scenario: p may first decline as the public begins to be convinced that the new parity is properly in line with fundamentals so it may last into the future. But as time goes by, uncertainty about the central bank's resolve may increase for various reasons. This hypothesis implies that p can be viewed as a U-shaped function of time. A third hypothesis, as suggested by Ghisellini (1992), assumes that there is a fixed cost of realignment, so realignment is infrequent, but the longer the time since last realignment, the more likely a new realignment will occur. This implies a positive relationship between p and time. Combining the above discussions, we use two separate formation rules for p, one is a direct measure of time since last realignment ($t^* \equiv ln(1+t)$), the other is a quadratic measure ($at^* + bt^{*2}$) aimed at capturing the U-curve effect (negative a and positive b).

The probability of a large adverse shock to the domestic economy relative to the foreign counterpart, q, can be measured in terms of various fundamental variables such as trade balance, industrial production, etc., while the expected size of devaluation, $\hat{c}^{e,d}$, can also be linked to the above variables, as well as to such fundamental positions as foreign exchange reserve, budget deficit, wages and inflation, and nominal variables such as liquidity. It should be noted that p may also depend on the government's financial positions such as deficit and foreign exchange reserves. Put together, we can isolate the independent effect of time since last realignment after controlling for these fundamentals.

We also incorporate some important institutional features of the EMS and evaluate their effectiveness in reducing realignment expectations. One such institutional arrangement is the fluctuation band, or the target zone. The target zone literature has shown on both theoretical and empirical grounds that the band has a stabilizing, or mean reverting effect on expected exchange-rate deviation from the central parity. In other words, the expected change in exchange rate deviation from the central parity is *negatively* correlated with the current deviation from the central parity. Although the models deal specifically with the *deviations from central parity*, the mean reverting result has been commonly interpreted in a naive way, which leads to the conclusion that the band has a stabilizing effect on *realignment* expectations. Changes in deviation from central parity and changes in central parity itself are equivalent only in the case of no realignment. So in general, when realignment is allowed, the stabilization property, at least in the form of negative correlation, may not apply. We include a variable representing the deviation from the central parity in our empirical estimation and examine whether the negative correlation holds for expected parity changes. This is crucial in evaluating the stability of the EMS.

Another feature of the EMS is the institutionalized coordination among member countries. The coordination efforts are aimed at strengthening member countries' positions in preventing and countering crises and speculations. We focus on the effectiveness of one such coordination – the introduction of the Basle-Nyborg agreements. Finally, the credibility and stability of the EMS can also be explored by studying the reaction of the foreign exchange market to a realignment. This is done employing a 'realignment dummy'.

The following is a complete list and definitions of the information variables.

- $C1, C2, \ldots$: Constant dummies corresponding to each central parity regime. Ten regimes for IL and seven for FF.
- $X1$: Log relative foreign exchange reserve position measured in terms of the DM.
- $X2$: The percentage change in budget surplus on a cash basis (Italy or France minus Germany).
- $X3$ The difference of the trade balance surpluses (Italy or France minus Germany).
- $X4$ Relative industrial production indices. Denote foreign (German) variable with a star, the definition can be written as

$$\ln\left(\frac{IP}{IP^*}\right) \qquad (7)$$

- $X5$ The position of the exchange rate within the band (x).
- $X6$ Form 1: The log of 1 plus the number of months since last realignment, denoted as t^*; Form 2: $at^* + bt^{*2}$.
- $X7$ An index of relative CPIs. Denote S as the exchange rate measured in terms of domestic currency value of one unit of DM, the index is written as

$$\ln\left(\frac{CPI}{CPI^* \times S}\right). \qquad (8)$$

- $X8$ An index of relative wages, i.e.:

$$\ln\left(\frac{W}{W^* \times S}\right). \tag{9}$$

- X9: Relative liquidity, i.e.:

$$\ln\left(\frac{L}{L^* \times S}\right). \tag{10}$$

- X10: DM/US$ exchange rate.
- X11: Jump dummy that takes the value 1 at the first month of realignment and 0 otherwise.
- X12: X1 multiplied by the slope dummy that equals 0 before the Basle-Nyborg agreements and 1 afterwards.
- X13: X5 multiplied by the same slope dummy as in X12.

The sources for the data used are listed at the end of the chapter. The frequency of our data is monthly, and the horizons we study are one month and three months. We look at the lira/DM and French franc/DM exchange rates since the beginning of the EMS.

ESTIMATION

In the previous section we argued that the estimation of the expected change in the central parity requires an estimation of the expected change in the exchange rate within the band. Our task is to explore the determinants of expectations of parity changes. To do this, we estimate the following equation:

$$\delta_t^j - (x_{t+j} - x_t) = Z_t'\beta + u_{t+j}, \tag{11}$$

where Z_t' is a vector of variables in agents' information sets at time t. Here we assume Z_t consists of all the information variables listed in the previous section. The disturbance term u_{t+j} has two components. One is the expectations error $(x_{t+j} - Ex_{t+j})$, the other is an error due to the imprecise measurement of expectations, or the existence of variables affecting expectations that are left out from the vector Z. The former is, under the assumption of rational expectations, orthogonal to any variable included in Z, depending on the severity of specification errors. In general, the expectation error always swamps the error due to mismeasurement, because, as is well known, the variance of the unpredictable component of exchange rates is very high. When $j > 1$ the expectation error follows a moving average process of order $j - 1$.

Equation (11) allows us to estimate, simultaneously, the expected change in the exchange rate within the band and the determinants of expected parity changes. Consider the linear projection:

$$\delta_t^j - E[(x_{t+j} - x_t)] = Z_t'\hat{\beta}, \qquad (12)$$

where $\hat{\beta}$ is a consistent estimate of β. Equation (12) shows that the projection of the interest-rate differential net of the realized exchange-rate changes within the band on information provides an estimate of the expected change in the central parity. The coefficient vector β will indicate the relation of the expected change in the central parity to fundamentals.

The basic strategy of this regression is inspired by the following observation. Under the assumption of linear rational expectations, the best estimate of the expectations of any economic variable is its projection on variables in agents' information sets at the time such expectation is formed. The property of this estimate is that the estimated residuals, which represent the 'surprises', are orthogonal to the variables used to form expectations. In that sense, information cannot be used more efficiently to form expectations, and therefore expectations are rational.

A problem with unrestricted projection using target zone data is that it fails to specify explicitly the restrictions implied by the presence of the target zone band, which is a part of the public's information set, and is non-linearly related to, and correlated with many other information variables. This may result in incorrect estimates of expectations. This problem is discussed by Chen and Giovannini (1992b), who propose a type of Box–Cox transformation which recovers the good properties of projection equations. This transformation cannot be used in the equation we estimate in this chapter, because it would not allow the easy joint estimation of expectations of realignments and exchange-rate movements within the band. However, we have verified that, in the case of the EMS, the errors that arise from not exploiting the information on exchange-rate bands are likely to be negligible (see also Svensson, 1991).

RESULTS

Tables 8.1 (plus 8.1a and 8.1b) and 8.2 (plus 8.2a and 8.2b) report the estimates of the projection equation over the one-month horizon, respectively for the lira and the French franc. Tables 8.1 and 8.2 contain the estimates over the full sample (March 1979 to January 1992), Tables 8.1a and 8.2a contain the estimates over the period from March 1979 to August 1987, while Tables 8.1b and 8.2b contain estimates over the period from September 1987 to January 1992. The breakpoint is the date of the Basle–Nyborg agreement (12 September 1987), of the Committee of Central Bank Governors, which strengthened the Exchange Rate Mechanism of the EMS by adopting a number of measures, including in

Table 8.1 One-month IL/DM expected devaluation: full-sample regression (March 1979–January 1992)

Variable	Coefficient	t-value	p-value
C1	−478.1773	−0.7268	0.4686
C2	−479.8048	−0.7349	0.4637
C3	−472.0257	−0.7249	0.4698
C4	−479.6472	−0.7355	0.4633
C5	−460.6358	−0.7099	0.4790
C6	−458.5521	−0.7096	0.4792
C7	−471.8912	−0.7329	0.4649
C8	−459.9705	−0.7188	0.4735
C9	−467.0552	−0.7313	0.4659
C10	−460.8237	−0.7251	0.4697
X1	6.4620	0.6659	0.5066
X2	−0.1873	−0.4917	0.6238
X3	126.6341	0.2778	0.7816
X4	−14.0219	−0.2477	0.8048
X5	0.5303	6.0541	0.0000
X6	−9.6477	−4.7456	0.0000
X7	−59.6633	−0.3861	0.7001
X8	8.5227	0.0721	0.9426
X9	−23.5367	−1.4285	0.1555
X10	19.6028	0.6498	0.5170
X11	−17.8491	−2.5136	0.0131

Diagnostics
  Number of observations 155
  Standard Error   16.636
  R-squared   0.457
  $F_{(21, 134)}$ 7.211
  Durbin–Watson   2.320

particular an extension of the use of the Very Short Term Financing Facility to finance intra-marginal interventions.

In the case of Italy, the variables whose coefficients tend to be consistently significant are X5 (the position of the exchange rate within the band), and X6 (time since last realignment – a variable meant to capture learning and reputation effects). The coefficient of X5 is always positive, indicating that a wider deviation from a central parity increases expectations of exchange-rate changes. Interestingly, it is not significant at the 5 per cent level in the period since the Basle-Nyborg agreements (Table 8.1b). The strong significance and the negative sign on the coefficient of X6 implies that a proven tough exchange-rate stance – represented by the lack of recourse to realignment for a long period – other things equal, seems to improve the credibility of the exchange rate regime. The jump dummy X11 has a large negative coefficient, and is sometimes significant. This suggests that the occurrence of a realignment

Table 8.1a One-month IL/DM expected devaluation: sub-sample regression (March 1979–3 August 1987)

Variable	Coefficient	t-value	p-value
C1	1.3754	0.0659	0.9476
C2	−11.0142	−0.8400	0.4033
C3	6.2068	0.3890	0.6982
C4	−2.0331	−0.1243	0.9014
C5	22.4409	1.1763	0.2428
C6	33.2140	1.6584	0.1010
C7	10.2432	0.6146	0.5405
C8	12.8307	1.1084	0.2709
X1	1.3248	0.0945	0.9249
X2	−0.2116	−0.4676	0.6413
X3	159.1566	0.2536	0.8004
X4	38.9896	0.4786	0.6335
X5	0.6434	4.9941	0.0000
X6	−10.5628	−3.4840	0.0008
X7	−37.4572	−0.2197	0.8266
X8	67.4376	0.4187	0.6765
X9	−39.3983	−1.6092	0.1114
X10	−35.6960	−0.7698	0.4436
X11	−15.7087	−1.6153	0.1100

Diagnostics
  Number of observations 102
  Standard Error 19.310
  R-squared 0.509
  $F(19, 83)$ 6.067
  Durbin–Watson 2.471

induces sharp revisions of realignment expectations. The fact that $X11$ is not significant after Basle-Nyborg (Table 8.1b) is not surprising: the realignment of the lira of January 1990 was only due to the narrowing of the fluctuation band of that currency vis-à-vis the ERM partners.

The results for the case of France are broadly similar to Italy's with $X5$, $X6$ being the most significant variables, i.e. the position of the exchange rate within the band and the time elapsed since last realignment are the most powerful sources of revision of expectations. The jump dummy $X11$ also exhibits negative significance in Table 8.2

Tables 8.3 and 8.4 report regression results for one-month projections over the whole sample for Italy and France, with slope dummies on $X1$ and $X5$ to capture the effects of Basle-Nyborg on the sensitivity of realignment expectations with respect to reserves and exchange rate position within the band. Tables 8.3a and 8.4a contain regression results for the three-month horizon. The slope dummies $X12$ and $X13$ are obtained by multiplying $X1$ and $X5$, respectively, by a series that equals 0 up to August 1987, and 1 thereafter.

Table 8.1b One-month IL/DM expected devaluation: sub-sample regression (September 1987–January 1992)

Variable	Coefficient	t-value	p-value
C1	−2301.4348	−2.0236	0.0497
C2	−2294.3506	−2.0177	0.0504
X1	26.9352	2.0824	0.0437
X2	0.4132	0.4327	0.6676
X3	687.5019	1.2733	0.2103
X4	−45.1056	−0.8098	0.4228
X5	0.2382	1.8003	0.0794
X6	−2.9499	−1.4582	0.1526
X7	−417.4870	−1.6094	0.1154
X8	67.4277	0.4962	0.6225
X9	−5.5523	−0.4192	0.6773
X10	32.8205	1.1532	0.2557
X11	−1.9425	−0.1953	0.8462

Diagnostics
Number of observations   53
Standard Error   7.856
R-squared   0.385
$F(13, 40)$ 3.236
Durbin–Watson   1.860

For Italy, the slope dummy on the position of exchange rate within the band, $X13$, is negative and significant for both one-month horizon (5.4 per cent p – value) and three-month horizon (2.8 per cent p – value), while the slope dummy $X12$ is not significant. The opposite holds for France: the slope dummy on the foreign exchange reserve position, $X12$, is positive and significant for both one-month horizon (5.6 per cent p – value) and three-month horizon (0.27 per cent p – value), while the slope dummy $X13$ is not significant. Overall, this evidence suggests that Basle-Nyborg agreement may have indeed strengthened the central bank's ability to defend the announced parity. However, such gains in credibility appear to have been achieved through different channels in the two countries: for Italy, exchange rate deviation from the central parity is less worrisome to the public (negative coefficient on $X13$) since Basle-Nyborg, probably because of the perceived availability of the Very Short Run Facility that may strengthen the central bank's ability to intervene and regulate the exchange rate within the band; for France, the gains in credibility primarily come from the strengthened exchange reserve positions.

The three-month projections (Tables 8.3a and 8.4a) contain some more interesting results. For the case of Italy, $X4$ (relative industrial production) becomes significant, with a negative sign indicating a decline in realignment probabilities when Italian industrial production

Table 8.2 One-month FFr/DM expected devaluation: full-sample regression (March 1979–January 1992)

Variable	Coefficient	t-value	p-value
C1	317.9150	3.2361	0.0015
C2	322.2156	3.4408	0.0008
C3	321.1153	3.4300	0.0008
C4	333.0882	3.4148	0.0008
C5	331.2239	3.3702	0.0010
C6	323.2528	3.2734	0.0013
C7	317.1123	3.2861	0.0013
X1	−13.3100	−2.2929	0.0234
X2	−0.2640	−1.2067	0.2296
X3	−93.8045	−0.4467	0.6558
X4	70.5748	0.9709	0.3333
X5	0.8730	7.6783	0.0000
X6	−9.1515	−4.2937	0.0000
X7	276.7218	1.9938	0.0481
X8	−22.4749	−0.2186	0.8273
X9	−21.5987	−1.0839	0.2803
X10	−8.4588	−0.4482	0.6547
X11	−13.9427	−1.4449	0.1508

Diagnostics
  Number of observations   155
  Standard Error   15.916
  R-squared   0.545
  $F(18, 137)$ 9.912
  Durbin–Watson   2.423

improves relative to that of Germany. For the case of France, X1 and X9 become significant at the 5 per cent level, with negative signs suggesting that stronger relative reserve positions and relative liquidity help reduce realignment expectations.

To visualize the projected devaluations arising from the equations we estimated, we plot the predicted values of the regressions, together with the dates of the actual EMS realignments (each indicated by the tip of a triangle). Figures 8.1 and 8.2 plot the predicted one-month devaluation (expressed in percent per annum) for the lira/DM and the FFr/DM respectively (the predictions are based on equations whose estimates are in Tables 8.3 and 8.4). Interpreting the figures in terms of the model on p.116, we observe that they imply unambiguously a positive p (perceived probability that the government follows an escape clause policy, and does not credibly peg the currency) throughout most of the sample. The figures also show that the market tends to anticipate a realignment in the one-month horizon at all times, but such anticipation becomes more pronounced (indicated by large spikes in the figures) in

Table 8.2a One-month FFr/DM expected devaluation: sub-sample regression (March 1979–August 1987)

Variable	Coefficient	t-value	p-value
C1	414.2165	2.9950	0.0036
C2	413.8643	3.1375	0.0023
C3	410.6509	3.1160	0.0025
C4	416.5870	3.0512	0.0030
C5	414.2206	2.9974	0.0036
C6	412.1694	2.9652	0.0039
C7	405.4981	2.9893	0.0037
X1	−20.2068	−2.4533	0.0162
X2	−0.2537	−0.6182	0.5381
X3	−110.4367	−0.3692	0.7129
X4	89.1508	0.7758	0.4401
X5	0.9472	5.8764	0.0000
X6	−7.3715	−2.3743	0.0199
X7	237.1713	0.9697	0.3350
X8	79.2739	0.3859	0.7006
X9	−32.3508	−1.0448	0.2991
X10	−28.5935	−0.9969	0.3217
X11	−11.2882	−0.8933	0.3742

Diagnostics
Number of observations   102
Standard Error   19.312
R-squared   0.575
$F(18, 84)$ 6.943
Durbin–Watson   2.415

the few months preceding realignments. The figures also highlight the importance of the information about the occurrence of the realignment: after the realignment the expected devaluation of the lira and of the franc turn sharply negative.

For comparison, Figures 8.1a and 8.2a report the observed one-month interest rate differentials. While there are visible spikes they do not appear to match the timing of realignments with good precision. Another noteworthy feature of Figures 8.1a and 8.2a is the familiar evidence of interest rate convergence for both countries (relative to Germany) over time. We cannot, however, find a corresponding drastic decline of realignment expectations in Figures 8.1 and 8.2, although the variability of the expected devaluation has decreased over time. In other words, interest rate convergence is not necessarily a full reflection of a decline in expected devaluation.

In order to get a clearer indication of the accuracy of the estimated predictions about the timing of realignments, we plot in Figures 8.3 and 8.4 the difference between the one-month and the three-month expected

Table 8.2b One-month FFr/DM expected devaluation: sub-sample regression (September 1987–January 1992)

Variable	Coefficient	t-value	p-value
X1	−18.8457	−2.5994	0.0127
X2	−0.3606	−3.4552	0.0012
X3	−50.9597	−0.3756	0.7091
X4	−31.7236	−0.7245	0.4727
X5	0.2597	2.1636	0.0361
X6	13.2109	2.4251	0.0196
X7	21.6307	0.3970	0.6933
X8	29.2768	0.5437	0.5894
X9	−8.6638	−0.8264	0.4131
X10	10.5750	0.7958	0.4305

Diagnostics
Number of observations 53
Standard Error 4.970
R-squared 0.414
$F(10, 43)$ 3.691
Durbin–Watson 1.885

devaluations (the term premia). Simple intuition tells us that a positive term premium implies the estimated probability of a realignment is higher in the next month than in the two months at the long end of the horizon. Figures 8.3 and 8.4 show that the term premium tends to rise sharply one month prior to realignments, implying that the timing of realignments is correctly anticipated.

In contrast, Figures 8.3a and 8.4a show the one-month vs three-month term premia directly calculated from the term difference of the interest rate differentials. They do not appear to anticipate the timing of realignments with any good precision. This evidence further demonstrates that the interest rate differential is not a precise measure of realignment expectations.

Finally, our fitted data in Figures 8.1, 8.2, 8.3 and 8.4 reveal large reverse of realignment expectations in the month immediately following realignments. Again, such negative expected realignments are absent in the figures constructed directly from interest rate differentials (Figures 8.1a, 8.2a, 8.3a and 8.4a).

In the above report, $X6$ takes the form t^*. When it is replaced by the alternative form $at^* + bt^{*2}$, we find some evidence of the so called 'honeymoon' effect, or the U-curve effect. As we can see from Table 8.5, the estimated coefficient $\hat{a}$ is consistently negative for both the lira and the French franc in both the one-month and three-month projection horizons. This also holds for $\hat{b}$ with an opposite sign. The coefficients in the one-month regressions are all significant at the 5 per cent level, but

Table 8.3 Final regression results with regime dummies: expected one-month IL/DM devaluation (March 1979–January 1992)

Variable	Coefficient	t-value	p-value
C1	−688.0799	−0.9628	0.3374
C2	−690.6784	−0.9710	0.3333
C3	−676.1609	−0.9540	0.3418
C4	−684.9434	−0.9650	0.3363
C5	−662.2425	−0.9396	0.3492
C6	−655.5832	−0.9334	0.3523
C7	−671.8954	−0.9596	0.3390
C8	−660.1667	−0.9479	0.3449
C9	−669.7942	−0.9650	0.3363
C10	−673.9213	−0.9738	0.3319
X1	2.4665	0.1594	0.8736
X2	−0.1933	−0.5125	0.6091
X3	298.6601	0.6427	0.5215
X4	−0.9510	−0.0169	0.9866
X5	0.6774	5.8305	0.0000
X6	−8.4593	−4.0102	0.0001
X7	−124.9686	−0.7844	0.4342
X8	43.1606	0.3646	0.7160
X9	−26.0058	−1.5849	0.1154
X10	7.6254	0.2416	0.8095
X11	−11.1960	−1.4228	0.1572
X12	9.2878	0.7399	0.4607
X13	−0.4418	−1.9414	0.0543

Diagnostics
 Number of observations 155
 Standard Error 16.471
 R-squared 0.476
 $F(23, 132)$ 6.922
 Durbin–Watson 2.270

they become less significant in the three-month regressions. The results indicate that lack of realignment initially helps dampen realignment expectations (negative slope of the U-curve when t^* is small), but as time goes on, this trend tends to be reversed (upward-sloping part of the U-curve). To assess which part of the effects matters more in practice, we calculate the number of months it takes to reverse the downward trend using the one-month regression results.[3] We find the turning point occurs roughly 22 months after a realignment for the case of the lira and about 42 months for the case of the franc. Time periods of such lengths are long enough for practical considerations. So we view the dampening effect of a clean realignment record on the market expectations as the dominating effect, which is consistent with the result obtained by using the proxy t^* alone.

Table 8.3a Final regression results with regime dummies: expected three-month IL/DM devaluation (March 1979–January 1992)

Variable	Coefficient	t-value	p-value
C1	−205.5754	−0.7205	0.4725
C2	−200.4904	−0.7039	0.4827
C3	−184.0127	−0.6502	0.5167
C4	−184.2734	−0.6480	0.5181
C5	−174.2544	−0.6173	0.5381
C6	−175.1046	−0.6229	0.5344
C7	−183.7843	−0.6560	0.5129
C8	−187.4939	−0.6720	0.5027
C9	−197.9485	−0.7112	0.4782
C10	−205.4887	−0.7417	0.4596
X1	−0.2918	−0.0401	0.9681
X2	−0.0223	−0.1992	0.8424
X3	135.2704	0.7845	0.4341
X4	−67.0406	−2.9483	0.0038
X5	1.1806	7.3367	0.0000
X6	−3.1201	−3.3994	0.0009
X7	19.9725	0.2943	0.7690
X8	−49.1452	−1.0143	0.3123
X9	−4.6889	−0.8648	0.3887
X10	−15.9043	−1.1238	0.2632
X11	0.1448	0.0476	0.9621
X12	7.3982	1.3353	0.1841
X13	−0.5789	−2.2083	0.0289

Diagnostics
  Number of observations   155
  Standard Error   6.898
  R-squared   0.625
  $F(23, 132)$ 19.330
  autocorrelations order   2
  Autocorrelation of errors:
    One period   0.193
    Last period   0.037

CONCLUDING REMARKS

In this chapter we have presented a methodology to explore the relationship between expectations of parity changes and economic variables. This methodology accounts for the expectation of exchange rate changes within fluctuation bands, and therefore should in principle yield more precise estimates of expected parity changes.

Interest rate differentials are commonly used as a proxy for realignment expectations. As Svensson (1991) has pointed out, however, the

Table 8.4 Final regression results with regime dummies: expected one-month FFr/DM devaluation (March 1979–January 1992)

Variable	Coefficient	t-value	p-value
C1	368.5814	3.5424	0.0005
C2	370.0584	3.7313	0.0003
C3	369.2664	3.7354	0.0003
C4	377.8181	3.6990	0.0003
C5	376.2023	3.6429	0.0004
C6	374.1967	3.5823	0.0005
C7	370.5824	3.6129	0.0004
X1	−18.2409	−2.9416	0.0038
X2	−0.2471	−1.1117	0.2682
X3	−84.2307	−0.4062	0.6852
X4	46.1439	0.6252	0.5329
X5	0.9458	7.6955	0.0000
X6	−7.5872	−3.3990	0.0009
X7	267.8869	1.9424	0.0542
X8	26.3587	0.2533	0.8004
X9	−19.6365	−0.9974	0.3204
X10	−18.3181	−0.9569	0.3403
X11	−12.1930	−1.2015	0.2317
X12	14.5593	1.9234	0.0565
X13	−0.2006	−0.6343	0.5269

Diagnostics
  Number of observations 155
  Standard Error 15.711
  R-squared 0.563
  $F(20, 135)$ 9.436
  Durbin–Watson 2.344

flexibility of exchange rates within the target zones makes such a proxy imprecise. This is confirmed in our study with a more carefully constructed realignment expectation measurement. In addition, our estimated expectations reveal some facts about realignment expectations that are not apparent in the interest rate differential proxy, such as a less than dramatic reduction in expected devaluation as implied by interest rate convergence, and more precision in expected timing of realignment than implied by the interest rate differential and its term premium.

The most important finding is that expected parity changes vary over time, and appear to be significantly related to a number of variables. The variables that have consistently high explanatory power are the length of time since last realignment (measuring the reputation of the central bank) and the deviation of exchange rates from central parity. The results indicate that in general the absence of realignments improves the central bank's reputation. Such an effect is strong in the short and

Table 8.4a Final regression results with regime dummies: expected three-month FFr/DM devaluation (March 1979–January 1992)

Variable	Coefficient	t-value	p-value
C1	195.8427	4.0488	0.0001
C2	195.1067	4.2145	0.0000
C3	195.7883	4.2517	0.0000
C4	198.5340	4.2608	0.0000
C5	191.7341	4.3632	0.0000
C6	191.2826	4.1282	0.0001
C7	187.3248	4.1287	0.0001
X1	−9.2245	−3.0188	0.0030
X2	0.0093	0.1770	0.8598
X3	28.4486	0.3100	0.7570
X4	1.7272	0.0795	0.9367
X5	1.3195	11.4652	0.0000
X6	−1.7053	−1.6346	0.1045
X7	70.1270	1.6173	0.1081
X8	75.3372	1.8853	0.0615
X9	−15.9054	−2.2699	0.0248
X10	−14.6836	−1.6717	0.0969
X11	0.8762	0.3458	0.7300
X12	6.4625	3.0575	0.0027
X13	−0.2650	−1.1693	0.2443

Diagnostics
Number of observations 155
Standard Error 6.303
R-squared 0.642
$F(23, 135)$ 16.974
Number of autocorrelations 2
Autocorrelation of errors:
    One period 0.057
    Last period 0.003

medium run, but in the long run, the trend may be reversed. This is consistent with the 'honeymoon' hypothesis and the presence of a fixed cost of realignments. We have also found that a change in regime is detectable after the Basle-Nyborg agreements.

In order to evaluate the performance of adjustable parity systems like the EMS it is tempting to assess whether the expectations of parity changes which we estimate here appear, according to given criteria, to be rational. Some of our observations in the previous section were indeed motivated by that question. The two most important results of our regressions are the positive significance of the variable X5, representing the percentage deviation of the exchange rate from the centre of the band, and the large turnround of expected parity changes following realignments. The first finding is opposite to the naive

REALIGNMENT EXPECTATIONS

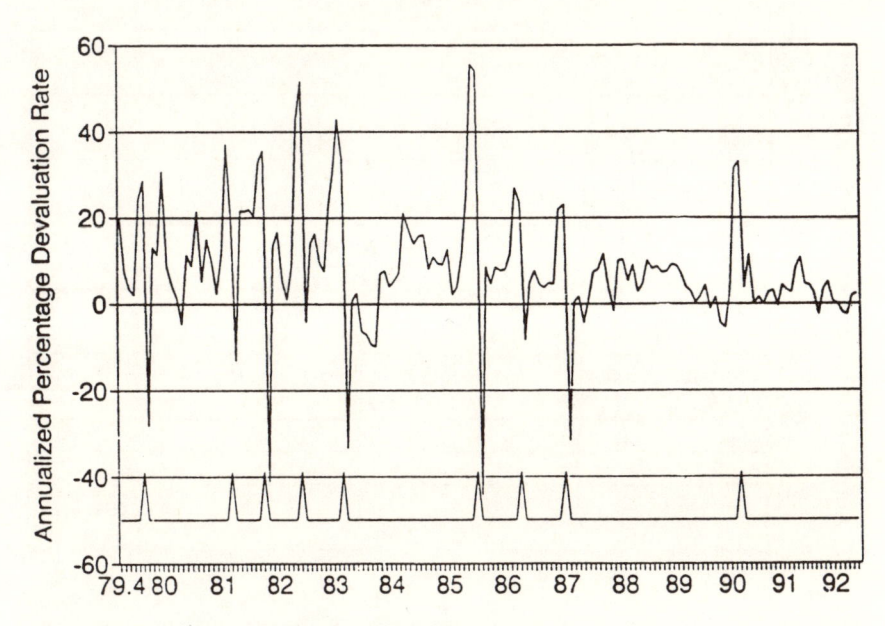

Figure 8.1 One-month expected devaluation, IL/DM

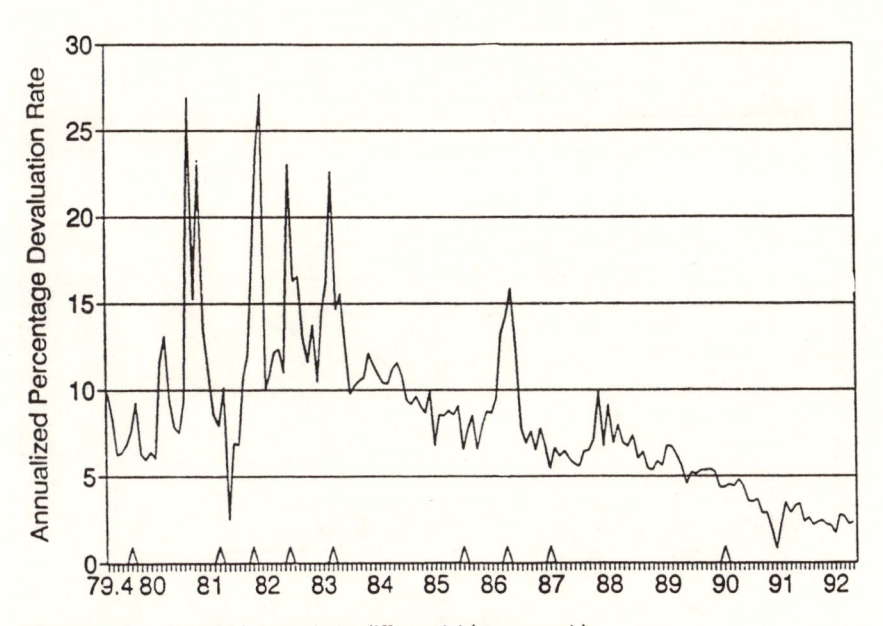

Figure 8.1a IL–DM interest rate differential (one-month)

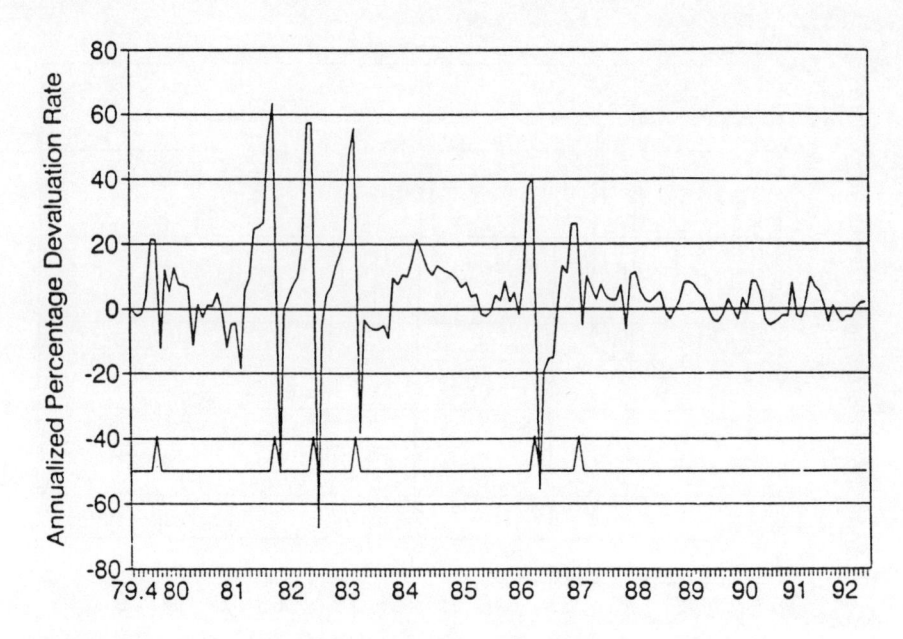

Figure 8.2 One-month expected devaluation, FFr/DM

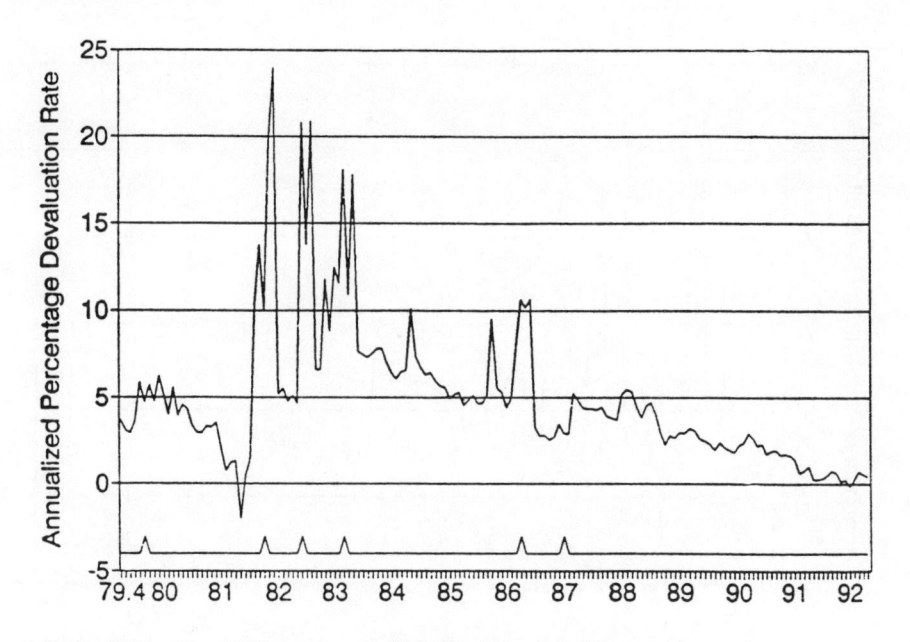

Figure 8.2a FFr−DM interest rate differential (one-month)

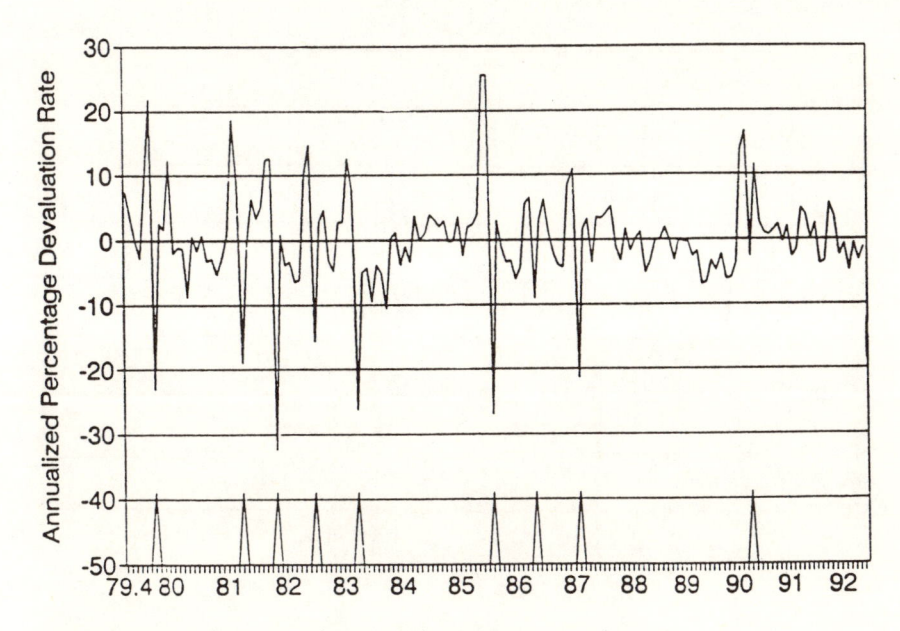

Figure 8.3 One-month vs three-month IL/DM term premium

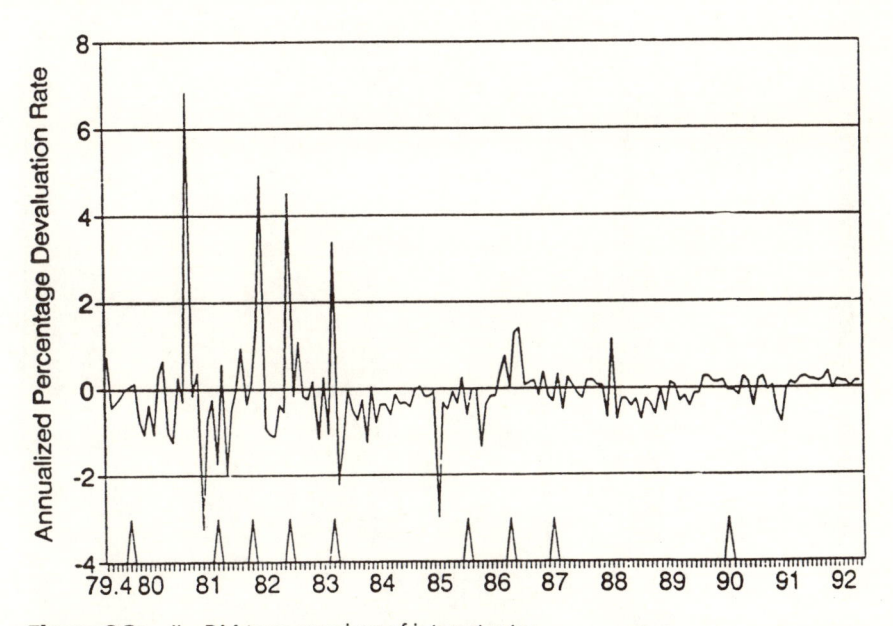

Figure 8.3a IL–DM term premium of interest rates

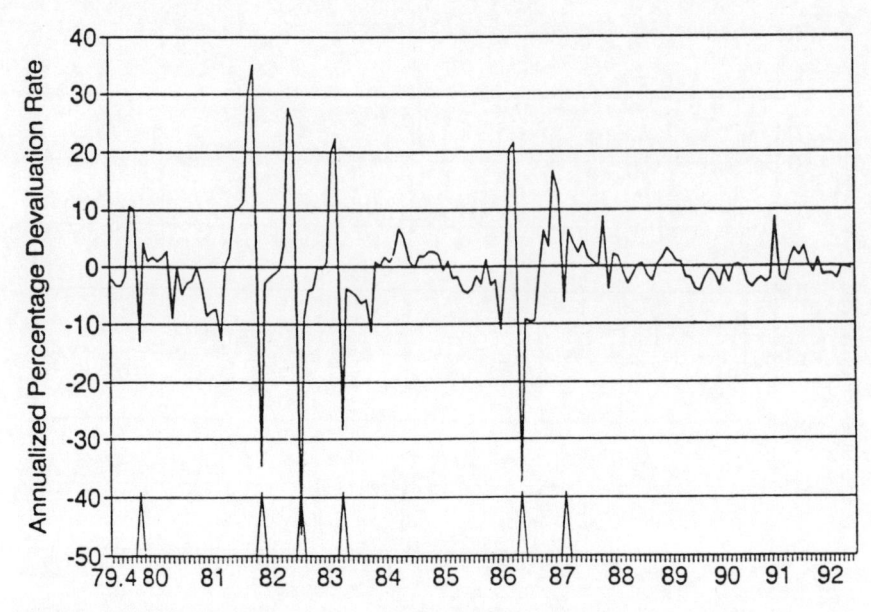

Figure 8.4 One-month vs three-month FFr/DM term premium

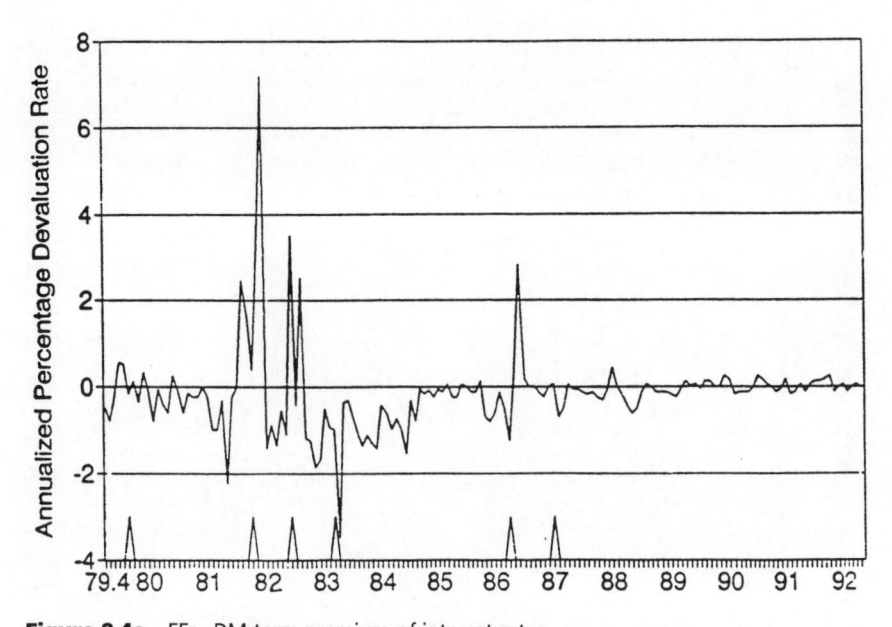

Figure 8.4a FFr−DM term premium of interest rates

Table 8.5 The 'honeymoon' effect: estimated coefficients $\hat{a}$ and $\hat{b}$ in the full projection equation with $X6 \equiv at^* + bt^{*2}$

Regression	a	b
One-month IL	−3.0357	0.0686
	(−3.8742)	(2.5591)
One-month FFr	−1.4222	0.0170
	(−3.4337)	(2.1384)
Three-month IL	−0.8002	0.0144
	(−2.5606)	(1.5264)
Three-month FFr	−0.2090	0.0035
	(−1.8091)	(1.3440)

Note: t-values in parentheses.

generalization of the 'stabilization effect' of the fluctuation band, a hallmark of recent target zone literature. Our evidence could be consistent with herd-like behaviour in the foreign exchange markets, which, however, is not necessarily inconsistent with rational expectations under imperfect information.

The second finding, that the estimates of expected parity changes after realignments are always negative – the DM is to be devalued relative to the lira and the franc – and large, together with the size and significance of the dummy variable representing the recent occurrence of a realignment in some cases, is difficult to interpret. There are two potential explanations for this puzzle. One is that market participants take larger-than-necessary short positions, and find the market is oversold after realignment. This could happen when speculators trying to bring down the parity overestimate the government's ability to defend the system.

An alternative explanation is that speculators abandon the market after having profited from the change in parity. This would be the case, for example, of fund managers who are given performance targets and do not have much of an incentive to active trading after those targets are met. As a result, information may not be efficiently used in the marketplace, with the resulting puzzling discrepancies between actual observations and predictions of models that assume rational expectations, such as ours. In general, the data at our disposal do not seem to provide evidence in support of the theory that adjustable parity systems are 'stable'. Indeed, two of the most significant empirical facts we have uncovered – discussed heretofore – are not inconsistent with the hypothesis that the fluctuation band generates insufficient stabilization on private realignment expectations, and that overspeculation or market inefficiency is present.

These suggestions, however, should not be taken as conclusive evidence in favour of market inefficiency. Such a test requires a structural model. While our evidence cannot be considered conclusive, it adds to other empirical regularities that characterize adjustable parity systems, the most prominent of which is perhaps the so-called 'capital-inflow problem' (see, for a discussion on the EMS, Giovannini, 1992). Our results, together with the empirical regularities studied in the literature on the capital-inflow problem, point to potential inherent instabilities of adjustable parity systems.

APPENDIX

This appendix contains an extension of the previous study. The extension covers a more recent sample period (up until August 1992, one month prior to Black Wednesday), and employs data from different sources and sometimes uses different definitions of variables. Such an extension is of interest for two reasons: first, it provides a check of robustness of the previous findings using a different sample; second, the more recent sample period may shed some light on information related to the onset of the September 1992 turmoil.

The results confirm the main conclusion of the previous study that the realignment expectation is related to the position of the exchange rate within the band and, to a far less extent, to macroeconomic fundamentals. The major difference is that the measure of gained credibility, 'time since last realignment', becomes insignificant. This is interesting because it may imply that credibility gained through refraining from realignment might have become less relevant in the later part of the EMS (before Black Wednesday), as realignments were virtually non-existent for much of that period.

The data used are downloaded from Datastream International's database. The definition of the log DM/$ exchange rate has been changed from the level to changes of the (log) exchange rate. The budget deficit variable is eliminated due to a data availability problem (it was not significant in the previous study anyway).

Detailed results are contained in the Tables 8A.1 and 8A.2. ($X5$ is defined in the same way as in the previous study, which is a measure of exchange rate position within the band, and the jump dummy is defined in the same way as $X11$.) As in the previous study, the most significant variable affecting realignment expectations is the exchange rate deviation from central parity. It is significant at the 5 per cent level for both currencies. Also as in the previous study, the regime dummies representing different central parity regimes are mostly significant. At the less stringent 10 per cent significance level, wage index and DM/$ exchange rate changes become relevant for the Italian lira, with the former playing a positive role on expectations (i.e. higher wage rate leads to higher expected devaluation), and the latter playing a negative

Table 8A.1 Regression result on one-month IL/DM expected devaluation (March 1979–August 1992)

Variable	Coefficient	Std Error	t-value	p-value
Regime 1	5573.3939	3226.3041	1.7275	0.0864
Regime 2	5486.9920	3202.6781	1.7133	0.0890
Regime 3	5554.6537	3171.4211	1.7515	0.0822
Regime 4	5528.3366	3182.3755	1.7372	0.0847
Regime 5	5572.9865	3170.3374	1.7579	0.0811
Regime 6	5589.0596	3160.7821	1.7683	0.0793
Regime 7	5522.2685	3143.2555	1.7569	0.0813
Regime 8	5545.5969	3130.4223	1.7715	0.0788
Regime 9	5486.3854	3135.1957	1.7499	0.0824
Regime 10	5402.4769	3109.8282	1.7372	0.0847
Reserve	−13.6325	36.3114	−0.3754	0.7079
Trade	−0.0027	0.0046	−0.5831	0.5608
Ind Prod	76.4447	222.0436	0.3443	0.7312
X5	0.2477	0.0497	4.9826	0.0000
TIME	−11.1295	13.7754	−0.8079	0.4206
CPI	−60.1843	664.9069	−0.0905	0.9280
Wage	989.9606	532.0787	1.8606	0.0650
Liquidity	0.4564	2.4244	0.1883	0.8510
Ch. DM/$	−282.1436	165.0311	−1.7096	0.0897
Jump dummy	0.0101	30.3328	0.0003	0.9997
Diagnostics				
Standard Error	68.141			
R-squared	0.258			
Restr R-squared	0.272			
$F(20, 132)$	2.469			
p-value	0.001			
Durbin–Watson	1.733			

role (a weakening of the DM relative to the dollar helps reduce lira realignment expectations). For the French franc, liquidity is significant at the 10 per cent level with a negative sign. The other macro variables remain insignificant.

To summarize, the extension of the earlier study to the more recent sample period further highlights the positive correlation between the exchange rate deviation from central parities and realignment expectations. Most macroeconomic variables remain statistically insignificant as in many studies. Refraining from realignment helped strengthen credibility in the earlier part of the EMS regime, but becomes irrelevant in the more recent sample, probably due to the virtual non-existence of realignment between late 1980s and the September turmoil in the EMS.

Table 8A.2 Regression result on one-month FFr/DM expected devaluation (March 1979–August 1992)

Variable	Coefficient	Std Error	t-value	p-value
Regime 1	−797.8893	5609.2684	−0.1422	0.8871
Regime 2	−171805.6345	76112.8009	−2.2573	0.0256
Regime 3	−167816.2258	75152.8685	−2.2330	0.0272
Regime 4	−173188.1746	78746.9664	−2.1993	0.0295
Regime 5	−187200.3418	84399.2306	−2.2180	0.0282
Regime 6	−182567.7014	87434.8777	−2.0880	0.0386
Regime 7	−191711.9635	90091.1724	−2.1280	0.0351
Regime 8	−199731.1924	91389.6847	−2.1855	0.0305
Reserve	−4499.9321	4607.1853	−0.9767	0.3304
Trade	−330.8366	225.7164	−1.4657	0.1450
Ind Prod	56581.2772	34270.4420	1.6510	0.1010
X5	0.1373	0.0590	2.3257	0.0215
TIME	2302.2738	4552.2777	0.5057	0.6138
CPI	−713.0030	1038.8478	−0.6863	0.4937
Wage	49684.8248	78732.7567	0.6311	0.5291
Liquidity	−96171.9034	53009.8028	−1.8142	0.0718
Ch. DM/$	156.5311	264.9690	0.5908	0.5557
Jump dummy	−12070.7084	17482.6726	−0.6904	0.4911

Diagnostics	
Standard Error	7612.569
R-squared	0.161
Restr R-squared	0.181
$F(18, 137)$	1.686
p-value	0.049
Durbin–Watson	2.008

DATA SOURCES

Exchange Rates: *Financial Times*. End of month observations.
Interest Rates: *Financial Times*. Eurodeposit rates. End of month observations.

$X1$:

- Germany: *Bundesbank external position. Monthly Report*, Table 12. Measured in millions of DM.
- France: *Banque de France Quarterly Bulletin*, Table 10, Counterparties de M3. Measures in billions of FFr.
- Italy: Banca d'Italia net external position, *Economic Bulletin*. Measured in Billions of IL.

Budget Surplus/Deficit:

- Italy: Treasury borrowing requirement. Bank of Italy.
- Germany: Federal finance on a cash basis. Data Resources, Inc.
- France: Public authority financial deficit (national accounts). *INSEE Comptes et Indicateurs Économiques.*

Trade Balances: OECD
Industrial Production: OECD. Index 1985 = 100.
Consumer Prices: OECD. Index 1985 = 100.
Wages:

- Italy: Contract wages. *International Financial Statistics.*
- Germany: Monthly wage and salary rate in the overall economy. Datastream International, Inc.
- France: Labour costs. *International Financial Statistics.*

X9:

- Germany and Italy: Liquidity of deposit banks, line 20, IFS.
- France: M1, IFS.

NOTES

1. Svensson (1991) develops an alternative measure of expected devaluation associated with realignment expectations: $\delta_t^j - E[(x_{t+j} - x_t) | \text{no realignment}]$. The key feature of this measure is that the second term is a *conditional* expectation, conditional on an information set that is generally smaller than the full set I_t, with the realignment events excluded from the latter. While desirable in the case of a few realignment observations, the conditional expectation of x cannot, in general, be correctly estimated from the data even with realignment observations excluded from the sample, since the possibility of a future realignment should be 'priced' by the market under rational expectations, and the sample x is conditional on both realignment and no-realignment possibilities.
2. We thank Charles Goodhart for suggesting this idea.
3. This is simply done by setting the derivatives of $at^* + bt^{*2}$ (with respect to t^*) to zero and solving for t^*.

REFERENCES

Barro, R.J. and Gordon, D.B. (1983), 'A positive theory of monetary policy in a natural rate model', *Journal of Political Economy*, 91, 589–610.

Bernanke, B. and Mishkin, F.S. (1992), 'Guideposts and signals in the conduct of monetary policy: lessons from six industrialized countries', manuscript, Columbia University.

Calvo, G. (1983), 'Trying to stabilize: some theoretical reflections based on the case of Argentina', in P. Aspe Armella, R. Dornbusch and M. Obstfeld (eds), *Financial Policies and the World Capital Market: The Problem of Latin American Countries*, Chicago, Chicago University Press, for NBER.

Chen, Z. and Giovannini, A. (1992a), 'The credibility of adjustable parities', mimeo, Columbia University, presented at the Ossola Memorial Conference, July.

Chen, Z. and Giovannini, A. (1992b), 'Estimating exchange rates under target zones', mimeo, Columbia University.

Collins, S. (1984), 'Exchange rate expectations and interest rate parity during credibility crisis: the French franc, March 1983', mimeo, Harvard University.

Collins, S. (1986), 'The expected timing of devaluation: a model of realignment of the European Monetary System', mimeo, Harvard University.

Diaz Alejandro, C.F. (1981), 'Southern cone stabilization plans', in W.R. Cline and S. Weintraub (eds), *Economic Stabilization in Developing Countries*, Washington, DC, Brookings Institution.

Dornbusch, R. (1982), 'Stabilization policies in developing countries: what have we learned?', *World Development* 10(9), 701–708.

Flood, R.P. and Garber, P. (1984), 'Collapsing exchange rate regimes: some linear examples', *Journal of International Economics*, 17, 1–13.

Flood, R.P. and Isard, P. (1990), 'Monetary policy strategies – a correction: reply to Lohmann', *International Monetary Fund Staff Papers* 37, 446–448.

Friedman, M. (1968), 'The role of monetary policy', *American Economic Review*, 58, 1–17.

Ghisellini, F. (1992), 'Credibility and hard currency options in the transition to economic and monetary union', mimeo, Ministero del Tesoro, Rome.

Giovannini, A. (1990), 'European monetary reform: progress and prospects', *Brookings Papers on Economic Activity*, 2, 217–292.

Giovannini, A. (1992), 'The capital inflow problem in the EMS', mimeo, Columbia University.

Lizondo, J.S. (1983), 'Foreign exchange futures prices under fixed exchange rates', *Journal of International Economics*, 14, 69–84.

Lohmann, S. (1990), 'Monetary policy strategies – a correction', *International Monetary Fund Staff Papers* 37 440–445.

Simons, H.C. (1936), 'Rules versus authorities in monetary policy', *Journal of Political Economy*, 44(1), 1–30.

Svensson, L.E.O. (1990), 'The foreign exchange risk premium in a target zone with devaluation risk', mimeo, IIES, Stockholm.

Svensson, L.E.O. (1991), 'Assessing target-zone credibility: mean reversion and devaluation expectations in the EMS', University of Stockholm, IIES seminar paper no. 493.

9

TOWARDS MONETARY UNION IN EUROPE – REFORMS OF THE EMS IN THE PERSPECTIVE OF MONETARY UNION*

Niels Thygesen

INTRODUCTION

Two major and interrelated upsets to the process towards monetary union occurred in the course of 1992/93: (1) several countries experienced far greater difficulties than anticipated by governments in getting the Maastricht Treaty ratified; and (2) a major crisis in the European currency markets in September 1992, followed by recurrent periods of turbulence, made the European Monetary System (EMS), viewed as the essential stepping stone to monetary union which the EMS was seen to shadow increasingly closely, look very vulnerable – indeed, as potentially incapable of surviving. Two currencies left the system and no fewer than four realignments took place in less than five months. Both of these events – popular disaffection with the objective of monetary union and a single currency and a breakdown of cooperation

* This chapter reviews a number of options to reform the EMS in the light of the currency turmoil if 1992/93. While greater flexibility – wide fluctuation margins and frequent small realignments – may now seem attractive to some countries, notably the United Kingdom, steps in this direction are likely to lead to increased instability and divergence while postponing for a long time advances towards monetary union. If anything, the fluctuation margins and the Basle-Nyborg agreement of 1987 providing mechanisms for the short-term defence of exchange rates need to be tightened up. The chapter also discusses the scope for strengthening monetary coordination in the European Monetary Institute which started on 1 January 1994, respecting the principle that monetary sovereignty should remain ultimately in national hands until the start of full monetary union and the setting-up of the European Central Bank.

between national monetary authorities – have raised serious doubts about the feasibility of the timetable for moving towards full monetary union foreseen in the Treaty signed in Maastricht in February 1992 (henceforth 'Maastricht'). The purpose of the present chapter is to discuss whether the approach to monetary union remains viable and, if so, how monetary unification could be resumed, possibly with a revised timetable.

Only two member states out of the 12 had ratified Maastricht within the timeframe foreseen of end-1992. Denmark voted 'no' by a small margin on 2 June 1992, but this result was reversed in a second referendum on 18 May 1993 after the Edinburgh European Council had granted Denmark significant exemptions in four important areas; one of them was to allow Denmark immediately to exercise its option, granted in a special Protocol in Maastricht, not to join the third stage of Economic and Monetary Union. The United Kingdom, which had already obtained this particular exemption in Maastricht along with a freer status in relation to some of the provisions applying in the second stage, is currently (June 1993) far advanced towards ratification. Although ratification has been challenged in the Constitutional Court of the Federal Republic of Germany and may be challenged in UK and Danish courts it now seems a safe assumption that Maastricht will be ratified by all 12 in the course of 1993. This implies that the new provisions of Maastricht can enter into force before the date of 1 January 1994 when some of them may prove essential to the resumption of monetary unification. The alternative scenario in which the new provisions remain unusable after 1 January 1994 will not be discussed further here.

The following sections are organized as follows: The next section looks at a number of specific reforms of the EMS, keeping in mind the differentiated requirements and starting points of the member states (and of the prospective new entrants in the EC). The third section attempts an overall evaluation of the scope for reforms; it explores, in particular, the limits of the so-called indivisibility doctrine, according to which national monetary sovereignty can only be effectively shared in the final stage of monetary union, since this doctrine poses the main challenge for the European Monetary Institute (EMI), the precursor of the European System of Central Banks, in convincing financial markets that the transitional arrangements are robust and deserve credibility. The final section offers some tentative conclusions.

PATHS OF REFORM IN EUROPEAN MONETARY UNIFICATION

Having watched the main elements which brought forward the 1992/93 crisis in European monetary arrangements it is tempting to ask – encouraged by the analysis of many North American observers: why not revert to *individual floating* for a period to accommodate the real or perceived differences in the environment for monetary policy within the EC? Martin Feldstein (1992) advocated this option forcefully in words that may now be close to the official UK position:

Even defenders of monetary union recognize that the loss of flexible nominal exchange rates makes it more difficult for countries to respond to shocks to demand that create local unemployment. A single European currency precludes adjusting national monetary policy and interest rates to offset shocks to demand that are greater locally than in the EC as a whole.

Feldstein does allow for the high probability that the option of flexible exchange rates will not appeal to several smaller countries in the EC which have come to appreciate the advantages of a very tight exchange rate link to the DM and do not think that they could produce policies of their own which are on average superior to what they could achieve by abandoning German leadership. The prescription for floating would only apply to the major EC countries, including the largest of them, Germany.

The reason why this option is regarded as undesirable by EC policy makers outside the United Kingdom is not just that it would for a long time close the road to monetary union. More importantly, it would also deny the reasons why the EMS was formed in 1978 and the lessons from its gradualist experience which have built up over nearly 15 years.

The Rome Treaty stated (Article 103) that economic policies and hence, *par excellence*, the exchange rates of member states was a matter of common concern. This principle, retained in the same article in Maastricht would in any case put severe constraints on the extent to which a member state would be allowed to rely on movements in its exchange rate to accommodate differences in performance and/or policy preferences. This principle in the Treaty was violated in the early years of the post-Bretton Woods period (1972–1978) and the response in 1978 was the start of the EMS, designed to constrain movements in the strong as well as in the weak currencies in the face of fundamentally similar shocks to all the European economies, e.g. US policy shocks or changes in the price of imported energy. The Germans were primarily concerned about the prospect of a weak US dollar trend triggering an unwarranted strong appreciation of the DM against all important EC trading partners – a concern not far from those of the 1990s. Other EMS participants feared the implications of the mirror image of this scenario: excessive devaluation of their weaker currencies and consequently additional inflation. The EMS was set up to contain the potential for additional divergence between the performance of the European economies which intra-EC exchange rate changes had revealed in the 1970s.

In short, the emerging view was that unless exchange-rate stabilization was made an explicit objective of policy, currency instability would persist. Even firm and apparently parallel monetary policies in two countries could not be relied upon to be enough to achieve an indirect objective of a stable exchange rate between their currencies, as demonstrated by the adoption in the mid-1970s by nearly all the main industrial countries of a strategy of designing policy consistently in terms of broadly similar monetary aggregates. Exchange rates were never less stable than in the early years thereafter.

There is no inclination in the main EC countries to relearn this early post-Bretton Woods experience. Admittedly, with the low inflation now prevailing in the EC, and a stronger commitment to maintain it more permanently, the risk of a repeat of the currency instability of the 1970s may look remote. Nevertheless, the events of 1992/93 have shown that such a repeat can not be excluded. Once formal policy commitments weaken and national elections are approaching with the prospects of significant policy shifts in the modified environment, the exchange rate can move far in a short time.

Currency fluctuations of the size experienced in some years in the 1970s and in 1992/93 would be seen, and rightly in my view, by Europe's business community, trade unionists and policy makers as highly undesirable and as incompatible with the realization of a well-functioning internal market in goods and services. The benefits of a single currency which had begun to be regarded as marginal towards the end of the long period of a stable EMS because the standard of comparison was so close to monetary union suddenly loom much larger.[1] With renewed instability all transaction and information costs related to exchange-rate changes rise towards earlier observed levels. At the same time, transition to a floating rate environment could not provide national governments with an additional policy instrument. Dissolving the EMS would remove an apparent constraint, but at the cost of introducing additional uncertainty in the ability to forecast the effects of other policy instruments, notably fiscal policy. One advantage of a monetary union and an EMS that has come to foreshadow it closely is that the effects of changes in budgetary policy became more predictable than in looser exchange-rate regimes.

Whatever the validity of the general arguments against a significant reversal to floating, the fact that two important currencies are currently floating and at least one of them – sterling – is unlikely to return soon to the system, implies that the proposal of Feldstein and others to allow floating as a temporary solution while targeting monetary policy to domestic objectives, is being adopted by some – voluntarily or by the force of circumstances. The question then becomes whether individual floating of one major currency could still be viewed with equanimity by the others or whether changes in the value of that currency should be constrained by a more formal monitoring procedure than simply building on the revised Article 103 and its multilateral surveillance provisions. This is where the idea of examining the suitability of the target zone proposal as a regime intermediate between a continuing EMS and individual floating comes into its own.

The target zone proposal was advanced in its most elaborate form in Williamson (1985) and subsequently expanded in Miller and Williamson (1987) into a more comprehensive scheme for international policy coordination by bringing in rules for fiscal policy as well as exchange- and interest-rate policy. The basic idea, however, goes back at least another decade,[2] and it is interesting to reflect that it was used as a framework for discussing how the then joint float management (the 'Snake') between five EC currencies could be extended to comprise all or most of the EC's then nine currencies. The analysis and the reasons why the target zone idea was not put into practice appear just as relevant in 1993 as 17 years earlier.

Then finance minister of the Netherlands, Wim Duisenberg – currently chairman of the Committee of EC Central Bank Governors – submitted a letter to his colleagues in July 1976. This was shortly after massive depreciations of the lira and sterling which had greatly weakened the competitive position of participants in the Snake (and a few months after the exit of the French franc from the Snake). Duisenberg complained about the absence of an effective EC framework for cooperation on exchange-rate issues. More specifically, he proposed a mutual surveillance procedure inspired by the IMF guidelines for floating centred on a set of mutually agreed target zones for the three main floating currencies (lira, sterling, French franc) and – presumably – for the Snake as a whole. The target zones would be defined in effective exchange rate terms; they would imply no positive obligation for a country to keep its exchange rate within the zone through interventions or domestic policy measures ('soft buffers'), only a presumption that no steps would be taken to push the rate away from the target zone. The latter would from time to time be reviewed and central rates realigned. Exit from the zone would trigger discussions of closer policy coordination.

This subtle but minimalist plan never materialized, though it may have inspired some of the ideas that went into the EMS one or two years later.[3] It failed for several reasons: it was considered too vague by those policy makers who were getting ready for the more ambitious EMS, and too open-ended by the Germans who feared they might be drawn into large interventions in support of currencies that had not themselves accepted real obligations. Finally, idealists objected on the grounds that the target zone proposal would create additional asymmetries and consolidate a two-speed monetary Europe.

The similarities with the current debate on reforming or reviving the EMS are indeed striking. Informed public opinion in the United Kingdom now appears to think the system should be made more flexible, possibly by extending more freedom to participants in realigning and in waiving their obligations than was available even in the early and most 'permissive' EMS period (1979–1983). In this spirit, *The Economist* recently (8 May 1993) proposed 're-entry' of sterling along lines similar to those of the Duisenberg plan.

If the United Kingdom were to seek to attach sterling to other European currencies in such a way – no doubt updating the proposal by presenting it in terms of sterling's exchange rate vis-à-vis the DM or the Ecu rather than the effective rate and by focusing more on wide fluctuation margins than on the other two dimensions of flexibility: frequent central rate changes and only negative obligations to support the zone – could other EC member states have an interest in accepting it? The balance of the arguments suggest not, while raising doubts as to whether the United Kingdom could even serve its own interests by 'participating' on these terms.

The core of the matter is that the target zone proposal in one of its more flexible variants appears in today's perspective as no more than a framework for monitoring a deviant currency and preparing its entry. This type of framework will be used anyway when the time comes to consider on what terms re-entry for the lira and sterling could take place. The competent EC bodies will need to examine at that point whether market exchange-rates for currencies which floated from September 1992 could be maintained within the EMS at the level established in the market. This judgement would focus on the competitiveness of their economies, i.e. on whether they have been improved sufficiently since 1992. There is no need to revise the operation of the system itself, only its rules of entry.

The point may be seen by some as almost purely semantic. But it is not. If the United Kingdom wishes to give the impression that it is again 'participating' in European monetary integration, a form of words could no doubt be found. The danger lies in the precedent such a position would set to other potential entrants and in the general impression it would create that the whole process of European monetary integration had drifted into such an agnostic and confused stage that even proposals which were rejected 17 years ago at the nadir of the European disintegration of the 1970s as being too vague could be entertained. The difference between on the one hand a group of countries that tries with some joint determination to peg their currencies as a strategic element in maintaining low inflation and on the other hand a potential participant in the club wishing to adjust its exchange rate regularly to avoid disequilibria more continuously is basic and can not readily be accommodated within the same system, as has been recognized recently by Williamson (1993) who distinguishes sharply between these two views of the exchange rate. One emphasizes its role as a nominal anchor in an anti-inflationary strategy; from time to time that may produce misalignments. The other stresses the need to prevent disequilibria from arising in exchange markets and hence foresees regular small realignments.

There remains one residual appeal of the target zone approach even to those who prefer to use their exchange rate as a firm nominal anchor: the approach could still put constraints on the behaviour of outsiders and hence be less destabilizing also to the cohesion of the first group clustering around a common nominal anchor. The major question for this group is whether a target zone arrangement for sterling could in practice provide better protection against further large currency movements and, particularly, additional competitive advantages for the UK economy, than simple individual floating for sterling. This must be unlikely, if the target zone is wide and flexible and if departures from it cannot be subjected to sanctions by the countries that have joined the first group. If so, the disadvantages of appearing to provide a general alternative to their approach to monetary union will be decisive in determining their attitude to the far-reaching flexibility sought by the United Kingdom.

Another question is whether it would serve UK interests in any meaningful economic sense, if sterling were to be accepted within a softer arrangement than has existed in any past incarnation of the EMS. Credibility effects, allowing lower long-term UK interest rates than if sterling were to float individually, would be unlikely, as the markets would perceive that the trend inflation rate had not been affected in any appreciable way relative to what the UK could achieve anyway by its own efforts. It would be more than difficult to envisage that the UK authorities could expect intervention support, if the target zone were to be wide and subject to regular revision; such support could, of course, not even be imagined, if the zone was only to be defended by negative obligations not to take steps that would push sterling away from the zone. And if there were to be positive obligations to defend the zone, the UK authorities would have to expect to provide the defence by unilateral interest rate hikes, though the latter could presumably be much more modest than was required in the (wide) EMS band of September 1992. If the hypothesis advanced in the previous section, viz. that the depreciation of sterling has overcorrected any previous misalignment, is correct, any subsequent appreciation of sterling may be easier to handle under individual floating than in a modified target zone system.

In short, the United Kingdom would appear to have no well-defined economic gains in prospect from obtaining a target zone arrangement with the EMS countries. There might be political gains. 'Rejoining' on a new basis could be presented to domestic opinion as a pragmatic reintroduction of an exchange-rate objective to reinforce domestic objectives of low inflation and as a partial victory over a European system which had become overly rigid and too intolerant of a country wanting to pursue a monetary policy better attuned to domestic conditions than a replica of policies in other EC countries. But there should, in case other EC countries accept the implications of this argument, be expression of firm determination that what is being put in place is a specific and temporary arrangement for the United Kingdom rather than a general reform of the EMS, converting it to more flexibility.

Having argued that neither individual floating nor target zone arrangements for those currencies that may request them would be desirable paths of EMS reforms it must be asked whether there exist reforms which appear at the same time economically desirable and politically feasible. This will be discussed in the following under three headings: (1) the width of fluctuation margins, (2) an updating of the defensive mechanisms of the Basle-Nyborg agreement, and (3) the role of realignments.

Margins of fluctuation

In May 1993 the EC currencies fall into three distinct categories: seven currencies [4] observe the normal margins of 2.25 per cent (and have done so continuously since the start of the EMS in 1979), two (escudo, peseta) observe margins of 6 per cent (used also by Italy 1979–1989), while three are individually floating. It is hard to conceive that a common prescription could be made for these diverse groups; in any case the theoretical arguments for choosing the width of the margins and the accumulated evidence of the EMS experience both warrant more careful examination.

Historically the width of the normal margins dates back to the European response to the widening of margins against the US dollar from ±1 to ±2.25 per cent which was introduced by the Smithsonian Agreement of December 1971. Since that step implied that the exchange rate between two EC currencies could change by as much as 9 per cent if they were to switch position between the ceiling and the floor of their respective margins against the US dollar – a degree of variability which was considered excessive in 1972 – the participants in the Snake chose to put each other's currencies on a par with the dollar in terms of predictability. This simple and logical response has now survived the floating of the dollar in 1973, the transition to the EMS in 1978/79, the subsequent tightening of that arrangement in the course of the 1980s, the liberalization of capital movements, and the formulation of a Treaty in 1991 setting out a blueprint for the transition to full monetary union in which the margin would by definition be reduced to zero. Given the increasingly arbitrary character of the margins, this attachment to a figure chosen more than 20 years ago is surprising.

The Delors Report on EMU (para. 57) did propose that the standard margins be narrowed to, say, ±1 per cent at the beginning of Stage II. This proposal was supported by the European Parliament and in various reports by private groups, though without any particular analytical underpinnings. The idea of narrowing margins as a general prescription never won wide favour among officials. When the Danish government proposed early in the 1991 Intergovernmental Conference on EMU that margins be narrowed for all participants to ±1.5 per cent from the start of Stage II, no other government supported the idea. EMS participants appear to have preferred on the one hand to accept wider margins as a transitional arrangement available on demand and on the other hand to retain the option to move unilaterally to narrower margins when individual circumstances permitted, as the Benelux countries have done de facto in recent years.

If one examines the target zone literature where the choice of margins is at times explicitly discussed a trade-off emerges between the removal of part of the residual autonomy available to a participant in the EMS contemplating a narrowing, and the benefits in terms of improved credibility of the central rates as the monetary authorities signal their decision by words or actions to move to narrower margins. While agreeing on the objective – to manage their currency with as little tension as possible at short-term interest rates a minimum distance above (and ideally just below) comparable German rates – countries observing the normal margins appeared for a while to interpret this trade-off in different ways. The Benelux currencies were managed – for some time in the late 1980s for the Netherlands, since the spring of 1990 for Belgium – within unilaterally narrowed margins against the DM. They were rewarded with near-complete convergence of their short-term rates with German ones in 1991/92 and most recently by a fall to levels slightly below them. France and Denmark by contrast wanted to retain the freedom of action of the normal margins. As long as there is (nearly) full confidence in the markets that the central rate will continue to be observed and that present margins will be defended, a strategy of retaining the normal margins while using short-term interest rates to keep the DM exchange-rate as close to the floor as possible should, in principle, enable short-term interest rates to move around a lower average level than the 'Benelux strategy' can deliver; the currency at the floor will be expected to revert towards the central rate hence allowing for an appreciation discount to be incorporated into the yield on short-term assets denominated in the currency. The size of the discount should rise with the width of the margins – provided the credibility of the central rate is unrelated to the width of the margins and to the position of the currency inside them.

These are, however, strong assumptions. France tested the limits of policy autonomy inside the normal margins in late 1991, well before the currency turmoil of 1992, and succeeded temporarily in keeping the French short-term rate below the German level. But France lost more than FFr50bn through interventions in support of the franc over the October 1991–January 1992 period; apparently the French policy was seen as unduly aggressive by market participants since it created fears that a devaluation might be in preparation. Once such fears arise the 'honeymoon effect' identified by Krugman within a credible target zone disappears and interest-rate differentials have to widen in favour of the weak currency. France decided the outflows were enough and raised short-term rates relative to Germany by around 50 basis points in early 1992; until the political uncertainties about ratification of Maastricht set in with the first Danish 'no' and the announcement of the French referendum in early June the French franc was maintained near the centre of the band. There is little doubt, judging from both actions and policy statements at the time, that France was attracted by the idea of shifting to a Benelux strategy of narrower margins. The currency turmoil since June 1992 has so far made the adoption of such a shift unfeasible, but it remains on the agenda.

Denmark and Ireland have shown a more permanent readiness to make full use of the margins than has France; they could hardly be tempted to opt for a unilateral narrowing of margins. Following the end-January devaluation of the punt, the Irish currency moved to the top of the margins; relatively high interest rates were maintained in order to facilitate the reflow of capital. With the uncertainty surrounding the exchange-rate policy of major non-ERM trading partners of both Denmark and Ireland (Sweden and the United Kingdom), these two EMS participants seem unlikely to narrow margins voluntarily. For Denmark there is an additional complication, viz. that Denmark has announced an opt-out from the third stage of EMU, so that steps aimed in that direction have little domestic appeal despite the Danish economy's relatively strong performance with respect to the Maastricht convergence criteria.

A tentative conclusion is accordingly that only France is likely to join the Benelux countries in maintaining (announced or unannounced) narrow margins vis-à-vis the DM. A scenario in which the normal margins of ±2.25 per cent remain the norm is therefore probable.

Indeed, the language of the official reports suggests that more flexibility, including wider margins, rather than less, may be in store. The official reports advocate a continuation of the practice in the EMS since the start of leaving the decisions regarding fluctuation bands to the national authorities; though the governors' report adds that 'experience with operating the EMS has shown that the width of the fluctuation band must be regarded as a matter of common concern', and that decisions 'should be preceded by close consultation taking due account of the same factors as those considered when the sustainability of the parity grid is examined' (Section IV,1). Remarkably, the text makes no reference to the provisions of Article 109j(1) according to which a currency must have observed the normal fluctuation margins for at least two years without devaluing in order to qualify for the final stage of monetary union. It is possible, of course, that the official committees thought that no member state needed to be reminded of this point, but the omission is still an indication of the extent to which the officials are currently trying to separate reforms in the EMS from the progress towards monetary unification which they were supposed to facilitate.

Whether countries should be given the choice of wider than normal margins must depend on the experience with such margins and their expected contribution to sustaining the system in the future rather than on tradition and established rights. The wide margins were initially offered to Italy in 1978 with the following provision (Annex to the conclusions of the Presidency of the European Council of 6 and 7 July 1978 in Bremen):

In terms of exchange-rate management the EMS will be at least as strict as the 'snake'. In the initial stages of its operation and for a limited period of time member countries not currently participating in the snake may opt for somewhat wider margins around central rates.

Italy chose this option because its inflation rate in 1978 was still well into double figures and some 7–8 per cent above that of Germany. Though the lira probably started life in the EMS from a comfortable position of some undervaluation after the massive depreciation of the

1970s, it was in retrospect a prudent strategy on the part of both Italian and other EC authorities to grant the temporary exemption of the wide band which could – and did – prevent Italy from having to realign more frequently than other participants. It also protected the lira against the need to face discontinuities in market exchange-rates at the time of realignments; the latter were never, in the nine cases of devaluations vis-à-vis the DM, so large as to prevent the new fluctuation margins from containing the previous market rate.

It may well be asked whether the 11 years from the start of the EMS to January 1990 when Italy narrowed the margins to the normal level was not an unduly long transition period. The initial turbulent phase of the first four years in the EMS when no inflation convergence got underway, the relatively slow subsequent convergence and the fact that Italy gave priority to removing controls on capital flows over the narrowing of margins help to explain why the process took long.

Spain joined the EMS in June 1989, also with a wide band. The country had only become a member of the EC in 1986, leading to very rapid integration of goods and services markets. Massive capital inflows had been observed and the peseta appreciated nominally; real appreciation was much stronger, since inflation was still running at a rate about 4 percentage points above Germany's, while the current account showed a large deficit. It was understandable that there was some uncertainty as to whether the exchange rate was in equilibrium. In any case, with inflation clearly above the EMS average, high interest rates were required. The peseta was near the top of the wide band for most of the more than three years after entry, but abnormal rates did not explode the system since they were in part offset by the expectation that the peseta would revert towards the centre of the margins. Somewhat similar comments apply to Portugal; the authorities had stabilized the escudo for about a year and a half before they took it into the EMS in April 1992, while also asking for a wide band. The latter no doubt helped the Iberian currencies in reconciling the need for – by EC standards – very high interest rates and the desire for a stable exchange rate with the main trading partners.

The United Kingdom authorities took sterling into the EMS in October 1990 also opting for the wide band (which had been refused in 1978). It saw itself in a situation similar to that of Spain, excess inflation being the most obvious source of policy divergence with the narrow margins group. But, as recession proved to be deeper and more protracted than expected, inflation was temporarily reduced to a rate well below the German one and the UK economy came to look more like some Continental economies, such as France and Denmark, with a need to keep interest rates as low as technically possible for domestic reasons. Efforts in this direction, political pressures for additional monetary ease and a marginally higher sensitivity to the decline in the US dollar than that observed for other EMS currencies drove sterling to the bottom of the wide band in the summer of 1992, which could not in these circumstances provide much of a buffer. Sterling was divergent from

August and higher interest rates were not considered a viable option. Having borrowed heavily in international markets to bolster resources for intervention the UK authorities gave up their defence of the currency and embarked on an aggressive lowering of short-term interest rates causing a fall in sterling of around 20 per cent relative to its EMS central rate.

The common element in the experience of the Iberian currencies and of sterling with the wide band is that, although the extra flexibility provided some additional monetary autonomy while the currencies were strong, it did not protect them in any significant sense in the currency crisis of 1992. On the contrary, the fact that these currencies had so far to fall and did move rapidly towards the floor of the band may have accentuated speculative pressures against them, because markets interpreted these moves as a signal of a possible devaluation. Obviously this issue is one that requires careful study of the comparative efficiency of interventions in the wide and in the narrow band, but the burden of proof would appear to be on those who believe that the wide band was helpful.

Even if this turns out not to be the case, a preliminary examination of the data suggests a wide band might still be regarded as useful in more normal times than during the exceptional economic and political turbulence of 1992. One should not expect to continue to fight yesterday's battles.

The present exchange-rate constellation should prove easier to defend than the one prevailing in the summer of 1992 because the earlier weak currencies have overadjusted and are now more likely to move up rather than down while the present weakness of the DM is now widely perceived by market participants. The currencies presently in the wide band or the two potential entrants, lira and sterling, which might want to ask for it, could be more in need of the upward flexibility provided by the wide band than of the buffer provided by an exceptional scope for weakening.

If such a scenario is realistic it would, however, be preferable that the required flexibility be used while the presently floating currencies are still outside the system. That would cause less tension with (and among) the currencies which have remained in the EMS and avoid undue pressure on the new entrants to reduce interest rates faster than their domestic situation warrants to observe their renewed exchange-rate commitments.

A desirable scenario would seem to be one in which the lira and sterling had shown stability in the markets for some time, possibly around somewhat higher levels than today, before entering straight into the normal margins. As regards Spain and Portugal discussions could begin in late 1993 as to a narrowing of their margins; at that time the results of the Spanish elections should have been fully digested by the financial markets. Again this recommendation hinges on the belief that the present exchange-rates in the two Iberian countries do not reflect any lack of competitiveness, rather the opposite. The markets are more likely to be impressed that the period of devaluations has come to an end if the two countries were to abandon their margins than if they stay with them. Such a change would also show that the two countries should be considered serious candidates for monetary union later in the 1990s, as is their – not unrealistic – wish. In short, in the course of 1994 the wide margins could be eliminated for those that presently use them, Italy would have come back also with the normal margins which the United Kingdom – for whom maintaining candidacy for monetary union currently holds no attraction – would still have a floating exchange-rate.

There is, incidentally, nothing in the situations or the preferences of the four EFTA-countries which are currently negotiating for membership in the EC to suggest that they would require or welcome having the option of entering the EMS with a wide band. Austria has pegged tightly to the DM for more than a decade, while the three Nordic countries all chose a narrow band when they announced their unilateral peg to the Ecu in 1990/91. All four have stated explicitly that they have accepted the provisions of Maastricht which apply to EMU and to the transition towards it.

Updating the Basle-Nyborg agreement

This agreement, negotiated in 1987 as a response to the speculative attacks preceding the realignment of January that year, made explicit an emerging consensus among central bankers. The EMS was to be defended, in a world of increasing capital mobility, by a mixture of three types of mechanisms: first, currencies should be allowed to move inside the margins in response to market pressures; second, interventions could be used to stem undesirably strong fluctuations – for that purpose the use of the Very Short Term Financing Facility was made more easily accessible to debtors; and third, if pressures persisted, short-term interest rate differentials should move to abate the tensions. If that still did not work, a realignment might have to be resorted to. The latter point is still not explicitly mentioned in the official text,[5] which is in itself significant. At the time the governors were anxious to be seen to regard realignment as a last resort only to be used in exceptional circumstances, since many of them regarded the January 1987 realignment as basically superfluous. Several governors expressed the view that, if a realignment did become inevitable, it should be sufficiently small to permit continuity of market exchange-rates, implying that realignments should at a maximum be twice the width of the margins, or 4.5 per cent, assuming that the weak currency would go to the top of the new margins. Avoiding jumps in market exchange rates around realignments was seen as strategically important in deterring future speculative attacks, since no immediate gains would then be made by speculators.

For a long time the provisions of Basle-Nyborg worked very well. The provisions were put to the test in early November 1987 in an almost textbook fashion, particularly since short-term interest rates were moved in opposite directions by Germany and France which effectively checked speculation. The agreement also survived well the complete removal of capital controls in eight EC countries by 1988/90, the accommodation of two important new currencies and the narrowing of the band for the lira in January 1990. In retrospect, it is amazing and encouraging that a simple rulebook could suffice for five years. A careful historical analysis of how several periods of moderate tension were handled would be instructive, also as an antidote to the gloom surrounding the recent performance of the EMS.

However, in the September 1992 crisis the agreement did become inoperative. Movements inside the margins did not provide an initial protective buffer, but appeared to trigger further large flows as exchange rates moved rapidly towards intervention limits. Interventions became very large and had to carry the main burden for longer than could be sustained, prompting the Bundesbank to invoke its initial understanding with the German government that even the presumed mandatory interventions could be suspended, as happened for the operations in support of the lira. Most would say that the main departure from the spirit of Basle-Nyborg was the failure to use the final short-term defence by moving short-term rates in a decisive fashion. But this could hardly have been done without prior institutional changes in the United Kingdom and Italy to protect the domestic financial markets better against the spillover effects of very high money market interest rates targeted at speculators. Finally, when realignments came, they were not exactly small, they were improvised rather than negotiated, and two countries felt compelled to leave the system altogether.

The breakdown in the regular official machinery was also evident in the absence of any formal meeting by the EC Monetary Committee or the Ecofin Council prior to the Italian devaluation in September and the very casual approach to the subsequent three realignments in November (peseta, escudo), January (punt) and May (peseta, escudo). This violated an earlier tradition in the EMS back in the early 1980s when realignments were equally large. They were then typically accompanied by domestic measures to underpin the shift in resources in the devaluing countries, the most notable examples being those of France in 1983 and Belgium in 1982. It is when a government is negotiating to obtain a devaluation, typically trying to achieve a maximum figure, that it is most sensitive to peer pressure in the Ecofin Council. It becomes much less sensitive when the currency has been devalued or has given up its commitments altogether. The EC countries are now faced with the task of trying to influence ex post the domestic adjustment that should have been decided at the time of the realignment. In the specific environment of 1992 that would have implied peer pressure on Italy and the United Kingdom to accelerate budgetary consolidation in the light of the substantial devaluations they were obtaining. A major boost to competitiveness enables a country to contemplate faster budgetary retrenchment. Symmetrically, countries that have not devalued should be prepared to accept more of a cyclical weakening of their budgets than they would otherwise have done. Neither the sequence of events in the currency markets nor the convergence requirements of Maastricht have been conducive to this kind of constructive dialogue.

Although both the rules and the spirit of Basle-Nyborg were shown to be inoperative, the recent official reports are not necessarily wrong in presenting the view that the system remains basically sound and that most of what needs to be done in the future could be achieved if the rules are adhered to. Outside turbulent periods that is still likely to be fully adequate. But a capacity to handle turbulence as well is essential to the survival of a system. What reforms could be envisaged to make the EMS more robust?

There are two types of mistakes an exchange-rate system must attempt to avoid. The first is to defend rates that are perceived by markets to be misaligned. The second is to give in to speculative pressures when rates are in good correspondence with fundamentals. In an earlier incarnation the EMS handled the former challenge quite well by regular realignments while the second pitfall hardly materialized. With Basle-Nyborg emphasis shifted to avoiding the second challenge while the first faded into the background for a time owing to better convergence. It reasserted itself in 1992. With the massive realignments that have taken place there could be an extended period of grace, as the devaluers gradually lose some of their gains in competitiveness. With the degree of inflation convergence currently in prospect it is unlikely that the formerly weak currencies will become overvalued for some time. During that period emphasis on meeting the second challenge could make a decisive contribution not only to preserving the cohesion of the present EMS participants but also to making it a pole of attraction for those who are currently outside.

The three elements in the short-term defences need not be changed, but the balance between them needs to be adjusted. In particular, some mechanism needs to be introduced to ensure that interest-rate responses are triggered early in response to external pressures. One way is, as discussed above, to discontinue the wide margins and to encourage further unilateral narrowing of them. This would have the double effect of (1) signalling greater determination to maintain the exchange-rate, and (2) requiring more rapid use of the two other defensive mechanisms.

Since the experiences of 1992/93 have demonstrated that interventions cannot in practice be unlimited it may be thought that the transition from these to interest-rate changes in the graduated series of responses has become more rapid. However, a greater awareness of limitations to interventions may tempt markets to test the resolve of the national authorities trying to defend their currencies. Announcing limits to interventions could be outright destabilizing, particularly if the national authority managing the weak currency is thought to be unwilling to use interest-rates actively, because then the next response has to be a realignment. It would be preferable to design mechanisms that offer incentives for the central banks to modify interest rates so as to check the need for intervention.

Two proposals have recently been formulated in this spirit, by Peter Bofinger and Graham Bishop respectively.[6] Bofinger's proposal is to suspend the requirement that a debtor central bank repurchase its own currency acquired by the creditor central bank in interventions. At present, the time limit within which repurchase has to be made is 3½ months (extended from 2½ in the Basle-Nyborg agreement), except for the relatively modest amounts under the debtor quotas in the short-term facility. This provision has been central to the functioning of the EMS in the past; because a debtor central bank knows that it must repurchase its currency not very far in the future, it has to generate a private capital inflow – or the government must borrow – to enable it to do so. This is an incentive to raise interest rates which would weaken with an extension of the credit period.

The Bofinger proposal could harden the reluctance of the creditor central bank to intervene at all, because it would risk being stuck with the increase in reserves for a long time. So a prior question is how it could still be obliged to intervene. If the obligation existed the creditor central bank would have an incentive to give a high weight to external pressures in designing its interest rate policy. By swift management of interest rates the creditor central bank could minimize the interventions which have now become too onerous. But in so doing it would lose much of its monetary autonomy. The Bofinger scheme would create a more symmetric system by increasing the pressure on the creditor central banks. Precisely for that reason its implementation would be resisted by the Bundesbank, at least as long as the German monetary authorities see themselves as cast more permanently in that role.

The Bishop scheme is explicitly asymmetric in that it is foreseen that a country which has lost a large amount of reserves through the intervention of other EMS central banks also loses its monetary autonomy. When reserves corresponding to a certain percentage of the domestic money supply – 15 per cent of M2, to be specific – have accumulated as balances with other EMS central banks, the creditors take over and presumably raise interest rates or take other measures to restore confidence in the debtor's economy. This prospect obviously gives a debtor a strong incentive to avoid being put into such a position of dependence – in short to take early action of the type that would otherwise be forced upon it later. This approach will appeal to those monetary authorities who see themselves as trendwise creditors, but hardly to the debtors. It may not even appeal to a large creditor central bank, because the task of assuming responsibility for another country's monetary policy at a time when political integration is only moderately advanced could become very burdensome for the creditor. It is an advantage in such a framework to have an international institution to oversee policy adjustments and take the political flak, rather than to project an individual foreign central bank into such a visible role. It must remain an open question whether even the creditor central bank will feel encouraged to take on the task.

Both the Bofinger and the Bishop plans, appealing as they are in pure logic, seem unlikely to enlist sufficient political support to materialize. The proposals may also make inadequate use of the emerging multilateral framework which will become an increasingly significant feature for the next few years as the EMI begins to operate. Hence there is a case for a third approach which remedies these weaknesses.

One element in the September 1992 crisis already noted in passing was that both strong and weak currency countries strongly resisted drawing the money supply and interest-rate implications required for interventions to fulfil a stabilizing purpose. The Bundesbank has prided itself on having proved able to sterilize 90 per cent of the interventions undertaken within a short period of time. Some of the weak currency countries similarly made an effort to sterilize fully; it is difficult, for example, to see any trace of the dramatic outflow from the United Kingdom in the monthly UK money supply figures for 1992.

It is a well-known property of a fixed exchange rate system that the higher the degree of combined sterilization of interventions the more unstable the system becomes. If all participants succeed in sterilizing completely stabilization would hinge only on the so-called portfolio effect: as additional volumes of financial assets denominated in the weak currency are held reluctantly an increasing premium return is required which dampens activity in the deficit country and conversely in the surplus country. Empirical work by Dominguez and Frankel (1993) and others suggest that this effect is modest, because even in turbulent periods interventions are small relative to the total size of the stocks of financial assets denominated in the respective currencies. Nearly fully sterilized interventions can therefore go on for a long time, because they reduce only marginally the tensions which prompted them.

This is the problem which the Bofinger and Bishop proposals address, though in a way that is likely to meet maximum resistance. If repurchase obligations for the deficit country were removed as proposed by Bofinger sterilization would become harder in the longer term for the surplus country which is accordingly likely to resist by intervening less and trying to push the burden of adjustment back on to the deficit country. If monetary autonomy is lost by the deficit country automatically once it has lost an important part of its reserves, the deficit country may resort too quickly to the instrument it can control, viz. a devaluation.

A more acceptable device might be one in which sterilization practices in both the surplus and the deficit country are monitored collectively on a continuing short-term basis. After 1 January 1994 the EMI is the institution designed to manage collective action. Its potential for discharging this task would be enhanced if a significant number of participating national central banks were to use the provisions of Maastricht[7] to entrust to the EMI the task of managing their foreign exchange reserves, in which case the EMI would itself undertake the interventions. No specific norms would be set for the degree of sterilization; discretionary judgements would be made from day to day as to whether the need for intervention was accelerating (in which case the degree of sterilization would be reduced), or decelerating (in which case no change in recent practice would be required). The scheme would be designed to speed up the transition from sterilized to non-sterilized interventions in circumstances where the gradualist approach of Basle-Nyborg is blocked and a risk is perceived that the deficit country will be tempted or forced into a devaluation not warranted by fundamentals.

The proposed scheme would be facilitated if the EMI were also to be empowered through bilateral contracts to manage domestic money market operations of the participating central banks. Such a pooling of operations was suggested during the work of the Delors Committee by Professor Lamfalussy (1989) in order to make all operations by each central bank more transparent to other participants while presenting a more common front to market participants. In the Lamfalussy proposal only operations were to be pooled, while no transfer of decision-making authority was to take place. The proposal did not meet with favour among the national central bankers, perhaps surprisingly since it was a minimalist proposal that could nevertheless have improved the efficiency of the operations and not only in an international sense. Preoccupied as the discussion was with the detailed blueprint for ultimate monetary union with a European System of Central Banks combining centralized decision-making with decentralized implementation of policy, the idea of early centralization of operations did not fit in very well. The experience of the 1992 currency crisis justifies a reconsideration of this reluctance. But in order to prevent speculative attacks from succeeding when they are basically seen as unwarranted some pooling of authority is now required.

As in the case of the proposals by Bofinger and Bishop the present proposal will be met with the objection that monetary sovereignty is transferred to an unacceptable degree. The following section takes up briefly the limits of the principle of the indivisibility of monetary policy.

Realignments

If the revised combination of defensive measures already contained in the Basle-Nyborg agreement proves insufficient the issue arises of how realignments, which may then become inevitable, should be handled. The questions centre on two interrelated issues: What size of realignments should be permitted? Who should take the decision?

Given the two types of 'errors' which an exchange-rate system may commit – trying to defend basically misaligned rates and giving in to speculative attacks not justified by fundamentals – the response to the two challenges should be different. In the former case, realignments should be sufficiently large to forestall for a long time any expectation that it will be followed by another. A recent example of a successful large realignment is that of the 10 per cent devaluation at the end of

January 1993 of the Irish punt, which arguably became misaligned as a result of the sharp depreciation of sterling, the currency of Ireland's dominant trading partner, and a rapid decline of UK interest rates. Subsequently the credibility of Irish exchange-rate policy was rapidly restored as expressed in terms of the simple test proposed by Svensson (1990) for currencies in a target zone. Currently Irish short-term interest-rates are slightly below German rates, a result that would hardly have been attainable following a smaller devaluation triggering expectations of more to come.

A sizeable realignment should, as was the case in the pre-1987 EMS, be accompanied by domestic measures designed to improve performance in terms of the Maastricht budgetary criteria. Such a realignment is accordingly a decision of high politics and could only be taken by the Ecofin Council.

Should the possibility of a small realignment of the type envisaged in Basle-Nyborg (and carried out in January 1987) remain as an option in the final months of Stage I and during Stage II? A mini-realignment would serve a different purpose from a large one. It would be designed as one additional and ultimate response in a chain of events in which the traditional short-term defensive instruments, even when revamped as suggested above, had proved inadequate to stem speculation which is basically seen as unwarranted.

Ideally this type of realignment should be superfluous if the other defences work well and participation in the EMS is confined to currencies that are not misaligned. The mere fact that realignments remain a possibility over the next few years is itself an invitation to speculation. By insisting on the retention of this form of continued flexibility the more stable currencies in the EMS are storing up trouble for themselves. In order to limit this cost realignments among these currencies should explicitly be restricted in the way that was implicit in Basle-Nyborg, i.e. to changes in central rates that do not cause any jumps in market exchange-rates. Furthermore, in order to protect the credentials of participants wishing to join the final stage of monetary union they should be confined to cases in which one or two currencies become divergently strong so as not to disqualify a country which has trusted its own initiative.

In these circumstances a mini-revaluation would appear only as a final response in monetary management. Since no domestic adjustments outside the monetary area would be required – that would not make sense given the small size – the question arises whether the decision could not be taken by the central bankers rather than by the Ecofin Council. This idea was discussed at times in the late 1980s, but it was dismissed not only by the political officials, but also by the central bankers themselves. Careful analysis is now required whether the strong attachment to stable exchange-rates demonstrated over the past six years by all countries which have observed the normal margins has not changed the balance of the argument in favour of leaving the decision to the machinery of central bank cooperation in the EMI.

THE LIMITS OF THE PRINCIPLE OF INDIVISIBILITY OF MONETARY POLICY

During the work of the Delors Committee the most difficult task was to define how the transition to monetary union was to take place. It was obvious that the starting point in the EMS was one in which monetary authority rested ultimately in national hands. The EMS is a system of rules, but relying in the end on the will of independent states to let their central banks cooperate. The incentives for them to do so were becoming visibly stronger than before in the course of the 1980s as economic performances began to converge and capital controls were removed. But the mere fact that realignments could occur made it obvious that in the end there was an escape route. The lack of central bank autonomy in several member states increased the likelihood that policy conflicts between countries would escalate quickly to the political level and create a public debate which would encourage market expectations that the system was becoming vulnerable. For a long time before the 1992 crisis these two elements receded into the background and central bank publications were able to offer a rosy picture that voluntary monetary cooperation was quite adequate to the task. Many central bankers would have preferred to leave matters like that and to adopt a very slow gradualist approach to monetary integration. They feared that forcing the pace towards monetary union would stir up political antagonisms, putting their regular task of managing the EMS at risk.

The European Council in 1988 asked the Delors Committee, consisting largely of central bank governors, (1) to study how EMU could be realized and (2) to propose concrete stages leading towards this objective. In meeting the former of these challenges the Committee outlined an advanced form of monetary unification with a federal central banking institution, issuing a single currency as soon as possible after the definitive locking of intra-union exchange-rates. Bini-Smaghi, Padoa Schioppa and Papadia (1993) have aptly termed the inspiration for this blueprint of monetary union 'national', in the sense that monetary policy in the union could be analysed in familiar terms from large individual countries rather than as an advanced form of international policy coordination. All monetary conflicts would be fully internalized inside the union.

This was clearly a system qualitatively very different from that of the existing EMS, even on an optimistic assessment of the state of monetary integration at the end of the 1980s. Accordingly, there was a long road to travel to the final stage and it is obvious from the nature of the proposal that the central bankers initially assumed that the transition would have to take many years. As the subsequent political debate preparing and negotiating the Maastricht Treaty began to set dates not too far into the future, the vagueness and the fragility of the preparations for the transition stood out even more clearly than before.

Paradoxically, the more the transition was telescoped into a few years, the less substantial the concrete provisions for transition became. Symbolically, the European System of Central Banks was no longer to be set up at the start of Stage II to begin the transition from coordination of independent national monetary policies to the formulation and implementation of a common policy in the final stage – only a temporary and preparatory EMI which looks like an only slightly modified Committee of Governors. It is possible to argue that the nomination by the European Council of a full-time EMI President, the requirement that the members of its Council exercise their collective functions without receiving political instructions, the possibility that national central banks will delegate some of their tasks to the new institution and, above all, the intended preoccupation of the EMI with planning for policy in the final stage will all tend to give the EMI a higher public profile and greater authority as a mediator/coordinator for the central banks than the Committee of Governors. But it is clear that de jure there will be very little the EMI can do to impose its authority. It will have to work by persuasion.

Is it possible to envisage a transition in which monetary authority is somehow shared between the national level and EMI? The Delors Committee deliberated long on this issue, but efforts to develop specific proposals under the heading of 'gradualism and indivisibility' had to be given up – not only because there was disagreement on the substance, but also because any precise description of a division of responsibilities would have been very difficult to draw up. It is obvious that there should be no doubt in financial markets as to who is responsible for any particular decision, but would that necessarily preclude the attribution of some clearly defined policy functions to the EMI? Could, for example, as was proposed by some members of the Delors Committee, two important instruments of monetary management – one external: interventions in third currencies, and one 'domestic': changes in European-wide reserve requirements – be assigned to the EMI while leaving other instruments in national hands?

It is tempting, but by now rather unproductive, to argue the case for such a division of responsibilities. The Germans – and some others – have indicated their firm opposition to any intermediate stage between the decentralized framework of the present and the federal model of the final stage and the transition and the role of the EMI. Nothing can change that as a legal reality. But still the environment within which policy making nationally or collectively takes place can be modified in ways that shift the incentive in voluntary coordination strongly towards collective action and management so that de facto the system begins to operate as a closer substitute for a common monetary policy.

Two changes in the environment appear central. The first which is occurring is to make the national central banks more independent of their respective governments. This will at the same time make them dependent on each other. In Maastricht it was argued to delay initiatives of this kind till the final days of transition to EMU, but since then several modifications in the status of the central banks have occurred or are underway, most significantly in France. The risk that incipient policy conflicts would quickly escalate to the political level has in the past severely constrained voluntary central bank cooperation in the EMS. The most dramatic event in the 1992 crisis was the public policy conflict between the Bundesbank and the British Treasury.

The second change in the environment for central bank cooperation will come about as the EMS tightens up without excessive flexibility of exchange rates (in the form of wide fluctuation margins or regular realignments) and becomes more symmetric. When the decision fully to dismantle capital controls was taken in 1988, the challenge of near-complete capital mobility prompted reflections on how to share monetary policy more efficiently in the long term and pushed the monetary authorities into tighter cooperation then. Notably, interest-rate convergence became stronger than in the past. Leadership in monetary policy began to be more widely shared among the participants as the relative financial weight of Germany declined. But this process was reversed by the shock of German unification and the exceptional need for the Bundesbank to maintain high interest rates in its wake. Leadership shifted back to Germany, not because it had a superior economic performance as in the mid-1980s, but because of the need to conduct the tightest monetary policy in the EC. This phase now appears to be over. As German interest rates decline in recession and the German stability performance is no longer superior to that of several other member states, the anchor function will widen to comprise all the countries conducting stable exchange rate policies – whether this development is planned or not. Germany will obviously continue to exercise the influence that its financial weight accords, but that is inevitably smaller than in the past. In this process the German attitude to even tighter forms of monetary cooperation should change and the limits of the doctrine of the indivisibility of monetary policy will be explored. As financial markets change their evaluation of Germany's economic prospects – as already seems to have happened during the recent period of surprisingly strong interest rate convergence – Germany will see its own interest in being less averse to testing new initiatives and procedures such as those advocated in the previous section for sharing monetary sovereignty. In this process the growing independence of the central banks of partner EMS countries will be a major determinant of the speed. Other countries are now showing their capacity to anticipate this new opportunity.

TENTATIVE CONCLUSIONS

Although the present state of monetary integration and of the prospects for resuming the advance towards monetary union is seen as unpromising and uncertain by most observers, and official proposals for reforms are extremely bland, there may nevertheless be some grounds for the apparent complacency and lack of initiative.

One element is that there is little risk of a repeat of the currency turmoil of 1992/93. The factors which produced the massive adjustments are no longer present. Weak currencies have, if anything, overadjusted and now appear more likely to rise than to fall. Those countries that maintained their central rates appear determined to continue. There is no need to prepare to fight anew yesterday's battle and good reason to resist any future attacks in the market. The alternative of a reversal to a much more flexible EMS is unattractive; continued convergence of inflation rates at a low level will make this gradually more evident.

There is a problem of how to reintegrate the presently floating currencies. The strategy that seems best is to wait until they have stabilized in the market and then invite them back at agreed central rates and with observance of the normal fluctuation margins. Wide margins would not help the new entrants and they could destabilize the system for the regular membership. On the contrary, those countries that can do so should be encouraged to narrow their margins further.

The Basle-Nyborg agreement of 1987 worked well until 1992 and is in need primarily of a change of emphasis in the short-term defences. Interest rate coordination must become the prime tool, but interventions are also necessary, provided their effects are to some extent allowed to work their way through to domestic money supplies and interest rates. Two recent proposals to this effect by Bofinger and Bishop are considered, for different reasons, unlikely to win political favour because they will be seen as unfairly burdensome or risky by either surplus or deficit countries. A third proposal is to monitor sterilization of interventions closely through the EMI in Stage II.

A reform of Basle-Nyborg in a direction of more symmetry should be tailored to the new reality that there is no longer an obvious tendency for Germany to retain the leadership role in the EMS. The anchor function will be broadened to comprise those countries that are prepared to accept a very tight EMS and take steps to make their central banks more independent. These developments will ease the constraint on the process of monetary unification imposed by the doctrine that monetary authority is indivisible.

NOTES

1 By the late 1980s intra-EMS exchange rate variability – measured by the standard deviation of monthly changes in bilateral rates – had been reduced to about one-fourth of what had been observed in the five-year period just before the EMS (1974–1978), see Gros and Thygesen (1992), Ch. 4, particularly pp.101–10.
2 Williamson (1977) and contemporaneous articles applied the concept to IMF surveillance and to his ideas for reviving European monetary integration.

3 The EC Monetary Committee and the Governors' Committee did introduce, in 1977, more regular consultations on exchange-rate issues. And the notion that there should be an exchange-rate related trigger for closer policy coordination survived in the form of the supplementary indicator of divergence – which has not, however, been much used in the EMS. – For a fuller account of the Duisenberg Plan, see Gros and Thygesen (1992), pp.39–41.
4 Counting the Luxembourg franc as a separate currency.
5 Press Communique of the Committee of Governors of 18 September 1987, reproduced in Gros and Thygesen (1992), p.99.
6 Bofinger (1993), Bishop (1993).
7 Article 6.4 of the Protocol of the EMI Statute.

REFERENCES

Bimi-Smaghi, Lorenzo, Padoa Schioppa, Tommaso and Papadia, Francesco (1993), 'The policy history of the Maastricht Treaty', paper presented at a conference 'The Monetary Future of Europe', organized by the Centre of Economic Policy Research in la Coruna, Spain, Banca d'Italia, February.
Bishop, Graham (1993), 'Is there a rapid route to an EMU of the few?', *Economic and Market Analysis*, 11 May, Solomon Brothers, London.
Bofinger, P. (1993a), 'Geldpolitische Koordination durch das Europäische Währungsinstitut', in *Europa vor dem Eintritt in die Wirtschafts-und Währungsunion*, Berlin, Duncker & Humblot.
Bofinger, P. (1993b), 'Währungsintegration durch eine Währungsunion in EG Kernländern', in R. Caesar and H.E. Scharrer (eds), *Europäische Wirtschafts-und Währungsunion durch Maastricht? Perspektiven der Wirtschafts-und Währungsintegration*.
Bofinger, P. (1993c), *Währungsintegration durch eine Währungsunion in den EG-Kernländern*, Würzburg University Economics Departement.
Committee of Governors of the Central Banks of the Member States of the European Community (1993a), *The Implications and Lessons to be Drawn from the Recent Exchange Rate Crisis*, Basle, 21 April.
Committee of Governors of the Central Banks of the Member States of the European Community (1993b), *Annual Report 1992*, Basle, April.
Dominguez, Kathryn M. and Frankel, Jeffrey A. (1993), *Does Foreign-Exchange Intervention Work*, Washington DC, Institute for International Economics.
Eichengreen, Barry and Wyplosz, Charles (1993), 'The unstable EMS', *Brookings Papers on Economic Activity* 1993: 2, Washington, DC.
Feldstein, Martin (1992), 'Does European Monetary Union have a future?', paper presented at a conference 'The Monetary Future of Europe', organized by the Centre of Economic Policy Research in la Coruna, Spain, December.
Gros, Daniel and Thygesen, Niels (1992), *European Monetary Integration: From the European Monetary System to European Monetary Union*, London, Longman.
Lamfalussy, Alexandre (1989), 'A proposal for stage two under which monetary policy operations would be centralised in a jointly-owned subsidiary', collection of Papers Annexed to the *Delors Report*, Luxembourg, Office of Publications of the European Community.
Miller, Marcus and Williamson, John (1987), *Targets and Indicators: A Blueprint for the International Coordination of Economic Policy*, Washington DC, Institute for International Economics.

Monetary Committee of the European Community (1993), *Lessons to be Drawn from the Disturbances on the Foreign Exchange Markets*, Brussels, 13 April.

Svensson, Lars E.O. (1990), 'The simplest test of target zone credibility', NBER working paper no. 3394, Cambridge MA, June.

Williamson, John (1977), *The Failure of World Monetary Reform*, London, Nelson.

Williamson, John (1985), *The Exchange Rate System*, Washington DC, Institute for International Economics.

Williamson, John (1993), 'Exchange Rate Management', *Economic Journal*, 103, 188–197.

10

HOW TO SAVE THE EMS

Barry Eichengreen and Charles Wyplosz

The September 1992 crisis in the foreign exchange markets threw a spanner in the works of European monetary unification. Was that crisis a one-time event reflecting exceptional disturbances to the European economy, in which case the Maastricht process can proceed as before? Or can such crises recur, in which case the three-stage transition to monetary union delineated in the Maastricht Treaty must be fundamentally rethought?

At one level, the September crisis did in fact reflect an exceptional disturbance to the European economy, namely German economic and monetary union (GEMU). That another disturbance as profound as GEMU is unlikely in the coming years might therefore appear reassuring. But the economic effects of GEMU cannot by themselves explain the timing or course of the crisis. Also at work were other sources of instability intrinsic to the Maastricht process. These intrinsic instabilities were not vented by the crisis; if anything they were heightened. They continue to pose a threat to the stability of the EMS and therefore to the goal of EMU.

Our analysis of the 'fault lines' running through the EMS (to quote John Major) rests on three pillars. First, we take the Maastricht Treaty seriously. We show how expectations that the treaty might be interpreted literally worked to destabilize the EMS. We show, in other words, that certain perverse and ill-advised provisions of the treaty were at the root of the crisis.

Second, we show that economic theory offers a coherent analysis of the forces working to destabilize the EMS. Theory may not have predictive power (if it did the authors of this chapter would be rich), but it can still be used to identify the factors making for financial instability.

Third, rather than simply posing assumptions about what foreign exchange market participants think, we base our analysis on what traders actually say. Much of our work is based on a postal questionnaire addressed to virtually every institutional trader in the European foreign exchange market.[1]

THE NEW EMS

To understand the crisis, it is first necessary to understand the European Monetary System. As set up in 1979, the EMS allowed periodic realignments of exchange rates to redress persistent external imbalances. Countries with high inflation rates and balance-of-payments deficits were allowed to devalue their currencies against other EMS countries. Eleven such realignments took place in the first ten years of the EMS.

Realignments were made possible by capital controls. Intervals of exchange-rate stability punctuated by occasional realignments were feasible because controls protected central banks' reserves against speculative attacks. If, for example, Italy sought to run looser monetary policy than Germany, huge quantities of financial capital did not flow instantaneously from Milan to Frankfurt, immediately exhausting the Banca d'Italia's reserves. The interest differential had to be large before arbitragers found it economical to incur the cost of circumventing Italian capital controls and thereby forced a realignment. Capital controls were not impermeable: they could not support a weak currency indefinitely, but they provided enough insulation to arrange for an orderly realignment.

Orderly realignments were further facilitated by the provision of international credit facilities. The Very Short Term Financing Facility prescribes unlimited interventions at the margin. This implies that the stronger currencies must be prepared to defend the weaker ones to the extent necessary.

The three central features of the original EMS – realignments, controls and concerted intervention – went by the board in 1992. Starting in 1987 realignments were dismissed as harmful; none took place from the beginning of that year until the crisis. The major EMS countries removed all significant capital controls. And new questions arose about whether strong-currency countries were actually prepared to provide unlimited support to their weak-currency partners.

This created the potential for instability. Ruling out realignments, whatever the anti-inflationary benefits in weak-currency countries, made relative price changes more difficult to effect. Balance-of-payments problems, reserve losses and exchange-rate instability followed inevitably. Eliminating capital controls, whatever its virtues in terms of resource allocation, left central banks bereft of protection. The burden of support was shifted on to strong-currency central banks, who could not afford the responsibility. In the face of full-scale speculative attacks, even Europe's largest country, Germany, found itself forced to create such large amounts of money when intervening in support of weak EMS currencies that its commitment to price stability was threatened. The EMS anchor – the DM – is simply too small in a world of full capital mobility to discharge its role in all circumstances.

For a time, the knowledge that countries wished to qualify for monetary union convinced the markets of governments' commitment to policies consistent with the maintenance of fixed rates. Figure 10.1 presents the one-year forward rate along the current spot rate against the DM for the major EMS currencies. By the beginning of 1992, nearly all currencies were credible: under the assumption that the forward rate reveals the market forecast for the exchange rate one year ahead, the markets did not anticipate movements outside the bands of fluctuation. But once the prospects for EMU were clouded by the Danish referendum, confidence in this commitment ebbed, as the survey results in Table 10.1 clearly show. The EMS became unstable, more so by virtue of the fact that GEMU had already thrown the entire system out of whack.

THE GERMAN UNIFICATION SHOCK

Most early analyses correctly predicted that an appreciation of the DM would be required to accommodate the economic effects of GEMU. They noted that public and private spending in Germany would rise following unification. Public spending was spurred by the need for infrastructure investment and the rise in unemployment compensation. Increased private spending in the east reflected consumption smoothing in anticipation of real wage gains. In the absence of a commensurate supply-side response, the pressure on home goods had to be accommodated by a real appreciation.

As the surge in spending consequent on GEMU shifted demand towards German goods, their price had to rise relative to that of foreign goods in order to clear domestic and international markets. This change in relative prices (in the real exchange rate) could be effected in three ways: higher inflation in Germany, lower inflation abroad, and a one-time revaluation of the DM. German policy makers understandably resisted a significant increase in domestic inflation. Although the Bundesbank made known its wish that the DM be revalued within the EMS it could not muster the unanimous agreement of ERM countries as required. France, pledged to its franc fort policy, vetoed any change in its parity vis-à-vis the DM. Britain, which had just entered the ERM, argued that a downward realignment against the DM would undermine the credibility of its new monetary strategy. The Bundesbank's offer of a realignment was rejected apparently repeatedly. With these alternatives closed off, the only remaining avenue for adjustment was deflation in other countries. But deflation is painful: it requires persistent demand restriction, which may in turn imply rising unemployment (Figure 10.2)

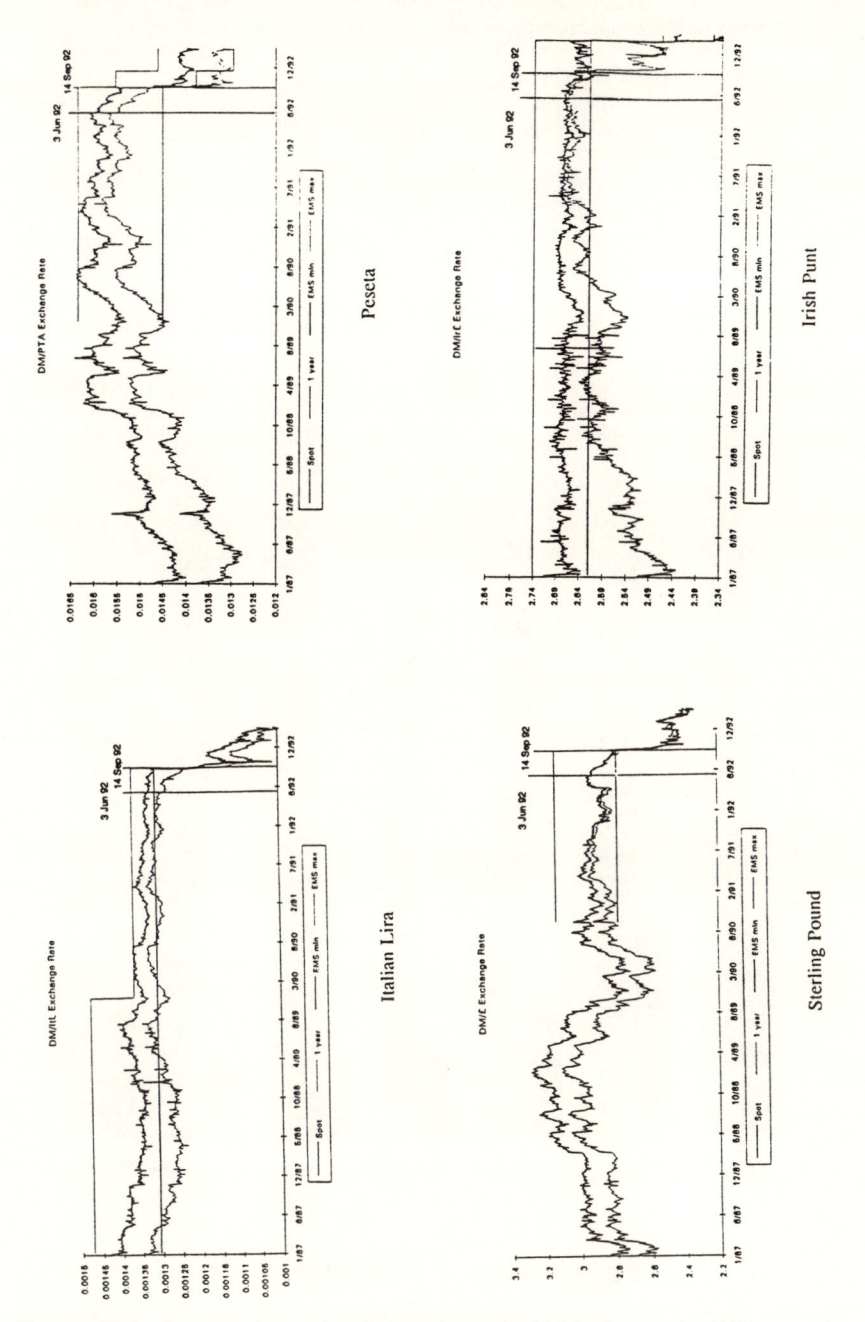

Figure 10.1 One-year forward and spot rates vs the DM for four major EMS currencies

Source: DRI

Table 10.1 Expecting imminent changes in ERM parities (*Question asked*: When did you first begin to think that changes in ERM exchange rates were imminent?)

Before the Danish referendum in June	21.8%
Just after the Danish referendum	46.6%
Upon hearing about public opinion polls in France during the run-up of the referendum	15.1%
Around the time of the Finnish crisis and devaluation	6.8%
Around the time of the Swedish crisis in September	6.8%
Other	9.1%

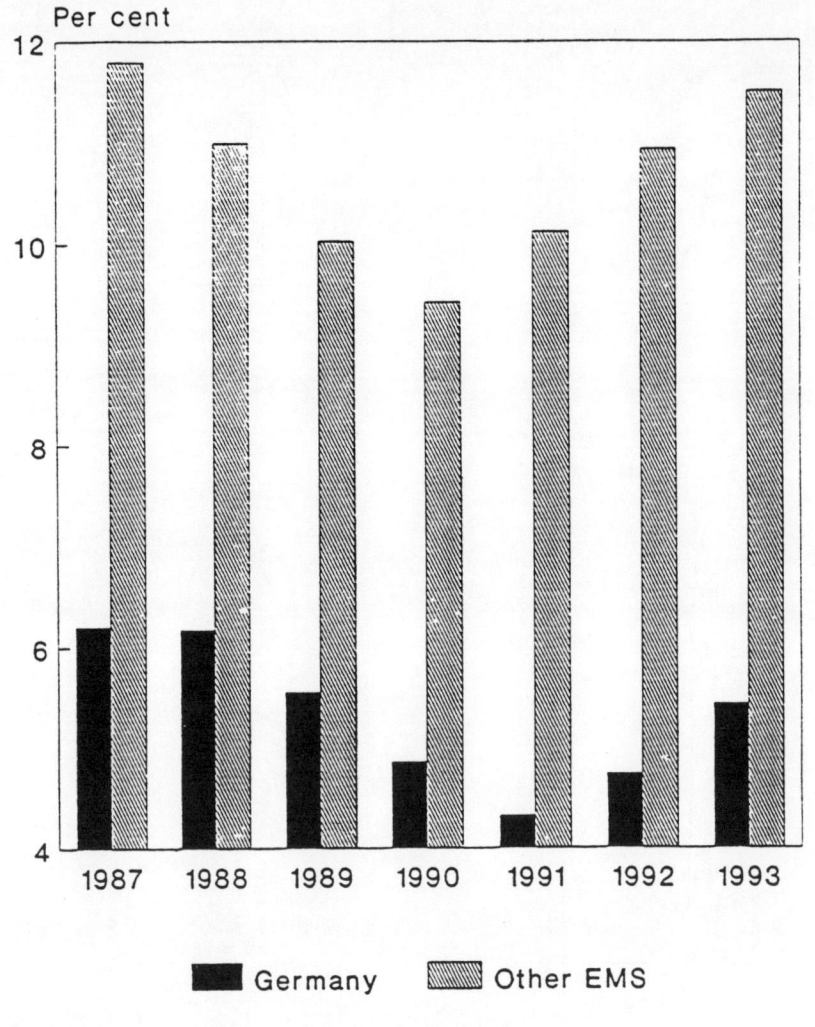

Figure 10.2 EMS-country unemployment rates, 1987–1993

Source: OECD *Economic Outlook*, December 1992.

and mounting opposition to the policy. If governments and unions resist carrying out this adjustment, markets may begin to doubt the credibility of their commitment to the prevailing exchange rate and test their resolve. This process of testing is what constitutes a speculative crisis.

THE COMPETITIVENESS PROBLEM

The simplest explanation for the September crisis is thus that Germany's EMS partners first vetoed a revaluation of the DM and then failed to carry out the deflationary adjustment required by the GEMU shock. German inflation did in fact accelerate after 1989, while inflation in Germany's EMS partners declined. The question is whether the decline in inflation rates in these other countries was sufficient to bring about the requisite adjustment in relative prices. Figure 10.4 (which displays labour unit costs relatively to Germany) shows that this is particularly questionable for three EMS countries: the UK, Italy and Spain, whose inflation rates relative to Germany's remained persistently high. These three were, not surprisingly, the first EMS countries to be attacked in September.

Even those countries which succeeded in bringing their inflation rates below Germany's might be unable to stay the course. Policies of austerity produced rising unemployment (Figure 10.2) and fostered opposition. Even if governments had succeeded for a time in deflating and maintaining competitiveness vis-à-vis Germany, there was the danger that opposition might reach boiling point, ruling governments might be deposed, and policies of austerity might be reversed.

Thus, the evolution of competitiveness provides a straightforward explanation for the September crisis. The attempt to fix parities once and for all first required other EMS countries to reduce their inflation rates to German levels. The shift in demand towards German goods consequent on GEMU then required them to reduce their inflation to below Germany's. Failure to do so implied deteriorating competitiveness, balance-of-payments weakness and reserve losses, as well as mounting unemployment. These facts became evident over the summer of 1992, and investors scrambled to get out of other EMS currencies before the inevitable devaluations ensued. The result was the September crisis.

LIMITATIONS OF THE EXPLANATION

If this is all there is to the story, the policy implications are straightforward. Exchange rate stability requires policy convergence. GEMU

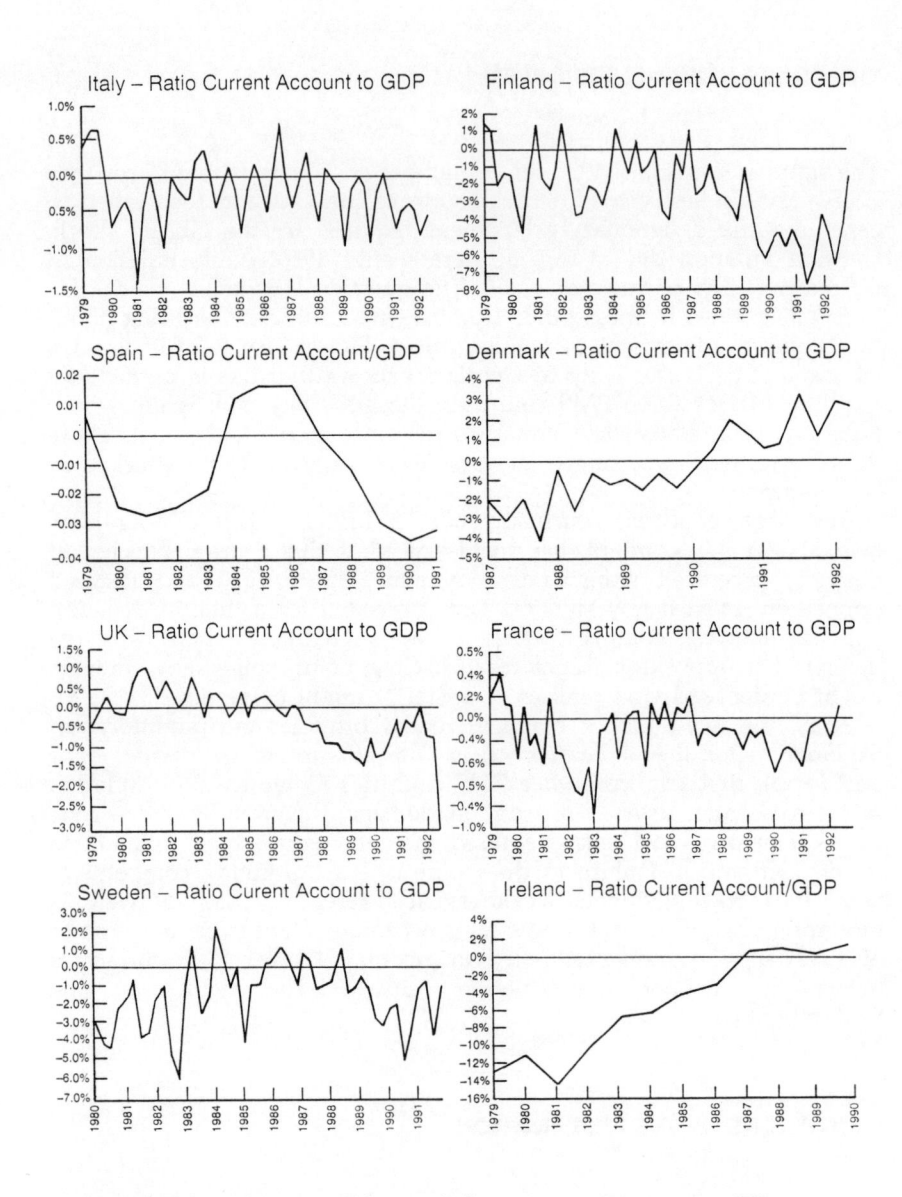

Figure 10.3a Further competitiveness indicators: current account to GDP
Source: IMF.

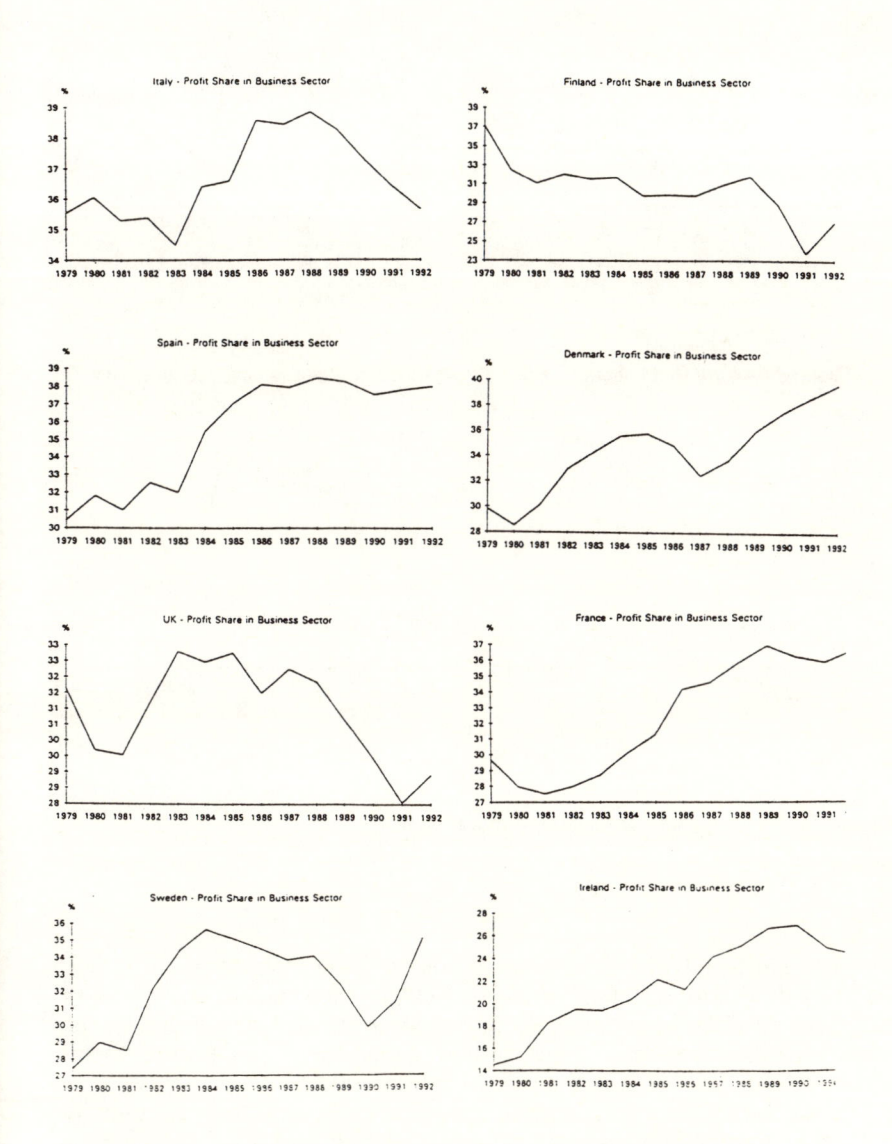

Figure 10.3b Further competitiveness indicators: profit share in business sector
Source: OECD.

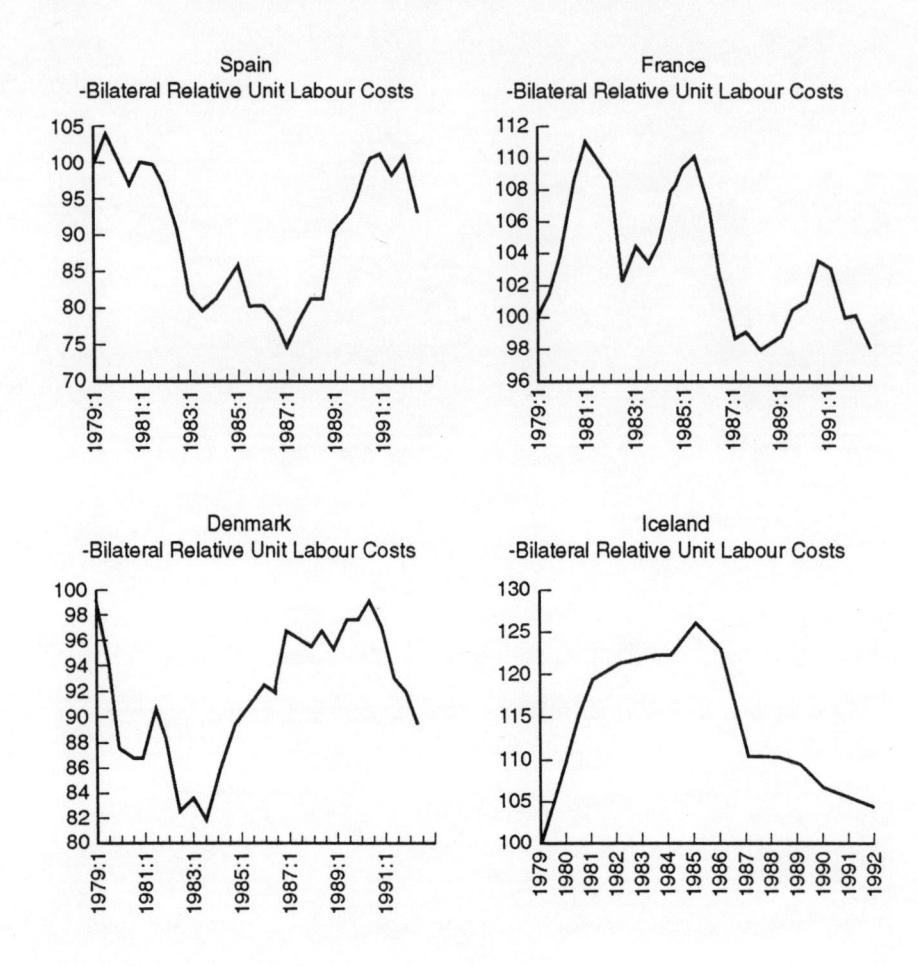

Figure 10.4 Unit labour costs relative to Germany

Source: OECD.

simply reinforced the pressure on other EMS countries to follow German-style anti-inflation policies, which they failed to do with sufficient resolve. Stabilizing EMS parities over the remainder of the transition therefore only requires that governments rededicate themselves to this task. This is the official interpretation

Unfortunately, the story is more complicated. Several facts sit uneasily with the competitiveness explanation. First, the timing of the crisis is wrong. GEMU occurred in 1990 but the EMS crisis only eventuated in 1992. Markets are forward looking: traders make profits if they succeed in anticipating events. It seems peculiar that the imbalances set afoot by

Table 10.2 Traders' evaluation of an ERM currency (*Question asked*: What factors do you consider when evaluating the outlook for an ERM currency?)

Prospective inflation	84.2%
Prospective trade performance	72.2%
The unemployment situation	61.6%
Interest rates	87.9%
Rate of growth of money supply	60.1%
Other	30.1%

GEMU should only have destabilized EMS parities more than two years afterwards.

Second, even countries like France which had undertaken adequate adjustment were attacked. In Eichengreen and Wyplosz (1993) we provide an extensive analysis of the evolution of relative prices, adjusting them for changes in labour productivity and other factors. While this does not undermine the view that countries like Italy had competitiveness problems, it provides little evidence that they existed in other countries like Denmark and France whose currencies were also attacked.

Third, currencies like the Spanish peseta were at the top of their EMS bands on the eve of their devaluation. If the markets perceived competitiveness problems, traders would have begun to sell pesetas in anticipation of difficulties, driving the currency down towards the bottom of its band before the fact. This did not occur as Figure 10.1 demonstrates.

Fourth, countries that were not attacked experienced the same rise in unemployment as countries that were. If rising unemployment was a signal that the commitment to exchange-rate stability might have to be abandoned, we should have observed the most serious speculative attacks on the currencies of countries where unemployment was the most serious problem. This was not the case as the example of Belgium shows. Consistent with this conclusion is the fact that public criticism of the EMS for spawning unemployment was as prevalent in the countries that were not attacked as in those that were.

Fifth, traders themselves did not look only at the fundamental determinants of competitiveness when assessing the prospects for European exchange rates. Table 10.2 confirms that competitiveness figures in their calculations. But Tables 10.3 and 10.4 suggest that other factors were also at play. Questions about why the weakness of some currencies led to weakness of others consistently elicited the response that the 'markets "tasted blood" (realized that there are profits to be made)'. This suggests that once the speculative attack got underway, it fed on itself and proved self-fulfilling.

Table 10.3 Contagion within the ERM (*Question asked*: Did the weakness of some ERM currencies late in the summer lead you to anticipate weakness of other ERM currencies?)

Yes: 90.2%	
Because:	
Devaluing countries are able to undercut competitors	53.4%
Markets 'tasted blood' (realized that there are profits to be made)	76.7%
Other	4.5%

Table 10.4 Contagion from outside the ERM (*Question asked*: Did the weakness of non-ERM countries (those of Finland, Sweden, Norway, for example) lead you to anticipate weakness of ERM currencies?)

Yes: 50.4%		No: 49.6%	
Because:		Because:	
Devaluing countries are able to undercut competitors	23.3%	ERM central banks can borrow from one another	22.6%
Markets have 'tasted blood' (realized that there are profits to be made)	42.9%	EC countries mostly trade with one another	24.8%
Other	3.8%	EC countries' financial markets are deeper	36.1%
		Others	1.5%

HOW THE MAASTRICHT TREATY PROVOKED A SELF-FULFILLING ATTACK

A self-fulfilling attack arbitrarily shifts the foreign exchange market between alternative disequilibria. That multiple equilibria can exist in foreign exchange markets was pointed out by Obstfeld (1986). He described a model in which a speculative attack not grounded in fundamentals can exhaust a central bank's foreign exchange reserves, forcing it to float the exchange rate. As the exchange rate floats downward, reserves flow back into the country, allowing the central bank to re-peg the exchange rate. But this exchange rate can be pegged at different levels. Obstfeld considers two possibilities: in one, a 'wet' government undervalues the new exchange rate (sets it at a lower level than prevailed before the speculative attack); in the other, a 'dry' government does not undervalue the new rate (sets it at a level at least as high as that which prevailed before the attack). When the markets (rationally) anticipate that the government is dry, no self-fulfilling speculative attack will occur. Because post-attack monetary policy will be at least as tight as the pre-attack policy (in order to prevent a nominal depreciation), no capital gains on foreign assets will be available, leaving investors with no incentive to attack the exchange-rate peg. But when the markets (rationally) anticipate that the government is wet, a self-fulfilling speculative attack can occur. Even if, in the absence of an attack, the stance of policy would be consistent with balance-of-payments equilibrium and the pegged exchange rate would be sustainable indefinitely, because investors anticipate that post-attack monetary policy will be looser than the pre-attack policy (in order to induce a nominal depreciation), capital gains on foreign assets are rationally anticipated in the event of an attack, which can occur despite the sustainability of the initial exchange rate in its absence.

This is in contrast to the seminal analysis of Krugman (1979), in which the exchange rate will be attacked only if there currently exists a competitiveness problem implying the eventual exhaustion of reserves. It is also in contrast to a variant of the Krugman model in which an attack occurs because policy is anticipated with certainty to shift in a more expansionary direction (because, for example, the unemployment associated with restrictive policy provokes domestic political opposition). Here policy changes if and only if a speculative attack occurs.

For this explanation to be compelling, there must exist an intrinsic reason why policy would shift in the event of an attack. The Maastricht Treaty provides one. The Treaty's entry conditions introduce the possibility of self-fulfilling attacks. Gaining entry to EMU requires exchange-rate stability. Specifically, one of the four convergence criteria specified in the Treaty requires countries to maintain exchange-rate stability (defined as keeping their currencies within their EMS fluctuation bands 'without severe tensions' for a minimum of two years prior to the inauguration of monetary union). A speculative attack forcing a devaluation that prevented a country from satisfying this requirement might, by eliminating the lure of EMU membership, induce its government to alter policy. Since the country, once driven out of the EMS, might no longer qualify for EMU, it would no longer possess an incentive to pursue the policies of austerity necessary to gain entry. A speculative attack could prove self-fulfilling. The plausibility of this explanation is buttressed by the behaviour of the UK, which, after having pursued high interest-rate policies, cut its discount rate in half as soon as it was driven out of the EMS – this despite no other obvious change in economic circumstances, no change in government, and not even a change in the identity of the Chancellor of the Exchequer.

Thus, although there already existed scope for speculative crises due to competitiveness problems, that scope was greatly widened by the perverse incentives built into the Maastricht Treaty. By withdrawing the prospect of early EMU participation in the event of exchange-rate instability, the treaty provided an incentive for governments to shift policy in more expansionary directions if attacked, thereby introducing the possibility that an attack might prove self-fulfilling.[2]

WHY SELF-FULFILLING ATTACKS CANNOT BE CONTAINED BY STANDARD METHODS

The obvious means of dealing with speculative attacks are to raise interest rates and to obtain foreign support. Neither is likely to be adequate in the circumstances described above.

Sufficiently high interest rates can rebuff the most concerted attack. Even if traders expect a 10 per cent devaluation in ten days with 75 per cent probability, the cost of borrowing at an annualized rate of 500 per cent will dominate the capital gains they can expect to reap by selling the currency now and buying it back following devaluation.

High interest rates are tolerable for short periods but if maintained for long become impossible to bear. Hence, if European central banks stopped defending their exchange-rate pegs, they must have grown convinced that high interest rates would prove impossible to reduce quickly. The Swedish case is illustrative. Towards the beginning of the crisis, the Riksbank raised its marginal rate to 500 per cent. But reserves did not flow back in as soon as the crisis passed. Even after turbulence in other markets died down, it proved possible to reduce rates only part way to pre-crisis levels. When reserve outflows accelerated again in November, it became necessary to ratchet rates back up, to even higher levels than before given the depletion of reserves. When it realized that no interest rate, no matter how high, would attract capital inflows and rebuilds of its foreign exchange reserves the Riksbank stopped defending the krona. Several other countries inside the EMS experienced the same inability to reverse the flow of capital.

Central banks were unwilling to maintain interest rates at high levels for extended periods for four reasons. First, high interest rates squeeze investment and hence depress activity. Second, they are passed through to mortgage payments, especially in countries like the UK and Ireland where mortgage rates are indexed. Third, they increase the cost of servicing public debt, especially in countries like Italy, Belgium and Ireland with high debt–GNP ratios. Fourth, they can destabilize the banking system, especially in countries like Sweden and Finland where banks were already weak. Traders regard a number of these channels as important. As shown in Table 10.5, 88 per cent of respondents thought that central banks worried that interest rate increases would worsen domestic economic conditions, while 69 per cent thought that central

Table 5.4 Why did central banks give up? (*Question asked*: In September, central banks ultimately gave up defending certain European currencies. What explains this decision?)

	Very important	Important	Not important
Central banks' reserves are always insufficient	23.3%	40.6%	30.8%
Central banks' reserves are insufficient now that most exchange controls in Europe have been removed	28.6%	38.3%	28.6%
Central banks worried that further interest rate increases would destabilize banking systems	21.8%	47.4%	24.1%
The Bundesbank worried that further intervention would threaten price stability	22.6%	45.1%	26.3%
Central banks worried that further interest rate increases would worsen domestic economic conditions	64.7%	23.3%	3.8%

Note: Row totals do not sum to 100%, because not all respondents answered all questions.

banks worried that interest rate increases would destabilize banking systems.

These costs can be minimized if high rates are only maintained for short periods. Banks can find alternatives to the discount window for a time. Governments can temporarily curtail the issue of short-term debt. Brief interest rate increases will have only a modest impact on the long-term rates upon which investment and mortgage obligations depend. But if rates have to be maintained at high levels for extended periods the costs may prove great.

The question, then, is whether the type of speculative attack experienced in 1992 requires a short or long period of increased interest rates. That a short period cannot permanently curtain adverse speculation follows from the existence of multiple equilibria. High rates can defer the speculative attack so long as they are maintained. But as soon as they are lowered, the markets have the same incentive as before to mobilize an attack. Neither a shift in domestic monetary policy nor an interlude of foreign support removes this incentive. In the presence of multiple equilibria like those described above, interest rates have to be maintained indefinitely at excruciating levels.

Given central banks' unwillingness to tolerate high interest rates indefinitely, the stability of EMS currencies turned on the provision of foreign support. The Act of Foundation of the EMS states unambiguously that support shall be unlimited:

Intervention shall in principle be effected in currencies of the participating central banks. These interventions shall be unlimited at the compulsory intervention rates. (Document 8, Section I, Article 2.2)

To enable interventions to be made in Community currencies, the participating central banks shall open for each other very short-term credit facilities, unlimited in amounts. (Document 8, Section II, Article 6.1)

With hindsight, it is obvious that no central bank would ever commit unconditionally to unlimited lending. A careful reading of contemporary commentary supports this scepticism. Thus, the German Finance Minister, Otto von Lambsdorff, told the Bundestag on December 1978:

The adjustment of the exchange rate has always been the responsibility of the Government and not of the Bundesbank. The Bundesbank has the responsibility to intervene, and the option not to intervene if it is its opinion that it is not able to do so.

For many years this distinction was incompletely appreciated. Through the early years of the EMS, capital controls and realignments obviated the need for unlimited intervention. The elimination of realignments and capital controls changed this. When the 1992 crisis erupted, the Bundesbank initially responded as previously, intervening to support the lira and acquiring some $4bn of foreign exchange in June. It grew increasingly worried at the sight of its ever-expanding reserves, however. By early September its target monetary aggregate M3 was rising at an annual rate of nearly 10 per cent (far above the target range of 3.5–5.5 per cent). It is plausible, therefore, that at this point the Bundesbank invoked their interpretation of the 1978 understanding that if the DM cannot be revalued the Bundesbank may legitimately refuse to intervene on the grounds that its monetary control is threatened. According to Neumann (1992), this clause had already been invoked in March 1983.

Over the weekend Bundesbank president Helmut Schlesinger reportedly sought to arrange a general realignment in return for a reduction in German interest rates. For reasons that remain unclear, a general realignment proved impossible to arrange. The Bundesbank then informed its partners that they should not expect further support when the markets reopened. Thus, by denying the German central bank its request for a DM revaluation, other countries subjected the Bundesbank to demands for intervention incompatible with its commitment to monetary stability. This prompted the German central bank to renounce its promise to intervene.

A complementary interpretation recalls the Bundesbank's opposition to the very idea of monetary union and then to a fixed date for its inauguration. It notes that the Bundesbank regarded monetary union as properly being the last step in a long process of convergence. It implies that the German central bank opposed a monetary union of more than a handful of strong-currency countries. In this view, the Bundesbank was far from devastated by events that drove countries like Italy and Britain from the EMS.

There is nothing incompatible about these two explanations. Both explain why unlimited support was not forthcoming in 1992 and make clear that governments cannot expect unlimited support in future crises.

THE WAY FORWARD: FEASIBLE AND INFEASIBLE OPTIONS

Where does the Community go from here? As we see it, the complete menu of options contains five entries. We list them in order of increasing likelihood.

Least likely is that the EC will succeed in completing the transition to EMU by proceeding as before. Our analysis makes clear that the events of September were more than a delayed reaction to a one-time shock. In addition they reflect intrinsic sources of instability that are still present. There remains ample scope for additional self-fulfilling speculative attacks repeatedly to destabilize the system until the transition to EMU is complete.

Marginally more likely is a shotgun wedding between Germany and France. If the two countries credibly commit to close harmonization of their monetary policies and to unlimited intervention of whichever currency weakens, the DM–FFr rate could provide a stable core to which other northern European currencies could attach themselves, creating a zone of exchange-rate stability. This scenario is implausible for political reasons, however, as Helmut Schlesinger emphasized in speech on 30 March 1993, Germany will not soon be given control of French policy, in the absence of which unlimited intervention is unpalatable to the Bundesbank. Germany can hardly be expected to grant a seat on the Bundesbank's board to a Bank of France official. Absent institutional innovations of this sort, a commitment to stabilize the DM–FFr rate can always be abandoned or reversed. Statements that the two governments 'desire' or 'intend' to stabilize the rate will not therefore be regarded as credible.

Only somewhat more likely is a quick move to EMU within the framework of the Maastricht Treaty. The treaty is commonly interpreted as implying that EMU cannot commence before 1 January 1997. In fact, it says that the European Monetary Institute and the Commission must report on who qualifies before the end of 1996, but nothing prevents them from reporting anytime after the inauguration of Stage II on 1 January 1994. In principle they can report on 2 January 1994. That a majority of EC countries must satisfy the convergence criterion is the binding constraint. Only six current EC members – Germany, France, Belgium, Denmark, Luxembourg and the Netherlands – are obvious candidates. Germany is likely to veto monetary union if it turns on the participation of a country like Ireland, Portugal or Spain with a recent history of exchange-rate instability and/or heavy debts. Admitting

Austria would help, but EC rules do not permit Austria to be considered on a separate track from Finland and Sweden.

More plausible in theory, though not in practice, is more exchange-rate flexibility over the transition. Wider bands would reduce the need for intervention and opportunities for speculative profits. The problem is that exchange-rate swings make the Common Agricultural Policy difficult to operate and create resentments due to import penetration and job shifting (witness the Hoover affair, when Hoover shifted jobs from Dijon to Scotland following sterling's depreciation). Large exchange-rate fluctuations are not tolerable for political economy reasons. Moreover, they exacerbate credibility problems. Wide bands provide scope for manipulating exchange rates; when the exchange rate drops it is not clear whether it is responding to market forces or if the government is pushing it down to steal a competitive advantage. More exchange-rate flexibility hardly seems the way to convince the markets that policy makers are really committed to less flexibility and ultimately to monetary union.

This leaves only one alternative: slowing down exchange markets. This solution has significant disadvantages, but it would bring to the exchange markets the kind of prudential regulation that exists on all other financial markets. Requiring that all open foreign exchange positions be matched, partly or fully, by a non-interest-bearing deposit with the central bank would amount to a tax on foreign exchange transactions (a 'Tobin tax'). An advantage of deposit requirements is that the implicit tax increases with the interest rate, therefore rising in times of foreign exchange market crisis. This device could not permanently support weak currencies, but it would provide time to organize orderly realignments, precisely the option not available in September 1992. Since it is not an administrative control, it would be permissible under the provisions of the Maastricht Treaty and the Single European Act.

A deposit requirement has disadvantages. It reduces the liquidity of the foreign exchange markets. This may discourage foreign investment and hinder efforts to develop on-shore financial centres.

We are not unaware of these drawbacks, which render us hesitant at best to recommend any form of restriction to capital movements. But we would emphasize that it is not enough for critics to point out the disadvantages of our proposal. They must offer an alternative. And they must show that their alternative is feasible. Proceeding as before is not. Neither are the other obvious options.

NOTES

1 In the second half of February 1993, we administered a questionnaire to all European traders listed in *The Currency and Instrument Directory* (1993). While some dealers may not be listed in this directory, it appears to come close to representing the population of foreign-exchange traders. We sent

out more than 500 questionnaires to all Europe-based individuals listed in the directory and got a response rate of 25 per cent.
2 Admittedly, the relevant protocol continues, 'In particular, the member state shall not have devalued its currency's bilateral central rate against any other member state's currency on its own initiative for the same period.' The 'on-its-own-initiative' proviso might provide a loophole permitting participation of some countries that were forced to devalue in 1992. But strong-currency countries like Germany would allow this loophole to determine the starting date of EMU only if it was crystal clear that the member state(s) in question satisfied the other convergence criteria. Projections for 1993, assuming no GDP growth in EC countries, show no country satisfying both the debt and deficit requirements. Spain and Portugal have projected budget deficits of more than 4 per cent, above the Treaty's 3 per cent reference value. Ireland's public debt remains 100 per cent of GDP, far above Maastricht's 60 per cent threshold. Unless these positions change dramatically, it seems unlikely that the 'own initiative' loophole would be allowed to determine the outcome.

REFERENCES

Bank Research Limited (1993), *Currency and Instrument Directory*, London, Bank Research Limited.
Eichengreen, Barry and Wyplosz, Charles (1993), 'The unstable EMS', *Brookings Papers on Economic Activity*, 1993:2.
Krugman, Paul (1979), 'A model of balance-of-payments crises', *Journal of Money, Credit and Banking*, 11, 311–325.
Neumann, Manfred (1992), 'Reflections on Europe's monetary constitution', *Central Banking*, 3, Winter 1992–93, 20–27.
Obstfeld, Maurice (1986), 'Rational and self-fulfilling balance-of-payments crises', *American Economic Review*, 86, 72–81.

11

A RETHINK FOR THE ECU?

Lord Cobbold

The main reasons for establishing the Ecu as a basket of existing currencies were:

1. To define a real value for the unit of account, in the absence of a central bank issuing Ecu. As a basket of defined quantities of each constituent currency, it could be put together and unbundled by the foreign exchange market.
2. To define a real interest rate which would be the weighted average of interest rates applicable to the constituent currencies.
3. To create a 'European' currency that was neutral in nationalistic terms.
4. To create a unit of account for accounting and settlement between Community institutions and governments.

The main achievements of the Ecu to date are:

1. The Ecu is widely used in Eurobond transactions.
2. Ecu Treasury Bills are issued by the Bank of England.
3. An Ecu clearing system is managed by commercial banks.
4. Ecu bank accounts and payment facilities are provided by banks.
5. The Ecu has on occasions established a market value that is independent from the sum of its constituent parts.
6. The Ecu is used as an accounting currency and for internal and external pricing by some European companies.

The Ecu's principal practical disadvantages are:

1. The Ecu is one more foreign currency (in addition to the existing 12 in the Community).
2. The Ecu is a 'political' hybrid – the 'Esperanto' factor.

3. The Ecu's value is not known outside professional circles.
4. There are no notes or coins in Ecu and no consumer goods are priced in Ecu.

Under the existing three-stage Maastricht plan for monetary union, the currency composition of the Ecu is fixed once the Treaty is ratified but its final value in terms of the other Community currencies will not be known until the close of business on the last business day before the beginning of Stage III, when its relationship with qualifying Stage III currencies will become fixed.

It will in theory be possible to issue notes and coins in Ecu before Stage III but it is hard to see them becoming widely used by consumers. For example, it is unlikely that banks and businesses will exchange Ecu notes and coins without charge to and from other currencies, given that values will be fluctuating in the open market.

It must also be remembered that there are considerable physical, cost and timing constraints to the introduction of notes and, in particular, coins. It is estimated that 200 coins are required per person making a total of 69 billion for the Community's 340 million population. These would take several years to mint.

The practical problems of introducing the Ecu as the new single currency for Europe under the existing Maastricht plans are such that the Ecu may well suffer the same fate as Esperanto earlier this century, unless some changes to the plans are made.

This chapter puts forward a two-point scheme to overcome the Ecu's difficulties:

1. Switch the definition of the basket in Stage II from fixed currency amounts to fixed percentage weights in the Ecu basket.
2. Fix the exchange rate of the Ecu to the DM from the beginning of Stage II at a whole number parity, namely DM1.00 = Ecu 1.00.

THESE SUGGESTIONS IN DETAIL

1. Article 109g of the Maastricht Treaty lays down that 'the currency composition of the Ecu basket shall not be changed'. This is usually interpreted to mean that the fixed currency amounts making up the Ecu are fixed from then on. If this is the case then suggestion 2 below cannot be realized. However, if the article is interpreted to mean that the percentage weight in the Ecu basket of each currency cannot be changed, then suggestion 2 becomes possible.

The difference is illustrated in Table 11.1. This lists the fixed currency amounts at the most recent official central rates effective from 29 January 1993 (rates for pound, lira and drachma are notional rates based on market rates at 29/1). Column (D) gives the equivalent exchange

Table 11.1 Ecu fixed currency amounts, central rates, % weighting and external value in DM at 29 January 1993

	(A) Fixed currency amount	(B) Ecu central rate	(C) % weight in Ecu basket	(D) Exchange rate v DM	(E) Value in DM
German mark	0.624200	1.952940	31.96	1.00000	0.6242
French franc	1.332000	6.549880	20.34	3.35390	0.3972
Italian lira	151.800000	1796.220000*	8.45	919.75200	0.1650
Dutch guilder	0.219800	2.200450	9.99	1.12670	0.1951
Belgian franc	3.431000	40.280200	8.52	20.62540	0.1663
Danish krone	0.197600	7.449340	2.65	3.81440	0.0518
Irish punt	0.008552	0.809996	1.06	0.41480	0.0206
Spanish peseta	6.885000	142.150000	4.84	72.78770	0.0946
UK pound	0.087840	0.808431*	10.87	0.41396 (2.4157)	0.2122
Greek drachma	1.440000	259.306000*	0.55	132.77700	0.0108
Portuguese escudo	1.393000	180.624000	0.77	92.48800	0.0151
			100.00		1.9529
A – currency amount fixed					
UK pound	0.08784	0.781176	11.24	0.4 (2.50)	0.2196
			100.37		1.9603
B – % weight fixed					
UK pound	0.08491	0.781176	10.87	0.4 (2.50)	0.2122
			100.00		1.9529

Notes: *notional central rates based on market rates of 29th January 1993; (A) = (B) × (C); (D) = (B) ÷ 1.95294; (E) = (A) ÷ (D).

rates versus the DM and column (E) gives the value of the fixed currency amounts in DM terms, totalling DM1.9529, i.e. the same as the DM/Ecu central rate.

Two sample scenarios are set out on the table, each assuming that the pound strengthens from 2.4157 to 2.5 versus the DM (0.41396 to 0.4 reciprocal). Everything else remains unchanged. In Example *A* the fixed currency amount is held constant at 0.08784. The result is that the percentage total moves to 100.37 and the Ecu value in DM terms rises to 1.9603, which is incompatible with the central rate of 1.95294.

In Example *B* the percentage weight in the basket is held constant and the currency amount therefore decreases to 0.08491 to compensate for the increased value of the pound. The percentage total remains at 100 and the Ecu value in DM terms remains at the central rate of 1.9529.

By holding the percentage weights constant and allowing the currency amounts to fluctuate, the Ecu becomes a function of the DM exchange rate, permitting implementation of suggestion 2.

2. The DM at 31.96 per cent has the largest percentage weighting in the Ecu basket. It is the dominant currency within the EMS and German interest rates provide the benchmark for other European rates.

The DM is the best-known currency in the Community. Apart from being the currency of the member state with the largest population (79 million or 23 per cent of the total), it is familiar to large numbers of people in neighbouring Holland, Belgium and Denmark and to travellers, traders and investors in all other member states. Without a full survey, the true figure cannot be established but a rough calculation suggests that at least 30 per cent of the Community's population is familiar with the value of the DM. This would compare with about 20 per cent for the pound, French franc and lira and 15 per cent for the peseta. The others would all rate less than 10 per cent, and the Ecu probably less than 1 per cent.

Prior to the September 1992 exchange rate crisis the Ecu central rate against the DM was 2.05586. Since 29 January 1993 it has been 1.95294. Fixing the DM/Ecu rate at 2.00 from the beginning of Stage II on 1 January 1994 would require only a very minor adjustment to the percentage weighting and the fixed currency amount. Once done, and given acceptance of suggestion 1 above, the Ecu would become fixed at DM 2.00.

Advantages of the scheme

1. The value of the Ecu becomes instantly recognizable to all who are familiar with the value of the DM.
2. German notes and coins would have an exact equivalent in Ecu terms.
3. New German notes and coins could be issued during Stage II showing both their DM and Ecu values.

4. The entire German note and coin issue would be valid and would aid the transitional process at the start of Stage III.
5. The 'basket' status of the Ecu is preserved but becomes largely cosmetic.

Possible disadvantages of the scheme

1. Would fixing the Ecu parity with the DM at 2.00 create problems for the German government and Bundesbank? Would they in any sense be underwriting the Ecu?

   To the extent that the Ecu is currently convertible, a holder of Ecu bonds or Ecu Treasury Bills can convert the proceeds into DM at a price within the existing ERM trading bands. The Bundesbank has an obligation to buy Ecu in the marketplace but can 'unbundle' its purchases with other member central banks. Under the new scheme the Ecu becomes a 'doppelmark'. The Ecu can no longer be devalued or revalued against the DM (although it will continue to fluctuate – within trading bands where applicable – against other member currencies). During Stage II member governments would underwrite the Ecu in proportion to their fixed percentage in the basket.

2. Would the scheme cause problems for the Ecu bond market?

   From the start of Stage II, Ecu bonds would become equivalent to DM bonds and any interest rate differentials would disappear. The spread of Ecu ten-year interest rates over German Bund rates narrowed to 0.4 per cent at the beginning of 1992 but bounced back to 2.2 per cent as a result of the 1992 EMS turmoil. It is now down again to 1.13 per cent. Given ratification of Maastricht in the UK and Denmark, it should fall further.

   The scheme would not therefore represent a radical step and should be popular with Ecu bond holders. It might be unpopular with Ecu borrowers, particularly in Italy. However, even under existing rules, Ecu borrowers in non-qualifying countries after the beginning of Stage III would face an Ecu tied to the DM. Furthermore, borrowers have benefited from the devaluation of the Ecu since September.

3. Would the scheme be regarded as an imposition of the DM and therefore be rejected by member governments and populations on nationalistic grounds?

   Inevitably there would be objections of this sort. However, there will be nationalistic objections about adopting the Ecu as a single currency under existing plans. At least the future value of the single currency would be clear from an earlier stage, which would assist enormously the whole transitional process. Government, banks and corporations would be able to start the planning and systems modification process at an earlier stage. Keeping the Ecu name (or adopting new names in some countries for the Ecu on the back of consumer polls) would soften the impact of DM imposition.

12

DETERMINANTS OF LONG-TERM INTEREST RATES IN SELECTED COUNTRIES: TOWARDS A EUROPEAN CENTRAL BANK POLICY DESIGN

Wolfgang Gebauer, Matthias Müller, Klaus J.W. Schmidt, Michael Thiel and Andreas Worms

INTRODUCTION

During the recent EMS crisis, interest rate policies were used in attempts to stabilize exchange rates: in countries with 'weak' currencies, monetary authorities increased the short-term money market rates to demonstrate their strong determination to defend existing parities as well as to discourage speculation financed by short-term loans. France succeeded with such a strategy. Other countries failed, with consequences ranging from 'temporarily' leaving the Exchange Rate Mechanism (ERM) (Italy and the United Kingdom), or 'enforced' devaluations (Spain and Portugal). On the other hand, the country with the – so far – strongest currency, i.e. Germany, lowered its short-term rates for the DM in an attempt to cooperate with the exchange rate stabilization efforts of European partner countries, and to react to the slowdown of economic activity at home as well as abroad. It should be noted that the official Bundesbank policy design still in formal existence, i.e. monetary targeting to secure price stability, would have required the contrary – an increase in money market interest rates.

These hints on recent 'monetary history' in Europe suffice to justify a scientific analysis of the role of short-term interest rates in order to derive policy-oriented lessons. In the present chapter we focus on short-term interest rates as determinants of long-term interest rates in selected European countries. This is, of course, a very narrow question. But our attempt to quantify the relative importance of short-term interest rates in such a limited sense nevertheless carries enormous weight, as it tackles the centrepiece of the process by which the effects of financial policies and events are transmitted to the 'real' side of the economy. The following study is, therefore, meant as a contribution to our understanding of the 'monetary' transmission process in selected EMS member countries.

As we are focusing on such a small slice of the rather complex issue of monetary transmission, it is necessary to state, at the very outset, the main insights on which the following research has been based. They are summarized in the following three points; the last one contains the 'real' justification for our question in terms of the monetary transmission process.

1. All monetary authorities in the EMS employ operating procedures for short-term interest rates on the domestic money market in order to implement their policy decisions. As a result, nominal money market interest rates are effectively controlled by central bank interest rate and bank liquidity measures. Therefore, we take the short-term interest rate, empirically represented by the three-month money market rate, as exogenously given in the sense of a policy-controlled magnitude, being determined outside our theoretical and empirical analysis.
2. In a European context, the German money market rate has been of particular importance due to the functional asymmetry within the ERM, at least during our investigation period (until December 1992). German interest rate policy has tended, in other words, to dominate money market rates in the partner countries.[1] More recently, and very likely for the foreseeable future, French interest rate policy will gain comparable importance, too. Therefore, our results for Germany and France will be interpreted with specific care, in particular as regards policy conclusions.
3. Recent research results on the newly rediscovered old issue of the monetary transmission process concern the effects of a changing relationship between nominal short-term and long-term interest rates on economic activity, i.e. on the business cycle, on employment, and on prices. Evidence for several countries suggests that this relationship, i.e. the term structure ('spread') of interest rates, has a strong predictive power for economic activity, which outperforms conventional existing explanations.[2] As the 'short end' of the spread is the money market rate controlled by monetary authorities, there is, at least in principle, a clear responsibility of central banks for business cycle developments. In short: interest rate policies of central banks are far from being 'neutral'.[3]

Based on these three 'fundamentals', we proceed in this chapter as follows: Next we discuss theoretical aspects of the relationship between short-term and long-term interest rates, together with some non-technical modelling considerations (for a detailed and more formal exposition, see Appendix 1). Our empirical results follow, together with suggested interpretations for Germany (D), France (F), the United Kingdom (GB), Italy (I), the Netherlands (NL) and Spain (E). The country sample has been put together with regard to data considerations; omitted countries limit, of course, the scope of our findings. Nevertheless, we cover all three types of 'currency behaviour' during the last EMS crisis: Stable (D, F, NL), devalued but remaining in the system (E), and devalued 'drop outs' (GB, I). Finally, we advance some conclusions on interest rates, economic activity and central bank policy.

THEORY

Variables

In theory, the nominal long-term rate of interest (RL) on the domestic financial capital market is supposed to be determined by the following magnitudes:

Domestic short-term interest rate (RS)
In the absence of market segmentation due to differing time to maturity, the long-term rate RL should be related to the short-term rate RS by interest rate arbitrage, eventually augmented by risk or liquidity premia for different times to maturity. An increase in the short-term interest rate should lead to a higher long-term rate, and vice versa (term structure effect). The argument is dealt with in the context of several versions of the term structure theory of interest rates. For example, according to the expectation hypothesis, the long-term interest rate RL depends solely on the expected evolution of the short-term interest rate. Other theories of the term structure also suggest a dependence of RL on the short-term interest rate, but allow for further variables of influence, too.

Real economic activity
Stronger economic activity (e.g. measured by industrial production IPX) should lead to higher loan demand to finance additional physical capital formation, thus tending to increase the price (interest rate) of long-term loans (and vice versa for recessions). Hence, a positive effect of economic activity on the long-term interest rate is postulated (real income effect). However, a reverse causation, running from interest rates to economic activity, may be suggested as well. Therefore, we are uncertain as regards sign and significance of a real income effect.

Inflationary expectations
According to Fisher, the nominal rate of interest should contain a premium for expected inflation in order to compensate for the foreseen decline in purchasing power of the unit of account.[4] Hence, increased inflationary expectations should lead, in theory, to an immediate increase in nominal interest rates of the same magnitude, and vice versa for falling inflationary expectations (Fisher effect). However, such an

effect may already be incorporated in the term structure effect, i.e. in the influence of the short-term nominal rate RS. Therefore, we are uncertain as regards the significance of a separate Fisher effect on the long-term interest rate, in addition to the structure effect.

Money stock

It is argued that monetary authorities, by directly influencing the monetary base, are controlling the money stock as well, given a reasonably stable money multiplier. If the growth of the money stock is expanded, the increased 'liquidity' is said to lower rates, and vice versa for a reduction in money stock growth. We are most sceptical of this liquidity effect, as the chain of causation runs, if at all, the other way round (see Introduction above, point 1). In addition, we would rather favour an endogenous money stock approach (see below).

Foreign short-term interest rates

Due to exchange rate expectations, risk considerations and/or specific currency preferences, international capital flows may be induced, which in turn will affect the domestic long-term interest rate. We postulate that the three-month Euro-$ interest rate (*RUS*) will take account of such influence, as exchange-rate expectations for the domestic currency should be reflected in the relevant foreign short-term interest rates. This view is based on the uncovered interest rate parity theorem. Hence, we will test for an interest parity effect: A higher foreign interest rate should induce a higher domestic (long-term) rate, and vice-versa for lower rates.

Market segmentation

The postulated effects of the short-term rates *RS* and *RUS* on the long-term rate *RL* deserve a closer look, as they involve three interrelated aspects: the associated risk, the time to maturity and the respective country (i.e. the respective currency). According to these aspects, three types of financial market segmentation can be identified:

1. Between different assets with the same time to maturity due to different risk characteristics (e.g. government and corporate bonds in a national capital market are not perfect substitutes for each other).
2. Between (otherwise homogeneous) assets of different time to maturity due to differing time preferences and/or production periods.
3. Between different national financial markets due to exchange rate risk and differing national institutional settings (e.g. investors are not indifferent between investing in French or in Brazilian currency).

Concerning segmentation type 1 we expect arbitrage to be sufficient to allow the long-term interest rate on government bonds *RL* to be interpreted as a representative interest rate on long-term capital.[5]

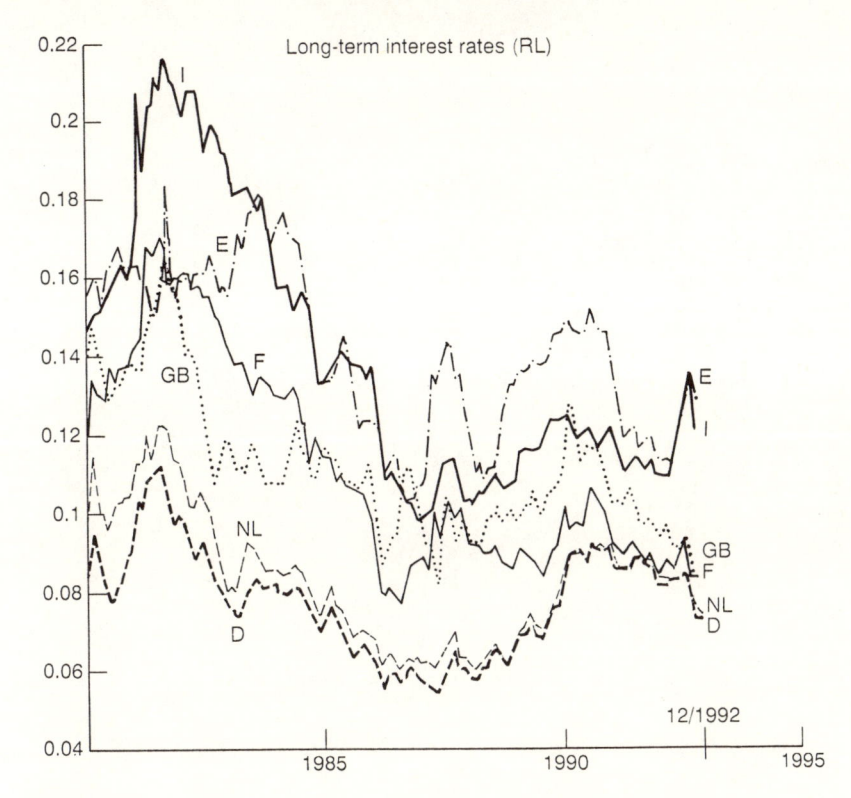

Figure 12.1 Long-term interest rates in selected European capital markets

Concerning segmentation type 2 we interpret the short-term money market rate *RS* as mainly influenced by the central bank (see Introduction above). Within the transmission of monetary policy, shifts of the short-term interest rate should induce movements of the long-term interest rate *RL* which – according to our assumption that there is no segmentation of type 1 – represents the price equilibrating demand and supply of financial capital.

Concerning segmentation type 3, i.e. the relation between interest rates of different countries (resp. different currencies), a large discrepancy should not occur if the participants in the respective national capital markets expect irrevocably fixed exchange rates according to the Maastricht Treaty. But although a convergence of interest rates can be found, Figures 12.1 and 12.2 show that there are still considerable differences.

From a theoretical point of view, such discrepancies deserve particular attention, as out assumption of UIP ('uncovered interest parity') together with a credible announcement of irrevocably fixed

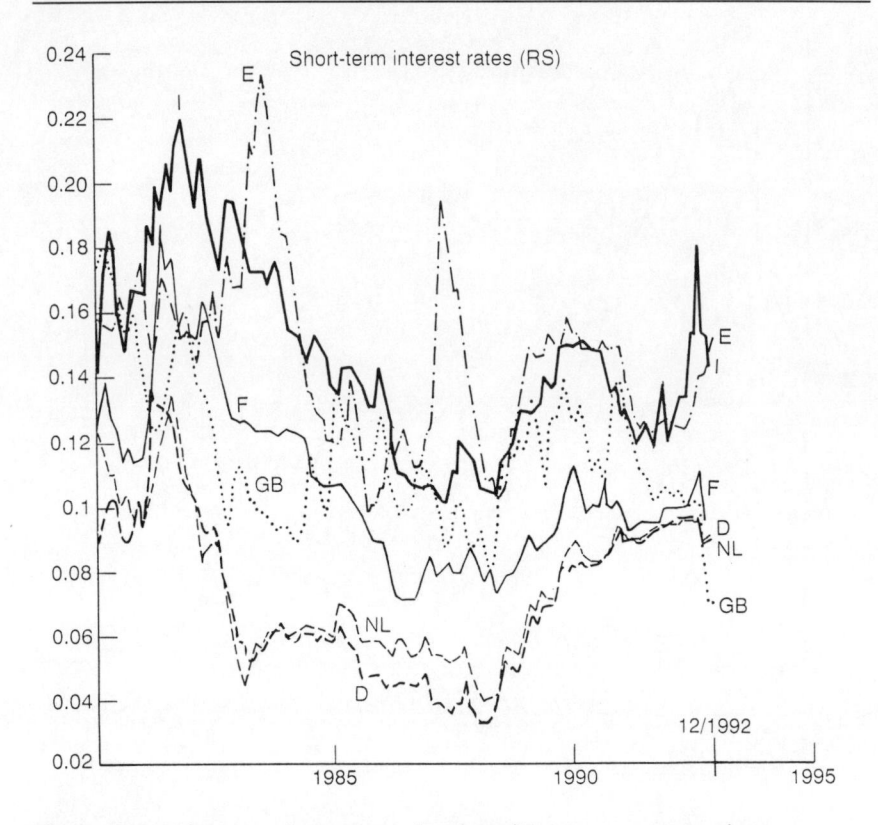

Figure 12.2 Short-term interest rates in selected European money markets

exchange rates should rule out such interest rate differences on assets with the same time to maturity and default risk. Therefore, the observed discrepancies between interest rates in Figures 12.1 and 12.2 can be explained (1) by expectations of future realignments and/or (2) by imperfect interest rate arbitrage between national financial markets.

1. Recent discussion of the Maastricht convergence criteria may lead market participants to expect a 'softening' concerning these criteria for entry into the third stage of EMU. But this in turn raises speculation on the time of entry of specific countries. Therefore, it seems that interest rates in countries like Italy or Spain incorporate a premium for the risk of not qualifying for EMU in the 'first round' and for a non-credible exchange rate policy.[6]
2. The integration of national markets to one European financial market has not yet been fully completed. Domestic firms often finance themselves with domestic resources only, and even large banks still operate mainly in their home country, as barriers to

market entry still exist.[7] This might suggest, that a shock in one country (e.g. a policy action by the national central bank) does not necessarily lead to strong reaction in capital markets abroad (segmentation type 3). In addition, it can be observed that firms in different countries prefer different forms of financing. Hence, arbitrage between national capital markets still appears to be imperfect.

As regards our research, we expect that changes in the short-term interest rate will imply different consequences for the various national capital markets in our European country sample: dissimilarities in market structures should find their expression in distinguishable determinants of the long-term interest rate.

Modelling considerations

In order to derive a testable empirical model, we use a comparatively new econometric modelling strategy – the 'LSE-approach'. Our basic motivation for the choice is twofold.

First, this new approach does not require specification, at the very outset of our analysis, of the 'right' theoretical model in order to derive testable implications as well as theoretically interpretable results. After all, this 'right' model is unknown anyway. Instead, we derive an empirical model by applying a general-to-specific modelling sequence. This means that we begin by formulating a general model in order to impose a few restrictions on the data generating process (DGP), a shorthand for the unknown mechanism which actually generated the observed data, a priori. This model comprises, in our case, all possible determinants of the long-term interest rate as outlined above. Therefore, it contains a most comprehensive economic content in view of existing theory.

Second, we hold that economic theory should describe and explain long-run phenomena as distinct from short-term impacts and events. This applies, in particular, to central bank policies and financial markets and events; continuity and longer-term strategies require corresponding research concepts. In essence, we are less interested to reveal the short-term factors which may have pushed away the EMS from its earlier 'equilibrium' position. Such a task can be, and meanwhile has been, handled by policy institutions like the EEC monetary committee, the Bank for International Settlements, or European central banks. Instead, we want to concentrate on those forces which *tend to push a phenomenon* (like the long-term interest rate in our case) *back to its long-run equilibrium* after a 'shock'.

This second motivation is justified by the idea that certain pairs (or even higher-dimensional vectors) of economic variables 'belong together' in the long run due to a causal relationship. A monetarist, for example, would argue that the money stock and the price level are such a pair of variables which should not diverge from each other by too large an extent. For the research presented here, we have chosen the short-term and long-term rates of interest, RS and RL, as such a pair of long-run related variables, with RS being possibly supplemented by further explanatory variables (see above). We suppose, for example, that RS and RL may drift away from each other in the short run such that their difference, the spread, will show a positive or a negative sign, implying a positive or 'inverse' yield curve. However, we hold that in the long run, given all particulars like market segmentation, there are economic forces which always tend to bring both rates together again, in the sense of a 'normal', long-run, equilibrium relationship.

In order to implement this view econometrically, the concepts of cointegration and error correction are utilized within the LSE methodology. The detailed modelling approach is explained in the Appendix. In the following, we present a condensed and less formal exposition.

To begin with, we formulated a fairly general model which explains the long-term interest rate by its own past history, the current and lagged short-term rate, and all other current and lagged variables as suggested by theory (see above). This so-called Autoregressive Distributed Lag (ADL) model was then statistically tested and repeatedly respecified in order to extract given explanatory power from a formulation as simple as possible. Particular attention was paid to the long-run, 'equilibrium' relationship between the level of the long-term interest rate RL, and the levels of the explanatory variables. Technically speaking, we checked for cointegration of variables.[8]

As a result, we arrived at a static long-run (or 'cointegrating') equation; the coefficients of this equation – the Ks – describe the equilibrium relation between RL, RS and those other Z^j-variables which proved to have a significant long-run effect in the ADL model (* denotes equilibrium values). Our notion of long-run equilibrium implies a static solution: no variable has a tendency to move away from its actual magnitude:

$$RL^* = K_1 \cdot RS^* + \sum_{j=1}^{J} K_{j+1} \cdot Z^{j*} + K_0. \qquad (1)$$

The deviation of the actual value of RL at time t and the equilibrium value RL^* as implied by the actual values of the explanatory variables RS and Z^j is termed 'equilibrium error' or 'error correction mechanism' (ECM). The greater the absolute value of ECM, the more is RL away from its equilibrium value:

$$ECM_t = RL_t - RL_t^* = RL_t - \left\{ K_1 \cdot RS_t + \sum_{j=1}^{J} K_{j+1} \cdot Z_t^j + K_0 \right\}. \qquad (2)$$

In the case of cointegration, ECM represents a *stationary* linear combination of the respective variables, i.e. the ECM cannot drift anywhere as time goes by but has an inherent tendency to revert to its mean value = 0; hence, *RL*, *RS* and Z^j cannot drift too far apart and *RL* is pushed back towards its long-run equilibrium value.

As our cointegrated variables have an error correction representation, we finally arrived at the following error correction model:

$$\Delta RL_t = \beta_1 \cdot \Delta RS_t + \sum_{j=1}^{J} \beta_{j+1} \cdot \Delta Z_t^j + \gamma \cdot ECM_{t-1} + L + \varepsilon_t \qquad (3)$$

where Z^j are our explanatory variables in addition to *RS*, *ECM* is the – already known – stationary linear combination of the levels of *RL*, *RS*, and the Z^j variables, *L* denotes higher order lags of the first differences of *RL*, *RS* and Z^j variables, and ε_t represents a stochastic error term. The parameters of our error correction model can be associated with three distinct effects as regards time horizon and adjustment process:

1. the short-run- (or 'differences'-) effect associated with the βs: how does the long-term interest rate change immediately in reaction to a contemporary change of the short-term interest rate (and/or, eventually, further (weakly) exogenous variables)? This is called the *'impact effect'*;
2. the long-run (or 'levels') effect associated with the *K*s: how does the long-term interest rate have to change in reaction to a change in the short-term interest rate and/or further (weakly) exogenous variables, such that long-run equilibrium is restored? This is called the *'long-run response'*;
3. if the long-run response differs from the impact effect, equilibrium is not achieved immediately after a disturbance, but adjustment takes time. A constant fraction γ of the lagged equilibrium error (the difference between the actual and the equilibrium long-term interest rate, or a 'weighted' long–short spread) is eliminated each period, motivating the expression 'error correction'. This is called *'feedback effect'*.

To sum up, we derived our final error correction model in four steps. First, the various estimates and associated tests of the ADL model were conducted to gain evidence on the information content of the variables (long-run and/or short-run information, or no information at all). Second, we estimated the cointegration equation (by OLS) and tested *ECM* for stationarity. Third, this *ECM* was inserted into a general error correction model, which was estimated (again by OLS) using appropriately transformed variables. Fourth, this model was simplified in a general-to-specific modelling sequence.

Table 12.1 Estimated coefficients of the error correction model

	Impact effect $\Delta RS_t \downarrow \Delta RL_t$ β_1	Long-run response $RS_t \downarrow RL^*$ K_1	Feed-back effect $ECM_{t-1} \downarrow \Delta RL_t$ γ	$\Delta RUS \downarrow \Delta RL_t$ β_2	$RUS \downarrow RL^*$ K_2	$\Delta\Delta_{12}pc \downarrow \Delta RL_t$ β_3	$RSD \downarrow RL^*$ K_3	$\Delta\Delta_{12}p \downarrow \Delta RL_t$ β_4	$\Delta_{12}p \downarrow RL^*$ K_4
D	0.26	0.44	−0.09	0.09	0.07	0.14	–	n.s.	n.s.
NL	0.39	0.60	−0.09	0.14	0.27	n.s.	n.s.	0.13	n.s.
F	0.30	0.45	−0.12	n.s.	n.s.	n.s.	n.s.	n.s.	0.40
I	0.29	0.48	−0.29	n.s.	n.s.	n.s.	n.s.	0.20	0.54
GB	0.39	n.s.	−0.10	0.08	0.39	n.s.	0.18	0.09	n.s.
E	0.32	0.33	−0.10	0.35	0.59	n.s.	0.27	n.s.	n.s.

Notes: The coefficients β_i, K_i and γ refer to the model specification (3) resp. (A.10) in Appendix 1; 'n.s.' means not significant at 5% significance level. For a detailed definition of all variables, see Appendix 3; small letters denote natural logarithms.

EVIDENCE

Main Results

Table 12.1 contains the most important estimated coefficients for the various countries. Detailed information on all coefficients of the models is given in Appendix 1 together with the relevant (misspecification-) test-statistics.

Despite considerable differences in the financial environment of the countries considered here, the most important of the estimated parameters are surprisingly similar. In all countries, the *impact effect* of the short-term on the long-term interest rate is around 0.3, ranging from 0.26 (Germany) to 0.39 (Netherlands, United Kingdom). Except Spain and the United Kingdom, the long-run response is considerably larger, ranging from 0.44 (Germany) to 0.60 (Netherlands). In Spain, the long-run response is 0.33 which is only marginally greater than the impact effect (0.32). In the United Kingdom though, there is no significant long-run response, suggesting strong segmentation of the markets for long- and short-term assets (segmentation type 2). In all countries except Italy, the feedback effect roughly amounts to 0.1 (0.09 in Germany and the Netherlands to 0.12 in France). In Italy, the feedback effect is 0.29; this may reflect larger opportunity costs of non-adjusting in a highly inflationary environment.

Besides the short-term interest rate, *further variables* affect the long-term interest rate: in all countries except France and Italy, the Euro-$ interest rate has both a long- and a short-run effect on the long-term interest rate. The effect is rather weak in Germany (0.09 = impact effect, 0.07 = long-run response), stronger in the Netherlands (0.14, 0.27) and the United Kingdom (0.08, 0.39) at least as regards the long-run response, and strongest in Spain (0.35, 0.59).

In countries which were outside the EMS most of the time, the German interest rate has a significant long-run effect: 0.18 in the United Kingdom and 0.27 in Spain. In all countries except Germany and Spain, the observed rate of inflation has an additional influence on the long-term interest rate. This effect is strongest in Italy: the impact effect is 0.2 and the long-run effect is 0.54. In France, only a significant long-run effect (0.4) can be observed, whereas in the Netherlands and the United Kingdom the rate of inflation only has a significant short-run effect (0.13 resp. 0.09). The nominal short-term interest rate may already contain information on inflationary expectations as stated by Fisher's theorem; hence our inflation effect should be due to an additional information content of the observed rate of inflation itself.

In Germany, a change of the growth rate of private credits positively affects the long-term interest rate (impact effect = 0.14). Such an effect was not significant in the other countries.

Interpretation

Following the general-to-specific procedure only a few variables proved to possess significant influence on *RL*. Quantity variables like income proxies, monetary and credit aggregates play no or only a minor role in determining long-term interest rates. This concentration on price variables (such as interest rates and price levels) indicates that there is no evidence for segmented capital markets in the sense of type 3 for the respective countries.

Despite domestic *RS*, further determinants of *RL* are the rate of inflation ($\Delta_{12}p$), the Euro-$ (*RUS*) and the German short-term interest rate (*RSD*). These variables indicate the existence of time-varying exchange risk premia.

According to the determinant of the long-run equilibrium rate *RL**, we suggest differentiation between three groups of countries within our sample:

Germany and the Netherlands: de facto monetary union

Germany and the Netherlands have in common that the domestic short-term interest rate and the Euro-$ interest rate solely determine *RL* in the long run. The long-term interest rate is mainly influenced by central bank activity (via *RS*) and international capital flows (via *RUS*) as a reflex of flexible exchange rates towards the rest of the world. Both countries have completely open capital markets and are founding members of the EMS. The impact effects (β_1, β_2) and the long-run responses (K_1 and K_2) in the Netherlands are larger than in Germany; this may indicate a larger volatility of the smaller Dutch capital market. We cannot exclude a risk premium in the short run, depending on the current rate of inflation in the case of the Netherlands.

In Germany, however, we observe a positive short-run effect of the growth-rate of private loans on *RLD* (see β_3), which can be interpreted as a (positive) interest-rate effect of (positive) credit-demand shocks

The lowest value of γ can be found in Germany and the Netherlands. γ describes the speed of adjustment of *RL* to *RL** (if no further disturbance occurs) and therefore the speed with which *ECM* moves towards zero. This can be interpreted as follows: In an uncertain environment it is more costly not to adjust to the (often) changing state of the world than in a traditionally stable environment where frequent adjustment is less necessary. Therefore, collecting relevant information is more promising in an uncertain world than in a relatively certain one, in which the probability of a changing environment is smaller. A change in the 'state of the world' will then first be noticed by the economic agents in an uncertain environment, while it will be detected later in a traditionally stable environment, thus leading to a lagged, slower speed of adjustment. If this holds true, the expected returns of collecting information about the 'state of the world' in Germany and the Netherlands are relatively small.

France and Italy: lacking credibility in the past
In France and Italy the domestic short-term interest rate and the rate of inflation determine the equilibrium long-term interest rate. We found no significant influence of foreign interest rates. The insignificance of *RUS* in the models of France and Italy might reflect efficient capital flow controls being in force during a considerable part of the sample period. In France and Italy the rate of inflation carries information about the path of *RL* independent of the information already contained in the nominal short-term interest rate.

This gives reason to assume that there exists a risk premium, as the long-run rate of inflation might be higher than the actual one.[9] Therefore, it was probably doubted that both countries would get inflation under permanent control. The rate of inflation as an additional long-term determinant of *RL* can be seen as a proxy for an exchange rate premium, reflecting the risk of devaluation in the sense of purchasing power parity.

There are differing results for both countries, too. On the one hand, the parameters are higher for Italy than for France, indicating a higher risk premium for Italy. Moreover, we observed no impact effect of the rate of inflation in France; this might be interpreted as a credibility advantage of French stabilization policy. While for France γ is slightly higher than the average value of all other countries (excluding Italy), the highest value for γ can be observed in Italy: the expected returns of collecting information about the 'state of the world' are high in this country.

The United Kingdom and Spain: outside a 'credibility zone' of the EMS
The information content of the German short-term interest rate (*RSD*) has already been incorporated in the domestic short-term interest rates of those countries joining the ERM together with Germany. The United Kingdom and Spain, however, entered the exchange rate mechanism relatively late. Therefore, it seems reasonable to find an additional influence of *RSD* on the long-term rates in both countries (*RLGB* and *RLE*), reflecting a relatively large degree of flexibility in their exchange rate system during our investigating period. In the United Kingdom and Spain, shifts in *RSD* directly caused the anticipation of devaluation. In contrast, no such effect occurred in France and Italy.[10]

Positive shifts in *RSD* raise long-term interest rates in both countries, which underlines the so far dominant German position. Surprisingly, *RSGB* was not significant in determining the British capital market rate in the long run. We suppose two factors to be responsible for this result: the dominance of international capital flows in London, and structural impediments in the domestic transmission of changing interest rates in Great Britain – there is a direct influence on discount houses only, as additional intermediaries on the monetary markets of the United Kingdom (firms in the United Kingdom are more market oriented than firms in Germany which rely heavily on banks).

In both countries the γ-values are within their average ranges, indicating similar costs of adjustment as in the other countries (except Italy). As in the Netherlands, the rate of inflation has a short-run impact on the long-term interest rate.

In all countries, movements in the short-term interest rate induce less than proportional shifts in the equilibrium long-term interest rate. As regards theory consistency, the static long-run results are at odds with the expectations theory which would require a slope coefficient insignificantly different from one. Thus, our findings are consistent with the empirical literature rejecting the expectations theory.[11] In the static long-run equilibrium, the term premium – the long minus the short-term interest rate – depends, *inter alia*, on the level of short-term interest rates, i.e. it is not a constant, but grows as short-term interest rates fall and vice versa.

CONCLUSION: INTEREST RATES, ECONOMIC ACTIVITY, AND CENTRAL BANK POLICY

We expected to discover different relations of long-term and short-term interest rates according to the hypothesis of market segmentation within the different countries as well as between them. Surprisingly, we found remarkably similar relations in the short as well as in the long run. Except in the case of the United Kingdom, the short-term interest rate proved to be an important magnitude in determining the level of nominal interest rates in the long run. To be sure, there are additional domestic and foreign factors of significant influence. Nevertheless, central bank policy definitively has to accept, as a result, responsibility for the longer-term developments of nominal interest rates on capital markets, and not only on the (short-term) money markets. This finding holds despite a substantially differing environment of institutional details in which central bank policy is conducted in the European countries under investigation.

What does such responsibility mean? Answering the question amounts to judging the role of the interest rate spread, as well as the role of the short-term and the long-term interest rates separately, in the transmission process of central bank policy. In economic theory, there are several views to suppose and explain a causal relationship running from interest rates to economic activity.[12] The conventional view holds that it is the long-term rate which, in comparison to some expected rate of return on physical capital, matters most for economic activity. Therefore, on this broad theoretical argument, our results stipulate that central banks, via their influence on the long-term interest rate, should accept a – maybe uncomfortably broad – responsibility for business cycle activity.

However, recent information on the magnitude and timing of interest rate effects in European countries is basically lacking. An attempt to get answers deserves a study of its own. Nevertheless, as a first step, it may be checked whether the causal relationship running from interest rates to economic activity can be sustained empirically. To get a better 'feeling' for the overall importance of our results, we therefore finally conducted causality tests for our European country sample, by asking whether (a) the interest rate spread, (b) the long-term capital market rate, and (c) the short-term money market rate each had a separate, significant causal effect on industrial production during our investigation period.[13] The results were mixed. For Germany, we found that our specific version of the spread between long-term and short-term interest rates has an econometric causal effect on domestic production: a larger positive spread (a steeper yield curve) causes higher industrial production, and vice versa. This result confirms the already existing evidence for Germany (see Introduction, point 3). In France and the United Kingdom, it was the short-term rate which showed a strong, and negative causal impact on domestic production. The UK result is particularly interesting, as it suggests an interest rate effect despite the non-existent link between short-term and long-term rates. In Italy, Spain and the Netherlands, our preliminary search for causality was futile.

The reason for the different roles played by interest rates in relation to economic activity may be found in a more extensive analysis of the investment and financing decisions of enterprises and financial intermediaries. Theory and evidence taken from corporate finance demonstrate that enterprises do not behave in the naive way assumed by macroeconomic theory in general. Informational and incentive arguments give a closer insight of financial instruments.[14] Industrial economics, on the other hand, suggests that if an enterprise has to regard the behaviour of potential newcomers in an oligopolistic market, investment decisions have to be modified, too. A simple calculation of net present values is no longer sufficient; strategic consideration and sunk costs have also to be taken into account.[15]

Two main policy implications emerge. First, central bank policies of the two countries presently dominating the ERM group, France and Germany, have real effects at home: falling short-term money market rates tend to stimulate their economies at home, and vice-versa. Given the dominance of both countries in Europe, such real effects may be 'exported' to the rest of the present ERM group – unless the linkage is cut by an exchange rate realignment or a departure from the exchange rate system. Both possibilities for 'escape' have been practised during the recent EMS crisis, thus a certain degree of policy autonomy in the devaluing and/or leaving countries. This is the presently accepted view resp. interpretation of short-term adjustment possibilities within the EMS.

Second, and related to our first point, there are longer-term implications for central bank stabilization policies. After all, we have meanwhile to face a general consent that the ultimate goal of price stability should be pursued with priority, on a national and a European level. In particular, it is generally accepted that responsibility for a stable price level rests with central banks, due to their alleged ability to control the growth of the stock of money. It is exactly this point which introduces a potential conflict with exchange-rate and/or business cycle policy intentions, as it is again the short-term interest rate which is used as central instrument ('lever') for attempting money stock control. The German example gives a striking recent example for this conflict: In order to reduce monetary growth, the Bundesbank tried to increase money market rates in autumn 1992, due to its pragmatic monetarist policy design still in use. But stimulating the economy, and cooperating within the ERM, required just the opposite: a policy of lowering short-term rates. At least in times of inflationary discrepancies and tensions, the instrument of interest rate policy cannot serve two conflicting purposes at the same time.

Our suggestion for a way out, and at the same time our proposal for a future European central bank policy design, is based on two main points:

1. Inflation is the result of a comprehensive policy mix, comprising not just central bank policy, but fiscal policy and income policy as well. Hence, the central bank should not be held responsible for inflation alone. This point has repeatedly been emphasized in the past by the Deutsche Bundesbank. It implies, for example, that fiscal policy will cause inflation in certain policy mix situations. Germany 1992/93 is an example of moderate inflation due to fiscal influences. Russia or Brazil 1992 as well as Germany 1922/23 provide examples of hyperinflation caused by the fiscal policy stance.

2. Monetary targeting has been downgraded in Western countries during the past decade. The reasons were, on the one hand, exactly the conflict of policy aims just mentioned. On the other hand, we had to register worldwide difficulties to define and control 'the' stock of money due to financial innovation and liberalization processes in financial markets. Indeed, there are good reasons to regard the money stock as an endogenous magnitude, being determined by interacting portfolio decisions of banks and their non-bank customers.[16] Therefore, the present policy design of 'pragmatic monetarism' still in official use is open to serious doubts. Our results, as well as recent research,[17] point to another, more promising policy design, which would in principle avoid the present policy conflict: to choose the term structure of interest rates, instead of the money stock, as the main indicator for central bank policy effects on economic activity.[18]

APPENDIX 1: ERROR CORRECTION MODELS FOR THE LONG-TERM INTEREST RATE ON SELECTED EUROPEAN CAPITAL MARKETS

Notation of variables

The notation of variables and operators is as follows: capital letters (X_t) denote the original value of variable X observed at time t, small letters denote the natural logarithm of the variable ($x = \ln X$) Every variable X is marked by the respective country code, i.e. Germany – D, France – F, Italy – I, Spain – E, the Netherlands – NL and the United Kingdom – GB. L^n is the lag-operator, defined as $L^n X_t = X_{t-n}$; Δ_n^d is the difference operator, defined as $\Delta_n^d = (1 - L^n)^d$; if n or d are equal to 1, they are dropped. Notice that $\Delta_{12} x$ can be interpreted as an annual growth rate of variable X. $a^m(L) = a_0 L^0 + a_1 L^1 + \ldots + a_m L^m$ is a polynomial in the lag-operator with m being the highest lag.

Empirical methodology: aspects of the LSE approach[19]

DATA GENERATING PROCESS

One of the basic concepts of the LSE-approach is the data generating process (DGP), a shorthand for the unobservable mechanism which actually generated the observed data. The DGP can be expressed as the joint density function of 'all' variables, i.e. somewhat informally, $D(S)$ with S being a row vector of variables. S can be divided into (X,M), with X being the 'relevant' variables and M being the 'marginalized' variables which are assumed to have no impact on the phenomenon under study (in this case: the volatility of long-term interest rates RL in selected European countries). Economic theory might give hints which variables are relevant (e.g. short-term interest rates RS) and which are irrelevant (e.g. number of sheep in Iceland). The 'irrelevant' variables are left outside; this first step from the DGP to an estimable empirical model is labelled 'marginalizing'. Next, we separate the variables X into endogenous and (weakly) exogenous variables.[20] This second step is called 'conditioning'. Again, economic theory might suggest which variable can be conditioned on which, as conditioning implies an assumption about the direction of causality. Here, for example, the expectation theory of the term structure of interest rates suggests that RL is an average of current and expected short-term interest rates and, hence, RL should be conditioned on RS. Of course, as mentioned above, further valid conditioning variables are likely to exist, which we label $Z^1, Z^2, \ldots Z^j$ (j=number of further valid conditioning variables). Obvious candidates, are, as mentioned in the text (see pp.191–192), the rate of inflation, economic activity, monetary aggregates, foreign interest rates, and so on.

Thus we get

$$X = (RL, RS, Z^1, Z^2, \ldots Z^j)$$

and

$$D(RL, RS, Z^1, Z^2, \ldots Z^j) = D(RL\,|\,RS, Z^1, Z^2, \ldots Z^j) \cdot D(RS, Z^1, Z^2, \ldots Z^j),$$

with the conditional distribution being the regression model and the marginal distribution being the exogenous process.

GENERAL-TO-SPECIFIC MODELLING

The ultimate goal is an empirical model which parsimoniously (i.e. with a small number of parameters) describes the essential features of the DGP and remains reasonably constant over time. Because an empirical model is thought of as being derived from the DGP through a reduction sequence of marginalizations, transformations and restrictions, it seems extremely unlikely that one specific ad hoc model can be a valid simplification of the DGP. Therefore, the starting point should be a fairly general model, thus imposing few restrictions on the DGP a priori, and to simplify it step-by-step through testable restrictions and transformations. If we can accept the general model and the restrictions imposed, we can also accept the specific model. Hence, the so called *general-to-specific modelling sequence*[21] starts with a general model with an unsystematic (white noise innovation) error term not containing any valuable information, and the marginalization should be monitored by (a) testing the validity of restrictions imposed, and (b) tests of whether the error term does not start to contain valuable information.

NON-STATIONARITY OF VARIABLES

The following subsections formalize this modelling approach and simultaneously account for a common problem in time series econometric non-stationarity.[22] Economic time series often violate the usual stationarity assumptions about variables, which are necessary for statistical inferences associated with standard estimation techniques such as ordinary least squares (OLS). In particular, variables often are integrated, i.e. they have to be differenced to become stationary.[23] A variable which has to be differenced d times to be stationary is called integrated of order d, or I(d). Because integrated variables need a special treatment, a test for the order of integratedness of the variables involved is necessary prior to modelling. The well known Dickey–Fuller-type tests[24] (DF, DF_C, $DF_{C,T}$, ADF_n, $ADF_{n,C}$, $ADF_{n,C,T}$) are appropriate for this. As could be shown by these tests, all variables of this investigation are I(1), i.e. difference-stationary, except *ipx*, the (natural logarithm of) the index of industrial production which is trend-stationary, i.e. it is stationary around a deterministic time trend (this holds true for all countries under consideration here). Removing the deterministic time trend by regressing the trend-stationary variable on a constant and a trend and then taking the residuals from this regression is appropriate to get a stationary variable; differencing as in the case of I(1) variables would be misleading.

AUTOREGRESSIVE DISTRIBUTED-LAG MODELS

In order to get a congruent model (i.e. an empirical model satisfying certain very desirable criteria)[25] for the long-term interest rate, it is recommended to start the general-to-specific modelling sequence with the following equation:[26]

$$RL_t = a(L) \cdot RL_{t-1} + b_1(L) \cdot RS_t + \sum_{j=1}^{J} b_{j+1}(L) \cdot Z_t^j + C + \varepsilon_t. \quad (A1.1)$$

Equation (A1.1) is a general autoregressive distributed-lag (ADL) model[27] of *RL* conditional on *RS* and *j* further valid conditioning variables Z^j. Since economic theory does not specify how quickly economic agents react, the orders of the lag polynomials can not be specified a priori but must be chosen on the basis of the data. Moreover, no sign restrictions on individual coefficients within the polynomials can be made since they essentially reflect the dynamics of adjustment. We estimated such ADL models for every country and tested whether they can be viewed as a valid statistical description of the DGP, especially, whether the residuals are white noise innovation errors (using the same tests described below). An *F*-test of the null-hypothesis $H_0: b_i(L) = 0$, $i = 1, \ldots, J+1$, provides evidence on the relevance of the respective variable; if the null can not be rejected, the respective variable can be marginalized.

STATIC LONG-RUN SOLUTION

The static long-run equilibrium solution of the ADL model is defined as the (unobservable) state in which the variables do not have any inherent tendency to move away from their actual values; in that case:

$$RL^* = RL_t = RL_{t-1} = \ldots = RL_{t-n},$$
$$RS^* = RS_t = RS_{t-1} = \ldots = RS_{t-n},$$
$$Z^{j*} = Z_t^j = Z_{t-1}^j = \ldots = Z_{t-n}^j, \forall j, \quad (A1.2)$$
$$\varepsilon_t = 0.$$

The lag-operators from (1), ($a(L)$ and $b_i(L)$, $\forall i$) then can be written as $a(L^0)$ and $b_i(L^0)$, $\forall i$, which in this case is equal to $a(1)$ and $b_i(1)$, $\forall i$.

In the static long-run equilibrium, equation (A1.1) can therefore be written as:

$$RL^* = a(1) \cdot RL^* + b_1(1) \cdot RS^* + \sum_{j=1}^{J} b_{j+1}(1) \cdot Z^{j*} + C \quad (A1.3)$$

which can be solved for RL^* and reformulated to yield the static long-run solution:

$$RL^* = \frac{b(1)}{1 - a(1)} \cdot RS^* + \sum_{j=1}^{J} \frac{b_{j+1}(1)}{1 - a(1)} \cdot Z^{j*} + \frac{C}{1 - a(1)}. \quad (A1.4)$$

For all analysed countries we computed the static long-run solution and tested whether $1-a(1)$ is significantly different from 0 (using PC-GIVE's unit-root t-test). If not, the static long-run solution would not exist.[28] Additionally we tested whether the $b_i(1)$ are significantly different from 0, which gives evidence on the influence of the explanatory variables on the dependent variable in the long run. With

$$K_i = \frac{b_i(1)}{1 - a(1)}, \forall i > 0 \quad (A1.5)$$

and

$$K_0 = \frac{C}{1 - a(1)} \quad (A1.6)$$

the static long-run solution can be rewritten in the following way:

$$RL^* = K_1 \cdot RS^* + \sum_{j=1}^{J} K_{j+1} \cdot Z^{j*} + K_0 \quad (A1.7)$$

which describes the static long-run solution of (1) as a theoretical construct. Since economic theory often deals with such types of equilibria, the static long-run solution should be consistent with economic theory which is one aspect of a congruent model.

COINTEGRATION

The static long-run solution can be computed directly from an ADL model like equation (A1.1), once the parameters of the ADL model are estimated. Alternatively, the Ks can be estimated directly performing a static regression in levels as described by Engle and Granger.[29] Equation (A1.2) then has to be reformulated to:

$$RL_t^* = K_1 \cdot RS_t + \sum_{j=1}^{J} K_{j+1} \cdot Z_t^j + K_0 \qquad (A1.8)$$

or to:

$$RL_t = K_1 \cdot RS_t + \sum_{j=1}^{J} K_{j+1} \cdot Z_t^j + K_0 + ECM_t. \qquad (A1.9)$$

This equation is called a *'cointegrating equation'* and can be estimated by OLS.[30] The estimated residuals of (A1.3) are called the *'equilibrium error'* or *'error correction mechanism'* (ECM). If the variables in the cointegrating equation individually are I(1) – as is the case here – but the ECM (i.e. a linear combination of those variables) is stationary, the respective variables are said to be cointegrated. Dickey–Fuller-type tests yield the appropriate test statistics, but critical values differ if the cointegrating vector has to be estimated. Intuitively, cointegration means that, although the variables involved can drift anywhere individually, they cannot drift 'too far' apart, but are tied together in the long run. Notice that cointegration is necessary for theory consistency. The estimated Ks (the cointegrating vector) describe the long-run response of RL on a movement in the respective variables. ECM describes the deviation of RL^* from RL: $ECM_t = RL_t - RL_t^*$.

ERROR CORRECTION MODEL

Dealing with I(1) variables, it is highly recommended to estimate a model which can be derived from the ADL model solely by reparameterizing, i.e. by algebraic tranformations without imposing additional restrictions. Such a model is called an error correction model.

$$\Delta RL_t = \beta_1 \cdot \Delta RS_t + \sum_{j=1}^{J} \beta_{j+1} \cdot \Delta Z_t^j + \gamma \cdot (RL_{t-1} - K_0 - K_1 \cdot RS_{t-1}$$

$$- \sum_{j=1}^{J} K_{j+1} \cdot Z_{t-1}^j) + \text{higher order lags}$$

$$(\Delta RL, \Delta RS, \Delta Z^1, \Delta Z^2, \ldots, \Delta Z^j) + \varepsilon_t. \qquad (A1.10)$$

The term in the brackets represents ECM_{t-1}; thus, (4) can be simplified to:

$$\Delta RL_t = \beta_1 \cdot \Delta RS_t + \sum_{j=1}^{J} \beta_{j+1} \cdot \Delta Z_t^j + \gamma \cdot ECM_{t-1}$$

$$+ \text{ higher order lags } (\Delta RL, \Delta RS, \Delta Z^1, \Delta Z^2, \ldots, \Delta Z^j) + \varepsilon_t.$$

(A1.11)

Error correction models are advantageous, both economically and econometrically. The parameters of an error correction model can be associated with three distinct and economically interpretable effects – 'impact effect' (βs), 'long-run response' (Ks) and 'feedback effect' (γ) – as already outlined in the text above. For cointegration, γ has to be significantly smaller than zero. The error correction model only contains I(0) variables in the case of cointegration and all statistical standard inferences are valid. Another advantage of this model is the usually low multicollinearity of the regressors. Notice, that cointegration is necessary (and sufficient) for error correction (Granger's representation theorem). If the variables involved were not cointegrated, ECM would be I(1) and would drop out as γ would not be significant. In that case, the model would hold only in differences and no long-run level information would enter the model.

Empirical evidence

The models presented in this subsection have been derived from a general-to-specific modelling sequence starting with a general error correction model estimated by the two-step procedure of Engle and Granger, as outlined above: in the first step, the cointegrating equation was estimated by OLS; in the second step, the residual of this cointegrating equation, the ECM, was inserted into the error correction model, which was estimated using appropriately transformed variables (again by OLS).[31] If more than two variables are involved in the cointegrating equation, OLS yields consistent estimates of the cointegrating parameters if and only if there exists exactly one cointegrating vector (there might be up to $n - 1$ cointegrating vectors for n integrated variables). We conducted both Johansen's trace and maximal eigenvalue tests and found evidence in favour of exactly one cointegrating vector for all countries.[32] Moreover, the OLS-estimates of the long-run parameters do not differ strongly from either the Johansen estimates or from those computed directly from a general ADL model, as described above. For cointegration, the ECM has to be stationary and we provide an ADF test for this.[33] Unfortunately, we could not reject the null of no cointegration in the case of Spain, even with 10 per cent error probability. The Spanish model, therefore, should be interpreted with care; but dropping ECME would lead to an inferior model, in which case the use of an ECM term sometimes is recommended, though cointegration might be statistically insignificant.[34]

The values shown in brackets below the estimated coefficients are heteroscedasticity consistent standard errors (HCSE) which would remain interpretable even if there were heteroscedasticity in an unknown way. Besides the well-known coefficient of determination (R^2) and the Durbin–Watson statistic (DW), we report additional descriptive statistics: the standard deviation of the residual (σ), the sum of squared residuals (RSS) together with the number of variables and observations, and three information criteria (Schwarz criterion – SC, Hannan–Quinn criterion – HQ, final prediction error – FPE). For models with no dummies, within-sample tests for parameter constancy are reported, both for the error variance and all parameters jointly (the error variance and the estimated coefficients).

Below, the most important misspecification tests are given which are based on the desirable properties of the residual: the models should have normally distributed residuals (test statistic: normality Chi-squared(2)), which are not autocorrelated (AR 1–7F) and have a homoscedastic variance (ARCH 7F, Xi^2 F); the linear functional form should be appropriate (RESET F). For F-tests, the degrees of freedom are given in parenthesis, and the error probability necessary to accept rejection of the desirable zero is added in brackets behind the test statistic. For the normality-Chi-squared(2) statistic, the 5 per cent critical value is equal to 5.99. Statistical inferences based on the model are only valid if no test rejects.[35] For some countries, the sample period is somewhat shorter than the maximum available sample period, because the model could not account for the volatility of the variables involved in the omitted period (some misspecification tests rejected if the model was estimated over the whole sample period).

GERMANY

Static long-run equation

Modelling RLD_t by OLS.
The present sample is: 1979 (1) to 1992 (12).

$RLD_t = 0.03868 + 0.4361\ RSD_t + 0.07303\ RUS_t$.

$R^2 = 0.847069$; DW = 0.147.
ECMD = Residual values of static long-run equation.
$ADF_{12}(ECMD) = -3.08$ (10% critical value = -3.06)

Error correction model

Modelling ΔRLD_t by OLS.

The present sample is: 1979 (2) to 1992 (12).

ΔRLD_t = 0.2515 ΔRLD_{t-1} + 0.2587 ΔRSD_t − 0.1081 ΔRSD_{t-1}
[HCSE]   [0.06521]   [0.043]   [0.05122]

+ 0.0938 ΔRUS_t + 0.1408 $\Delta \Delta_{12} pcD_t$ − 0.09288 $ECMD_{t-1}$
   [0.01614]   [0.04362]   [0.0271]

+ 0.007215 $D90(2)_t$.
   [0.0001768]

R^2 = 0.616033; σ = 0.00165184; DW = 1.97.
RSS = 0.0004365700254 for 7 variables and 167 observations.
Information criteria: SC = −12.64; HQ = −12.7177; FPE = 2.84293e-006.
Normality Chi-squared(2) = 3.1803.
AR 1- 7F(7,153) = 1.313 [0.2477].
ARCH 7F(7,146) = 2.0246 [0.0557].
X_i^2 F(13,146) = 0.72542 [0.7360].
RESET F(1,159) = 0.059253 [0.8080].

Actual versus fitted values of ΔRLD

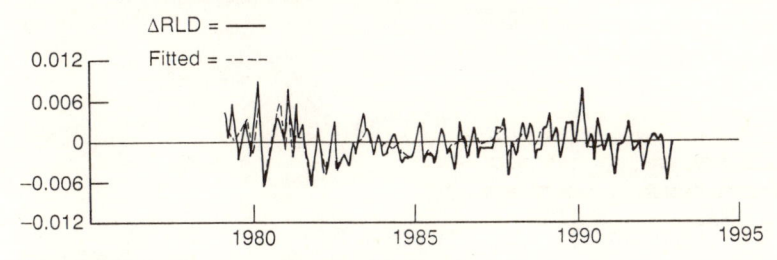

Figure 12A.1   Error correction model, Germany

THE NETHERLANDS

Static long-run equation

Modelling $RLNL_t$ by OLS.
  The present sample is: 1983 (6) to 1991 (12).

$RLNL_t$ = 0.01408 + 0.5965 $RSNL_t$ + 0.2652 RUS_t

R^2 = 0.729857; DW = 0.0814.
ECMNL = Residual values of static long-run equation.
$ADF_1(ECMNL)$ = −3.345 (5% critical value = −3.36. 10% critical value = −3.04).

Error correction model

Modelling $\Delta RLNL_t$ by OLS.

The present sample is: 1983 (7) to 1992 (12).

$\Delta RLNL_t =$ 0.2693 $\Delta RLNL_{t-1}$ + 0.3906 $\Delta RSNL_t$ − 0.1446 $\Delta RSNL_t$
[HCSE]   [0.08692]   [0.0435]   [0.05762]

+ 0.1373 ΔRUS_t + 0.1342 $\Delta \Delta_{12} pNL_t$ − 0.08664 $ECMNL_{t-1}$
[0.03462]   [0.04036]   [0.0196]

R^2 = 0.678051; σ = 0.00115891; DW = 2.00.
RSS = 0.0001450511042 for 6 variables and 114 observations.
Variance instability test: 0.160956; joint instability test: 1.03792.
Information criteria: SC = −13.3253; HQ = −13.4109; FPE = 1.41375e-006.
Normality Chi-squared(2) = 3.2444.
AR 1- 7F(7,101) = 0.56763 [0.7806].
ARCH 7F(7,94) = 0.61977 [0.7384].
X_i^2 F(12,95) = 0.7791 [0.6704].
RESET F(1,107) = 1.7704 [0.1862].

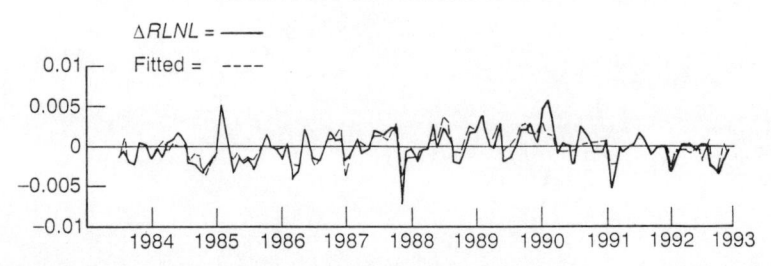

Figure 12A.2 Error correction model, the Netherlands

FRANCE

Static long-run equation

Modelling RLF_t by OLS.
The present sample is: 1980 (5) to 1992 (8).

RLF_t = 0.03964 + 0.4485 RSF_t + 0.3997 $\Delta_{12} pF_t$.

R^2 = 0.932298; DW = 0.192.
$ECMF$ = Residual values of static long-run equation.
$ADF_{1,C}(ECMF)$ = −3.598 (10% critical value = −3.53).

Error correction model

Modelling ΔRLF_t by OLS.

The present sample is: 1980 (6) to 1992 (8).

$\Delta RLF_t = 0.189\ \Delta RLF_{t-1} - 0.115\ \Delta\Delta RLF_{t-2} + 0.3024\ \Delta RSF_t$
[HCSE]   [0.07402]   [0.04361]   [0.04739]

$\qquad + 0.04\ \Delta\Delta_{12}m1F_{t-3} - 0.1182\ ECME_{t-1} + 0.01204\ D87(5)_t.$
$\qquad\quad$[0.01277]   [0.02952]   [0.0004853]

$R^2 = 0.529946$; $\sigma = 0.00237242$; DW = 1.95.
RSS = 0.0007936007742 for 6 variables and 147 observations.
Information criteria: SC = −11.9257; HQ = −11.9981; FPE = 5.8581e-006.
Normality Chi-squared(2) = 4.5064.
AR 1- 7$F(7,134)$ = 0.25788 [0.9688].
ARCH 7$F(7,127)$ = 0.79693 [0.5912].
$X_i^2\ F(11,129)$ = 0.44553 [0.9323].
RESET $F(1,140)$ = 0.17912 [0.6728].

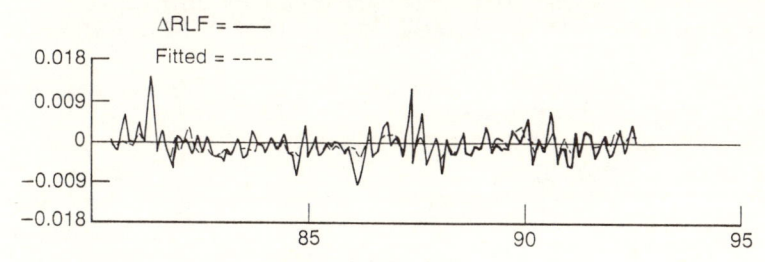

Figure 12A.3 Error correction model, France

ITALY

Static long-run equation

Modelling RLI_t by OLS.
The present sample is: 1982 (5) to 1992 (12).

$RLI_t = 0.02513 + 0.4756\ RSI_t + 0.5388\ D_{12}pI_t.$

$R^2 = 0.974734$; DW = 0.591.
ECMI = Residual values of static long-run equation.
$ADF_{1,C}(ECMI) = -5.268$ (1% critical value = −4.44).

Error correction model.

Modelling ΔRLI_t by OLS.

The present sample is: 1982 (6) to 1992 (12).

$\Delta RLI_t = 0.362\ \Delta RLI_{t-1} - 0.181\ \Delta\Delta RLI_{t-2} + 0.294\ \Delta RSI_t$
[HCSE] [0.06167] [0.06147] [0.03669]

$- 0.1283\ \Delta RSI_{t-4} + 0.1444\ \Delta\Delta RSD_{t-4}$
[0.03252] [0.05741]

$+ 0.1538\ (\Delta RUS_{t-1} + \Delta RUS_{t-5}) + 0.1955\ \Delta\Delta_{12} pI_t$
[0.02424] [0.07162]

$- 0.06011\ (\Delta\Delta_{12} m3I_t - \Delta\Delta_{12} m3I_{t-1} + \Delta\Delta_{12} m3I_{t-2})$
[0.02354]

$- 0.2891\ ECMI_{t-1}.$
[0.04558]

$R^2 = 0.694807$; $\sigma = 0.00216225$; DW = 2.06.
RSS = 0.0005516877715 for 9 variables and 127 observations.
Variance instability test: 0.0920293; joint instability test: 1.2178.
Information criteria: SC = −12.0034; HQ = −12.1231; FPE = 5.00664e-006.
Normality Chi-squared(2) = 0.82365.
AR 1- 7$F(7,111)$ = 1.171 [0.3252].
ARCH 7$F(7,104)$ = 0.69392 [0.6770].
$X_i^2\ F(18,99)$ = 1.5342 [0.0941].
RESET $F(1,117)$ = 3.7401 [0.0555].

Actual versus fitted values of ΔRLI

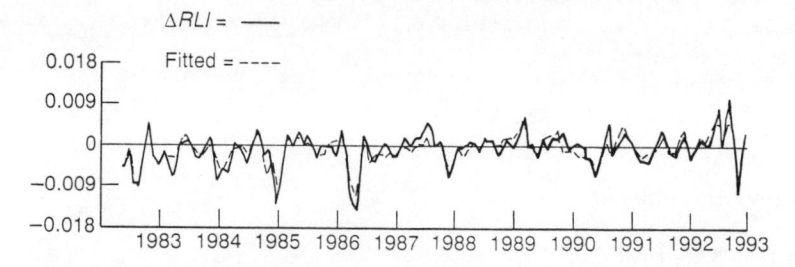

Figure 12A.4 Error correction model, Italy

UNITED KINGDOM

Static long-run equation

Modelling $RLMGB_t$ by OLS.
The present sample is: 1979 (1) to 1993 (1).

$RLGB_t = 0.06376 + 0.1756\ RSD_t + 0.3859\ RUS_t.$

$R^2 = 0.787269$; DW $= 0.349$.
$ECMGB$ = Residual values of equation 1.
$ADF_{1,C}(ECMGB) = -6.436$ (1% critical value $= -4.43$).

Error correction model

Modelling $\Delta RLGB_t$ by OLS.

The present sample is: 1980 (3) to 1993 (1).

$\Delta RLGB_t = 0.3526\ \Delta RLGB_{t-1} + 0.3909\ \Delta RSGB_t - 0.2741\ \Delta RSGB_{t-1}$
[HCSE]   [0.06419]   [0.04134]   [0.052]

$\qquad + 0.08285\ \Delta RUS_t + 0.09138\ \Delta\Delta_{12} pGB_t - 0.1047\ ECMGB_{t-1}$
$\qquad$ [0.03064]   [0.04071]   [0.02462]

$\qquad + 0.0108\ D87(6,7)_t.$
$\qquad$ [0.0005537]

$R^2 = 0.66145$; $\sigma = 0.00251694$; DW $= 1.86$.
RSS $= 0.000937574717$ for 7 variables and 155 observations.
Variance instability test: 0.136568; joint instability test: 0.966337.
Information criteria: SC $= -11.7879$; HQ $= -11.8695$; FPE $= 6.62106\text{e}{-}006$.
Normality Chi-squared(2) $= 0.86047$.
AR 1- 7$F(7,141) = 0.83928$ [0.5565].
ARCH 7$F(7,134) = 0.1047$ [0.9980].
$X_i^2\ F(14,133) = 1.3501$ [0.1869].
RESET $F(1,147) = 0.023353$ [0.8788].

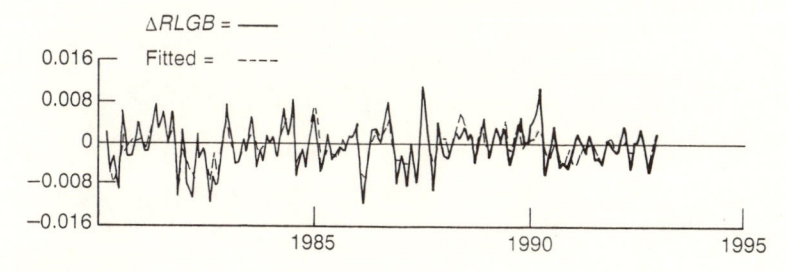

Figure 12A.5 Error correction model, UK

SPAIN

Static long-run equation

Modelling RLE_t by OLS.
The present sample is: 1984 (4) to 1992 (12).

$RLE_t = 0.0249 + 0.327\ RSE_t + 0.2696\ RSD_t + 0.5905\ RUS_t$.

$R^2 = 0.7362$; DW = 0.169.
ECME = Residual values of static long-run equation.
$ADF_1(ECME) = -3.243$ (10% critical value = -3.46).

Error correction model

Modelling ΔRLE_t by OLS.

The present sample is: 1984 (3) to 1992 (12).

$\Delta RLE_t = 0.2952\ \Delta RLE_{t-1} + 0.3133\ \Delta RSE_t + 0.3525\ \Delta RUS_t$
[HCSE]   [0.06067]   [0.03497]   [0.05856]

$\qquad - 0.1618\ \Delta\Delta RUS_{t-1} - 0.1032\ ECME_{t-1}$.
$\qquad\ \ $ [0.06166]   [0.03978]

$R^2 = 0.637334$; $\sigma = 0.00274301$; DW = 2.01.
RSS = 0.0007448864279 for 5 variables and 104 observations.
Variance instability test: 0.256927; joint instability test: 1.5438.
Information criteria: SC = -11.6234; HQ = -11.699; FPE = 7.88584e-006.
Normality Chi-squared(2) = 0.66941.
AR 1- 6$F(6,93)$ = 0.87002 [0.5201].
ARCH 6$F(6,87)$ = 1.3394 [0.2485].
$X_i^2\ F(10,88)$ = 0.77758 [0.6499].
RESET $F(1,98)$ = 2.8484 [0.0946].

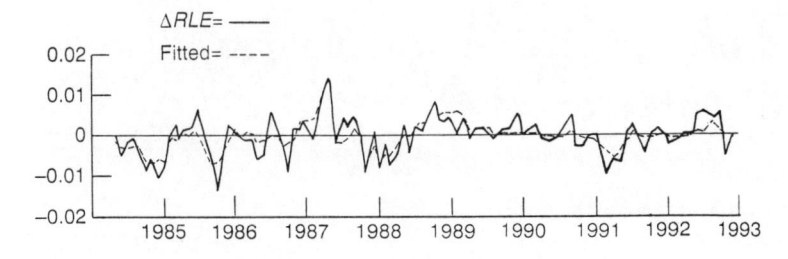

Figure 12A.6 Error correction model, Spain

APPENDIX 2: INTEREST RATES AND ECONOMIC ACTIVITY: EVIDENCE FROM GRANGER-CAUSALITY TESTS

Our goal is to study the impact of interest rates on real economic activity. The concept of *Granger-causality*[36] is a rather simple econometric tool to address this question empirically. A variable X is said to Granger-cause another variable Y (here: the detrended index of industrial production as a monthly proxy for real economic activity) if lagged X-values have explanatory power for the contemporary Y in addition to lagged values of Y. The explanatory variable here is either the equilibrium error, i.e. roughly, the '(term) structure of interest rates', or the long- resp. short-term interest rate for themselves. Formally, our Granger-causality test is based on the following regression equation:

$$ipxDT_t = C + \sum_{i=1}^{6} \alpha_i \cdot ipxDT_{t-1} + \sum_{i=1}^{18} \beta_i \cdot XJ_{t-1} + \varepsilon_t \quad (A2.1)$$

with $X1 = ECM$, $X2 = RL$ and $X3 = RS$. If the null hypothesis, H_0: $\beta_i = 0$, $\forall i$, can be rejected with low error probability α, the variable XJ Granger-causes *ipxDT* (DT = detrended). We decided to take the detrended index of industrial production as the dependent variable (instead of a growth rate) because this index proved to be trend-stationary (instead of difference-stationary, as all the other variables). Hence, we investigate whether interest rate variables Granger-cause deviations of the index of industrial production from its long-run growth path; these deviations might be associated with the business cycle. We chose a lag-length of up to 18 months for the explanatory variables because investment decisions (based on interest rates) might take a relatively long time to be reflected in real economic activity. The following table contains the error probability α of rejecting H_0: $\beta_i = 0$, $\forall i$, for the respective variables and countries.

Table 12A.1 Granger-causality tests

	D	F	I	E	NL	GB
ECM	0.05*	0.44	0.63	0.13	0.29	0.18
RL	0.29	0.10	0.26	0.55	0.82	0.22
RS	0.18	0.01*	0.37	0.28	0.53	0.007**

Notes: * 5% > α; ** 1% > α.

In Germany, the equilibrium error Granger-causes real economic activity, whereas individual interest rates do not. This is quantitatively similarly true for the Netherlands and Spain, as the error probability of rejecting Granger non-causality of the equilibrium error is much lower than for the individual interest rates; but unfortunately, this effect is statistically not significant at conventional significance levels. The results for these countries therefore have to be interpreted with much care. In France and the United Kingdom, though, it is mostly the short-term interest rate which matters for real economic activity. In Italy, no variable is significant.

We concentrate in our interpretation on those values which have shown themselves to be highly significant. The strong causal effect of short-term interest rates on real economic activity in *France* and the *United Kingdom* is underlined by the fact that most of the financing of private enterprise is short term in these countries, which is in the case of France due to credit controls in the long-term credit market up to 1987.

In *Germany*, where the interest rate spread proved to be significant, a major part of the total credit volume is medium and long-term, and most of the borrowing of enterprise takes the form of bank credit. The relations between banks and enterprises are often close and long-term oriented. In this setting, price terms in the credit contract might not play a major role as compared to a situation of frequent changes of loan contractors. This may be one explanation why long-term financing is chosen even in the face of an upward-sloping yield-curve.

France removed credit controls in 1987, and since that time, the share of long-term credit on total credit has risen remarkably from 6.8 per cent in January 1987 to 13 per cent in November 1992.[37] It can be expected that the importance of longer-term financing will increase still further in the future.

The low levels of significance for the tested causality relationship in *Italy* and *Spain* might reflect the inflationary environment, as price terms in credit contracts play only a minor role in high-inflation countries. Furthermore, the information content of the long rates is limited, since they may not fully reflect market expectations: financial markets in Spain are relatively 'thin', and central bank interventions in the Italian bond market tend to distort its price signals.

For the *Netherlands*, we found low levels of significance for the tested causal relationship, too. This might be due to using credit ceilings as an instrument of central bank policy.[38]

APPENDIX 3: DATA AND DATASOURCES

The subsequent Tables 12A.2 to 12A.7 contain a short explanation of all variables used in this investigation, together with the maximum available sample size and the datasource.

Table 12A.2 Germany

Variable	Sample	Explanation	Source
GBD	79M1–92M12	Government bonds in circulation (Bil. DM Nominal Value)	Deutsche Bundesbank
GCD	79M1–92M12	Credits of commercial banks to the public sector (Bil. DM)	Deutsche Bundesbank
IPXD	79M1–92M12	Index of industrial net production (1985=100)	Deutsche Bundesbank
M1D	79M1–92M12	Money Stock M1 (Bil. DM)	Deutsche Bundesbank
M3D	79M1–92M12	Money Stock M3 (Bil. DM)	Deutsche Bundesbank
PCD	79M1–92M12	Credits of commercial banks to private non-banks (Bil. DM)	Deutsche Bundesbank
PD	79M1–92M12	Consumer Price Index (1985=100)	Deutsche Bundesbank
RLD	79M1–92M12	Yield to maturity of public bonds (% p.a.)	Deutsche Bundesbank
RSD	79M1–92M12	3-month interest rate on the Frankfurt inter-bank money market (% p.a.)	Deutsche Bundesbank
RUS	79M1–92M12	3-month interest rate on Euro-dollar (% p.a.)	Deutsche Bundesbank
D90(2)		Impulse-dummy; 1 in February 1990, 0 otherwise; date of announcement of GMU	

Table 12A.3 The Netherlands

Variable	Sample	Explanation	Source
CNL	79M1– 92M12	Banks, claims on non-bank residents NSA (Mil. NLG)	BIS
IPXNL	79M1– 92M12	Industrial production total (excl. construction) SA (1985=100)	Centraal Bureau voor de Statistiek
LCNL	79M1– 92M12	Banks, long-term claims on non-bank residents (incl. secs. and real estate) NSA (Mil. NLG)	BIS
PNL	79M1– 93M1	Consumer price total (1985=100)	Centraal Bureau voor de Statistiek
RLNL	79M1– 93M1	Yield on government bonds (% p.a.)	Centraal Bureau voor de Statistiek
RSNL	79M1– 93M1	3-month AIBOR (% p.a.)	BIS
SCNL	79M1– 92M12	Banks, short-term claims on non-bank residents NSA (Mil. NLG)	BIS

Table 12A.4 France

Variable	Sample	Explanation	Source
CF	79M1– 92M11	Banks: claims on the economy, credits NSA (Bil. FFr)	BIS
IPXF	79M1– 93M1	Industrial production, total (1985=100)	OECD
LCF	79M1– 92M11	Banks: long-term claims NSA (Bil. FFr)	BIS
M1F	79M1– 93M1	Money supply M1, residents (Bil. FFr)	Banque de France *Statist. Monetaires*
M4F	79M1– 93M1	Money supply M4, residents (Bil. FFr)	Banque de France *Statist. Monetaires*
PF	79M1– 93M1	Retail prices, total index (1985=100)	BIS
RLF	79M1– 93M1	Yield on government bonds (% p.a.)	Banque de France *Bulletin Trimestriel*
RSF	79M1– 93M1	3-month interbank loans rate (% p.a.)	OECD *Main Economic Indicators*
D87(5)		Impulse-dummy, 1 in May 1987, 0 otherwise; interest rates reacted drastically to Euro-$ interest rates in this month (source: Banque de France, *La monnaie en 1987*, p. 56)	

Table 12A.5 Italy

Variable	Sample	Explanation	Source
CI	79M1–92M11	Banks, domestic loans NSA (Bil. ItL)	BIS
GDI	79M1–92M10	Deposit money banks: claims on central government (Trillions ItL)	IMF *Inter. Fin. Statistics*
IPXI	79M1–92M11	Industrial production total excl. construction NSA (1985=100)	BIS
M1I	79M1–93M1	Money supply M1 NSA (Bil. ItL)	Banca d'Italia
M3I	79M1–92M12	Money supply M3 NSA (Bil. ItL)	Banca d'Italia
PCI	79M1–92M11	Deposit money banks: claims on private sector (Trillions ItL)	IMF *Inter. Fin. Statistics*
PI	79M1–93M1	Consumer price general index (1990=100)	BIS
RLI	79M1–93M1	Yield on government bonds (% p.a.)	Banca d'Italia
RSI	79M11–93M1	3-month ord. treasury bills, gross of tax (% p.a.)	BIS

Table 12A.6 United Kingdom

Variable	Sample	Explanation	Source
IPXGB	79M1–93M1	Industrial production, production industries excl. construction NSA (1985=100)	BIS
M4GB	82M6–93M1	Private section liquidities SA (Mil. GB£)	Bank of England *Monetary Statistics*
M0GB	79M1–93M1	Money supply; narrow monetary base (Mil. GB£)	Bank of England *Monetary Statistics*
PGB	79M1–93M1	Retail prices all items (1987=100)	BIS
RLGB	79M1–93M1	Yield on government bonds (medium terms) 10 Years (% p.a.)	Bank of England *Quarterly Bulletin*
RSGB	79M1–93M1	3-month sterling interbank deposits (Mil. GB£)	BIS
D87(6,7)		Impulse-dummy, −1 in June 1987, 1 in July 1987, 0 otherwise; period of extreme exchange rate fluctuations and central bank interventions (source: BIS, *58. Jahresbericht*, 1988, p.193)	

Table 12A.7 Spain

Variable	Sample	Explanation	Source
CE	83M1– 93M1	Crédito total – morosos (Bil. ESP)	Banco de España
IPXE	82M7– 92M9	Index of Industrial Production, SA	IMF *Inter. Fin. Statistics*
M1E	79M1– 93M1	Money supply M1 (Mil. ESP)	Banco de España
M3E	79M1– 93M1	Money supply M3 (Mil. ESP)	Banco de España
PCE	83M1– 93M1	Crédito comercial + deudores con garantia real + otros deodores a plazo (Bil. ESP)	Banco de España
PE	79M1– 93M1	Consumer Price Index	IMF *Inter. Fin. Statistics*
RLE	79M1– 93M1	Yield on government bonds more than 2 years, secondary market (% p.a.)	OECD, *Financial Statistics*
RSE	79M1– 93M1	3-month interbank rate (% p.a.)	Banco de España

NOTES

1 See Gros and Thygesen (1992), pp.144–156; Fratianni and von Hagen (1992), pp.75–98; and Beyer and Schmidt (1993).
2 Evidence is presented by Harvey (1991) and Schmidt (1993) for Germany, Estrella and Hardouvelis (1991), and by Hardouvelis (1988) for the United States. A survey is given by Hesse and Roth (1992); Friedman and Kuttner (1991) concentrate on the spread of government bonds and private enterprise bills in the USA with a similar result. All of them found a stable relation of term premia or risk premia incorporated in interest rates and real economic growth, suggesting the use of interest rate relations as predictors of economic activity.
3 This view implies our critical distance from the recent 'real business cycle' approach.
4 For an interpretation, see e.g. Gebauer (1982).
5 For the purpose of this chapter it is sufficient to assume that the interest rate on government bonds develops like the representative interest rate on capital. This is equivalent to the assumption of a constant default-risk-premium for different interest rate levels.
6 See Andersen and Risager (1991); Agénor et al. (1992).
7 See Steinherr and Gilibert (1989); Vives (1991).
8 Of n variables are stationary in first differences and if there exists a stationary linear combination in the levels of these variables, they are said to be cointegrated; see Appendix for details.
9 See Modigliani and Shiller (1973).

10 In France and Italy such shifts do not influence the risk-premia of the currencies.
11 See Shiller (1990) for a survey.
12 The traditional starting point is Wicksell's famous distinction between the money rate of interest and the natural rate. This line of thought has been followed up to recent research on macroeconomic portfolio theory and Tobin's q.
13 See Appendix for a short exposition of method and results.
14 See Fazzari et al. (1988). Their results suggest important effects of the availability of internal funds on physical investment by firms in various industries.
15 See Pindyck (1991). For example, it might be desirable to continue a production which is no longer profitable due to changed exchange rates and/or sales prices because closing down the production and restarting it after conditions have changed would be costly, too (hysteresis).
16 See Gebauer (1993).
17 See Lown (1989); Fama (1990); Mishkin (1990a,b, 1991); Frankel and Lown (1991); Jorion and Mishkin (1991); Emery and Koenig (1992); Robertson (1992) for a strong (multicountry) evidence that the term structure does have significant ability to forecast changes in inflation.
18 See Gebauer (1989).
19 See Gilbert (1986); Eitrheim and Nymoen (1988); Granger (1990); Charemza and Deadman (1992), Doornik and Hendry (1992).
20 See Engle et al. (1983) for a classification of statistical exogeneity concepts.
21 See Charemza and Deadman (1992), Ch. 4.
22 A variable is called (weakly) stationary if its mean, variance and autocovariance are constant through time.
23 For a comparison of stationary and integrated time series c.f. Engle and Granger (1991), pp.1–6.
24 See Dickey and Fuller (1979).
25 Such, that it can be viewed as a 'good' simplification of the DGP; the most important implications of congruency will be addressed below. See Hendry and Ericsson (1991) for details.
26 The variables used in this investigation are explained in detail in Appendix 3. The notation of variables and operators are explained below together with all relevant information about the estimated empirical models for the long-term interest rate.
27 ADL models are appropriate models to start with, because they contain most of the widely used empirical models as special cases. See Charemza and Deadman (1992), pp.80–86.
28 Thus, suggesting a lack of cointegration; see below.
29 See Engle and Granger (1987).
30 The OLS-estimator yields even super-consistent estimates of the Ks, but the standard errors are not interpretable, if the variables involved are I(1); see Stock (1987). Strictly speaking, this is only true if the cointegrating vector is unique, but for n integrated variables there might exist up to $n-1$ cointegrating vectors. Thus, one has to test for the number of cointegrating vectors if $n > 2$.
31 The various estimates and associated tests of the ADL models, which preceded the estimation of the error correction models, provided additional evidence on the information content of the variables (long-run and/or short-run information, or no information at all).

32 See Johansen (1988) and Johansen and Juselius (1990); Dickey et al. (1991) provide a short survey of the Johansen procedure.
33 Critical values are taken from Charemza and Deadman (1992), Table 3; notice that the standard DF-critical values are not appropriate if the cointegrating vector is estimated.
34 See Muscatelli and Hurn (1992), p.12.
35 Details on all tests are given in Doornik and Hendry (1992).
36 See Granger (1969).
37 Commission of the European Community (1991), p.34.
38 Commission of the European Community (1990), P.28.

REFERENCES

Agénor, Pierre-Richard, Bhandari, Jagdeep S. and Flood, Robert P. (1992), 'Speculative attacks and models of balance of payments crises', *IMF Staff Papers*, 39, 357–394.

Andersen, Torben M. and Risager, Ole (1991), 'The role of credibility for the effects of a change in the exchange-rate policy', *Oxford Economic Papers*, 41, 85–98.

Beyer, Andreas and Schmidt, Klaus J.W. (1993), 'Ist das Europäische Währungssystem symmetrisch? - Ein alternativer empirischer Ansatz', Geld-Währung-Kapitalmarkt-working paper no. 29, December.

Charemza, Wojciech W. and Deadman, Derek F. (1992), *New Directions in Econometric Practice - General to Specific Modelling, Cointegration and Vector Autoregression*, Aldershot.

Commission of the European Community (1990), 'The Netherlands', *Economic Papers* 81, July.

Commission of the European Community (1991), 'France', *Economic Papers*, country study 5, July.

Dickey, David A. and Fuller, Wayne A. (1979), 'Distribution of the estimators for autoregressive time series with a unit root', *Journal of the American Statistical Association*, 84, 427–431.

Dickey, David A., Jansen, Dennis W. and Thornton, Daniel L. (1991), 'A primer on cointegration with an application to money and income', *Federal Reserve Bank of St Louis Review*, March/April, 58–78.

Doornik, Jurgen A. and Hendry, David F. (1992), *PC-GIVE (Generalized Instrumental Variables Estimators) - An Interactive Econometric Modelling System*, Version 7, Oxford.

Eitrheim, Øyvind and Nymoen, Ragnar (1988), 'LSE-Skolen i Økonometri', *Arbeidsnotat av Norges Bank*, Oslo, October.

Emery, Kenneth M. and Koenig, Evan F. (1992), 'Do interest rates help predict inflation?', *Federal Reserve Bank of Dallas Economic Review*, Fourth Quarter, 1–18.

Engle, Robert F. and Granger, Clive W.J. (1987), 'Co-Integration and error correction: representation, estimation, and testing', *Econometrica*, 55, 251–276.

Engle, Robert F. and Granger Clive W.J. (eds) (1991), *Long-Run Economic Relationships - Readings in Cointegration*, Oxford.

Engle, Robert F., Hendry, David F. and Richard, Jean-Francois (1983), 'Exogeneity', *Econometrica*, 51, 277–304.

Estrella, Arturo and Hardouvelis, Gikas A. (1991), 'The term structure as a predictor of real economic activity', *Journal of Finance*, 46, 555–576.

Fama, Eugene F. (1990), 'Term structure forecasts of interest rates, inflation and real returns', *Journal of Monetary Economics*, 25, 59–76.

Fazzari, Steven M., Hubbard, Glenn R. and Petersen, Bruce C. (1988), 'Financing constraints and corporate investment', *Brookings Papers of Economic Activity*, 1/1988, 141–195.
Frankel, Jeffrey A. and Lown, Cara S. (1991), 'An indicator of future inflation extracted from the steepness of the interest rate yield curve along its entire length', Federal Bank of New York research paper No. 9122, June.
Fratianni, Michele and Hagen, Jürgen von (1992), *The European Monetary System and European Monetary Union*, Boulder, San Francisco, Oxford.
Friedman, Benjamin M. and Kuttner, Kenneth N. (1991), 'Why does the paper-bill spread predict real economic activity?', NBER working paper no. 3879.
Gebauer, Wolfgang (1982), *Realzins, Inflation und Kapitalzins - Eine Neuinterpretation des Fisher-Theorems*, Berlin, Heidelberg, New York.
Gebauer, Wolfgang (1989), 'Zinsstrukturtheorie und Zentralbankpolitik', Norbert Bub, Dieter Duwendag and Rudolf Richter (eds), *Geldwertsicherung und Wirtschaftsstabilität, Festschrift für Helmut Schlesinger zum 65. Geburtstag*, Frankfurt, 71–86.
Gebauer, Wolfgang (ed.) (1993), *Foundations of European Central Bank Policy*, Heidelberg.
Gilbert, Christopher L. (1986), 'Professor Hendry's econometric methodology', *Oxford Bulletin of Economics and Statistics*, 47, 283–307; reprinted in Granger (1969).
Granger, Clive W.J. (1969), 'Investigating causal relations by econometric models and cross-spectral methods', *Econometrica*, 37, 424–438.
Granger, Clive W.J. (ed.) (1990), *Modelling Economic Series*, Oxford.
Gros, Daniel and Thygesen, Niels (1992), *European Monetary Integration - From the European Monetary System to European Monetary Union*, London, New York.
Hardouvelis, Gikas A. (1988), 'The predictive power of the term structure during recent monetary regimes', *Journal of Finance*, 43, 339–356.
Harvey, Campbell R. (1991), 'Interest rate based forecasts of German economic growth', *Weltwirtschaftliches Archiv*, 127, 701–718.
Hendry, David F. and Ericsson, Neil R. (1991), 'An econometric analysis of U.K. money demand in monetary trends in the United States and the United Kingdom by Milton Friedman and Anna J. Schwartz', *American Economic Review*, 81, 8–38.
Hesse, Helmuth and Roth, Gisela (1992), 'Die Zinsstruktur als Indikator der Geldpolitik?', *Kredit und Kapital*, 1/1992, 1–25.
Johansen, Søren (1988), 'Statistical analysis of cointegration vectors', *Journal of Economic Dynamics and Control*, 12, 231–254.
Johansen, Søren and Juselius, Katharina (1990), 'Maximum likelihood estimation and inference on cointegration - with applications to the demand for money', *Oxford Bulletin of Economics and Statistics*, 52, 169–210.
Jorion, Philippe and Mishkin, Frederic S. (1991), 'A multicountry comparison of term-structure forecasts at long horizons', *Journal of Financial Economics*, 29, 59–80.
Lown, Cara S. (1989), 'Interest rate spreads, commodity prices and the dollar: a new strategy for monetary policy?', *Federal Reserve Bank of Dallas Economic Review*, 13–26.
Mishkin, Frederic S. (1990a), 'What does the term structure tell us about future inflation?', *Journal of Monetary Economics*, 25, 77–96.
Mishkin, Frederic S. (1990b), 'The information in the longer maturity term structure about future inflation', *Quarterly Journal of Economics*, 105, 815–828.
Mishkin, Frederic S. (1991) 'A multi-country study of the information in the

shorter maturity term structure about future inflation', *Journal of International Money and Finance*, 10, 2–22.

Modigliani, Franco and Shiller, Robert J. (1973), 'Inflation, rational expectations and the term structure of interest rates', *Econometrica*, 40, 12–43.

Muscatelli, Antonio and Hurn, Stan (1992), 'Cointegration and dynamic time series models', *Journal of Economic Surveys*, 6, 1–43.

Pindyck, Robert S. (1991), 'Irreversibility, uncertainty, and investment', *Journal of Economic Literature*, 29, 1110–1148.

Robertson, Donald (1992), 'Term structure forecasts of inflation', *Economic Journal*, 102, 1083–1093.

Schmidt, Klaus J.W. (1993), 'The (term) structure of interest rates as a predictor of real economic growth: an econometric analysis for Germany', W. Gebauer (ed.), *Foundations of European Central Bank Policy*, Heidelberg, 165–189.

Steinherr, Alfred and Gilibert, Pier-Luigi (1989), 'The impact of financial market integration on the European banking industry', CEPS Financial Markets Unit Research Report No. 1, Brussels.

Stock, James (1987), 'Asymptotic properties of least square estimators of cointegrating vectors', *Econometrica*, 55, 1035–1056.

Vives, Xavier (1991), 'Banking competition and European Integration', in A. Giovannini and H. Mayer (eds) *European Financial Integration*, Cambridge, 9–31.

13

IS THERE AN 'EMS EFFECT' IN EUROPEAN LABOUR MARKETS?

Michael Artis and Paul Ormerod

The UK's decision to participate in the exchange rate mechanism (ERM) of the European Monetary System (EMS) is widely understood to be, among other things, an attempt to share in the counter-inflationary benefits of the System. There can be little doubt in fact that membership of the ERM will have some effect on the labour market, and will impact on the course of wages and prices, employment and real wages. Indeed, if we take the real wage experience of existing (non-German) ERM members as an appropriate guide, the effects could be quite dramatic. For example, Figure 13.1 indicates a pronounced slowdown in real wage growth over the period since the System was initiated in every country except Germany and the UK itself. The purpose of this chapter is to analyse the wage inflation process in the main ERM economies over the period from the early 1970s with a view to asking whether there is a detectable 'EMS effect'.

We first review the theory underlying the argument that participation in the ERM has particular counter-inflationary implications. For the estimation of wage-price systems this theory has some clear consequences. The remainder of the chapter is devoted to following up those consequences. Thus in the second main section of the chapter we present evidence on the inflation process in five ERM countries – Germany, France, Italy, the Netherlands, and Belgium. A key feature is that when inflation is modelled as an autoregressive process, it appears that for each of the countries under review, German inflation enters significantly at some point during the EMS period. We treat this as evidence of an effect upon inflation expectations, and in the third main section we present estimates of wage inflation processes incorporating these inflation expectations. While we find in each case evidence consistent with the EMS having caused a disruption in labour market behaviour, the chief long-run result that we obtain is that after this difficult

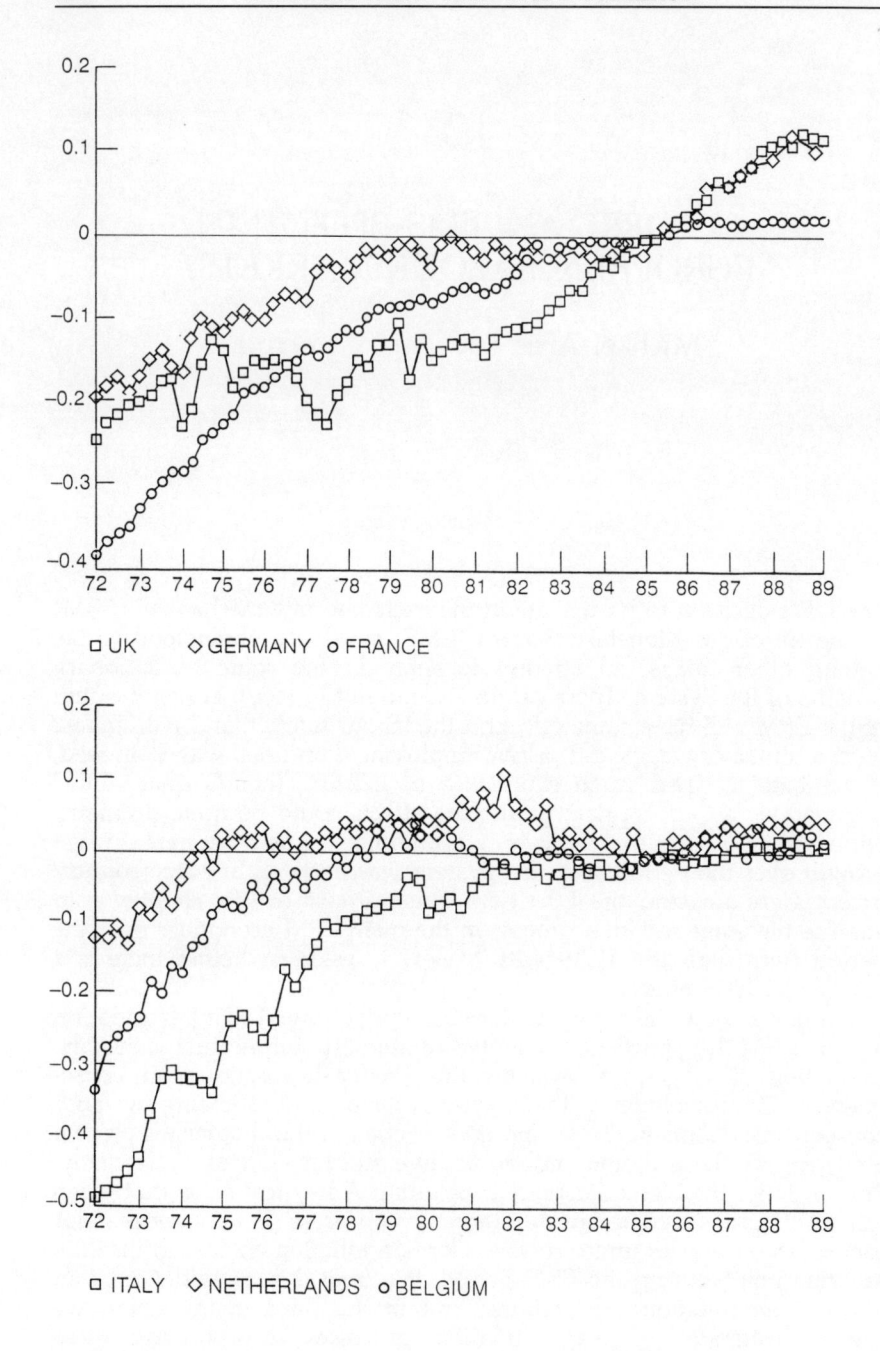

Figure 13.1 Log real wages in six countries

Table 13.1 Converging on the German standard

	Pre-EMS		EMS	
	1961Q1–1971Q4	1972Q1–1979Q1	1979Q2–1984Q4	1985Q1–1989Q2
A: Inflation rates (% p.a.); consumer prices				
Germany	2.90	4.98	4.45	1.06
France	4.02	9.16	10.55	3.52
Netherlands	4.22	7.43	4.80	0.63
Belgium	3.08	7.86	6.71	2.25
Italy	3.97	13.04	14.88	6.01
UK	4.43	12.75	9.67	4.88
Excluding UK:				
Mean	3.64	8.49	8.28	2.69
SD	0.54	2.65	3.95	1.94
Range	1.32	8.06	10.43	5.38
B: Simple correlation matrices of inflation rates[a]				
	France	Netherlands	Belgium	Italy
Germany	0.2,0.9	0.7,0.9	0.6,0.8	0.3($\times 10^{-2}$),0.9
France		0.3,1.0	0.7,0.9	0.9,1.0
Netherlands			0.8,0.8	0.3,0.9
Belgium				0.6,0.9

Note: [a] The first figure in each pair is the simple correlation of quarterly consumer price inflation for the period 1972Q1–1979Q1, the second for the period 1979Q2–1989Q2.

transition, national country wage inflation processes tend to resume their previous form, but with the important difference that they now incorporate a strong tie to German inflation. A final section provides some conclusions.

THE EMS AND INFLATION 1979–1989

Initial screening of the data provides strong prima facie evidence of a shift in the data-generating processes underlying wage and price behaviour in a number of the ERM countries. For example, the upper panel of Table 13.1 shows how, over the EMS period – especially in its latter part – consumer price inflation in the ERM countries was brought down from the high levels of the 1970s. In the process, inflation divergence among these countries was reduced. Analysis of this process (see e.g. Weber, 1991, for a detailed discussion) suggests that while member countries adjusted to the framework for counter-inflationary policies provided by the ERM at different speeds, the experience can be described as one of 'converging on the German standard'. Figure 13.2

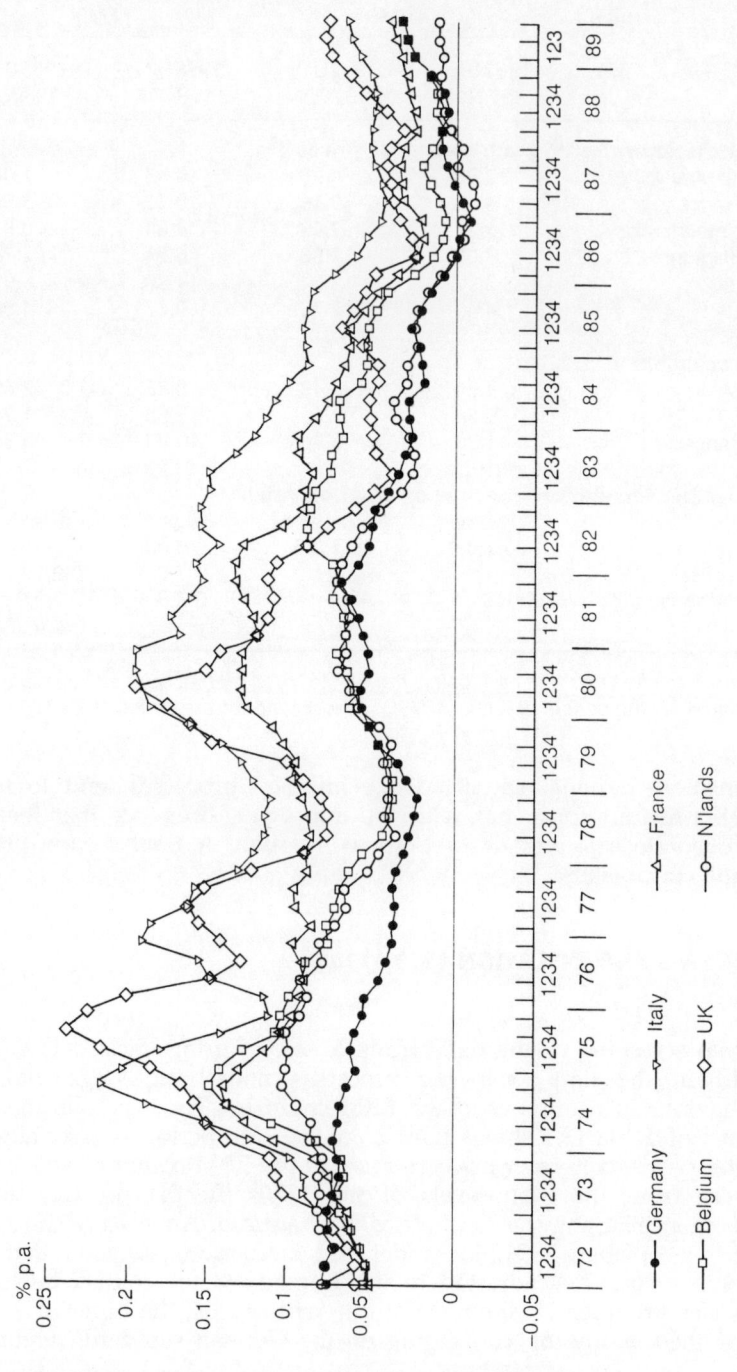

Figure 13.2 Consumer price inflation, 1972Q1–1989Q3

provides similar evidence in graphical form, illustrating more clearly the failure of the UK to preserve its own counter-inflationary gains, achieved – and lost – outside the ERM framework. The lower panel of Table 13.1 which tabulates the correlation matrix of consumer price inflation, comparing pre- and post-EMS periods, confirms the picture of convergence on the German standard.

If members of an exchange rate union succeed in holding their bilateral exchange rates against a low-inflation leader, inflation is certain to fall. This is not in dispute. The key issue is whether bringing inflation down in such a framework is distinctive in any significant way. There are at least two (not mutually exclusive) ways in which membership of the ERM could lower inflation. In the first, a high-inflation country which nonetheless succeeds in holding its nominal exchange rate 'fairly fixed' against low-inflation Germany, will experience a sustained loss of competitiveness and rising unemployment. Eventually, through a simple Phillips curve mechanism this process will bring inflation down towards the German level and the loss of competitiveness will then stabilize. While this means of reducing inflation offers no added gain against the alternative of deflating outside the System, the policy makers of the countries concerned might still find it preferable to join the System for counter-inflationary reasons because the rise in unemployment would otherwise be unacceptable and the desired reduction in inflation infeasible. However, in the literature, more attention has been paid to the idea that the EMS (ERM) offers a counter-inflationary framework which affords an added gain by making the reduction in inflation cheaper in terms of output and employment. The dominant model of the way in which inflation reduction within the EMS differs from inflation reduction outside it is the 'German leadership' model which has been put forward most notably by (among others) Melitz (1985), Giavazzi and Giovannini (1988) and Giavazzi and Pagano (1988). An informal summary of the model as it applies to the EMS runs as follows. The model is a version of the Barro–Gordon reputational model (Barro and Gordon, 1983a, 1983b). Germany acts as the low-inflation anchor; due to the independence of the Bundesbank or more generally to a high rate of inflation-aversion on the part of the German public, the Barro–Gordon 'reputational equilibrium rate of inflation' is particularly low in Germany. By committing to a stable exchange rate against the DM, non-German members of the ERM raise the profile and the credibility of their own counter-inflationary declarations. Credibility with domestic agents increases because the external commitments in effect raise the penalty which attends infraction of counter-inflationary promises. The EMS 'custom' of only permitting exchange rate realignments which under-accommodate cumulated inflation differentials puts pressure on governments and wage- and price-setting agents. The result is a reduction in the 'equilibrium' inflation rate outside Germany. In effect, non-German participants can import the Bundesbank's reputation. Joining the EMS is beneficial in reducing the unemployment and output costs of a successful counter-inflation policy for this reason.

In terms of an older vintage of inflation model (see e.g. Paldam, 1980), joining the EMS makes German inflation projections a credible component in domestic inflation expectations and thus affords a means of reducing the cost, in terms of unemployment, of the process of winding down such expectations. The reputational model therefore suggests an added gain in reducing inflation within the framework of the EMS. However, empirical verification of the added gain has not proven easy to find. Dornbusch (1991), for example, provides a notably cautious assessment. Giavazzi and Giovannini (1988, 1989) address the issue by presenting forecasts derived for the EMS period from VARs in wages, prices and output conditional on import prices and money supply estimated over a pre-EMS period. The resort to an atheoretical approach is advantageous in avoiding the need to specify a structure and the identification of change in that structure as 'EMS-induced' and in this way neatly turns the Lucas critique to positive account. But there are problems, both with the economic interpretation that can be placed upon parameter non-constancy in this case (see Kremers, 1990, for an argument to this effect) and with the statistical interpretation: the parameter change detected is not identified as significant. Nonetheless, the principal findings are suggestive, for the pre-EMS VAR appears to overpredict inflation for the EMS period and the results for the UK are in a different direction from those for full EMS members. It also seems that the results are sensitive to the *date* identified as the beginning of an EMS effect – not unreasonably in light of what we know, informally, about the way in which countries handled their membership of the System.

Artis and Nachane (1990) employ bivariate cointegration techniques to test for convergence on the German standard; but while they find that German inflation rates are pairwise-cointegrated with inflation rates in other ERM member countries after the inception of the EMS and not before, this finding also extends to the United Kingdom, thus undermining its attribution to an EMS effect. The EMS (ERM) effect, if there is one, cannot be distinguished from a more general global disinflation effect. By contrast, Kremers (1990) has employed a structured approach in his analysis of the Irish case and is able to reach the conclusion that Irish disinflation policy did derive credibility from the government's participation in the EMS.

Taking the 'augmented Phillips curve' approach at face value, successful adherence to the EMS for an erstwhile high-inflation country must involve either a direct credibility effect in the formation of inflation expectations, a change in the structure of the wage setting mechanism, or a change in the value of the determinants of that mechanism. Clearly these possibilities are not mutually exclusive and in practice one might expect to see elements of each of these responses: while it might always be argued that structural change in wage setting is an artefact of econometric techniques that fails to detect 'deep structure' parameters, the fact is that we have to live with such techniques. Looked at in this way the agenda for research is clear: first identify inflation-expectations generators, then look for evidence of credibility effects in these generators. Second, estimate wage determination equations using inflation expectations derived in ways that allow for any credibility effects detected in the first stage, then look for signs of parameter shift and institutional explanations. In the next section some evidence on the first part of this programme is presented and discussed.

INFLATION EXPECTATIONS

Autoregressive processes are known to provide a plausible and hard-to-beat standard for inflation projections, though in Artis et al. (1984) we provide evidence that a 'Keynesian' cost-based approach provides a slightly better one.[1] Accordingly, in testing for the significance of a German contribution in the formation of inflation expectations, we take an autoregressive (AR(4)) process as the base.

It is known from previous work and from informal knowledge of the events of the period, that credibility effects, if they existed, took time to be consolidated. The early phase of operation of the EMS, for example, was implemented by some member countries as a crawling peg and there were frequent realignments of exchange rates. Weber (1991) has documented the accretion of EMS credibility effects in respect of monetary growth, interest rates and exchange rates in some detail, confirming that ERM member countries adapted to the System at differing speeds. In searching for evidence of a German contribution to the inflation process under the EMS, we therefore work with a flexible break-period.[2] The AR(4) schemes were also further refined by the use of country-specific information derived from the OECD's *Economic Survey* for the country in question and by reference to an OECD study of inflation in France. These information sources were used where appropriate to justify the use of dummy variables where significant institutional change occurred (signalling, for example, a change in prices policy).

Quarterly data (non-deseasonalized) pertaining to consumer price inflation were employed, with inflation represented as four-quarter overlapping log differences. The results of following the approach outlined are summarized in Table 13.2. They provide an encouraging degree of support for the German leadership model: namely, that over time the relevance of German inflation for other ERM participants becomes more clearly established. Thus the results for France – where the break between pre-EMS and EMS is put at the end of 1982, just ahead of the Mitterrand U-turn – suggest that German inflation becomes a significant influence on French inflation after that time, where it was not before. Dummies corresponding to institutional change identified from the sources described are needed to eliminate some otherwise quite severe negative serial correlation in this case. For Italy a breakpoint occupying several quarters – 1979Q4–1982Q1 – is indicated: again, there

Table 13.2 The German content of inflation predictors

France

Pre-EMS			EMS		
1972Q1–1982Q3			1982Q4–1989Q3		
$\Delta_4\text{lfp}(-1)$	1.408	(12.75)	$\Delta_4\text{lfp}(-1)$	1.376	(9.26)
$\Delta_4\text{lfp}(-2)$	−0.483	(4.44)	$\Delta_4\text{lfp}(-2)$	−0.552	(3.62)
Df2	−0.015	(2.63)	$\Delta_4\text{lgp}(-4)$	0.223	(2.08)
DF6	−0.021	(3.73)			
DF7	0.023	(4.08)			
$\bar{R}^2$	0.947			0.964	
SE(% mean)	5.00			8.64	
χ^2 Serial correlation (LM4)	1.92			3.66	
Functional form	2.68			0.42	
Normality	1.23			0.66	
Heteroscedasticity	0.38			0.29	

Italy

Pre-EMS			EMS		
1972Q1–1979Q3			1982Q1–1989Q2		
$\Delta_4\text{lip}(-1)$	0.839	(14.33)	$\Delta_4\text{lip}(-1)$	0.748	(5.51)
			$\Delta_4\text{lgp}(-1)$	0.504	(3.52)
il2	0.024	(3.47)	$\Delta_4\text{lip}(-4)$	−0.004	(0.04)
il3	0.030	(4.91)			
il4	−0.015	(1.92)			
$\bar{R}^2$	0.933			0.981	
SE (% mean)	8.80			6.36	
χ^2 Serial correlation (LM4)	5.52			5.59	
Functional form	0.04			1.63	
Normality	0.83			0.19	
Heteroscedasticity	5.72			5.10	

is no significant German inflation term present before the break, but there is one after it. Institutional adjustments suggest, as in France, considerable scope for dummy variables and some are needed to eliminate serial correlation. In the Belgian estimates serial correlation proved a considerable problem and with only limited evidence for the imposition of dummy variables the equation for the period up to 1979Q3 was estimated on the assumption of an autocorrelated error process (equation (A)). An extension of the period to 1981Q4 (equation (B)) was

Table 13.2 *(Continued)*

	Belgium (A)				
	Pre-EMS			EMS	
	1972Q1–1979Q3			1979Q4–1989Q2	
$\Delta_4 lbp(-1)$	1.081	(8.33)	$\Delta_4 lbp(-1)$	1.167	(7.35)
$\Delta_4 lbp(-2)$	−0.242	(2.10)	$\Delta_4 lpb(-2)$	−0.373	(2.70)
$\Delta_4 lgp(-2)$	0.179	(2.82)	$\Delta_4 lgp(-2)$	0.237	(2.93)
DB2	0.019	(6.30)			
MLH estimation	$\bar{R}^2$			0.962	
With autoregressive	SE (% mean)				10.98
error structure	χ^2 correlation (LM4)			10.35	
	Functional form			0.01	
	Normality				1.05
	Heteroscedasticity			0.05	

	Netherlands				
	Pre-EMS			EMS	
	1972Q1–1983Q1			1983Q2–1989Q3	
$\Delta_4 lnp(-1)$	0.885	(14.36)	$\Delta_4 lnp(-1)$	0.748	(5.32)
$\Delta_4 lgp(-1)$	0.604	(3.85)	$\Delta_4 lgp(-1)$	0.503	(2.68)
$\Delta_4 lgp(-2)$	−0.400	(2.18)	$\Delta_4 lgp(-2)$	−0.256	(1.21)
NL1	−0.011	(2.19)			
NL2	−0.013	(3.44)			
$\bar{R}^2$	0.941			0.895	
SE (% mean)	6.91			36.08	
χ^2 Serial correlation (LM4)	3.63			1.53	
Functional form	1.99			0.20	
Normality	1.06			2.45	
Heteroscedasticity	0.23			0.40	

much more successful, however. German inflation is a significant influence in both pre-EMS estimates as well as in the post-EMS estimate. For the Netherlands, dummy variables based on institutional evidence proved important in dealing with serial correlation and a breakpoint at 1983Q1/Q2 was identified. German inflation is significant in both periods. Finally, German inflation itself is found to be a notably stable process, only two one-quarter dummy variables being needed to remove serial correlation from an equation for the whole period.[3]

The evidence provided by the behaviour of autoregressive price-

Table 13.2 *(Continued)*

Belgium (B)			Germany		
1972Q1–1981Q4			1972Q1–1989Q2		
$\Delta_4$lbp(−1)	1.154	(13.79)	$\Delta_4$lgp(−1)	1.366	(13.38)
$\Delta_4$lbp(−2)	−0.333	(4.01)	$\Delta_4$lgp(−2)	−0.412	(4.04)
$\Delta_4$lgp(−2)	0.787	(5.66)	D79Q3	0.011	(2.56)
$\Delta_4$lgp(−3)	−1.270	(5.79)	D86Q1	−0.010	(2.42)
$\Delta_4$lgp(−4)	0.663	(4.34)	$\bar{R}^2$	0.963	
DB2	0.019	(7.45)	SE (% mean)	10.84	
$\bar{R}^2$	0.986		χ^2 Serial		
SE (% mean)	4.57		correlation	5.98	
χ^2 Serial			Functional form	0.0005	
correlation (LM4)	5.40		Normality	0.10	
Functional form	0.23		Heteroscedasticity	1.00	
Normality	1.71				
Heteroscedasticity	0.0002				

Notes: Constant terms included in the estimation are not reported.
Country dummies shown are 0,1 variables, taking the value unity for the periods:
France: DF2 1977Q1; DF6 1982Q3; DF7 1974Q1; Italy: IT2 1976Q2–1977Q1; IT3 1974Q1–1974Q4; IT4 1075Q1–1975Q4; Belgium: DB2 1974Q1–1974Q4; Netherlands: NL1 1977Q4; NL2 1982Q4–1983Q1; Germany: D79Q3 1979Q3; D86Q1 1986Q1.

inflation equations is, therefore, rather clear. A country's participation in the ERM of the European Monetary System has – sooner or later – provided an occasion for German inflation to enter significantly into the AR process describing that country's inflation. Germany's own inflation process, meanwhile, has remained remarkably stable. All of this is consistent with the German leadership model.

WAGE DETERMINATION

The second stage of the programme is to insert the inflation predictors into wage determination equations and to examine whether additional EMS influence is present in the form of structural change in the wage determination process. A general form for the wage determination process, which can be viewed as an error correction model of the real wage or as a hybrid augmented Phillips curve/real wage resistance process is as follows:

$$\dot{w}_t = \alpha + \beta_1 \dot{w}_{t-1} + \beta_2 \dot{p}_t + \beta_3 XD_t + \beta_4 (w/p)_{t-1} + \beta_5 D_i + u_t \quad (1)$$

where $\dot{w}$ is the rate of inflation, $\dot{p}$ the expected inflation rate, XD a proxy for excess demand in the labour market (unemployment), $(w/p)_{t-1}$ the real wage lagged i periods and D_i a sequence of dummy variables dictated by institutional information. A striking general characteristic of the data – already displayed in Figure 13.1 – is the way in which, in all of the non-German ERM participating countries, realized real wage behaviour has been modified, with a marked slowing down or even stagnation in the rate of growth of real wages shortly after the inception of the System. The behaviour of real wages in the UK affords a striking contrast in this respect. Another characteristic of the data revealed by estimation is that the change in trend of realized real wages emerges after a period in which previous relationships undergo some disturbance, corresponding *inter alia* to sharp institutional change in some cases. The OECD's series of *Economic Surveys* provides an invaluable source of comparative evidence in this respect. Institutional adjustment involving a mix of temporary incomes policies and the modification or elimination of formal indexing arrangements is a common theme in the OECD's *Surveys* for these countries at this time. The work of Barrell and his associates (Barrell, 1990; Barrell et al., 1990) provides further important evidence on the significance of institutional adjustments in the ERM countries. If all of these adjustments are credited to the EMS effect then that effect may comprise a combination of two influences: first, the intrusion of German inflation into predictors for domestic inflation; second, a possible modification, following a period of sometimes chaotic adjustment, of wage determination processes. However, the institutional adjustments may simply be the correlate of the intrusion of German inflation into expectations, with little additional effect remaining to be discerned in the estimation. Residual adjustment is accomplished by change in the determinants of wage inflation, notably change in the rate of unemployment.

Figure 13.3 is a reminder of the extent to which rising unemployment has taken the strain in the downward adjustment of inflation. That evidence could support a position of scepticism about the presence of 'added value' in inflation-reduction within an EMS framework, suggesting instead that while membership of the ERM can guarantee the reduction of inflation, that reduction will simply be effected by the necessary rise in unemployment.

The results of the estimation are shown, country-by-country, in Tables 13.3–13.7. In estimating equation (1) long-run dynamic homogeneity was imposed where this was supported by the data. The imposition was effected by subtracting $\Delta_4 lw_{-1}$ from each side of equation (1) and imposing the value of the coefficient on the inflation expectations term on the RHS at a value equal to the complement of that on the inertia term. In other words, we estimate with $\Delta_1 \Delta_4$ on the LHS and a composite term $(\hat{p} - \Delta_4 lw_{-1})$ on the RHS. The $\hat{p}$s are drawn from the fitted values of the preferred autoregressive inflation equations listed at Table 13.2.[4] For the EMS period, this means that German inflation is incorporated into the wage inflation estimates via its influence on the expectations terms.[5]

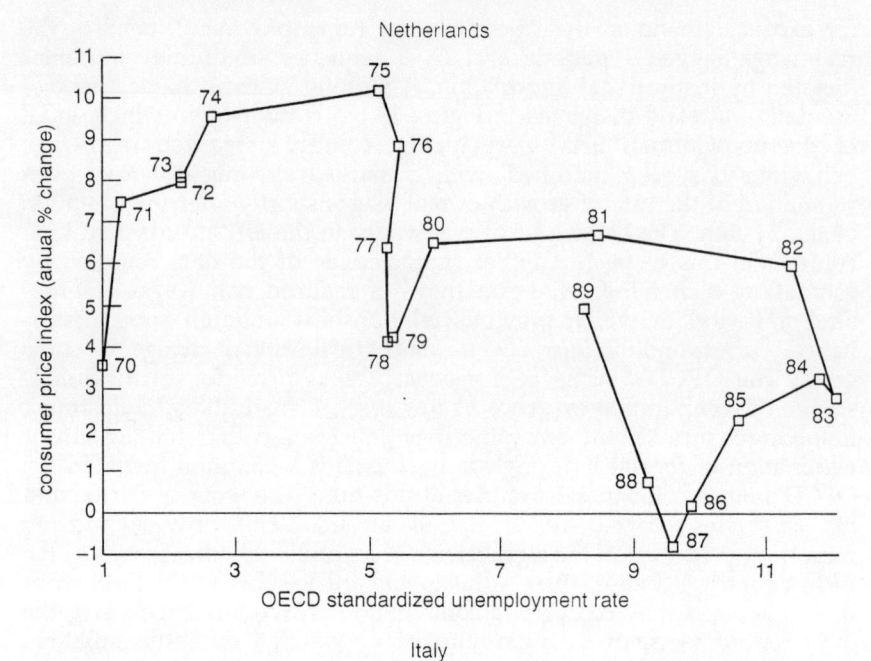

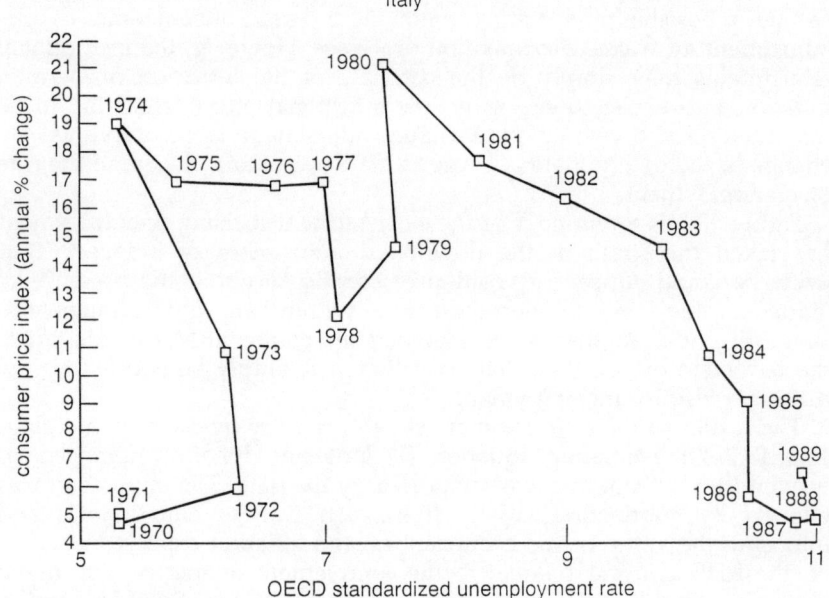

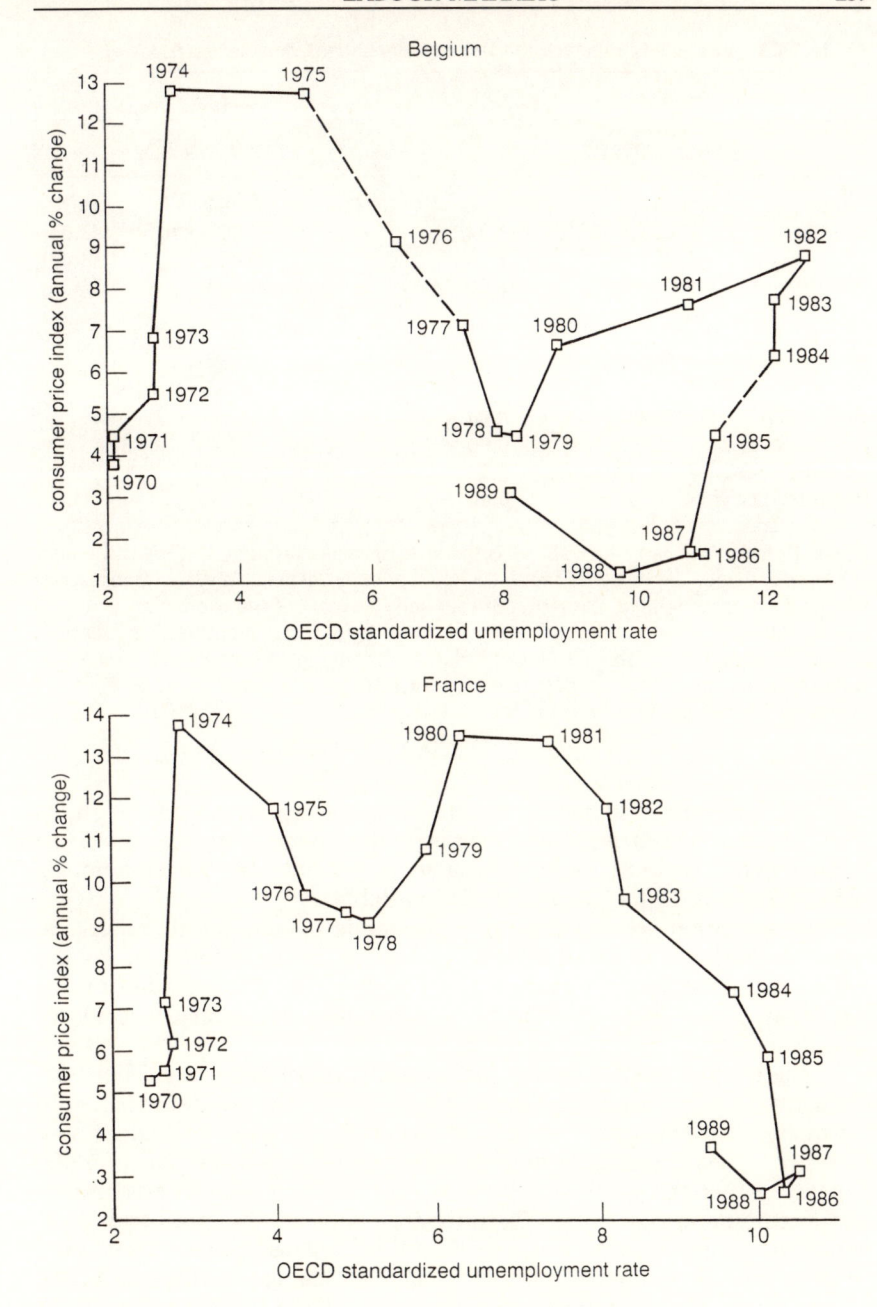

Figure 13.3 Inflation and unemployment, 1970–1989

Table 13.3 Wage determination in Germany (dependent variable: $\Delta_1\Delta_4 ldew$)

Pre-EMS			EMS		
1972Q1–1979Q3			1979Q4–1989Q2		
GPW1	0.534	(3.45)	GPW2	0.604	(4.32)
DEUNP	$-0.001(\times 10^{-1})$	(1.34)		$-0.003(\times 10^{-1})$	(3.65)
LGERW(−4)	−0.321	(2.18)		−0.406	(3.47)
TIM	0.002	(2.00)		0.003	(4.05)
			D81Q2	−0.029	(2.43)
$\bar{R}^2$	0.309		$\bar{R}^2$	0.445	
χ^2 Serial correlation (LM4)	8.54			8.82	
Functional form	0.60			0.03	
Normality	0.54			1.06	
Heteroscedasticity	0.40			0.19	

Notes: Definition of variables: DEUNP is the level of unemployment. LGERW is the (log of) the real wage. TIM is a time trend, D81Q2 a dummy variable. GPW1,2 impose long-run inflation homogeneity, the term representing the value of the expression ($\hat{p}_G - \Delta_4 ldew_{-1}$), with $\hat{p}_G$ imposed as the fitted value from the appropriate inflation predictor equation (cf. Table 13.2). Lag order is indicated in parentheses following the variable name. Data shown in parentheses are t-statistics. Constant terms were estimated but are omitted from the reporting.

While long-run dynamic homogeneity was supported for four out of five of our countries, for Belgium the data support short-run homogeneity, so there is no inertia term present and the equation is estimated with $(\Delta_4 lw - \hat{p})$ as the LHS variable.

The estimation was conducted with standard econometric criteria in mind; in addition to the diagnostics supplied in the country tables the period estimates were subjected to a variety of recursive stability tests. All those shown pass the Cusum-squared test at customary levels of significance.

We now turn to discuss the individual country estimates. Those for Germany are reported in Table 13.3. Whilst the wage process in Germany, like the price process, is generally very stable and of low variance, a change in behaviour is discernible around the end of 1979. Separate equations were consequently estimated for sub-periods ending and beginning at that point. The difference between the 'pre-' and 'post' equations is essentially that sensitivity to unemployment rises very sharply indeed as unemployment itself rises. Otherwise the coefficient values in the two equations are very similar. Long-run homogeneity of wage inflation is accepted in both periods, at least when a dummy for 1982Q2 is present in the second equation; in the absence of this dummy, the equation suffers from negative 4th order serial correlation.

The results reported for France in Table 13.4 reflect our finding of a

Table 13.4 Wage determination in France (dependent variable: $\Delta_1\Delta_4 lfw$)

	Pre-EMS			EMS	
	1972Q1–1982Q3			1986Q1–1989Q2	
FPW1	0.286	(5.20)	FPW2	0.240	(3.57)
FRUNP	−0.002(×10⁻²)	(1.88)	FRUNP(−1)	−0.005(×10⁻³)	(1.32)
LFRW(−4)	−0.089	(2.03)		−0.163	(2.18)
TIM	0.001	(1.66)		0.006(×10⁻¹)	(4.92)
D82Q2	0.017	(2.45)			
$\bar{R}^2$	0.515		$\bar{R}^2$	0.895	
χ^2 Serial correlation (LM4)	2.64			11.43	
Functional form	0.19			2.74	
Normality	0.61			0.20	
Heteroscedasticity	1.42			0.22	

Notes: Definition of variables: FRUNP is the level of unemployment, LFRW is the (log of) the real wage. TIM is a time trend. D82Q2 a dummy variable. FPW1,2, impose long-run inflation homogeneity, the term representing the value of the expression ($\hat{p}_F - \Delta_4 lfw_{-1}$), with $\hat{p}_F$ imposed as the fitted value from the appropriate inflation predictor equation (cf. Table 13.2). Lag order is indicated in parentheses following the variable name. Data shown in parentheses are t-statistics. Constant terms were estimated but are omitted from the reporting.

lengthy period of disturbance from the end of 1982 to the beginning of 1986 – spanning the Mitterrand U-turn and its consequences. We did not find it possible to make sense of the data set when this period was included. Omitting it, it is possible to estimate satisfactory equations, supporting long-term homogeneity and with perhaps surprisingly little change in structure. Recalling our earlier finding (Table 13.2) of a substantial EMS effect on inflation expectations, it appears that this is a principal avenue for such an effect in France.

Table 13.5, which logs the results obtained for Italy, suggests some similarities with the French experience. Again, there is a lengthy period of disturbance, though not quite so long as in the French case. A German influence mediated through inflation expectations is present in the post-transition period (Table 13.2). The inflation process itself is subject to a number of institutional disturbances both before and during the transition, but post-transition it is arguably not greatly different in fundamentals from its pre-EMS form.

Belgium (Table 13.6) is a different case. There is no lengthy transition period, although there is a break at the end of 1981. German inflation is significant in the expectations term in both periods. The specification of the wage–inflation relationship, post-break, is notable for the elimination of the significant time trend present in the pre-EMS relationship. A reduction in the rate of growth of the bargaining equilibrium real wage is indicated, which could be presented as an adjustment of aspirations

Table 13.5 Wage determination in Italy (dependent variable: $\Delta_1\Delta_4 liw$)

Pre-EMS			EMS		
1972Q1–1979Q3			1982Q1–1989Q2		
IPW1	0.472	(5.63)	IPW2	0.514	(3.64)
ITUNP(−4)	−0.007(×10^{-3})	(0.28)	ITUNP(−1)	−0.001(×10^{-2})	(1.01)
LIRW(−4)	−0.583	(4.25)		−0.706	(3.27)
TIM	0.009	(4.13)		0.002	(2.83)
IT2	0.028	(3.00)	D86Q1	−0.028	(3.69)
IT5	0.059	(4.99)			
D75Q1	0.056	(3.50)			
D76Q1	−0.052	(3.20)			
$\bar{R}^2$	0.827		$\bar{R}^2$	0.623	
χ^2 Serial correlation (LM4)		2.39		7.60	
Functional form		0.76		0.28	
Normality		3.48		1.65	
Heteroscedasticity		0.41		0.41	

Notes: Definition of variables: ITUNP is the level of unemployment, LIRW is the (log of) the real wage. TIM is a time trend: D75Q1, D76Q1, D86Q1 are dummy variables. IT2 is a dummy variable for 1976Q2–1977Q1; IT5 is a dummy variable for 1973Q2–1973Q3. IPW1,2, impose long-run inflation homogeneity, the term representing the value of the expression ($\hat{p}_l - \Delta_1 liw_{-1}$), with $\hat{p}_l$ imposed as the fitted value from the appropriate inflation predictor equation (cf. Table 13.2). Lag order is indicated in parentheses following the variable name. Data shown in parentheses are t-statistics. Constant terms were estimated but are omitted from the reporting.

on the part of the Belgian workforce – an EMS effect in the wage equation specification.

Finally, Table 13.7 gives the results for the Netherlands. German inflation was always important for the Netherlands, both before and after the EMS, however dated, and more important than in Belgium. The structure of the wages equation was found to be remarkably stable provided some turbulent periods associated with the first oil price shock were omitted from the beginning of the period.

The estimates provided in Tables 13.3–13.7 permit computation of summary measures of real-wage rigidity and real wage inflexibility. A wide variety of definitions of real-wage rigidity exists. The measure computed here is simply the ratio of the coefficient on own-country price inflation to (the modulus of) that on unemployment. This ratio, in effect, computes the proportionate increase in unemployment required to stabilize wage inflation when price inflation accelerates by a point. Since, according to equation (1), wage inflation depends on expected price inflation to the extent β_2, and on unemployment to the extent (−) β_3, a fall in β_2 or a rise in β_3 would reduce the measure of real-wage rigidity. Further, our representation of the expectations process makes

Table 13.6 Wage determination in Belgium (dependent variable: $\Delta_4 lbwpe$)

Pre-EMS			EMS		
1972Q1–1981Q4			1982Q1–1989Q2		
BEUNP(−1)	−0.003(×10^{-1})	(2.83)	BEUNP(−2)	−0.002(×10^{-1})	(3.77)
LBRW(−4)	−0.277	(5.47)		−0.440	(5.73)
TIM	0.003	(3.65)			
D75Q1	0.039	(2.95)			
$\bar{R}^2$	0.795		$\bar{R}^2$	0.600	
χ^2 Serial correlation (LM4)	4.94			7.42	
Functional form	0.95			0.16	
Normality	0.64			0.34	
Heteroscedasticity	1.61			0.53	

Notes: Definitions of variables: BEUNP is the level of unemployment, LBRW is the (log of) the real wage. TIM is a time trend, D75Q1 a dummy variable. For Belgium, the data support short-run dynamic homogeneity, and the dependent variable expresses this as $\Delta_4 lbwpe = \Delta_4 lbw - \hat{p}_B$, with $\hat{p}_B$ imposed as the fitted value from the appropriate inflation predictor equation (cf. Table 13.2). Lag order is indicated in parentheses following the variable name. Data shown in parentheses are t-statistics. Constant terms were estimated but are omitted from the reporting.

Table 13.7 Wage determination in the Netherlands (dependent variable: $\Delta_1 \Delta_4 lnw$)

Pre-EMS			EMS		
1974Q1–1980Q4			1981Q1–1989Q2		
NPW1	0.553	(4.33)	NPW2	0.433	(5.72)
NLUNP	−0.001(×10^{-1})	(1.92)	NLUNP(−1)	−0.001(×10^{-2})	(0.95)
LNRW(−4)	−0.302	(2.73)		−0.269	(3.18)
TIM	0.001	(1.88)		0.001	(3.87)
$\bar{R}^2$	0.529		$\bar{R}^2$	0.500	
χ^2 Serial correlation (LM4)	8.54			3.18	
Functional form	0.16			0.93	
Normality	0.48			0.93	
Heteroscedasticity	0.36			0.02	

Notes: Definitions of variables: NLUNP is the level of unemployment, LNRW is the (log of) the real wage. TIM is a time trend. NPW1,2, impose long-run inflation homogeneity, the term representing the value of the expression ($\hat{p}_N - \Delta_4 lnw_{-1}$), with $\hat{p}_N$ imposed as the fitted value from the appropriate inflation predictor equation (cf. Table 13.2). Constant terms were estimated but are omitted from the reporting.

Table 13.8 Change in the structural characteristics of the wage inflation process[a]

	Germany	France	Italy	Belgium	Netherlands
Real wage rigidity	−0.9	−0.8	3.4	0.4	5.6
Real wage inflexibility	−1.0	−0.8	−0.8	−1.0	9.0

Note: [a] Figures show the proportionate change between the pre-EMS and EMS period. See text for definition of terms.

expected inflation dependent on past own-inflation to an extent which tends to fall between the pre-EMS and the EMS period itself. Thus, if the dependence of inflation on past own-inflation is denoted α, our measure of real wage rigidity is computed as $\alpha\beta_2/|\beta|$. In Table 13.8 we plot the extent to which this measure changes from the pre-EMS to the EMS period. As can be seen, declines are limited to Germany and France. There is a small rise for Belgium and large increases (factors of 3.4 and 5.6 respectively) for Italy and the Netherlands. If a reduction in real wage rigidity is a good thing, the EMS does not appear to have been favourable in this sense. In the lower half of the table, we record the change in real-wage inflexibility. This is simply the ratio of the coefficient on the time trend to the coefficient on the (modulus of) the unemployment term, measuring the unemployment cost of the real wage trajectory. A reduction in the trajectory or a rise in the sensitivity of wages to unemployment reduces the ratio. Inflexibility, in this sense, has fallen everywhere except in the Netherlands, where it has risen sharply, according to our point estimates.

CONCLUSIONS

In this chapter we have examined wage inflation in the principal ERM countries with a view to establishing the presence or otherwise of an 'EMS effect'.

Screening of the data provides strong prima facie evidence that the data-generating processes underlying wage determination in France, Italy, Belgium and, to some extent, the Netherlands changed markedly some time after the countries joined the ERM. For example, not only was the average rate of wage increases far lower in the post-ERM period than in the period preceding entry, but also the correlation of both price and wage inflation rates between the countries increased in the post-ERM period. Further, graphical inspection of the relationship between inflation and unemployment in France, Italy and Belgium shows a clear break in the early 1980s, the period when the ERM became a firm framework.

In the wage bargaining process, theory indicates that such shifts could stem from the combination of Germany's dominance of the system and that country's strong counter-inflationary record. In seeking more formal evidence for these shifts, we carried out an econometric investigation into wage determination in the ERM countries.

Two sets of evidence were examined. First, we modelled expectations of price inflation by an AR process, and investigated for the direct impact of German inflation on these processes both before and after ERM entry. Second, after incorporating the inflation expectations variable as one of the explanatory factors, we examined the wage equations themselves for structural shifts around the time of the coalescing of the ERM.

For Germany itself, the autoregressive process describing price inflation was the same in both the pre- and post-ERM periods. There is evidence that the coefficient on the pressure-of-demand variable has become more important post-ERM, although in other respects the process of German wage/price determination remained the same after the formalization of the ERM in the early 1980s. To some extent, the same is true in the Netherlands, where, however, real wage rigidity has moved in the opposite direction.

In France and Italy, in the autoregressive schemes modelling price expectations, German influence emerges strongly in the post-ERM period. For Belgium, German influence is present in both the periods.

In terms of the wage equation in the above three countries, the experience of both France and Italy is again different from Belgium, although strong evidence of an EMS effect exists in all three countries. In Belgium, there appears to be a very sharp downward shift in the implied rate of increase of the real wage sought by the labour force. In France and Italy, the overall structure of the wage equation remains relatively unchanged post-ERM entry, with the exception of course of the modification of the expectations process. However, in both countries there was a period of disturbed transition shortly after ERM entry which we found very difficult to incorporate satisfactorily into econometric equations.

Overall, our estimates suggest strong support for the view that German inflation is a relevant factor in ERM member country price-expectation formation and hence in labour market behaviour. To this extent, the presumption of 'added gain' in deflating within the framework of the ERM is sustained. It is also clear that there have been important transitional effects, mediated through institutional adjustments and some longer-run impacts on the structure of the wage determination process.

Finally, to the extent that the inflationary process has not been brought into line by the reduction of inflationary expectations or by short or long-term structural changes, the residual adjustment has been accomplished by rising unemployment. In the period in question unemployment has risen strongly in all the countries concerned.

APPENDIX: THE EMS AND LABOUR MARKETS: A FURTHER LOOK

The foregoing chapter defines what an EMS effect might be and can be construed as an attempt to parameterize it. The results are less than resounding in a number of ways. First, there is little evidence of an EMS effect of a type that involves a shift in the wage equation, and what shift there is is not always in a favourable direction. Second, the effect which is mediated through expectations in the analysis, where inflation expectations in the EMS countries appear to embody information about German inflation after the EMS has established itself, is not unambiguous. While consistent with an 'EMS effect', the evidence does not discriminate decisively against rival hypotheses. In any event it is obvious that the EMS countries have paid a high price in unemployment to get their rates of inflation down to (or, now in some cases, somewhat below) German levels. However calculated, the sacrifice ratios of the EMS countries are not low when compared with similarly constructed calculations for other countries (see Table 13A.1, where sacrifice ratio data drawn from Schelde-Andersen (1992) are presented). According to ranking-by-characteristics exercises like those by Calmfors and Driffill (1988) or Bean (1992), most EMS countries have 'bad' characteristics which make them least able to cope with inflationary shocks and least able to effect disinflations which are cheap in unemployment and lost output. Of course, this observation is itself ambiguous. European sacrifice ratios may be higher than elsewhere, yet still lower than they would otherwise have been given the unfavourable starting position. Nevertheless, the fact is that the current state of European labour markets makes it difficult to draw very optimistic conclusions regarding the size of the EMS effect.

Non-wage labour costs

While the majority of studies focusing on labour market behaviour do so using data on wages, the overall performance of the system is also a function of non-wage labour costs, most notably payroll taxes and surcharges of a similar type of which social security systems are commonly, albeit often notionally 'financed'. There may also be significant non-wage labour costs arising from private provision of pensions and fringe benefits. Where these additional costs are proportional to wage costs, the *responsiveness* of the labour market to shocks may well not be greatly affected by their presence. However, it is clear that the presence of a substantial 'wedge' of non-wage labour costs, however structured, is likely to be employment-reducing. At times when unemployment is high in any case, the premium on government action to remove or reduce its contribution to those costs is obviously high. Figure 13A.1 (reproduced from the *Financial Times*) provides a convenient recent summary of the comparative significance of these costs. They are notably higher, especially in Germany but to a degree

Table 13A.1 Sacrifice ratios

	U	Y1	Y2	Y3
USA	0.85	1.35	0.40	0.30
Japan	0.70	0.50	0.10	−0.30
UK	3.40	0.90	0.60	0.20
Germany	6.40	2.20	1.20	1.60
France	2.15	0.50	0.50	0.20
Italy	1.40	0.65	0.45	0.20
Belgium	3.00	6.10	0.90	0.50
Denmark	1.25	0.90	−0.15	0.15
Ireland	3.35	0.30	0.50	0.50
Netherlands	4.95	1.85	0.80	1.10

Notes: Sacrifice ratio calculations can be very sensitive to choice of base and end-date. In the estimates quoted above those for U are calculated as the quotient of the cumulative increase in unemployment between 1979/81 and 1986/89 and the change in the rate of inflation (consumer prices) over the same period. Columns Y1, Y2 and Y3 are based on output losses, being calculated as the quotient of the cumulative loss of output from 1979 to (respectively), 1982, 1985 and 1988 and the change in inflation between 1979/81, and respectively 1984, 1987 and 1990. The choice of dates and averaging removes most of the idiosyncratic features of the data.

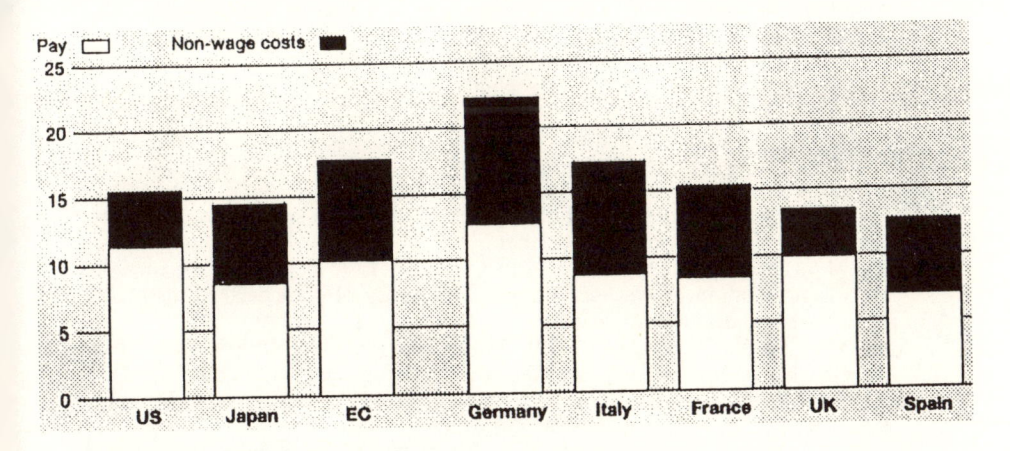

Figure 13A.1 Manufacturing labour costs, 1991 (US$ per hour)

elsewhere in Europe (though with the notable exception of the UK), than in the USA or Japan. This gives good reason for thinking that direct fiscal action may be called for to complement the labour market responses evoked by the counter-inflationary framework of the EMS.

NOTES

A good deal of the work that has gone into this paper was done while Michael Artis was a Nuffield Foundation Social Science Research Fellow. It was completed during this author's tenure of a research grant from the Leverhulme Trust. The support of both institutions is gratefully acknowledged. In addition the authors are grateful to members of the Macro-modelling Study Group for constructive comments on an earlier version which was delivered at the London School of Economics in May 1991.

1 Kremers (1990), in his work on the Irish economy, also successfully employs such an approach.
2 It nevertheless can also be shown for a breakpoint fixed at 1979Q1/Q2 that AR(4) predictors for our group of countries are improved by adding in German inflation for the EMS period, but not before. The exceptions are the UK, where German inflation is not relevant in either period, and the Netherlands, where German inflation is important both before and after EMS, though more so after the EMS was created. See Artis (1990), Artis and Nachane (1990).
3 Results for the United Kingdom are not reported; however, results obtained for this case do not include any significant influence from German inflation for any period. (See also Artis and Nachane, 1990.)
4 For Belgium in the EMS period, equation (B) was used.
5 This assumption embodies an exclusion restriction that can be tested. We therefore looked to see whether *additional* terms in German inflation (up to three lags thereof) contributed significantly to the explanatory power of the estimating equation. The results supported the exclusion restriction in every case with the exception of Italy, where German inflation entered at lags one and three – with coefficients of opposing sign and of similar magnitude. This dynamic effect appeared difficult to rationalize and has been omitted from the results shown in Table 13.5.

REFERENCES

Artis, M.J. (1990), 'Il Sistema Monetario Europeo come struttura anti-inflazione', *Revista di Politica Economia*, December.

Artis, M.J., Farmelo, F., Murfin, A. and Ormerod, P. (1984), 'Price expectations and wage inflation in Western Europe', University of Manchester Department of Economics, discussion paper no. 42.

Artis, M.J. and Nachane, D.M. (1990), 'Wages and prices in europe: a test of the German leadership hypothesis', *Weltwirtshcaftliches Archiv*, 126, 59–77.

Barrell, R.J. (1990), 'Has the EMS changed wage and price behaviour in Europe?', *National Institute Economic Review*, 132, May.

Barrell, R.J., Darby, J. and Donaldson, C. (1990), 'Structural stability in European wage and price systems', National Institute Discussion Paper, no. 188.

Barro, R.J. and Gordon, D. (1983a), 'A positive theory of monetary policy in a natural rate model', *Journal of Political Economy*, 91, August.
Barro, R.J. and Gordon, D. (1983b), 'Rules, discretion and reputation in a model of monetary policy', *Journal of Monetary Economics*, July.
Bean, C. (1992), 'European unemployment: a survey', LSE, Centre for Economic Performance, discussion paper no. 71.
Calmfors, L. and Driffill, J. (1988), 'Bargaining structure, corporation and macro performance', *Economic Policy*, 6, 14–47.
Dornbusch, R. (1991), 'Problems of European monetary integration', in A. Giovannini and C. Mayer (eds), *European Financial Integration*, Cambridge, Cambridge University Press.
Giavazzi, F. and Giovannini, A. (1988), 'The role of the exchange rate regime in disinflation: empirical evidence on the European Monetary System', in F. Giavazzi, S. Micossi and M. Miller (eds), *The European Monetary System*, Cambridge, Cambridge University Press.
Giavazzi, F. and Giovannini, A. (1989), 'Interpreting the European disinflation: the role of the exchange rate regime', in F. Giavazzi and A. Giovannini (eds), *Limiting Exchange Rate Flexibility: the European Monetary System*, Cambridge, Mass., MIT Press.
Giavazzi, F. and Pagano, M. (1988), 'The advantage of tying one's hands', *European Economic Review*, 32, 1055–1082.
Kremers, J.J.M. (1990), 'Gaining policy credibility for a disinflation', *IMF Staff Papers* 37, March, 116–145.
Melitz, J. (1985), 'The welfare costs of the European Monetary System', *Journal of International Money and Finance*, 4, 485–506.
Paldam, M. (1980), 'The international element in the Phillips curve', *Scandinavian Journal of Economics*, 216–239.
Schelde-Andersen, P. (1992), 'OECD country expansion with disinflation', in A. Blundell-Wignall (ed.), *Inflation, Disinflation and Monetary Policy*, Proceedings of a conference at the Reserve Bank of Australia.
Weber, A. (1991), 'Reputation and credibility in the European Monetary System', *Economic Policy*, 12, 57–102.

14

THE IMPLICATIONS OF DIFFERENT LABOUR MARKET REGIMES IN EUROPE AND THE LESSONS FROM GERMAN UNIFICATION FOR THE EMS AND EMU

Heiner Flassbeck

INTRODUCTION

The implications of different labour market regimes for the future of the EMS and the creation of EMU are only mentioned in passing. The main points of the discussion are the questions of central bank autonomy in matters of monetary policy, the technical form of a rigid EMS, and fiscal policy convergence. This is astonishingly similar to the preparations for the currency union in Germany: at that time official announcements and scientific publications hardly touched on the problem of wage determination in East Germany. In the meantime this has changed. There is now barely a single observer who does not emphasize the massive role of wage developments in the lasting weakness of the East German economy. There are well-founded fears that in moves towards currency union the same mistake will be made in Europe. Although details about the form of a reformed EMS are being discussed, the central question, whether and for how long the wage policy regimes in the countries concerned will permit stable exchange rates, is being ignored.

In reality it was the divergent wage policy developments which finally played a large part in the breaking up of the EMS. Great Britain and Italy especially were not successful in their attempts to maintain their competitiveness at fixed exchange rates through wage discipline. France, far more successful in this respect, was, in spite of considerable speculation, finally able to defend its exchange rate. Every reform of the monetary system and every currency realignment will be judged in terms of whether it supports or even forces the required degree of wage discipline. Technical details of the currency regime therefore play a small role, and the fact that the currency regime of the western world is nothing more than a wage standard is crucial. The paper money currencies can only fulfil their purpose if price stability is guaranteed through a wage policy based on the trend in productivity. This may not sound too displeasing, since it is already well known that a monetary policy geared towards stability, if possible with the help of an independent central bank, is responsible for price stability. Stable prices alone, however, are not sufficient.

The significance of price stability continually has to prove itself as a necessary condition for achieving an acceptable level of growth and employment in order to retain its acceptance in society. If these aims cannot be fulfilled to a sufficient extent, price stability and the autonomy of the central bank become a chimera. What made countries such as the Federal Republic of Germany and Japan so successful and stable in the past was not a permanent restrictive monetary policy to force price stability, but an expansion of the money supply in line with the potential for growth, which was guaranteed stability by the basic consensus of tariff partners and society to stand by the requirements (without inflation). Only this kind of policy guarantees good supply conditions from the monetary side because it keeps interest rates sufficiently low to allow a high level of investment.

But even this kind of policy is not sufficient to guarantee the stability of a system of fixed exchange rates or of a currency union. A situation could arise whereby member countries of a fixed exchange rate system or a currency union permanently show fundamentally different real growth rates despite the same levels of prices and interest rates. The level of investment in the partner countries would therefore vary and real incomes would grow at different rates. This would be acceptable if such a society did *not* aim to bring standards of living into line with each other. If a currency union is considered as a preliminary step towards a political union, as in the case of Germany, political tension without a system of income redistribution between regions is unavoidable. As the German experience again shows, comprehensive systems for income redistribution themselves can, however, only be implemented with far-reaching political consensus on the part of the regions and the political parties involved. As EMU is considered explicitly as a preliminary step towards a 'European Union', the effects of divergent rates of growth and their causes must be analysed.

Different rates of growth are, as will be shown here, predominantly the result of the wage policy regime at the microeconomic level and not merely a consequence of exogenous influences or political decisions. The wage policy regime determines what kind of effects the behaviour of entrepreneurs will have on capital returns and how much pressure there is for other firms to follow suit.

Two central questions will be examined below: first, what kind of wage policy regime at the microeconomic level is suitable for promoting dynamic management and therefore investment, and second, what kind of wage policy regime is required at the macroeconomic level to maintain the competition between economies and to guarantee price stability.

DECENTRALIZED VERSUS CENTRALIZED WAGE NEGOTIATIONS[1]

Given different exchange rate policy conditions, how are changes in competitiveness at the level of the individual firm translated into changes in competitiveness for the whole economy? Looking through the theoretical literature on foreign trade shows that such a question is dealt with neither in 'real' nor in 'monetary' theory, in such a way as really to help us in our task. The link between the firm level and the macro level is hardly to be found in modern literature, although older studies provided some preliminary work.[2]

Economic theory's lack of interest in finding out about questions of the efficiency of adjustment processes still stems from the one-sided orientation towards equilibrium as the beginning and end of every analysis. Equilibrium is only abandoned as a result of the overcoming of individual shocks, and the restoration of equilibrium through a change in price or quantity fulfils the aim of an insight into theoretical economics.[3] Only a few authors, whose theories have for the most part not yet found an important place in economics,[4] still interpret the world as a series of disequilibria at the micro and macro levels from which they develop a dynamic reference model. Only a dynamic model, based on the microeconomy, enables relevant economic policy conclusions to be drawn, because this is the only way in which the core of what makes up the dynamics of market economies can be captured. It is far more than a methodical difference as to whether it is a question of how flexible prices or flexible exchange rates can restore a certain initial equilibrium after a shock, or whether it is a question of how flexible prices or flexible exchange rates influence the ability of the system to adapt in view of the incentive mechanisms for the 'creation' of dynamic development. The dynamics of the market system and its superior efficiency in overcoming exogenous shocks are based on the permanent existence of temporary disequilibria and not on the quickest possible restoration of a general equilibrium. Flexible prices, wages, interest rates and exchange rates must always permit temporary rigidity if the correct signals for the evolution of the system are to be given.

The economics of general equilibrium is just not capable of analysing such a system, because the time requirement of rigidity tends systematically towards zero. Comparative statics can only show that there are equilibrium solutions if prices are sufficiently flexible. It can, however, be shown how large a change in output is possible if prices are sufficiently rigid for the dynamic evolution of the system.[5]

Nonetheless, attempts have been made at more detailed analyses of partial rigidities and the significance of wage rigidity especially is being discussed more and more.[6] The question is, however, almost always whether and how wage rigidity can be compensated by the flexibility of other prices, especially by exchange rate flexibility at the macroeconomic level. This is the classical analysis of overcoming shocks which in principle characterized the discussion in the 1960s about the 'assignment problem'. At the level of the individual firm and the adjustment processes which take place independently of price flexibility, however, this does not happen.

Strictly speaking, economic theory offers concepts for analysing competitiveness at only two levels:

1. At the level of the individual firm competing in a clearly defined market segment with rivals who, in terms of the availability of resources and technology, are all in a similar position. This is the area of business management market share analysis.
2. At the level of regionally separable conglomerates of firms from various branches of industry which are characterized by interregional immobility of the factors of production (land, labour and capital). This is the area of the classical theory of international trade.

With mobility of labour, capital and raw materials, deviating profit levels are generally not possible for the firms in individual regions. Migration takes place, which leads to a quick equalization of prices. In a very simple model of equal international and factor mobility, competition problems at the firm level arise in the course of the evolutionary process. These are solved by offensive cost reductions or defensive adjustment (bankruptcy), but the average competitiveness of a *regionally* diversified conglomerate is never threatened. All regions (nations) would progress at exactly the same rate, since the migration of labour and capital allow neither typical regional preferences nor the identification of an individual with the region in which he or she already lives. This also implies that the share of the state and the structure of state-produced goods and services fully conform to the preferences of the mobile suppliers of labour and capital. Any deviation from the level and structure of the desired state share would cause emigration and force the state to reverse such exogenous intervention. The level of state intervention in all regions would converge.[7]

Even these simple observations show that interregional or international comparisons of competitiveness, that is the attempt to analyse the relative adaptability of conglomerates in one area, is only useful if a large proportion of the factors of production is immobile. Immobility is, however, not the only necessary requirement. For measurable and noticeable changes in the competitiveness of conglomerates of firms within an area a non-market (disequilibrium) adjustment of prices to changes in threshold productivity is required as well.

The real or 'pure' theory of international trade explains – for a given quantity of resources – the exchange of goods and services between regions whose economic relations are characterized by immobility of the most important factors of production (labour, capital and land). The rates of exchange (relative prices, terms of trade) are determined by production costs and then lead to welfare gains for all regions concerned, compared with no trade if the absolute production advantages of particular goods were divided equally between sectors and regions. But even a one-sided allocation of absolute cost advantages can allow welfare-increasing trade, because the division of labour allows better use of the available resources (the principle of comparative cost advantages). Despite immobility of the most important factors of production there is a (long-run) tendency towards equalization of factor prices, as the prices of goods which are produced using abundant factors fall and through additional demand increase the scarcity of these factors and vice versa (Heckscher–Ohlin theorem).

As the theory of international trade was illustrated by the classical authors in quantities, it was often interpreted as if prices and costs expressed in money terms have nothing to do with the evolution of international trade. This is a misconception.[8]. The classical theory of international trade has only been built up and interpreted in this way because the classical authors wanted to prove the advantages of free trade between economies with different allocations of immobile factors. The emphasis of the theory of comparative costs clearly shows this aim. As a rule the classicalists believe that international trade is steered by absolute costs of production, expressed in money terms. Although the differences between prices are in the end determined by the differences in the (real) allocation of immobile factors, it does not matter a priori whether absolute or comparative real advantages determine the absolute difference between prices. The theory of comparative advantage shows simply that examining the absolute advantages of a firm or a country alone does not show whether an expansion of trade would still lead to welfare gains.

If, however, the absolute money costs actually do determine the evolution of trade flows and one takes into account that labour, as a factor that is being used directly, just as labour that was used in other periods (stored-up labour), called tangible capital, is by far the most important immobile factor of production, an analysis of the evolution of advantages and disadvantages in international trade which is not merely a welfare analysis cannot avoid recognizing the significance of changes in the cost of labour in its current form (nominal wage) or in the form of lower efficiency of the capital inputs as a result of a change in labour productivity.[9]

From these observations comes the very central conclusion often overlooked in 'modern' real analyses of developments in foreign trade (investigations of the rate of technical progress, patent registrations, factor productivity, etc.). The monetary regime selected in an economy for domestic and international matters also determines the (dynamic) evolution of an economy's foreign trade. The (real) allocation of factors determines the rate of increase of labour productivity, but it does not dominate the process which leads to the determination of prices (and the price level) and which finally fixes the level of employment and the balance of payments.

In principle there are two methods for converting an improvement in the production process (which is normal for western economies and involves a shift of the supply curve for the whole economy to the right) to a higher real income:

1. At constant nominal wages and constant nominal demand (money supply) the price level falls, corresponding to increases in productivity growth.
2. With anticipation of growth in productivity through pay negotiations the price level remains constant at increasing nominal wages and a money supply increasing in line with growth in production.

The type of exchange rate system then determines the exact adjustment requirements for open economies and the emergence, as well as the duration and extent of (temporary) deviations from equilibrium. With absolutely fixed exchange rates the following possibilities exist:

1. Price levels falling at different rates depending on the average increase in productivity in the individual countries indicate the need for a forced adjustment of the country's development with the most dynamic competitor. Disequilibria at the macroeconomic level may be barely visible since adaptation vis-à-vis competitors must take place at the level of the individual firm and in the very short term in order to be able to remain in the market. This is the principle of interregional adaptation applied at the international level and it implies a classical analysis on the basis of mobility of all factors and atomistic determination of prices and wages.

    This case will not be pursued further, as it is only of theoretical interest. In practice no wage or monetary policy regime of this kind – independent of the degree of mobility of factors and therefore the degree of competition in the factor markets – has ever been successful, although it comes closest to the ideal of the intervention-free economy.[10] The same arguments exist against permanent deflation as against permanent inflation.[11]
2. In principle, anticipation of the rate of productivity growth through nominal wage increases in competing countries (with immobile labour) prevents such a national requirement for adjustment, since the national price levels only differ in terms of the share of services in national output and export prices are the same. Such a statement is, like the classical theory, based on a mark-up hypothesis for the explanation of the national price levels. The adjustment requirements derived from such a hypothesis only affect the macroeconomic level (wage negotiations) without excluding the pioneering profits of individual firms (or sectors) and the corresponding losses elsewhere. The differential profits of the pioneer are smaller than in

the first case, as the pioneer must bear the average wage increase and therefore cannot reduce prices or realize profits to the full extent of the increase in productivity.

Macroeconomically, measurable differences in competition can only be explained under such a regime through deviations in productivity changes from the principle of totally fixed exchange rates and/or from the principle of adjustment of changes in the nominal wage, because 'unavoidably' differing national rates of inflation are included in pay negotiations or integrated institutionally (indexation). In this way problems of competition arose in systems with 'fixed but adjustable' exchange rates.

In order to reduce the complexity of reality in the centre of the adjustment process, the most simple dynamic model for analysis of changes in competitiveness will be used here. The starting point of all considerations is the improvement of a production process for a certain ('pioneer') firm's tradeable product in the observed country. The productivity of the immobile factor labour rises. At the same wage rate and the same level of output, the firm's costs fall. For the sake of simplicity, let us assume that the pioneer firm's productivity increases from the average for the whole economy to twice this rate. If the firm uses the reduction in costs to reduce prices immediately and to the full extent, it can increase its market share, even if this process results in an increase in the size of the total market.

The following assumptions will also be made, which merely simplify things without affecting the centre of the argument:

- Wage negotiations take place – either centrally or decentrally – at the end of a certain period. Wage increases can, however, be passed on in full in the form of higher prices.
- The price level abroad remains unchanged.
- The price elasticity of demand for the pioneer firm's products is normal in both domestic and foreign markets. This assumption may be risky for individual firms, but for the 'average' pioneer firm it is fair and realistic.

With fixed exchange rates and annually, *centrally* agreed wage rates on the basis of an anticipation of the increase in productivity for the whole economy at constant prices, conditions result such as those which were characteristic of the whole world in the 1960s or of the EMS for most of the 1980s. In very centralized pay negotiations, rates of wage increase are set at the beginning of each year according to the expected increase in labour productivity. If such a rule for finding wages is valid for all the countries participating in international trade, the average price competitiveness for the whole economy does not change, the real exchange rate remains constant and, as long as non-price changes are excluded, market shares remain the same. But what happens at the level of the individual firm?

Can pioneer firms, which enter the market with more efficient production processes, be successful? With a strategy of the highest possible market penetration, as has been assumed here, the pioneer firm can reduce the price of its product to the extent of its productivity increase, which is above the average for the whole economy. With normal price elasticities of demand this price reduction would lead to a corresponding increase in quantity demanded and a larger market share. For the duration of the pay agreement (normally one year) the domestic price level will fall in line with the weight of the pioneer firm's goods in the representative household's basket of goods. The same is true for the price level in foreign trade. With fixed exchange rates the real exchange rate (on a price and cost basis) falls, and the country's total market share increases.

Both change as soon as the new pay round at the start of the next period is completed. The average productivity increase for the whole economy causes the negotiating parties to agree on higher pay increases so that the price level for the whole economy returns to its previous level, and therefore remains constant from year to year. This increase in wages, which in the case described here is caused by higher productivity in just *one* firm signifies an increase in costs of the immobile factor (increase in labour costs per unit) for all other firms, which is reflected in lower profits or higher prices there. In contrast, the pioneer firm retains much of its original advantage, since its wages only increase in relation to the weight of its product in the basket of goods, and its labour costs per unit therefore remain lower than before. If increased costs are passed on in the form of higher prices, other firms' market shares in foreign markets fall if the competitive situation there remains the same. The country's real exchange rate then returns to its previous level.

The wage increase corresponding to the average productivity increase for the whole economy obviously has the function in this regime of equalizing differences in productivity growth between trading partners *without* eliminating the success and the incentives for the pioneering firm. In such a regime trading partners with very different rates of growth or very different structures of preferences and shares in foreign trade can keep the borders for goods open as long as the mobility of the other factors is not restricted.

In the case of *decentralized* pay agreements changes in wages are a function of the changes in productivity and profits in the individual firm. Whether and to what extent a price reduction will lead to an increased market share in this case depends on the speed and extent of the adjustment of wages to changes in productivity and/or profits. It is inevitable that the pioneer firm will at the time of the adjustment of wages lose most or even all of its advantage gained through innovation, so that the other firms at home and abroad – unlike with centralized pay negotiations – are only forced to adjust for a short time. Under the regime of a full adjustment of wages the profit level and the individual market shares may remain unchanged, leaving the pioneer firm successful neither at home nor abroad.

With 'normal' exchange rate policy conditions as have been assumed so far, the effect on the *whole economy* of an adjustment process in the wake of the 'disturbance' of equilibrium by a pioneer firm is absolutely identical in all imaginable cases. The market share of the whole regional conglomerate of firms investigated remains the same over a time span long enough to allow for equilibrium. This is trivial, as such a result consistent with the theory is a priori preconditioned by the inclusion of market ('equilibrium') factor price adjustments into the model.

The result of the adjustment *below* the average for the whole economy is by no means trivial. With decentralized pay negotiations the market share of the pioneer firm may also remain constant. The pioneer firm cannot maintain its advantage beyond the period of the pay agreement. With centralized pay negotiations, however, the gain in market share of the pioneer is final, the other firms must accept losses (in profits and/or in market share) and have the chance to regain the lost ground only through their own creativity. This is a central point: the explanation of market economic dynamics can only be based on microeconomic foundations if equilibrium at the level of the firm does not mean always returning to the old production level. Reaching a new equilibrium point (production level) requires that – at least for a sufficiently long period of time and for a sufficiently small economic unit – an adjustment of factor prices to the changes in profit does not happen.

On the other hand, a system of decentralized wage negotiations means that structures are conserved and the ability of firms to adjust is weakened, since they are to a large extent released from the pressure of adjusting to new conditions and they do not have the full incentive for 'creative destruction'. In this way such a regime reduces the competitiveness of the economy in the longer term. Moreover, a system of decentralized pay deals is only conceivable if the interregional and intersectoral mobility of labour is very low and/or the degree of organization of employees in trade unions is very low. Intersectoral mobility or pay deals for a whole sector create, however, the innovative incentives and the sanctions which are essential for dynamic economic development.

THE ROLE OF THE STATE AND PUBLIC INTERVENTION IF LABOUR IS IMMOBILE

The content of the preceding analysis can be summarized in a single sentence: competition problems always occur when a society does not recognize the limits of the production and sales opportunities which it itself has determined and so tries to force through income demands which are not justified in reality. In a closed economy this manifests itself in rising prices and finally, if there is money illusion, in low real income again. In an open economy it manifests itself firstly in rising prices (loss of competitiveness) and then in the loss of market shares on the world market and falling employment.[12] With fixed exchange rates these undesirable trends can only be corrected through withdrawal of the excessive nominal demands. The only function of flexible exchange rates is to facilitate this withdrawal by (unconsciously) exploiting money illusion. This also provides a direct solution to the 'problem of the state', much discussed in the preamble to Maastricht. Any change in the level and structure of state involvement which is not accepted by society and entails competing private demands will lead sooner or later to rising prices, which in turn will disrupt external development. It is not the increase in state involvement which causes an external problem, but only ever its non-acceptance by the population.

This also deals straight away with the 'tax burden problem' mentioned in Germany in connection with the location debate: in a country which – compared with the average of her trading partners – is characterized by stable price development without having to follow a permanent restrictive monetary policy, there is no reason to reduce state involvement or the tax burden on businesses *for external reasons*.

This can easily be illustrated. Let us assume that a state has an extremely high tax ratio and extremely high defence expenditure compared with its trading partners. This may lead to important public areas such as infrastructure, education or environmental protection having to be neglected. This means that the real purchasing power of private households will rise less sharply than in other countries, while businesses will have less investment funds and a worse complementary public infrastructure at their disposal. In turn this will indirectly reduce the chances of an increase in the purchasing power of households. Overall, growth and productivity in this country will be lower than in other countries, as defence expenditure is 'unproductive' both in the eyes of private households and in the eyes of the world market. There will, however, be no external problems in this country if the necessity of such defence expenditure is accepted by everybody for overriding reasons. If the overall political situation changes and defence expenditure and taxes can therefore also be lowered, it will undoubtedly not lead to an improvement in the external situation, but to an earnings trend which adapts itself to the new, 'more productive' circumstances.

The same applies to two countries which have the same level of state involvement but a completely different structure of public expenditure. Let us take one country with high 'unproductive' defence expenditure and one with high 'productive' expenditure on infrastructure and a small defence burden. If both countries have stable prices, i.e. they have adapted to the production opportunities in each case, there is no competition problem. The same rules as those for high defence expenditure apply for – what is in terms of international competition – 'unproductive' expenditure on environmental protection. Here too it is always a matter of social adaptation to the resulting lower productivity in international terms, not a *ceteris paribus* comparison of expenditure on environmental protection in two different countries.

In this respect discussion of comparative tax burdens or state involvement is generally not very relevant. Because there is the 'compensation mechanism' of wage development, the tax burden is no criterion for assessing the international competitiveness of a national economy. In the last 40 years this mechanism has worked better in Germany than in any other economically comparable country in the world. The relatively low inflation since 1950 is direct proof of this. This is the key to economic policy. The internal and external value of money cannot be separated. If internal stability is achieved, external stability cannot be lost; and only in times of an unsuitable currency system, e.g. the 1970s, could this realization be temporarily forgotten.

THE MACROECONOMIC REGIME

Contrary to what is asserted time and again, the preservation of international competitiveness for a national economy overall is in no way a task of economic policy which requires a large number of different activities and the subordination of internal goals to external adaptation. The maintenance of competitiveness in the sense of retaining adaptability to new and what are in principle unforeseeable events is far more a problem of the currency and wage regime, which is applied to real developments and adapts to them in each case. If this regime or even only parts of it are unsuitable for promoting the adaptability, all other measures for preserving a country's competitive position are condemned to failure in the long run. Conversely it is true that, with a suitable currency and wage regime which reacts flexibly, there are practically no limits to the freedom of a country to set and achieve its own goals in terms of social, environmental or defence policy.

This largely reduces the problem of preserving international competitiveness to the question of creating sufficient wage and/or exchange rate flexibility. The question as to which of these two variables should/can be made to bear the main burden of adaptation was a central feature of the debate on flexible versus fixed exchange rates in the 1950s and 1960s. For the most important advocates of flexible exchange rates[13] it was purely and simply the assumed rigidity of wage rates that justified flexible exchange rates. The assumption of rigid wages, however, was a theoretical 'device' of the Keynesian revolution, making it more than surprising that otherwise neoclassical and/or monetarist authors used this assumption to defend flexible exchange rates. This paradox must be reflected on briefly to be able to show how a consistent conception of economic policy can be backed up today, i.e. in the light of the events and theoretical upheavals of the 1980s.

The rigidity of nominal wages by no means only affects the external situation of a country. As the Keynesian revolution showed with great clarity, if nominal wages are rigid, there is also no endogenous mechanism internally for creating full employment. Fiscal policy is then required time and again to stabilize effective demand and employment by means of an accommodating monetary policy. It is precisely with this constellation of economic policy that resorting to changes in exchange rates becomes unavoidable in order to *make* wages flexible enough externally – by exploiting money illusion.[14] Competitiveness is permanently at risk because, as the Phillips curve logic of such a policy dictates,[15] internal price stability is permanently at risk.

It is completely different in the case of a conception of economic policy which also concentrates on wage flexibility in achieving its internal goals. The overcoming of Keynesianism by the monetarist counter-revolution undoubtedly produced such a conception. As emphasized at the start, a constant increase in the money supply can in principle only be successful in terms of price stability *and* employment, i.e. in the realization of a Phillips curve which is vertical in the long term, if nominal wages are flexible enough.[16] It is precisely then that external problems in the sense of the preservation of competitiveness can generally be solved, as there is sufficient price stability. In this conception flexible exchange rates are expendable in order to preserve external equilibrium.

In the case of a monetarist conception of economic policy there is only one class of phenomenon that demands flexible exchange rates. If two countries pursue constant expansion of the money supply with different target concepts with regard to the 'right' long-term (neutral) inflation rate (i.e. approximately 2 and 4 per cent), the exchange rate has to be changed by precisely this difference per period to preserve competitive neutrality.

It follows from these considerations that two types of international policy coordination are necessary in order to exclude changes in exchange rate for ever ('currency union'). In the first instance all the countries involved would have to agree on an internal assignment which imposes the main responsibility for the preservation of full employment on either wages policy or monetary/fiscal policy. This is clearly a very difficult form of policy coordination to handle, requiring as it does the ability to agree on how, at what times and in what economic situations money illusion is present and can be exploited.

If, however, all the governments involved are of the opinion that money illusion is not in any case large enough to base a conception of policy on, only coordination of the 'correct' long-term (neutral) inflation rate is necessary. This problem does not really exist, however, as it is possible to agree on an arbitrary inflation rate, and such agreement is in any case preferable to a permanent change in the exchange rate or even flexible (market-determined) rates.

These considerations show just how close the interdependence of the goals of 'external equilibrium, a high level of employment and stable prices' is. The simple assignment of goals and means which came out of the monetarist counter-revolution is:

- monetary policy – price stability,
- wages policy – employment,
- exchange rates – external balance,

and is only tenable under very restrictive assumptions. It is inconsistent in terms of external security if it is not assumed that different degrees of neutral inflation in different countries are unavoidable.

The assignment of monetary policy to price stability and wages policy to employment, which in terms of internal economics is expedient, must in any case be modified externally. Money supply policy is the attempt to 'objectify the money supply', that is to say the attempt to remove money supply policy from day-to-day politics and to assign responsibility for employment to nominal wages policy. With increasing internationalization of the money and goods markets more and more limits are being put on such a policy in a narrow national framework. The shifting of demand for domestic currency beyond frontiers (expansion of currency area) cannot be met with national money supply control, for example. Nor can monetary policy ignore changes in exchange rates which go far beyond the path of competitive neutrality marked out by purchasing power parity.

A system of fixed exchange rates has a very similar function when it comes to the assignment of responsibility for wages policy. Even with fixed exchange rates nominal wages policy is directly relevant to employment through the decline in competitiveness.[17]

THE GERMAN LESSON

Such a system works if any misconduct by the actors at national level is sanctioned directly. Excessive wage increases will entail negative labour market effects, bringing about a correction of wage development. Unemployment is generally cushioned socially by means of insurance in order to involve employees in the costs of their misconduct and to limit the shifting of this burden on to the anonymous 'state'. That is to say the area from which misconduct comes in the case of immobile labour is punished for the misconduct in a way that makes it seem worthwhile for those involved to obey the rules of the system.

If labour were mobile, such problems would not exist from the outset, as wages would quickly rise in the low-wage country and fall in the high-wage country without more unemployment arising anywhere than in the case of immobility. Mobility of labour is frequently misunderstood, however, and its effects were politically misused time and again in the course of the German currency union to justify rapid harmonization of wage levels in East and West. The argument that the market had forced the rapid harmonization of the wage level in East Germany with that in West Germany through the migration of labour is not tenable, however.

If the borders are opened between two countries with different capital resources and different wage levels at an exchange rate which just stabilizes production in both countries, i.e. is competitively neutral, migration from the low-wage country to the high-wage country will start if labour is perfectly mobile. Labour will become short in the low-wage country, and a labour surplus will arise in the high-wage country. This will put pressure on wages to level out – they will rise in the low-wage country and fall in the high-wage country. It is vital that unemployment does not occur in either of the two countries. In the low-wage country the labour market is characterized by a labour shortage, not by high and rising unemployment. The fact that wage development there has detached itself from productivity development is purely a market result under the conditions of the labour shortage.

In the case of East and West Germany this illustration of a market process does not get to the bottom of the matter. Falling unemployment in West Germany despite massive immigration, and rising unemployment in East Germany despite emigration would, according to the laws of the market, have demanded rising wages in West Germany and falling wages in East Germany. Migration could not be prevented even then. It is plainly untrue to say that migration can be stopped by rapid wage harmonization if the low-wage country is far inferior to the high-wage country in competition on the goods market. In this case the difference in income is only replaced by a difference in demand for labour. This is at least as important in terms of migration as a difference in income. The fact that there is not greater migration despite the extreme differences in the labour market situation between West and East Germany shows just how little mobility there is even in Germany.

Currency union in the case of immobile labour can function easily enough if *only* the responsibility for the currency itself is centralized, with all other sanction mechanisms remaining at the level (in the area) which is characterized by mobility of labour or centralized wage negotiations. Under these conditions at least the same goal combination is achieved as at present and the readiness of the richer countries to pay is not overstrained. In other words it is not currency union as such that is a problem. The currency of a united Europe can be just as stable as a national currency if all the parties involved share the basic conviction that inflation does not solve real problems, but creates new ones. Vital factors are the design and decision-making mechanisms of the central bank, together with the framework in which the other decision-makers operate.

The point is, however, that European currency union is not planned as purely a currency union. European currency union is seen by virtually all those responsible as a step in the direction of political union, at least in the sense of a confederation of states. The logical outcome of this is the shifting of additional responsibilities to the joint institutions of the European Commission and European Council, with cohesion funds, regional funds and structural funds being instruments for, in addition to standardizing currency conditions, providing harmonization aid for poorer regions with the aim of accelerating and facilitating the catching-up process.

It is precisely here that the real problems of the Maastricht Treaty begin. The national sanction in the wake of wage misconduct is weakened without their being a provision which would permit the other members of the currency union to assess why this undesirable trend is occurring and allow them to react as they saw fit – even with sanctions. This is possible in the case of budgetary policy misconduct, but in the case of wage policy misconduct the partner countries can only make references to general obligations to consult.

It might be argued that the barrier to entry into a currency union is so high with regard to inflation rate that only countries with the necessary social consent will be able to participate in any case. However, this fails to take account of the fact that the design of the currency union and the shifting of further responsibilities to the Council and Commission change conditions decisively. Even countries which demonstrated good conduct when there were strict national sanction mechanisms will adapt their behaviour to the new conditions. There will be a temptation for low-wage countries to maximize their share of the central funds available through selfish conduct.

There is in any case a tendency for all those involved to unload the responsibility for undesirable trends on to the state. This is given a new dimension in the case of the European Community. Poorer countries will try to move richer ones to share more than would otherwise be possible. Their means of doing this is to bid up national wage negotiations, that is to say misconduct in the sense of the union. Even if this means high regional unemployment, it may be worthwhile. The employed have higher real wages and unemployment is either kept directly lower by joint interventions or its social consequences are alleviated more than would be the case without European transfer mechanisms. The quantitative effect of such conduct can only be speculated about, but its occurrence is inevitable.

It is certain, therefore, that a currency union on these terms will produce poorer results with regard to inflation and/or employment levels than a currency union which retains the sanctions for misconduct in the region in question. This means that even if some means of price stability would be preserved in Europe as is the case in the most stable countries, the European Phillips curve would move to the right, i.e. unemployment would be higher at any inflation rate than it is now. The readiness of richer countries to pay transfers can also be overstrained

The differences in wage levels in Europe will be large for a long time to come. At present Portugal has the lowest wage level with approximately 4 Ecu an hour and Germany the highest with approximately 20 Ecu (including incidental wage costs). Announcement of a political union must lead to a response at European level from trade unions and employers' associations as well. If, as in the united Germany, the trade unions and employers were to join forces quickly on a Europe-wide basis in order to harmonize wage-setting systems and to avoid direct competition in collective bargaining, it would represent a great threat to the European economy. The trade unions would have to try to achieve rapid harmonization of wages to avoid pressure on the high-wage countries to reduce wages. The employers would have a similar interest so as to keep competition from the low-wage countries to a minimum. If, trusting to the harmonization mechanisms of the community, the low-wage countries were to accept this, all would be united in an attempt to assign maximum responsibility for the undesirable trends to the joint central institution. This institution too would be interested in the first instance in accepting such responsibility in order to prove its importance to the whole. In this way the need of not overstraining the readiness of the prosperous states to pay transfers could actually be violated so badly that European union as a whole would be endangered.

If there is anything to be learnt from German unification and the rapid currency union, then it is this: as soon as the social forces of the area within whose borders centralized wage negotiations take place or within whose borders labour is mobile no longer bear the social and financial responsibility for undesirable developments, wages are no longer exclusively the outcome of the negotiations of a bilateral monopoly, but are marked by all those concerned attempting to involve a third party, the 'state', in the responsibility. Owing to a power vacuum on the employers' side the results in Eastern Germany may deviate particularly markedly from the market result in open national economies where there is immobility of labour, i.e. the productivity orientation of wages, but in the European treaty the aspiration of the poorer countries 'to reduce the differences in the level of development of the various regions' (Article 130a) basically shows that currency union is to be accompanied by effective measures on the part of the joint authorities.

In principle there are two ways of designing a currency union. First, as a pure currency union, in which, with the exception of monetary policy, all important functions of economic policy and therefore all sanctions for misconduct remain at a national level. The immediate advantage of such a currency union compared with the system of largely fixed exchange rates practised today is hardly worth mentioning. The transaction advantage barely shows favourably in the books if the system of fixed exchange rates also succeeds in keeping the markets for goods and capital open. Such a pure currency union is open to all countries which want to submit to the constraints of its policy of stability, irrespective of their level of affluence.

Second, one can see European currency union as the preliminary stage of political union and, as in the Maastricht Treaty, soften the character of a pure stability community accordingly, i.e. sanction misconduct not only in the national framework. In this case rules have to be drawn up to prevent the readiness of the richer countries to pay from being overstrained. The Maastricht Treaty has tried to do this consistently in the area of fiscal policy. Wages policy, by far the more important factor in overall economic terms, is not even mentioned.

Politically this form of currency union can also be achieved if the richer countries' readiness to pay in accordance with the terms of the contract can be relied upon. It is questionable whether this is the case. Experiences in the united Germany show that policy tends to overestimate the readiness of the population to pay in principle and not call upon the readiness to pay which exists to a great enough extent.

Unlike a pure currency union, however, this type of currency union is not open to any number of countries with very different levels of affluence. Each admission of a country with below-average income threatens compliance with the aforementioned secondary consideration. The option of 'deepening *and* broadening' the community only exists if the countries to be admitted already have above-average income. This is true in the case of Austria, Norway and Sweden, currently the most important candidates for admission.

It is, however, fatal to have an income threshold like this as an admission criterion. If the community does not remain open to the poorest countries as well, redistribution within the existing community loses its legitimacy. In that case it is only historical chance (the Iron Curtain opening 'too late', for example) that decides whether a country will be able to enjoy redistribution from the richer countries to the poorer or not. In a changing Europe such a policy is bound to come to grief sooner or later.

CONCLUSION

The analysis presented here focuses on *two* arguments:

1. The wage regime (decentralized or centralized) at the micro level largely determines the ability of a country to increase its affluence in dynamic competition.
2. The wage regime at the macro level (adaptation to productivity and international price level) is vital to the stability of the currency system.

This produces *one* central conclusion: fixed exchange rate systems or currency unions which are not a direct preliminary step towards political union only function if they contain *no* precautions to cushion undesirable national trends with measures at the supranational level.

This can easily be explained using the above two arguments. Different wage regimes at the micro level can easily be maintained if different levels of income in the countries are not regarded as a problem in political terms. If harmonization of differences in affluence by means of joint measures is planned, however, the results are paradoxical. In this case the countries which have exposed themselves to greater pressure to conform in the structural change through centralized wage negotiations must pay for other countries choosing a slower rate of structural change. This cannot be wise in principle.

Different wage regimes at the macro level can only be maintained from the outset if there is no national sanction for misconduct, but supranational cushioning. This is not wise, as it provokes morally hazardous behaviour which is condemned to political failure in many respects.

NOTES

1 Pages 252–262 are based on an analysis carried out by the DIW for the Federal Minister for the Economy. Flassbeck (1992).
2 See for example Angell (1922), pp.116 onwards, and the works of Taussig (1927) and Ohlin (1967).
3 For an analysis of shocks and a critical appraisal of the theory of flexible prices see Flassbeck, Horn and Zweiner (1989).
4 Cf. Schumpeter (1954).
5 Cf. especially Flassbeck, Horn and Zweiner (1989).
6 Cf. Branson (1983), Dornbusch et al. (1977) and Frisch (1988).
7 As a rule, this effect is not, in reality, achieved by existing states through migration, but through an 'equalization of living conditions', as it is referred to in Germany, with the help of state measures and general compulsory regulations.
8 Cf. especially Ohlin's (1967) critique of this interpretation of the classical doctrine. Cf. also J. Viner (1937), pp.473 and 484.
9 In this respect the now accepted international standard for measuring changes in price competitiveness, the so-called real exchange rate on the basis of individual wage rates, has a thorough theoretical legitimacy.
10 Cf. Hayek (1967).
11 Cf. Keynes (1936).
12 Incidentally also stated explicitly by Keynes in his critique of neoclassical wage theory. Cf. Keynes (1936), pp.262 onwards.
13 Cf. Sohmen (1973) among others.
14 Keynes saw this very clearly, cf. Keynes (1936), p.270. Yet Keynes understood enough of the dynamics of highly speculative markets to reject flexible (market-determined) rates, cf. Keynes (1930), Vol. V, Chapter 21, pp.324 and 325.
15 Cf. Flassbeck and Vesper (1986), p.143.
16 Cf. Flassbeck (1987) and Koll (1988), on the logic of these correlations.
17 This too is evident in Keynes (1936), pp.262 onwards. Cf. also the fundamental work of Bosch and Veit (1966).

REFERENCES

Angell, J.W. (1922), 'International trade under inconvertible paper', *Quarterly Journal of Economics*, May, 359–412.
Bosch, A. and Veit, R. (1966), 'Theorie der Geldpolitik', *Wirtschaftswissenschaftliche und wirtschaftsrechtliche Untersuchungen*, 3.
Branson, W.H. (1983), 'Economic structure and policy for external balance', *IMF Staff Papers*, 30, pp.39–66.
Dornbusch, R., Fischer, S. and Samuelson, P.A. (1977), 'Comparative advantage,

trade, and payments in a ricardian model with a continuum of goods', *American Economic Review*, 67(1).

Flassbeck, H. (1982), 'Was ist Angebotspolitik?', *Konjunkturpolitik*, 28(2/3), 75–138.

Flassbeck, H. (1987), 'Geldmenge, Löhne und Beschäftigung', *Vierteljahrshefte zur Wirtschaftsforschung*, 3, 157–161.

Flassbeck, H. (1992), 'Theoretische Aspekte der Messung von Wettbewerbsfähigkeit', *Vierteljahrshefte zur Wirtschaftsforschung*, 1/2.

Flassbeck, H., Horn, G.-A. and Zweiner, R. (1989), 'Rigide Preise, flexible Mengen - Ansätze zu einer dynamischen Analyse von Angebots- und Nachfrageschocks', *Sonderheft*, 149.

Flassbeck, H. and Vesper, D. (1986), 'Konjunkturzyklus, Beschäftigung und Inflation - Bemerkungen zu alternativen wirtschaftspolitischen Strategien', in H.J. Krupp, B. Rohwer and K.W. Rothschild (eds), *Wege zur Vollbeschäftigung*, Freiburg, Rombach, 124–146.

Friedman, M. and Roosa, R.V. (1967), *The Balance of Payments: Free versus Fixed Exchange Rates*, American Enterprise Institute for Public Policy Research, Washington DC.

Frisch, G. (1988), 'Wechselkurs oder Geldmenge als Schockabsorber', *Wirtschaftspolitische Blätter*, 35(1), 27–34.

Hayek, F.A. von (1967), 'The theory of complex phenomena', in F.A. von Hayek, *Studies in Philosophy, Politics and Economics*, London.

Keynes, J.M. (1930[1971]), 'A treatise on money - the applied theory of money', in *The Collected Writings of John Maynard Keynes*, Vol. VI, London and Basingstoke.

Keynes, J.M. (1936), 'The general theory of employment, interest and money', in *The Collected Writings of John Maynard Keynes*, Vol. XII, London and Basingstoke.

Koll, W. (1988), 'Geldmenge, Löhne und Beschäftigung - Gesamtwirtschaftliche Bedingungen für mehr Beschäftigung bei Stabilität', *Vorträge und Aufsätze*, 120.

Ohlin, B. (1967), *Interregional and International Trade*, 2nd edn, Cambridge, MA.

Schumpeter, J.A. (1954), *History of Economic Analysis*, Oxford.

Sohmen, E. (1973), *Wechselkurs und Währungsordnung*, Tübingen.

Taussig, F.W. (1927), *International Trade*, New York.

Viner, J. (1937), *Studies in the Theory of International Trade*, New York.

15

THE NEED FOR REAL CONVERGENCE IN A MONETARY UNION

Paul de Grauwe

INTRODUCTION

Major decisions to move towards a monetary union were taken with the signing of the Maastricht Treaty. Many questions and doubts continue to exist, however. In particular, doubts exist as to whether the degree of 'real' convergence is strong enough to make a smooth working of the future monetary union possible.

In this chapter we analyse the need for real convergence (defined as the convergence in the growth rates of output and employment). In order to do so, we also contrast the need for real convergence with nominal convergence (i.e. the convergence of national inflation rates).

THE NEED FOR NOMINAL CONVERGENCE

A necessary condition for a well-functioning monetary union is that inflation rates should be the same throughout the union. In a similar way, fixed exchange rate systems (like the EMS after 1987) can only function satisfactorily if inflation rates are equalized across the participating countries. This 'nominal convergence' requirement is essentially the same for monetary unions and for fixed exchange rate regimes.[1]

One of the interesting features of this nominal convergence requirement is that it is relatively easy to achieve in the context of a monetary union, whereas it appears to be hard to reach in the context of fixed exchange rates. As a result, most fixed exchange rate arrangements tend to collapse, whereas relatively few monetary unions do.

Table 15.1 Cumulative differentials of national (regional) inflation rates

	Standard deviation	Range
Fixed Rate systems		
Bretton Woods (1961–68)	6.1%	20.0
EMS (1987–92)	6.4%	17.7
Monetary union		
W. Germany (1986–90)	0.5%	1.0

Note: The range is defined as the difference (at the end of the period) between the price index of the country (*Land*) with the highest rate of inflation and the price index of the country (*Land*) with the lowest rate of inflation.

As an illustration of this striking difference in the ease with which nominal convergence is achieved in different monetary regimes, we show the divergences in regional inflation rates in West Germany (a monetary union) and compare these with those observed in fixed exchange rate regimes. We selected the Bretton Woods System during the sixties and the EMS during its fixed exchange rate period of 1987–1992. The results are shown in Table 15.1. They indicate that in the two fixed exchange rate regimes the cumulative national inflation differentials were 10 to 20 times higher than the cumulative differential observed between the German *Länder* during a period of comparable length.[2]

Why is it that the nominal convergence requirement is so much more difficult to achieve in the context of fixed exchange rate regimes than in a monetary union? The reason is very simple. Inflation in a country is the loss of purchasing power of the money issued by the monetary authorities of that country. In fixed exchange rate systems, each country maintains its own central bank and its own money. Therefore, the existence of different monies, managed by different institutions with different preferences and policy objectives, makes divergences in national inflation rates almost inevitable. This is not the case in a monetary union where the same money circulates everywhere, and is managed by the same central bank.

In this sense a fixed exchange rate regime is fundamentally different from a monetary union. In the former regime nominal convergence is very difficult to achieve. As a result, this monetary regime tends to disintegrate over time. In a monetary union, however, nominal convergence is achieved almost automatically and stops being a problem.

The previous analysis has important implications for the transition to EMU in Europe. The Maastricht Treaty has defined tight nominal convergence requirements as a *precondition* for starting a monetary union. This is very paradoxical. The tight convergence criteria for inflation are easily met within monetary unions. They are most unlikely to be observed between countries maintaining separate currencies, except when some of these countries (like the Netherlands) completely abandon their monetary sovereignty. Thus the paradox is that the Maastricht Treaty imposes inflation convergence as a condition for the regime shift to monetary union, while the available evidence indicates that one needs the regime shift to achieve tight nominal convergence. It appears, therefore, that the Maastricht nominal convergence requirement will be an obstacle to monetary union instead of being a condition which facilitates the transition to monetary union.

THE NEED FOR REAL CONVERGENCE

The conditions for nominal convergence, as discussed in the previous section, are relatively well understood. What is less clear, however, is whether *real* convergence, i.e. convergence of growth rates of output and employment, is a condition for a successful monetary union, and for a successful fixed exchange rate regime.

When one compares monetary unions with other monetary arrangement one is struck by the fact that within monetary unions the degree of real convergence does not seem to be stronger than outside monetary unions. In the following tables we present some evidence. Table 15.2 shows measures of short-term and long-term divergences of the growth rates of output between the member states of the EMS and between the regions of the same countries. The striking feature of this table is that on average the degree of divergence of the growth rates of output does not seem to be lower between regions of the same monetary union than between countries. This is true both for the measures of short-term (yearly) divergences of growth rates as for the measures of long-run divergences.

The same conclusion holds true for the growth rates of employment (see Table 15.3). There is no evidence here either that the degree of real convergence is larger within monetary unions than outside it. In fact the contrary seems to be true. The growth rates of employment seem to diverge more between regions of the same monetary union than between countries which do not form a monetary union.

The contrast with nominal convergence is great. In the previous section we noted that nominal convergence tends to be much stronger within than outside monetary unions. This is certainly not the case with real convergence. The evidence even seems to suggest that the opposite is true. This evidence is not confined to Europe. When one compares the US with Europe, we observe similar phenomena. The degree of real divergence between the US-regions is at least as important as the degree of real divergence between the European countries.[3]

Why is it that real convergence is not a stronger force within monetary unions than outside monetary unions? The answer is provided by the theory of optimum currency areas.

Table 15.2 Short-term and long-term divergences in regional and national growth rates of output (yearly percentage change)

	Long-run divergence	Short-run divergence
Countries (1976–90)		
OECD	0.48	1.66
EMS	0.48	
Regions		
France (1976–86)	0.78	2.04
W. Germany (1976–86)	0.51	1.09
Netherlands (1976–86)	0.71	3.85
Spain (1981–86)	1.45	3.59
UK (1976–88)	0.72	1.40

Note: The long-run divergence of regions is defined as the standard deviation of the average regional growth rates over the relevant periods. For nations we have the same definition. The short-run divergence is defined as the average of the yearly standard deviations of the regional (resp. the national) growth rates.

Sources: The national data are from OECD, *Economic Outlook*; the regional data are from Eurostat, Banque de données régionales.

Table 15.3 Short-term and long-term divergences in regional and national growth rates of employment (yearly percentage change)

	Long-run divergence	Short-run divergence
Countries (1976–90)		
Whole sample	0.30	1.13
EMS	0.26	
Regions		
W. Germany (1976–87)	0.38	0.63
France (1976–87)	0.38	0.70
Italy (1984–87)	0.89	2.18
Spain (1981–86)	2.00	2.88
UK (1982–86)	0.96	1.11

Note: The long run divergence of regions is defined as the standard deviation of the average regional growth rates over the relevant periods. For nations we have the same definition. The short run divergence is defined as the average of the yearly standard deviations of the regional (resp. the national) growth rates.

Sources: The national data are from OECD, *Economic Outlook*; the regional data are from Eurostat, Banque de données régionales.

REAL CONVERGENCE AND THE THEORY OF OPTIMAL CURRENCY AREAS (OCA)

According to the OCA theory, countries that are subjected to asymmetric shocks (real divergence) will experience adjustment problems in a monetary union if they lack flexibility in real wages and/or in movements of labour. In this case the cost of the union will be large. Put differently, countries (regions) in a monetary union can afford a lot of real divergence if there is a sufficient degree of real wage flexibility and/or labour mobility. Thus, according to the OCA theory, the need for real convergence is inversely related to degree of wage flexibility and labour mobility. There is therefore no presumption that countries or regions in a union should experience less real divergence than countries who do not form a monetary union. In fact it is possible that countries or regions who form a monetary union actually experience more real divergence because, being more economically integrated, their industrial structures are more highly specialized, so that they are more likely to be hit by asymmetric shocks.[4]

The relation between real convergence and the degree of flexibility of the labour market (i.e. flexibility of real wages and mobility of labour) needed to sustain a monetary union is represented graphically in Figure 15.1. On the horizontal axis we set out the degree of flexibility of the labour markets. On the vertical axis the degree of real divergence is set out. Countries or regions that experience a high divergence in output and employment growth need a lot of flexibility in their labour markets. This relationship is represented by the upward sloping line AA. Countries or regions located below the AA line can form a union without 'excessive' adjustment costs. Countries above the AA line will experience a lot of adjustment costs if they form a monetary union.

In Figure 15.1 we have placed the EC above the AA line and the USA below. This is in a sense arbitrary, because we do not really know for sure that the EC does not form an optimum currency area.[5] We are, however, much less uncertain about the relative positions of the EC and the USA. Note that we have placed the USA at about the same vertical level as the EC, expressing the fact that the degree of real divergence in the USA is not much different from the real divergence observed in the EC countries. The major difference between the USA and the EC seems to be the degree of flexibility of labour markets.

Many recent empirical studies have documented this difference in the degree of flexibility of the labour markets in the USA and in Europe. For example, there is ample evidence that real wages in Europe respond less to unemployment than in the USA.[6] Similarly, there is ample evidence that labour mobility is much higher within the USA than it is between member countries of the EC.

It should be noted that we can also locate individual countries in the graph. For example, we have put West Germany on the right hand side

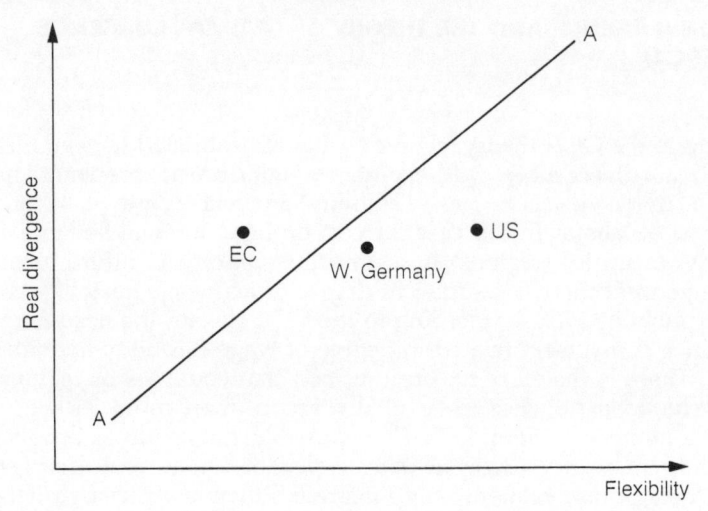

Figure 15.1 Trade-off between real divergence and flexibility

of the AA line. Here also there is no evidence that the degree of real divergence between the German *Länder* is smaller than between the EC countries (see above). There is, however, evidence that the degree of labour mobility between German *Länder* is significantly higher than between EC countries.[7]

The challenge for the EC is to move to the other side of the AA line, i.e. to make a monetary union less costly. How can this be achieved? There are essentially two strategies. One is to reduce the degree of real divergence, the other is to increase the degree of flexibility.

The difficulty of the first strategy is that the degree of real convergence is to a large extent dependent on factors over which policy makers have little influence. For example, the degree of industrial specialization matters in determining how important asymmetric shocks are. There is very little policy makers can do, however, to change regional specialization patterns. As was argued earlier, it is not inconceivable that economic integration will in fact increase real divergence.

The only realistic option, therefore, seems to be to increase the flexibility of the labour markets (real wages and/or labour mobility). This strategy implies a reform of labour market institutions, which will not be easy to implement. Nevertheless there is some evidence that steps in this direction can be taken. In Belgium, for example, legal changes were introduced at the end of the eighties allowing the government to step in and to reduce wages if they have trended away from those observed in the seven main trading partners of Belgium. Active incomes policies can be used as a substitute for a lack of flexibility in the labour market, so that a monetary union becomes less costly. We come back to this issue in the next section.

REAL CONVERGENCE AND THE EMS

The conditions for the successful functioning of a fixed exchange rate system are essentially the same as those that are needed to run a monetary union smoothly. Countries with rigid labour markets (i.e. low real-wage flexibility and low mobility of labour) will find it costly to fix their exchange rates in the face of asymmetric shocks. When such a shock occurs, the temptation will be great to use the exchange rate in order to introduce more flexibility in an otherwise rigid system. Here too flexibility must be enhanced in order to sustain a fixed exchange rate regime.

In the previous section, we mentioned the Belgian competitiveness law which has been instrumental in achieving a certain amount of real-wage flexibility. The main feature of the law is that if real wages in Belgium increase faster than in seven of their major partners, or if Belgian exports decline relative to the exports of these seven trading partners, the government can intervene in the wage bargaining process, so as to improve the competitive position of the Belgian economy. Although the law has, as yet, not been invoked, its existence has exerted a disciplinary effect on wage bargaining, allowing Belgium to maintain its competitiveness relatively unchanged. The recent devaluations of some EC currencies, however, have again put pressure on the competitiveness of the Belgian economy, and will challenge the authorities actually to use the law.

The Belgian example indicates that it is possible to devise schemes that introduce more flexibility in labour markets, thereby allowing the country to use substitute policies to exchange rate policies. The fact that these substitutes exist increases the credibility of the fixed exchange rate arrangement.

REAL CONVERGENCE AND FISCAL POLICIES

In the context of the OCA theory much attention has been paid to the need to centralize part of the national budgets in a monetary union so as to allow for automatic regional transfers when asymmetric shocks occur. This idea has led to many proposals to combine a monetary union with some budgetary union.[8]

The recent monetary unification of Germany testifies to the power of that argument. It also shows its limitations, however. We represent the effects of a budgetary union graphically in Figure 15.2. Without a budgetary union the AA_1 line shows the combinations of real divergence and flexibility which one needs to form a monetary union. Clearly, Germany as a whole (i.e. West plus East Germany) was situated above this line before 1990. The budgetary union changed all that. Graphically we represent such a budgetary union by an upward shift of the AA line

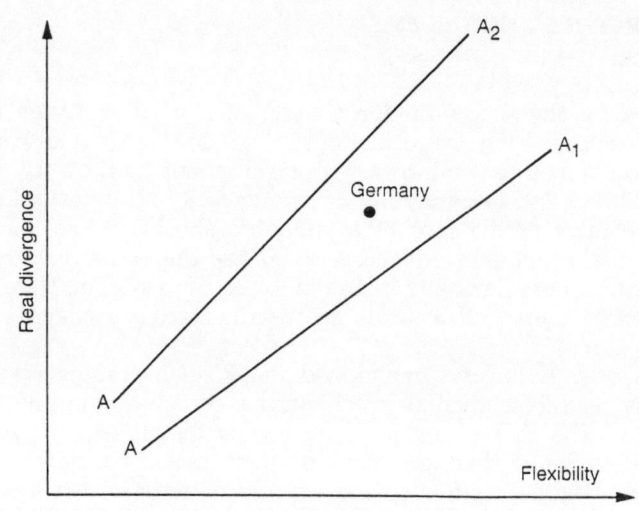

Figure 15.2 Trade-off between real divergence and flexibility: the role of a budgetary union

to AA_2. Germany as a whole now falls below this line. Put differently, the budgetary union had the effect of sustaining a monetary union between two regions by allowing for major transfers to the region hit by a sizeable negative shock.

The sizes of the transfers that appear to be necessary to sustain the German union, however, are so large that it cannot be repeated in countries that do not share the same intense national identification as the two parts of Germany do.

The limitation of budgetary centralization, as a means to sustain a monetary union, is also shown by the experience of Italy and Belgium. The high degree of budgetary centralization (including the social security system) has led to a situation where regional transfers occur in the same direction on a permanent basis. Thus, in these two countries the north has been transferring massive amounts of taxpayers' money to the south for at least twenty years, without any sign of a reversal of these transfers.

One of the reasons why regional transfers, initially intended to be temporary, acquired a permanent character, is that they also lead to moral hazard problems. More specifically, the regional transfers have reduced the need for labour mobility. As a result, the mobility of labour from the south to the north is diminished (in the case of Italy) or never occurred (in the case of Belgium). This also implies that unemployment rates become permanently higher in the south.

Table 15.4 presents some evidence of labour mobility between Italian regions. We compare it with Germany. It is striking to find that despite very large differences in unemployment between the north and the

Table 15.4 Average flows of immigrants plus emigrants of regions to and from the rest of the country (as a percentage of population of the region)

	1975	1980	1987	1975–87 (yearly average)
W. Germany	1.32	1.33	1.07	1.21
	(1.06)*	(1.06)*	(0.85)*	(0.98)*
Italy	0.78	0.68	0.53	0.66

Note: * these numbers excluded the German 'city-states' Bremen, Hamburg and West Berlin.

Source: Eurostat, Banque de données régionales.

Table 15.5 Regional unemployment rates in 1989 (by percentage)

	Standard	Maximum	Minimum	Difference
W. Germany	2.3	10.9	3.2	7.7
Italy	6.4	21.8	4.1	17.7

Source: Eurostat, Banque de données régionales.

south of Italy (see Table 15.5), labour mobility between the Italian regions is much smaller than labour mobility between the *Länder* of West Germany.

The existence of large transfers that, in addition, become permanent due to moral hazard problems, reduces the flexibility of the adjustments in the monetary union. Over time, the AA_2 line shifts back downwards, leading to the possibility that the country may cease to be an optimum currency area.

The permanence of the regional transfers also has strong political effects. It erodes the consensus in the country that the union benefits everybody. If nothing is done about it, the risk exists that the country splits.

The foregoing discussion highlights the need to limit the degree of centralization of national budgets. Although some budgetary centralization in Europe may be called for, the limits of such a centralization will be quickly reached.

CONCLUSION

In this chapter we have analysed the need for real convergence in a monetary union. It was argued that real convergence (i.e. convergence in the growth rates of output and employment) is not required as such. The need for real convergence depends on the degree of flexibility of labour markets. Monetary unions can withstand a lot of real divergence if their labour markets are sufficiently flexible.

The challenge for the Community is not so much to reduce the existing real divergence (which in any case cannot easily be influenced by policy measures), but to increase flexibility of the labour markets. In this context we discussed the Belgian 'competitiveness' law which is an attempt at introducing flexibility in the wage formation process as a substitute for exchange rate policies. The Belgian example indicates that there exist such substitutes to exchange rate policies.

Finally it was argued that the need for centralizing a part of the budget in order to improve the functioning of a monetary union has been overstated in the traditional theory of optimum currency areas. This theory calls for automatic and reversible regional transfers. Reversibility, however, is difficult to achieve in the presence of moral hazard problems. As the transfers tend to move in the same direction for decades, the social consensus to maintain the union in the regions which have to foot the bill is undermined.

NOTES

1 Obviously it does not mean that inflation rates should be identical at all times. Temporary or relatively small deviations in regional (national) inflation rates are often observed and do not endanger the union of the fixed exchange rate arrangements. In addition, to the extent that inflation differentials reflect different productivity growth rates, they are not a matter of concern and they can coexist in a monetary union. See de Grauwe (1992).
2 Lack of available data prevented us from computing differentials for comparable periods.
3 Some evidence is provided by Krugman (1992).
4 See Krugman (1991) on this issue.
5 On this issue see Eichengreen (1990), de Grauwe and Vanhaverbeke (1991), Bayoumi and Eichengreen (1992). The consensus emerging from empirical studies is that the EC-12 probably does not constitute an optimum currency area, while a subset of the EC probably does. See also von Hagen and Neumann (1991).
6 See Bruno and Sachs (1985), Grubb, Jackman, Layard (1983).
7 See de Grauwe and Vanhaverbeke (1991) who show that the degree of labour mobility in Germany is at least ten times higher than between EC countries.
8 The best-known proposal was formulated in the seventies in the McDougall Report (EC Commission, 1977). See also Wyplosz (1991).

REFERENCES

Bayoumi, T. and Eichengreen, B. (1992), 'Shocking aspects of European monetary unification', CEPR discussion paper no 643.
Bruno, M. and Sachs, J. (1985), *Economics of Worldwide Stagflation*, Oxford, Basil Blackwell.

de Grauwe, P. (1992), 'Inflation convergence during the transition to monetary union', CEPR discussion paper.
de Grauwe, P. and Vanhaverbeke, W. (1991), 'Is Europe an optimum currency area? Evidence from regional data', CEPR discussion paper no 555.
EC Commission (1977), *Report of the Study Group on the Role of Public Finance in European Integration* (MacDougall Report), Brussels.
Eichengreen, B. (1990), 'Is Europe an optimum currency area?', CEPR discussion paper no 478.
Grubb, D., Jackman, R. and Layard, R. (1983), 'Wage rigidity and unemployment in OECD-countries', *European Economic Review*.
Krugman, P. (1991), *Geography and Trade*, Cambridge, MA, MIT-Press.
Krugman, P. (1992), 'Geography and growth', in F. Torres and F. Giavazzi (eds), *The Transition to EMU*, Estoril, Banco de Portugal.
von Hagen, J. and Neumann, M. (1991), 'Real exchange rates within and between currency areas: how far away is EMU?', discussion paper, Indiana University.
Wyplosz, C. (1991), 'Monetary Union and Fiscal Policy Discipline', CEPR discussion paper no 488.

APPENDIX 1

MONEY MARKETS AND FOREIGN EXCHANGE INSTRUMENTS IN THE TRADING ROOM

Florence Sirel

This appendix provides a technical description of the characteristics of the major and more commonly used financial instruments available for trading activities, putting into perspective their rules, the markets on which they are traded and the risks involved.

It is by no means a comprehensive or an exhaustive description of these instruments especially given the extraordinary creativity prevailing in financial activities. The instruments described here include those that may be traded, but do not include those for which no market or little tradeability exists, such as investment vehicles and instruments designed for the long-term financing requirements of companies.

The appendix is divided into four parts which examine key features of the instruments in the following markets:

1. the physical markets, which include:
   - money markets,
   - foreign exchange markets,
   - securities markets;
2. the financial futures markets;
3. the swaps markets;
4. the financial options markets.

PHYSICAL MARKETS (CASH, CURRENCIES, SECURITIES MARKETS)

Historically and until financial futures and options markets were created, the physical markets were the only financial markets available to traders.

Deposits

Deposits are made between banks and major corporates on the basis of interbank and intercompany uncommitted approved lines. Maturities vary from one day to several months and sometimes years. Interest rates are based on the local prevailing interbank offered rate plus a premium reflecting the credit risk of the counter-party receiving the deposit. Most common trading maturities vary from one day to 180 days.

Short-term deposit interbank lines are also the basis for most derivative lines, i.e. swap lines, the latter being a function of deposit lines.

OVERNIGHT DEPOSITS
Short-term deposits for a maturity of 24 hours, often used between banks located in different countries availing themselves of the time lag between the depositor's closing hour and the receiving bank's closing hour.

INTRADAY DEPOSITS
Very short term deposits of a maturity of less than 24 hours initiated during a business day and coming to an end before the end of business.[1]

Foreign exchange markets

The outright foreign exchange markets broadly distinguish between major currencies (primarily US$, DM, yen) and other currencies. For the latter cross-rates are derived from exchange rates between major currencies.

Currencies for which the foreign exchange market is not liquid or that are prone to wide swings vis-à-vis more liquid currencies are sometimes referred to by traders as 'exotic' currencies.

A second distinction is made concerning the timing of the exchange of currencies:

SPOT FOREIGN EXCHANGE
Instantaneous exchange of two currencies.

FORWARD FOREIGN EXCHANGE
Exchange at a future date of one currency for another currency on the basis of the spot exchange rate plus or minus the interest rate actualized differential between the two currencies, with reciprocal delivery on an agreed date.

The exchange of currencies (purchase and sale) may be replaced with a loan (received or granted) and thus at maturity the transaction may be settled with the payment of the interest rate differential between the two currencies.

FORWARD FORWARD FOREIGN EXCHANGE
Agreement between two banks (or corporates) to borrow or deposit a

specified amount at a given date in the future for a specified period of time at a rate either prepaid or paid in fine. Both counter-parties are at risk on the capital.

Securities markets

These markets are dominated by instruments issued by governments which are representative of the stock of public debts.

TREASURY BILLS AND TREASURY BONDS

They are the most widely known types of government debt instruments and a number of them, issued in the major industrialized countries under various names, are actively traded internationally.

Whether they are treasury bills and bonds in the USA, gilts in the UK, BTF, BTAN or OAT in France, *Scheine* in Germany, their characteristics vary according to maturity and timing of interest payments.

Non-government instruments include a great variety of negotiable instruments.

SHARES

They are representative of the companies' capital.

BONDS

They are negotiable long-term financial instruments issued at either fixed, variable (floating) or indexed rate. They are issued for a minimum of five years in France. The reference for indexed rate may be a monetary or a bond index or even a composite index such as a stock exchange index (for example 'CAC 40 Index' in France). The performance of the issuer's stock is also used as a reference.

CERTIFICATES OF DEPOSIT

Negotiable instruments issued by banks or companies (called *billets de trésorerie* in France when issued by companies). They may be issued in local or foreign currencies, including the Ecu. Interest can be prepaid, paid in fine or paid at regular intervals.

REPURCHASE OBLIGATIONS (REPOS)

Repos, also called in France: *prêt de titres* or *mise en pension*.

Agreement whereby a sale of securities (with transfer of ownership) is tied to a repurchase obligation for the seller. This is to be distinguished from the French *réméré*, under which the repurchase is a mere faculty reserved to the seller who may or may not exercise it.

NEGOTIABLE MEDIUM-TERM NOTES

Called in France *Bons à moyen terme négociables*.

When these notes are fairly liquid they are often used as collateral for deposits.

Bons de caisse in France, *Schuldscheine* in Germany are anonymous bearer certificates issued by banks primarily to private customers rather than to corporates. They are merely mentioned here because of their bearer form which makes then freely transferable. They are not used, however, in interbank trading.

FINANCIAL FUTURES MARKETS

Financial futures are standardized transactions carried out on organized exchanges. They consist in firm commitments to deliver (or to purchase) at a set future date a given quantity of a financial asset at a price agreed on the transaction's date. All financial futures are constructed so that traders may secure a financial asset at a given price at a future date.

The main difference between cash and financial futures is the fact that financial futures are transacted on organized exchanges through licensed dealers. The technicalities of the exchanges (clearing mechanism, deposits, margin calls and restitutions) entail a number of consequences: no counter-party risk is incurred by participants, and no delivery risk. Amounts are standardized and so are delivery dates.

Financial futures exchanges are tightly supervised by regulators and monetary authorities.

There are three major categories of financial futures on the basis of the underlying assets:

1. currency futures;
2. interest rate futures;
3. stock market indices futures.

Currency futures

The purpose of a currency future is to set today the exchange rate for a currency at a given date in the future.

Interest rate futures

They are divided into two main types depending on whether they are based on securities or on loans (or borrowing). The latter are future (or forward) rate agreements (FRA).

CONTRACT TO BUY OR SELL FUTURE FIXED RATE NEGOTIABLE SECURITIES
Exclusively traded on organized exchanges they are based on fixed rate negotiable securities such as bonds or Treasury bills and bonds. Examples of such contracts include:

- '10 year French government bond' traded on Matif;
- 'Treasury bill (90 days)' traded on the Chicago Mercantile Exchange (CME).

FORWARD AND FUTURE RATE AGREEMENTS

Agreements to fix interest rates today for a future loan or investment at a certain date in the future, without any commitment regarding the completion of the loan or investment. They do not entail any movement of capital. At maturity one party pays the other an agreed interest rate differential.

Forward rate agreement

They are transacted over the counter, outside organized financial futures exchanges.

Future rate agreement

They are transacted on organized financial futures exchanges only. Examples of such contracts include:

- 'Pibor' (90 days) at Matif;
- 'Eurodollar (90 days)' at the Chicago Mercantile Exchange (CME).

Stock market indices futures

Based on an index representing the price curve of a set of quoted securities, these notional contracts are the most abstract financial futures as the underlying asset is not materialized. These futures meet hedging requirements of a diversified real life portfolio, for example: 'CAC 40 index' at Matif.

Features of selected financial futures:

10 year French Government bond at Matif (interest rate future): long term financial future based on fictitious government bonds with a residual life of seven to ten years. Quoted on four quarterly dates. Nominal amount: FFr500,000 bearing interest at 10 per cent per annum. Reimbursed in fine. This contract is used in hedging strategies against long-term exposure to interest rate risk.

Ecu bond, based on long-term Ecu bonds with a residual life of six to ten years. Quoted on two quarterly dates. Nominal amount Ecu 100,000. Reimbursed in fine.

Major financial futures exchanges and their major contracts

As a conclusion to this part it is noteworthy that financial futures markets have contributed to regaining liquidity on cash markets following periods of tight liquidity in the recent 1992–1993 financial upheavals. Although this may only be a temporary phenomenon as the sound development of financial futures is based on liquid underlying assets, it is an interesting feature of these markets.

Table A1.1 Major currencies financial futures contracts

Location	Exchange	Currency quotes against US Dollar	Jan–Dec 1992 vol.[a]
Chicago	Chicago Mercantile Exchange (CME)	• Yen (JPY)	4,520,356
		• Deutsche Mark (DM)	11,593,174
		• Swiss France (SFr)	5,134,717
		• Sterling pound (GBP)	3,053,428
		• Canadian dollar (CAD)	1,171,640
Singapore	Singapore International Monetary Exchange (SIMEX)	• Yen (JPY12.5m)	54,224
Tokyo	Tiffe	• Yen (US$50,000)	86,008

Note: [a] Source: *Futures and Options World*, February 1993, p.56.

SWAPS

Swaps deserve a special mention at this point as they are used more and more in conjunction with other financial instruments.

Three types of swaps may be distinguished:

1. interest rates swaps;
2. foreign exchange swaps;
3. currency swaps, which combine the exchange of currencies and interest rates.

Historically, currency swaps were the first type developed in the early 1970s. Because swaps allow counter-parties to exchange their local access conditions to capital markets, they have enabled counter-parties to access indirectly markets to which they normally would not have had access.

Swaps provide cost effectiveness and enhanced legal protection over cash transactions, which explains their impressive success.

They may be transacted between two or more counter-parties, on a scale of sophistication from simple to complex instruments. There are no organized markets for swaps. Swaps are transacted within the range of uncommitted interbank/intercompany authorized lines.

Swaps have greatly contributed to the growing integration of capital markets, as the mechanics of the various types of swaps reviewed hereunder can testify.

Interest rate swaps

They consist in the exchange of offered and bid rates of a principal

Table A1.2 Major interest rates financial futures contracts

Location	Exchange	Contract	Jan–Dec 1992 vol.[a]
Chicago	Chicago Board of Trade (CBOT)	• US T. bond (US$100,000) • US T. note (US$100,000) • 5 yr T. note (US$100,000)	70,003,894 11,217,938 6,441,193
	Chicago Mercantile Exchange (CME)	• Eurodollar (90d.) ($1m) • Treasury bill (90d.) ($1m)	60,531,066 1,337,061
Paris	Marché à Terme International de France (Matif)	• French gov. bond (FFr 500,000) • Pibor (90d.) (FFr5m) • Ecu bond (100,000) • Long term FFr[b] • Medium term FFr[c]	31,002,844 6,430,780 1,354,012 – –
London	London International Financial Futures Exchange (LIFFE)	• German Bund (DM250,000) • Sterling (3 months) (£500,000) • EuroMark (DM1m) • Long gilt 15 yr (£50,000) • Italian bond (Itl200,000,000) • Euro Swiss (SFr1m) • Eurodollar (90d.) ($1m)	13,604,523 11,296,327 12,173,431 8,804,629 3,773,105 1,970,438 709,305
Tokyo	Tokyo international financial futures exchange Tokyo stock exchange	• Euroyen (Y100m) • 10 yr Jap. gov. bond	14,967,769 11,868,127
Sydney	Sydney futures exchange	• Bank bills (90d.) (A$500,000) • 3 yr T. bond (A$100,000) • 10 yr Aust. gov. bond (A$100,000)	5,697,786 5,434,795 4,253,374
Singapore	Singapore International Monetary Exchange (SIMEX)	• Eurodollar (90d.) (US$1m) • Euroyen (Y100m)	5,039,745 2,472,931
Frankfurt	DTB	• German Bund (DM250,000)	5,327,846

Notes: [a] Source: *Futures and Options World*, February 1993, p.56.
[b] As of January 1993.
[c] As of June 1993.

amount so as to determine the amount of interest to be exchanged for each period over time. There are two kinds of interest rates swaps:

1. the exchange of a fixed rate for a floating rate (coupon swaps);
2. the exchange of a floating rate for another floating rate (basis swaps).

In practice only the net amount of the interest rate exchange is actually paid. There is no delivery of capital, hence no delivery risk.

The extraordinary success of interest rates swaps makes them the most commonly used swaps, with a large secondary market worldwide. The market has developed a quasi-standardized 'plain vanilla swap': a US dollar swap, being a domestic fixed rate swapped against three or six months LIBOR (London Inter-Bank Official Rate). Fixed rate payments are annual while refixing of floating rate may be quarterly or semi-annual. Common maturities are three to four years. As a result other interest rates swaps may be valued with reference to standardized swaps and this is reinforced through the use of a common valuation method (zero coupon).

Currency swaps

In a currency swap both parties exchange the servicing of their respective debts (principal and interest) in two different currencies. The difference between a currency swap and an interest rates swap lies in the fact that in a currency swap the capital amounts are in two different currencies which are actually swapped.

Mechanically the currency swap works like two crossed loans (*crédits croisés*) where parties exchange roles vis-à-vis their respective creditors. In currency swaps the US dollar plays a pivotal role vis-à-vis other currencies, primarily the Swiss franc, the yen, the DM, the pound sterling and the Canadian dollar. Common maturities are one to five years.

Foreign exchange swaps

A foreign exchange swap is a double and simultaneous foreign exchange transaction, where one transaction is a spot and the other a forward transaction. In other words, in one single contract a sale and a purchase of the same currency are transacted with the same counter-party. A foreign exchange swap may also be looked at as a double money market transaction with a funding in one currency and a loan in another. Foreign exchange swaps, as opposed to currency swaps, are short-term instruments.

On the technical side a foreign exchange swap is also different from a currency swap due to the capitalization of the interest rate differential to obtain the term rate, whereas the differential in a currency swap is paid periodically over time.

Both swaps are hedging instruments for foreign exchange risk exposure, either short term (foreign exchange swap) or long term (currency swap). When used in a speculative fashion, uncovered, they create a foreign exchange position, and therefore a risk for the company or the bank.

There are various forms of foreign exchange swaps:

Straight foreign exchange swaps

Parties exchange two currencies at a spot exchange rate. At maturity both currencies are reimbursed at the previously agreed term rate. Under this transaction there are two double capital transfers (principal + interests).

Currency swaps without initial exchange

One capital transfer only is carried out.

Currency swaps without any transfer of capital

In a pure arbitrage perspective such swaps afford cover against foreign exchange losses. They do not permit foreign exchange gains. They are very similar to forward foreign exchange over a longer period of time.

Foreign exchange swaps may be used in association with forward foreign exchange, saving two cash transactions, thus providing for off-balance sheet rather than balance-sheet positions.

OPTIONS

Under an option contract a maximum purchase price (or a minimum selling price) of an asset (currency) is fixed for a given period of time up to a certain date in the future, in consideration of the payment of a 'premium'. The novelty of options lies in the availability of the price fixing over a period of time rather than at maturity. It should be noted, however, that in a few instances, options may be exercised exclusively at maturity: they are called European options versus American options.

The two main features of options are:

1. an option to purchase (a call);
2. an option to sell (a put).

'Exercise price'

The 'exercise price' of an option – which is the predetermined price (rate) for the purchase or sale of the underlying asset (currency) – varies in relation to the spot price of the underlying currency. It may be higher

Table A1.3 The four major basic positions on options

Trader's position	Call	Put
Purchase	Right to purchase	Right to sell
Sale	Obligation to sell	Obligation to purchase

or lower than or equal to the spot price and determines, therefore, three different categories of options as a function of pricing:

Options at the money   when the 'exercise price' on the starting date or on any later date is equal to the spot price of the asset.

Options in the money   there are two types depending whether the option is a call or a put.

  A *call* is *in the money*   when the exercise price is less than the spot price of the asset.

  A *put* is *in the money*   when the exercise price is higher than the spot price of the asset.

Options out of the money   different depending on whether the option is a call or put.

  A *call* is *out of the money*   when the exercise price is higher than the spot price of the asset.

  A *put* is *out of the money*   when the exercise price is lower than the spot price of the asset.

Risks of purchasers and sellers

DEGREES OF RISK

The degree of risk varies between purchasers and sellers as their respective rights and obligations *are asymmetrical*.

The option gives the purchaser a right but no obligation to buy or sell vis-à-vis the seller, the agreed amount of currency (or other asset). So the premium paid by the purchaser to the seller takes the asymmetrical situation into consideration.

On the other hand the seller has an obligation to buy or sell at the agreed price which puts him in a 'standby' position until the purchaser exercises the call or put.

LIMITED RISK FOR THE PURCHASER AND UNLIMITED RISK FOR THE SELLER

The premium paid by the purchaser of a call or a put is comparable to an insurance against price fluctuation. Hence the purchaser's risk is limited to the amount of the premium paid to the seller.

In a selling position, the premium received from the purchaser compensates for the commitment to sell at the agreed price. Consequently, the seller's profit is limited to the premium when the purchaser does not exercise the option, whereas in case of exercise of the put or call *potential losses* are *unlimited* due to price fluctuation.

Strategies of purchasers and sellers on options markets

Sellers of calls or puts may cover their positions, hence limit their risk through purchasing (or selling) the underlying currency on the spot or forward markets. These strategies have developed extensively in recent years, but it is by no means proven that they have contributed to increasing exchange-rate or interest-rate volatility.

While the present work does not attempt to describe the valuations of options, which requires the presentation of mathematical models and 'indicators' taken into account by traders as a function of their positions, it is, however, of interest to note that the same valuation method (the Black & Scholes model) is used almost universally. As a result, for a given volatility, the effect of other parameters, whatever their complexity, is minimized.

Various types of option

Based on the nature of the underlying assets a distinction is made between three types of option.

CURRENCY OPTIONS (ALSO KNOWN AS FOREIGN EXCHANGE OPTIONS)

The underlying asset is the value of a currency relative to another currency (the US$ in a majority of deals).

A currency option gives the purchaser of the option a right to purchase or to sell a spot or a forward position of a given currency for a period of time until maturity at a predetermined rate fixed at the time of purchase of the option.

Currency options are either traded on exchanges (and in that case they are similar to financial futures, being standardized contracts cleared and settled through the exchange which operates a clearing house), or they are traded over the counter as customized agreements between two counter-parties.

Maturity dates for exchange-traded options coincide with the end of each quarter of the year and the height of activity is recorded in the days preceding maturity dates, when options are sold prior to maturity. Most common maturities are within four months.

INTEREST RATE OPTIONS

In the case of interest rate options, the underlying asset is a financial instrument generating an interest rate (such as securities, government bonds, etc.), forward contracts ('10 year French government bond' at Matif, etc.) or a loan under a future rate agreement (FRA, see above).

Under an interest rates option the purchaser (holder) of the option has the right to borrow (or to lend) at a predetermined rate a given amount of money over a stated period of time, in consideration of the 'premium' (paid to the seller of the option).

CAPS, FLOORS AND COLLARS

Cap (ceiling rate)

Under a cap the purchaser acquires a guarantee to borrow 'at a predetermined *maximum fixed interest rate*' a certain amount of money for a given period of time.

Floor

In a reverse mechanism to a cap, the purchaser of a floor acquires a guarantee to invest at a predetermined *minimum interest rate*, a given amount of money for a given period of time. There are no organized exchanges for caps and floors. Deals are transacted over the counter.

Collar

This is a *combination* of a cap and a floor (also known as 'tunnel'). It provides the right to borrow or invest at rates that range within predetermined *maximum and minimum rates*. The special feature of a collar is to provide for a band of rates within high and low limits. An advantage with a collar is to pay a reduced premium since the latter is equal to the difference between the premium of a cap and that of a floor. The collar, however, will not provide full benefit from a positive development in interest rates.

OPTIONS ON SECURITIES AND STOCK INDICES

Options on shares

These provide the right to purchase (call) or to sell (put) a given number of shares of the stock of a company at a predetermined price until (or at) a given date in the future. Options on shares are traded over the counter as well as on organized exchanges such as MONEP.[2] They provide the only instrument for forward transactions on stocks.

Options on stock indices

Through stock indices traders are able to cover large investment portfolios, the compositions of which are close to the securities used in the index. In France the stock index CAC 40 is the basis of an option contract traded at MONEP.

DERIVATIVES

Derivatives have met the requirements of treasurers who have mastered the techniques of swaps and options and need new tools to expand further the range of their dealings more flexibly and at a lower cost. A whole new range of instruments was thus successfully created including:

- swaptions;
- composite options (options on options);
- 'look-back' and 'average look-back' options;
- Asian options;
- extinguishable options.

Swaptions

A swaption is an option on a swap. It gives the purchaser of the swaption the right to do a swap over a determined period of time under conditions predetermined at the time of contract.

A *call swaption* provides the right to be lender of funds at a predetermined interest rate over a set period of time. A *put swaption* gives the right to become a borrower of funds at a predetermined interest rate over a set period of time.

A premium is paid for both instruments in consideration for the right to exercise the option. Swaptions are short-term instruments (commonly up to three months) based on long-term financial instruments (up to five to seven years).

Composite options

The underlying asset of a composite option is an option. Holders of composite options may exercise a right to purchase (or to sell) at a predetermined rate (exercise price) up to a set maturity date, an option whose characteristics have been predetermined.

This instrument is particularly suited to respond to tender offers, taking into consideration the chances of bids and the foreign-exchange/interest-rate conditions from the bidding to the acceptance date. The premium due on composite options is lower than on standard options.

'Look-back' and 'average look-back' options

Under a *look-back option* the holder acquires the right to purchase (or sell) the underlying currency *at the best rate* over the period of time specified which is the life of the option. The option is only exercised at maturity in order to choose the best rate from all available rates of the period.

In view of the greater flexibility afforded by look-back options the premium is substantially higher than that of standard options. At maturity the settlement is made in cash without delivery (or receipt) of the underlying currency.

This instrument makes it possible for corporates that do not monitor rates closely, still to enjoy the best rates over a given period of time. It is thus equivalent to an insurance against a loss of opportunity.

An *average look-back option* gives the purchaser the right to purchase (or sell) *at the average rate* of the period. The premium paid for this option is no higher than that of a regular option. This option is used primarily to guarantee rates for sales and purchases over a period of time.

Asian options

There are two types of Asian options and they are similar in concept to average look-back options.

Classical Asian options
This is a call or put of a European type option (exercisable at maturity only) that guarantees an average rate calculated on the basis of a predetermined number of dates regularly spaced in time (fixing dates), the last date being the maturity date.

Generalized Asian options
In this type of Asian option the fixing dates do not have to be spaced in time regularly. In addition, the average rate may be weighted by different amounts on each fixing date. The company that purchases a generalized Asian option is free to determine the various amounts and fixing dates.

Extinguishable options

An extinguishable option is cancelled automatically when the price of the underlying asset (currency) reaches a limit referred to as the extinction point and that point occurs before maturity. Extinguishable options have therefore two built-in references: the exercise price and the extinction rate. With a call the extinction rate is lower than the exercise price. It is the reverse with a put.

Such options afford a good hedging against a rate decrease (with a put) or a rate increase (with a call) at a low premium due to the possibility that the instrument (hence the cover) be terminated before maturity.

CONCLUSION

Financial activities have grown extensively with the globalization of financial markets as a result of the easing of capital controls and the emergence of the innovative instruments described in this appendix. A number of these instruments have been developed as tools for operating in global markets under hedging as well as speculative strategies.

While markets have become more volatile, at the same time new hedging instruments have been created to cover increased rate volatility. The interplay of interest-rate strategies and exchange-rate (currencies) strategies in a world of uneven regulatory constraints is what makes the markets extremely reactive to ever-changing 'indicators'.

The major options and contracts quoted on organized markets and exchanges are summarized in Tables A1.4 to A1.8

Table A1.4 Major currency options quoted on organized markets

Location	Exchange	Options contract; currency quoted against US dollar	Jan–Dec 1992 vol.[a]
Philadelphia	Philadelphia Stock Exchange (PHLX)	• Mark 62,500 option • Yen 6.25m option • SFr 62,500 option • Sterling £31,250 • Canadian Dollar (CAD)	7,966,240 1,305,042 434,432 788,769 188,860
Chicago	Chicago Mercantile Exchange (CME)	• Yen option • Mark 125,000 • GBP option	1,518,409 6,354,248 597,352
Amsterdam	European Options Exchange	• Guilder $10,000 option	537,892

Note: [a] Source: *Futures and Options World*, February 1993, p.56.

Table A1.5 Major interest rate options quoted on organized exchanges

Location	Exchange	Options contract	Jan–Dec 1992 vol.[a]
Chicago	Chicago Board of Trade (CBOT) Chicago Mercantile Exchange (CME)	• US T. bond option (15 yr) • US T. note option (10 yr) • Eurodollar (90d.) option (US$1m)	20,258,740 2,564,191 13,762,628
Paris	Marché à Terme International de France (Matif)	• 10 yr French gov. bond option • Pibor (90d.) option • Ecu bond option	10,047,391 2,000,034 82,820
London	London International Financial Futures Exchange (LIFFE)	• German Bund (6–10 yr) option • Euromark option • Italian bond option	2,749,670 1,964,405 395,354
Sydney	Sydney futures exchange (SFE)	• Aust. gov. bond (10 yr) option • Bank bills (90d.) option	745,994 610,458
Frankfurt	DTB	• German Bund option	498,324

Note: [a] Source: *Futures and Options World*, February 1993, p.56.

Table A1.6 Major stock indices contracts quoted on organized exchanges

Location	Exchange	Contract	Jan–Dec 1992 vol.[a]
Chicago	Chicago Board of Trade (CBOT)	• Major Market Index (MMI)	360,879
	Chicago Mercantile Exchange (CME)	• Standard and Poor 500 ($500)	12,414,157
Osaka	Osaka Securities Exchange	• NIKKEI 255 (Y1,000)	11,395,469
Paris	Marché à Terme International de France (Matif)	• CAC 40 (FFr200)	3,601,476
Frankfurt	DTB	• DAX (DM100)	3,271,055
Singapore	Singapore International Monetary Exchange (SIMEX)	• NIKKEI (Y500)	2,989,243
London	London International Financial Futures Exchange (LIFFE)	• FTSE 100 (£25)	2,618,629
New York	New York Futures Exchange	• NYSE composite Index $500	1,315,438

Note: [a] *Source: Futures and Options World*, February 1993, p.58.

Table A1.7 Major stock indices options contracts quoted on organized exchanges

Location	Exchange	Options contract	Jan–Dec 1992 vol.[a]
Chicago	Chicago Board Options Exchange (CBOE)	• Standard and Poor's 100 option • Standard and Poor's 500 option	62,427,272 13,420,174
	Chicago Mercantile Exchange (CME)	• Standard and Poor's 500 option	2,209,529
Frankfurt	DTB	• Dax option (DM10)	13,944,986
Paris	Marché d'Options Négociables de Paris (MONEP)	• CAC 40 option index FFr200 • CAC 40 long term option	3,170,782 547,495
Geneva	Swiss Options and Financial Futures Exchange (SOFFEX)	• Swiss market index option (SMI)	7,793,949
Stockholm	Stockholm Options Market (SOM)	• Swedish OMX index options	5,605,059
Amsterdam	European Options Exchange (EOE)	• EOE index option	2,452,238
Tokyo	Tokyo Stock Exchange (TSE)	• TOPIX option (Y10,000)	48,666

Note: [a] Source: *Futures and Options World*, February 1993, p.56.

Table A1.8 Contracts on the Paris financial futures and options exchanges

Exchange	Contract	Launching date	Jan–Dec 1992 vol.[a]
Marché à terme international de France (Matif)	**Interest rates financial futures**		
	• 10 yr French gov. bond (FFr500,000)	February 1986	31,002,844
	• 90d. French T. bill	June 1986	Quotations terminate in March 1989
	• Pibor (90d.)	Sept. 1988	6,430,780
	• EURODEM (90d.)	April 1989	Quotations discontinued in 1991
	• BTAN (4 yr)[b]	June 1989	
	• Ecu bond	Oct. 1990	1,354,012
	• Long term French franc	Jan. 1993	
	• Medium term French franc	June 1993	
	Stock indices contracts		
	• CAC 40 (FFr200)	Nov. 1988	3,601,476
	Options contracts		
	• 10 yr French gov. bond options	Jan. 1988	10,047,391
	• Pibor option (90d.)	March 1990	2,000,034
	• EURODEM option (90d.)	April 1990	–
	• Ecu bond option		82,820
Marché des options négociables de Paris (MONEP)	• CAC 40 option index	November 1988	3,170,782
	• CAC 40 long term option index	September 1987	547,495

Notes: [a] *Source: Futures and Options World*, February 1993, pp.56–58.
[b] Contract launched jointly by Matif SA and OM France Corp. on 1 June 1989.

ANNEX: A NOTE ON LEVERAGE

Exchange-traded instruments are subject to 'deposits', which generally represent 2 to 5 per cent of the nominal amounts. These 'deposits' allow dealers to use an instrument which has not been paid for in full. Gains or losses, corresponding to the variations of the instrument's value, are compared to the initial 'deposit': this constitutes the leverage of the instrument.

The leverage effect enables traders to take speculative positions, i.e. to keep open positions in anticipation of favourable rate developments.

Speculative positions are also possible with over-the-counter trades, such as FRA which require no initial 'deposit' or margin calls.

NOTES

1. Intraday transactions are also carried out on other financial instruments. See below, pp.285 and 289.
2. MONEP = Marché des Options Négociables sur Actions de Paris.

REFERENCES

Bank for International Settlements (1993), *Central Bank Survey of Foreign Exchange Market Activity in April 1992*, Basle, March.
Bordenave, Philippe (1990), 'L'inversion de la courbe des taux: une nouvelle habitude à prendre', *Revue Banque*, 505, May, 517.
Boulat, Pierre-Antoine and Chabert, Pierre-Yves (1992), *Les Swaps*. Masson, 1992.
Commission Bancaire (1991), *Le Risque Systémique*, presentation to the XIIIth Banque de France seminar, Nov.
Futures and Options World (1993), February issue.
Lefebvre, Francis (ed.) (1991), *Nouveaux Instruments Financiers*, Befec & Associés, Bureau Francis Lefebvre.
Matif S.A. (1992), annual report.
Option Finance (1992), March issue.
Option Finance, Dossiers et Fiches Pratiques (1989, 1990, 1991, 1992).
Wapler, Nicolas (1988), *Les Futurs*.

APPENDIX 2

THE ECU MARKETS AND THE EMS CRISIS

Taoufik Kharroubi

THE ECU BOND MARKET

Issues reduced to a trickle in the second half of 1992

During 1992, various issuers used the Ecu as the benchmark currency for their loan stock: 91 loans totalling 19.94 billion Ecu of which 22.8 per cent related to European institutions, 26.6 per cent to the public sector, 37.5 per cent to financial institutions and 13.1 per cent to industrial and commercial companies (source: Luxembourg Stock Exchange).

But the Danish 'no' vote to ratification of the Maastricht Treaty (June 1992) and uncertainties over the creation of European Monetary Union dissuaded the principal names from placing issues on the Ecu market during the second half of the year.

France did not complete its 1992 programme of Ecu issues which should have risen to some 15 per cent of total state loans. Only two *obligations assimilables du trésor* (OATs) were allocated for tender to a total value of 2,025bn Ecu (1,500m OAT April 2022 and 525m OAT March 2002). This position has been justified by the high level of interest rate spread between French Treasury loans denominated in Ecus and those denominated in francs, noted during the second half of 1992. During October, the UK postponed its issue of notes.

From the beginning of July, the lack of interest on the part of the institutional clients became obvious. The suspension of listings by market-makers in London from 23 July 1992 led to a virtual halt on the London market, to the profit of Paris where the SVT continued their activities with Ecu OATs, but within a declining market. The monetary crisis in September settled nothing, but rather aggravated the problems of liquidity. Dealing was nevertheless continued in benchmark stocks (OAT 9.5 per cent 2000, OAT 8.5 per cent 2002 and UK 9.125 per cent

2002) which were part of the basket of securities within the Matif Long-term Ecu contract.

The political uncertainties relating to ratification of the Maastricht Treaty by the UK and Denmark weighed heavily on the market, as did the position of Germany on the single European currency (a decision which would revert to Parliament even if the Treaty were adopted) and the shocks suffered by the European Monetary System during September.

A hesitant revival in the first quarter of 1993

After the uncertainties over the future of the EMS, which became evident during 1992, the Ecu bond market showed signs of revival during the first quarter of 1993. Now, in spite of the dangers which are still present regarding ratification of the Maastricht Treaty, investors are returning bit by bit to the Ecu market. This resumption of confidence has also led issuers to return to the Ecu bond markets – and loans for central government remain the most sought-after. The ten most popular bonds all total above 500m Ecu. They are generally the benchmark for maturity and so allow traders to deal across rate differentials on the most liquid stocks.

In view of this, the French Treasury issued 2.0bn Ecu of five-year BTAN at 7.51 per cent (the same rate as the franc BTAN benchmark) on 23 February 1993. Such a sizeable issue had not been effected on the market since 2 June 1992.

There are good reasons for believing that the new five-year Ecu benchmark is opening fresh opportunities for investors. This liquid issue, given top rating and support from the SVT bonds, represents an important stage in the development of the Ecu market. France is now the only country equipped with Ecu benchmark stocks across the majority of segments on the interest rate curve (5, 10 and 30 years). Moreover, given the instability of short-term rates, the Ecu basket has shown its economic usefulness. Exchange risks can be covered more easily with the Ecu than with other currencies which involve higher rates.

With short-term rates at a very high level, it became very costly for investors to maintain positions in component currencies. During what has come to be called the monetary crisis of autumn 1992, rates of the Ecu basket were kept at a lower average, which represented an important advantage in terms of the cost of porterage.

INSTRUMENTS DERIVED FROM ECU INTEREST RATES

The following forward markets in Europe and New York now offer Ecu contracts:

- Matif
- LIFFE
- FINEX

LIFFE (London's forward market) and Matif (the forward market in Paris) each offer interest rate risk management instruments denominated in Ecu. Paris also offers a futures option contract. Henceforth, the use of the Ecu on the derivative markets will be principally for long-term Ecu contracts.

The long-term Ecu contract: an instrument at the service of economic dealers

Since October 1990, Matif SA has made the long-term Ecu contract available on the bond market, an instrument which gives standardized coverage against the risk of interest rate variations. On average, nearly 1bn Ecu were processed daily between January and June 1992 with a record of 2bn on 4 June 1992 (19,514 lots). The forward market then experienced reduced activity, following on the slowdown in the primary and secondary market. At the worst point of the crisis, the contract performed its role of testing and price determination, so allowing dealers to make use of a particularly effective covering instrument.

A well arbitraged contract

The presence of dealers effecting arbitrage operations assures the economic dealers a balanced price reflecting the fundamental parameters from the underlying markets (a question of knowing the price of the bond, support for the contract and the short-term cost of money). A well arbitraged market takes account of the interactions between the spot market and the forward market and confirms the effective nature of the spread of information. A forward price which does not take account of all the information available in the market offers dealers risk-free profits (setting up cash and carry or reverse cash and carry operations).

Comparison of forward prices from a traditional arbitrage model with prices effectively seen in the market allows evaluation of continuing arbitrage opportunities. The forward price (adjusted by the similarity factor) ought to be equal to the underlying price (in this case, the OAT as the less expensive to deliver) increased by the cost of porterage and of a secondment of the possible coupon. The comparison between theoretical and real rates underlines the well arbitraged character of the long-term Ecu contract.

However, some discrepancies (of some 15 average basis points) appear, particularly during the SME's monetary crisis. The non-integration of costs does not explain this difference. A slight risk premium added to the short-term benchmark rate gives perfect adequacy between the issued prices of the arbitrage model and the rates seen in the market. The arbitrage profit chart allows us to determine support levels for forward contracts. The risk of changing to a bond which is less expensive to deliver is reduced. During the monetary crisis, different bonds were able to become contract supports. This might also explain the slight discrepancy described above. Arbitrages between different bonds appeared to be effective.

So the long-term Ecu forward contract is well arbitraged. Those involved in the Ecu markets maintain good transmission of information. This can be interpreted as a sign of the efficiency of the markets vis-à-vis Ecu interest rates.

THE FUTURE OF DERIVATIVE INSTRUMENTS DENOMINATED IN ECUS

The development of Ecu-denominated derivative instruments will depend on the progress of monetary union. Because of the growing number of paper issues denominated in Ecus, it seems that sovereign states will play a determinant role in their relations with investors. The Paris market benefits from strong political will concerning the Ecu market. Benchmark for the Ecu bond market, France is undertaking an ambitious programme of issues (15 per cent of total loans) on medium- (BTAN) and long-term maturities (OAT 6–30 years).

France has supported the market with its bonds denominated in Ecus by issuing, on several occasions, OATs to the profit of the *Fonds de soutien de rentes* (FSR). Created in 1937 and updated in 1986, the FSR has a particular status as a body. Its principal task is to intervene in the secondary market for public debt in order to guarantee the good standing of the state's signature compared with other borrowers and to bring liquidity to the market.

Bonds issued to the benefit of the FSR do not contribute towards the financing of the government budget since it cannot be the object of a closed sale. FSR dealings are the subject of loans/borrowings or of delivered pensions for short periods with selected compensation (essentially SVT). This confirms the commitment of the state in supporting paper already issued on the one hand and offers help (facilitating repo operations) on the other to the principal players in the public debt market.

The Paris market has developed – and launched at the start of May 1993 – a project called the Integrated System for Ecu Settlement (*Système intégré de règlements en Ecus*, SIRE). The purpose of this system is to facilitate the conclusion of settlement for bond transactions (securities and negotiable debt) denominated in Ecus. Thanks to the RELIT system within SICOVAM (the Paris securities payments centre) and to SATURNE within the Bank of France (payment of negotiable debt) the settlements system handles the simultaneous settlement of cash and the delivery of bonds and allows different dealings to be concluded the same day (settlement/delivery of bonds, transfer of cash between the payment parties and payment and international movement of bonds).

The Matif's three-month Ecu project might succeed in the same way. Its launch will depend on the expectations of the market and on short-term issues (Treasury bonds) from sovereign states (eg France, UK, Germany). In 1989, Matif SA joined the GLOBEX network – a 24-hour-a-day electronic quotation and negotiation system. By making use of the exclusivity of all the Ecu contracts on this network, Matif offers confirmation of its strategy in this area.

INDEX

absolute costs 254
adaptive error-learning model 67
  see also economic models
adjustable parities 113–14, 130–1
  see also parities
ADL *see* autoregressive distributed lag models
anonymous bearer certificates 283–4
arbitrage 302–3
Asian options 294
Austria 181–2
autoregressive distributed lag models 196, 197, 206
autoregressive processes:
  in economic projections 233, 24S
autonomous monetary policies 12
  see also monetary policies

Balassa-Samuelson effect 23
Balladur, Edouard 2
Bank of England 85–6, 87, 93, 96, 97, 199
Bank of Spain 15, 25
bank supervision 15
banking systems:
  Italy 7
  and Maastricht Treaty 15
  see also central banks
Banque de France 13, 15
Barrell, R.J. 237
Barro-Gordon reputation model 231
Basle-Nyborg agreement (1987) 12, 118, 120, 121, 122, 163
  revision of 153–8
bearer certificates 283–4
Belgium:
  and ERM 2, 149
  inflation 229, 233, 234, 235, 236
  interest rates 16
  labour market 274, 275

monetary policies 70
pay determination 7, 240, 241–2, 243, 244, 245
  see also Benelux countries
Benelux countries:
  and ERM 2, 12, 149
  see also Belgium; Netherlands
Bertola-Svensson test 69
Bishop, Graham 156–7
Bofinger, Peter 156–7
bond markets 283, 300–4
Bretton Woods systems 143, 144, 270
bribery and corruption 71
Britton, A.J.C. 85
budget deficits 12
budgetary centralization 275–7
  see also monetary policies
Bundesbank 12, 15, 88, 89, 96, 162, 180–1, 203
business cycles:
  and interest rates 190
Butler, Michael 87

call swaptions 293
Callaghan, James 84
capital controls 5, 184
capital inflow 22, 24–5
  see also investment
capital movements 199
  liberalization of 5, 12, 25, 68–9
caps *see* ceiling rates
Cassa Integrazione Guadagni (Italy) 61
causality tests:
  on interest rates 202
CBI *see* Confederation of British Industry
ceiling rates 292
central banks 8, 12, 15, 85–6, 178–9
  behaviour of 116
  Committee of Governors 120, 145
  cooperation between 162
  European System of 15, 142, 161

independence of 13, 15, 87, 161–2
and interest rates 190, 195, 201–4
  see also banking systems
Central Europe:
  and EMS 2, 103–9
centralized pay determination 252–8
  see also pay determination
certificates of deposit 283
CIG *see* Cassa Integrazione Guadagni
Clarke, Kenneth 98
classical Asian options 294
cointegration techniques:
  in economic models 2–8, 209, 224, 232
collars 292
Commission Bancaire (France) 15
Committee of Governors of the Central Banks 120, 145
Common Agricultural Policy 182
comparative cost advantages 254
competitiveness *see* economic competitiveness
composite options 293
Confederation of British Industry 86, 89
consumer price index *see* CPI
consumer prices 69–70, 90, 230, 233
  see also prices
contagion:
  in ERM 175–81
convergence:
  and EMS 275
  in EMU 269–79
  nominal 269–71
  real 271–8
convergence targets 4, 12, 99–100
  see also ERM
cooperation *see* monetary cooperation

corruption *see* bribery and corruption
costs:
  absolute 254
  comparative 254
  labour 62, 63, 73, 90–1, 174
  non-wage labour 6, 246–8
  production 254
counter-inflationary methods 231–3
  see also inflation
CPI:
  Portugal 34–5
  Spain 18–19, 21
crawling-peg exchange rate 33–4, 233
  see also exchange rates
credibility effects:
  of EMS 67–9, 147
crisis mentality theory 116
currency crises *see* monetary crises
currency futures 284
currency options 291, 295
currency swaps 288
currency unions 262–7
  see also EMU
current account deficits:
  Spain 25

data generating process 195, 204–5
  see also economic models
decentralized pay determination 252–8
  see also pay determination
Delors, Jacques 5
Delors Report (1989) 88, 148, 158, 160
Denmark:
  and EMS 11
  and ERM 2, 12, 49, 95, 142, 149–50
dependent economy model 21–2, 23
  see also economic models
deposits 282, 299
  see also foreign exchange markets
deregulated financial markets 97
  see also financial markets
derivative instruments 292–3
  Ecu denominations 33–4
Deutsche Bundesbank *see* Bundesbank
the deutschmark *see* Germany

devaluation 116–17, 124–6, 131–2
  France 13
  Ireland 1, 3, 41, 45, 49–55
  Italy 4
  Portugal 1, 3
  Spain 1, 2–3, 4, 20, 29
  United Kingdom 4, 94
Dickey-Fuller tests 208
direct bargaining:
  and pay determination 27
domestic demand:
  Portugal 33
  Spain 23–4
domestic interest rates *see* individual countries
domestic traded goods 21, 34, 70
  see also traded goods
'dry' governments 176–7
Duisenberg, Wim 145, 164
Durbin-Watson statistic 210

Eastern Europe:
  and EMS 2, 103–9
Ecofin Council 96, 98, 154, 164
economic activity 191, 201–4
  general equilibrium 252–8
  regional economics 253, 254, 271–2, 276–7
economic competitiveness 146, 171–3, 175, 177–8, 252–8, 260–2
economic crises *see* monetary crises
economic models 91
  adaptive error-learning 67
  autoregressive distributed lag 196, 197, 206
  Barro-Gordon reputation 231
  cointegration techniques 208, 209, 224, 232
  data generating process 195, 204–5
  dependent 21–2, 23
  error correction 197–8, 204–16
  escape-clause 116
  of exchange rates 56–8, 176–7
  general-to-specific 205
  of inflation 231–2
  of interest rates 56–8, 190, 195–8
  monetary policy games 116
  of parity changes 114–19

projection-equation technique 116–19
  static long-run solutions 206–8
  variables in 204, 205–6, 223
Economic and Monetary Union *see* EMU
economic stabilization 103–9
economic variables 195–6
the Ecu 5–6, 8, 184–8
  creation of 184
  currency composition 185–7, 188
  derivative instruments 303–4
  exchange rate of 185–7, 188
  hard Ecu project 6, 88
  private market 8, 17, 88
  problems of 184–8
Ecu bond market 300–4
Ecu interest rates 301–3
Ecu zone:
  creation of 104–7
Ecu zone Exchange Rate Mechanism 106–7
Ecu zone Stabilization Fund 105–6
Ecu zone Surveillance Board 104–5
elections:
  France (1993) 13–14
  Ireland (1993) 51
  United Kingdom (1979) 84–5
EMI *see* European Monetary Institute
employment *see* labour market
EMS:
  benefits of 227
  and Central Europe 2, 103–9
  creation of 143, 167, 179–8
  credibility effects 67–9, 147
  crises in 11–17, 166–71, 300–4
  and Denmark 11
  and Eastern Europe 2, 103–9
  Ecu zone 104–7
  and EMU 141–65
  enlargement of 2
  and ERM 16–17
  fluctuation margins 148–53
  and France 120, 122–8, 132, 134, 175

INDEX

future of 16–17, 181–3
and German unification 166, 168, 171, 174–5, 262–6
and Germany 145–6
and inflation 227, 229–49
and institutional coordination 118, 237
and Italy 61–83, 120–8, 131, 133
and labour markets 227–49
and pay determination 236–44, 262–7
reactions to 1
and real convergence 275
and realignment expectations 113–40, 158–9, 167–8, 194
and Spain 175
structure of 167–8
success of 1
target zone 117–18, 144–7
and United Kingdom 87–8, 145–6
EMU:
Basle-Nyborg agreement (1987) 12, 118, 120, 121, 122, 153–8, 163
benefits of 144
commitment to 3–4
convergence in 269–79
and EMS 141–65
and labour market 6–8
and Maastricht Treaty 141–2, 177, 181–2
and monetary crises 141
problems of 1, 3, 146
public opinion of 141–2
reform of 142–59, 162–3
transition to 11–12, 15, 16–17, 20, 87, 103, 141–65
and unemployment 3, 6, 7–8
energy supplies 86–7
England *see* United Kingdom
ERM:
and Belgium 2, 149
and Benelux countries 2, 12, 149
contagion in 175–81
convergence targets 4, 12, 99–100
crises in 1–2, 11–17, 49–50, 95
and Denmark 2, 12, 49, 95, 142, 149–50
and EMS 16–17

and France 1, 2, 4, 11–17, 149, 150
and Germany 2, 142
and Greece 2
and Ireland 1, 3, 12, 39–60, 149–50
and Italy 1–2, 3–4, 12, 16, 76, 150–1
and Maastricht Treaty 2, 4, 12, 176–81
and Netherlands 149
and Portugal 1, 3, 33–8, 151–3
reactions to 2
reform of 5
and Spain 1, 2–3, 18–32, 151, 152–3
and United Kingdom 2, 3–4, 12, 16, 84–103, 142, 143, 146–7, 151–2
error correction models 197–8, 204–16
escape-clause models 116
the escudo *see* Portugal
Europe *see* Central Europe; Eastern Europe; Single European Market
European Central Bank 15, 105
European Community:
and Central Eastern Europe 103–9
and United States 143
European Community Commission 5
One Market, One Money 1
European Community Monetary Committee *see* Ecofin Committee
European Council 142, 150
European Court of Justice 99
European Monetary Institute 5, 8, 17, 142, 157–8, 161, 181
European Monetary System *see* EMS
European Monetary Union *see* EMU
European Policy Forum 93
European System of Central Banks 15, 142, 161
exercise prices 289–90
exchange rate calculations 90
exchange rate convergence *see* convergence targets
exchange rate equilibrium 28
fundamental 91–2
Exchange Rate Mechanism *see* ERM

exchange rate stabilization 12, 114, 130, 135, 143–4, 162
exchange rates:
control of 182
crawling-peg 33–4, 233
of Ecu 185–7, 188
in Ecu zone 106–7
expected changes in 81
FEER 91–2
fixed 12, 114, 157, 251, 255–6
fixed but adjustable 11–12, 113–14
floating 16, 142–4
fluctuations 13
Ireland 41–3, 44, 45–8, 56–8
Italy 61, 63, 65–7
models of 56–8, 176–7
Portugal 34, 35–8
setting of 254
Spain 18–26, 28–30
United Kingdom 85–6, 87, 89–90, 91–2, 97
external debts:
Ireland 52, 53–4
extinguishable options 294
EZSB *see* Ecu zone Surveillance Board

FEER *see* fundamental exchange rate equilibrium
Feldstein, Martin 143, 144
financial futures 285–6, 298
financial markets:
deregulated 97
see also foreign exchange markets
Finland 181–2
fiscal policies *see* monetary policies
the Fisher effect 191–2
fixed but adjustable exchange rates 11–12, 113–14
see also exchange rates
fixed cost realignment 117
see also realignment expectations
fixed exchange rates 12, 114, 157, 251, 255–6
see also exchange rates
flexible exchange rates *see* floating exchange rates
floating exchange rates 16, 142–4
see also exchange rates
floors 292

fluctuation band *see* target zone
fluctuation margins 148-53
  see also EMS
Fonds de soutien de rentes 303
foreign exchange markets 281-99
  and capital controls 5
  crises in 11
  deposits 282, 299
  deregulated financial 97
  financial futures 284-9, 298
  forward 282-3, 301-2
  options 289
  physical markets 281-4
  securities 283-4
  spot 282
foreign exchange options *see* currency options
foreign exchange reserves 105
foreign exchange swaps 288-9
foreign interest rates 192
  see also interest rates
foreign support:
  for national interest rates 178, 179-81
foreign trade 105-6
  France 13
  free 254
  Ireland 52
  non-traded goods 20-1, 23-4, 26
  Portugal 33-4
  Spain 23-4, 26
  theory of 253-5
  trade flows 254
  traded goods 20-1, 22, 23-4, 256-8
forward foreign exchanges 282-3, 301-2
forward rate agreements 285
the franc *see* France
France:
  devaluation 13
  and EMS 120, 122-8, 132, 134, 175
  and ERM 1, 2, 4, 11-17, 149, 150
  foreign trade 13
  general election (1993) 13-14
  and Germany 12, 15, 181
  inflation 13, 229, 233, 234
  interest rates 2, 14, 16, 189, 199, 200, 202, 212-13, 218, 220

monetary policies 15-16, 203-4
pay determination 240-1, 245
pay policies 13
political problems 2, 4
risk premia 12, 13, 15, 16
under Balladur 2
unemployment 13
free trade 254
  see also foreign trade
FSR *see Fonds de soutien de rentes*
fundamental exchange rate equilibrium 91-2
  see also exchange rate equilibrium
future rate agreements 285

GDP:
  Ireland 47-8, 53-4
  Italy 65-6, 71
  Portugal 33
  Spain 23
general equilibrium economics 252-8
  see also economic activity
generalized Asian options 294
general-to-specific models 205
German leadership model:
  of inflation reduction 231, 236
German unification 7, 12
  currency union 250, 264-6
  effects of 168, 174-5
  and EMS 166, 168, 171, 174-5, 262-6
  and labour markets 262-6
  and monetary policies 275-7
  and pay levels 250, 262-6
Germany:
  economic problems 12
  and EMS 145-6
  and ERM 2, 142
  and France 12, 15, 81
  inflation 229, 233-6
  interest rates 2, 12, 14, 16, 17, 189, 190, 198, 199-200, 202, 210-11, 218, 219
  and Ireland 46-7
  labour costs 90-1, 174
  labour mobility 276-7
  monetary policies 203-4
  pay determination 240, 245
  unemployment 263

and United Kingdom 85, 87, 90-1, 94, 98
GLOBEX network 304
Granger-causality tests 217-18
Granger's representation theorem 209
Great Britain *see* United Kingdom
Greece:
  and ERM 2
gross domestic product *see* GDP

Hannan-Quinn criterion 210
hard core countries 12
hard Ecu project 6, 88
  see also the Ecu
health and safety standards 7
Heckscher-Ohlin theorem 254
honeymoon effect 117, 149
Howe, Geoffrey 87

Iberian currencies *see* Portugal; Spain
IGC *see* Intergovernmental Conference (1990)
IMF *see* International Monetary Fund
immobile labour 258-60, 263
  see also labour markets
incomes *see* pay
inconsistency triangle 12
individual floating *see* floating exchange rates
indivisibility principle:
  of monetary policies 160-2
industrial goods 21-2, 23, 54
industry:
  investment in 202-3
  production costs 254
inflation 144, 171
  Belgium 229, 234, 235, 236
  causes of 203
  counter-inflation 231-3
  and EMS 227, 229-49
  France 13, 229, 233, 234
  Germany 229, 233-6
  and interest rates 6
  Ireland 41, 43, 232
  Italy 61, 63, 229, 233, 234
  models of 231-2
  Netherlands 229, 235
  Portugal 3, 35
  and public expenditure 69-76, 178
  ranking-by-characteristics 246

INDEX

Spain 2, 18–20, 25
  and unemployment 67–8, 237–9
  United Kingdom 4, 85–6, 89–90, 92–5, 97–8, 100, 229
inflation differentials 63
inflation expectations 233–6
inflation inertia 23
inflationary expectations 191–2
institutional coordination: in EMS 118, 237
interest rate cuts 94
interest rate differentials 128–9
interest rate futures 284
interest rate models 56–8, 190, 195–8
interest rate options 291
interest rate parities 114–15
  uncovered 193–4
  see also parities
interest rate realignment 194
interest rate swaps 286–8
interest rates 295
  Belgium 16
  and business cycles 190
  causality tests 202
  and central banks 190, 195, 201–4
  foreign support for 178, 179–81
  France 2, 14, 16, 189, 199, 200, 202, 212–13, 218, 220
  Germany 2, 12, 14, 16, 17, 189, 190, 198, 199–200, 202, 210–11, 218, 219
  Ireland 46–7, 54–5
  Italy 198, 199, 200, 213–14, 218, 221
  levels of 178–81
  long-term 2, 6, 14, 46, 189–226
  Netherlands 16, 198, 199–200, 211–12, 218, 220
  short-term 2, 6, 14, 46–7, 189–90, 191–8
  Spain 24, 189, 199, 201, 216, 218, 221
  Sweden 178
  term structure 190, 202
  United Kingdom 6, 94, 146–7, 189, 198, 199, 201, 202, 214–15, 218, 221
Inter-Governmental Conference (1990) 88

International Monetary Fund 89, 105, 145
international trade *see* foreign trade
intraday deposits 282
investment:
  capital inflow 22, 24–5
  in industry 202–3
  in Italy 61–2
  in Portugal 34
  in Spain 23–4, 28
Ireland:
  devaluation 1, 3, 41, 45, 49–55
  economic structure 43, 45, 47–8, 54
  election (1993) 51
  and ERM 1, 3, 12, 39–60, 149–50
  exchange rates 41–3, 44, 45–8, 55–6
  external debts 52, 53–4
  foreign trade 52
  GDP 47–8, 53–4
  and Germany 46–7
  historical background 39–41
  industrial goods 54
  inflation 41, 43, 232
  interest rates 46–7, 54–5
  labour market 54
  sterling link 39–41, 45, 46–7
  taxation 48
  unemployment 3, 43, 48
  and United Kingdom 3, 39–41, 45, 46–7, 54–5
Irish pound *see* Ireland
Italy:
  banking system 70
  devaluation 1–2, 4
  domestic policies 3
  economic structure 61–7, 76–80
  and EMS 61–83, 120–8, 131, 133
  and ERM 1–2, 3–4, 12, 16, 76, 150–1
  exchange rates 61, 63, 65–7
  GDP 65–6, 71
  inflation 61, 63, 229, 233, 234
  interest rates 198, 199, 200, 213–14, 218–21
  investment in 61–2
  labour market 61–2, 67–8, 75–7, 79
  labour mobility 276–7
  monetary policies 61–2

pay determination 242, 245
pay policies 3, 4, 61, 62–5, 67–8, 76
pay levels 63–4, 67–8, 70–1, 72–3, 74, 78
productivity 61, 63, 65, 76–7
public expenditure 4, 62–3, 69–76, 77, 79, 81
public sector borrowing 71
social welfare 71, 73, 75
taxation 71–2, 75
unemployment 61–2, 66–8, 75

Japan 247, 248
job losses *see* unemployment
Johansen tests 209

Keynesian economics 233, 260–1
Krugman, Paul 177

labour costs 62, 63, 73, 90–1
  non-wage 6, 246–8
  Germany 90–1, 174
labour market flexibility 273–4
labour markets:
  Belgium 274, 275
  differences in 250–62
  and EMS 227–49
  and EMU 6–8
  flexibility of 7
  France 13
  and German unification 262–6
  immobile labour 258–60, 263
  Ireland 54
  Italy 61–2, 66–8, 75–7, 79
  job losses 61
  non-competitive 22
  public sector employment 61
  rigid 275
  Spain 20, 26–7, 30
  strike action 27
  temporary contracts 26–7
  trade unions 27
  United Kingdom 6
  working hours 7
  see also unemployment
labour mobility 253, 263, 276–7
labour productivity *see* productivity levels
Lamfalussy, Alexandre 158

Lamont, Norman 92, 93, 94–5, 96–8
Lawson, Nigel 4, 86–8, 89
Layard analysis 7
Leigh-Pemberton, R. 93, 97, 99
leverage 299
liberalization:
  of capital movements 5, 12, 25, 68–9
limited risks 291
living standards 72–3
London School of Economics see LSE approach models
long-term interest rates 6, 189–226
  France 2
  Germany 2
  Ireland 46
  relation to short-term 190, 191–201
  see also interest rates
look-back options 293
Louvre Agreement (1987) 86
LSE approach models:
  of interest rates 7, 195, 196, 204–9
Lucas critique 232
Luxembourg see Benelux countries

Major, John 89, 166
market penetration 12, 257–8
market segmentation 192–5
Matif SA 302, 304
models see economic models
monetary asymmetry 12
monetary cooperation 12, 15
monetary crises 116–17
  and EMS 1–2, 11–17, 49–50
  and EMU 141
monetary policies 260–2
  autonomous 12
  Belgium 70
  budgetary centralization 275–7
  coordination of 261–2
  France 15–16, 23–4
  and German unification 275–7
  Germany 203–4
  indivisibility principle 160–2
  Italy 61–2
  national 4, 12, 142–3, 144–5
  Portugal 33, 37–8
  pragmatic 204

  and real convergence 275–7
  rules of 144–5
  Spain 20, 25
  and stabilization 114
  United Kingdom 4, 93
monetary policy games 116
monetary speculation 135, 154, 281–99
monetary targeting 204
monetary transmission 190–1
monetary union see EMU
money stocks 192
multinational corporations see transnational corporations

NAIRU 7
  see also unemployment
national monetary policies 4, 12, 142–3, 144–5
  see also monetary policies
negotiable medium-term notes 283–4
negotiable securities 284
Netherlands 145
  and ERM 149
  inflation 229, 235
  interest rates 16, 198, 199–200, 211–12, 218, 220
  pay determination 243, 244
nominal convergence:
  in EMS 269–71
  see also convergence
non-accelerating inflation rate of unemployment see NAIRU
non-competitive labour markets 22
  see also labour markets
non-traded goods 20–1, 23–4, 26
  see also foreign trade
non-wage labour costs 6, 246–8
  see also labour costs

OATs see obligations assimilables du trésor
obligations assimilables du trésor 300–1
Obstfeld, Maurice 176–7
OCA see optimal currency areas
oil prices 33, 61, 86–7
One Market, One Money (EC) 1

optimal currency areas 271–2, 273–4
option contracts 289–94, 297
  on shares 292
  on stock indices 292
overnight deposits 282
overvaluations 11–12

parities:
  adjustable 113–14, 130–1
  deviations from 117–18
  expectations of 113–40
  of interest rates 114–15
  measurement of 114–28
  purchasing power 21
  variables in 116–19
pay determination 27, 67, 76
  Belgium 240, 241–2, 243, 244, 245
  centralized 252–8
  decentralized 252–8
  effects of 256–8
  and EMS 236–44, 262–7
  France 240–1, 245
  Germany 240, 245
  Italy 242, 245
  Netherlands 243, 244
pay levels 7, 227–8
  and German unification 262–6
  Germany 250
  Italy 63–4, 67–8, 70–1, 72–3, 74, 78
  Portugal 36–7
  public sector 27, 70–1
  Spain 25–6, 27
  Visco equation 67–8
pay policies 6–7
  convergence of 7
  differences in 7
  Italy 3, 4, 61, 62–5, 67–8, 76
  Belgium 7
  France 13
pay restraint 250–1
pension systems 62
periphery countries 12
the peseta see Spain
Phillips curve mechanism 231, 232–3, 236
Plaza Agreement (1985) 86
population migration 75
Portugal:
  CPI 34–5
  devaluation 1, 3
  domestic demand 33
  economic structure 34, 35–8
  and ERM 1, 3, 33–8, 151–3
  exchange rates 34, 35–8

INDEX

foreign trade 33–4
GDP 33
inflation 3, 35
investment in 34
labour market 3, 34–5
monetary policies 33, 37–8
pay levels 36–7
pay policies 34
public sector borrowing 36, 38
recession 33
and Spain 33
unemployment 33
the pound *see* United Kingdom
PPP *see* purchasing power parity
pragmatic monetarism 204
see also monetary policies
price expectations 67
price stability 251
prices 63–5, 255–6
consumer 69–70, 90, 230, 233
CPI 19–20, 21
domestic goods 34, 70
industrial goods 21–2
RPI 90, 92
of services 21–2, 70
private Ecu market 8, 17, 88
see also the Ecu
production costs 254
productivity agreements 27
productivity levels:
improvements in 255–8
Italy 61, 63, 65, 76–7
Spain 22, 23–4
projection-equation technique:
of economic models 116–19
public consumption:
Spain 23–4
public expectations:
of realignment 116–17
public expenditure:
and inflation 69–76, 178
Italy 4, 62–3, 69–76, 77, 79, 81
public opinion:
of EMU 141–2
public procurement 71
public sector borrowing:
Italy 71
Portugal 36, 38
United Kingdom 100
public sector employment:
Italy 61
see also labour market
public sector pay:

Italy 3, 70–1
Spain 27
see also pay levels; pay policies
purchasing power parity 21

ranking-by-characteristics:
of inflationary shocks 246
real convergence:
in EMU 271–8
see also convergence
realignment expectations:
of EMS 5, 113–40, 158–9, 167–8
fixed costs of 117
of interest rates 194
measurement of 114–28
negative 135
public expectations of 116–17
variables in 116–19, 129–30
recession:
United Kingdom 92–5
regional economics 253, 254, 271–2, 276–7
see also economic activity
RELIT system 303
repurchase obligations 283
retail price index:
United Kingdom 90, 92
risk characteristics 192–3
risk premia:
France 12, 13, 15, 16
risks:
degrees of 291
limited 291
RPI *see* retail price index

sacrifice ratios:
of non-wage labour costs 246–8
safety *see* health and safety standards
SATURNE system 303
Schlesinger, Helmut 180, 181
Schumpeter, Joseph 103
Schwarz criterion 210
securities markets 283–4
self-fulfilling attacks 175–81
containing of 178–81
service industries 21–2, 23, 70
shares 283
short-term interest rates 6, 189–90
foreign 192
France 2
Ireland 46–7

relation to long-term 190, 191–201
see also interest rates
Single European Market 4, 182, 194–5
SIRE *see* Système intégré de règlements en Ecus
Smithsonian Agreement (1971) 148
the snake 145
Social Chapter 7
social security 7, 61–2, 71
social welfare:
Italy 71, 73, 75
soft buffers 145
Spain:
CPI 18–19, 21
current account deficit 25
devaluation 1, 2–3, 4, 20, 29
domestic demand 23–4
domestic policies 2
economic structure 22–3
and EMS 175
and ERM 1, 2–3, 18–32, 151, 152–3
exchange rates 18–26, 28–30
foreign trade 23–4, 26
GDP 23
inflation 2, 18–20, 25
interest rates 24, 189, 198, 199, 201, 216, 218, 221
investment in 23–4, 28
labour market 20, 26–7, 30
and Maastricht Treaty 15
monetary policies 20, 25
pay levels 25–6, 27
pay policies 3, 20, 25–6, 27
peseta sustainability 28–9
and Portugal 33
productivity levels 22, 23–4
public consumption 23–4
unemployment 2–3, 26–7
speculation *see* monetary speculation
spot foreign exchanges 282
spread of interest rates *see* term structure
stabilization:
of exchange rates 12, 114, 130, 135, 143–4, 162
and monetary policies 114
standard of living *see* living standards
static long-run solutions:
to economic models 206–8
sterilization practices 157–8

INDEX

stock market indices futures 285, 296
strike action 27
  see also labour market
Svensson, L.E.O. 139
swaps 286–9
swaptions 293
Sweden 181–2
  interest rates 178
Système intégré de règlements en Ecus 303

tangible capital 254
target zone:
  of EMS 117–18, 120, 144–7
  fluctuation margins 148–53
taxation 258–60
  Ireland 48
  Italy 71–2, 75
temporary contracts:
  and labour market 26–7
term structure:
  of interest rates 190, 202
Thatcher, Margaret 4, 84–8, 89, 93
time-inconsistency 100
trade flows 254
  see also foreign trade
trade unions 27
  see also labour market
traded goods 20–1, 22, 23–4, 256–8
  domestic 21, 34
  foreign 21
  see also foreign trade
transnational companies 54
treasury bills and bonds 283
tunnels *see* collars

UIP *see* uncovered interest parity

UK *see* United Kingdom
uncovered interest parity 193–4
  see also interest rates
unemployment 170, 175
  and EMU 3, 6, 7–8
  France 13
  Germany 263
  and inflation 67–8, 237–9
  Ireland 3, 43, 48
  Italy 61–2, 66–8, 75
  Portugal 33
  rises in 237
  Spain 2–3, 26–7
  United Kingdom 98
  of young people 13
  see also labour markets
unemployment compensation 61
United Kingdom:
  devaluation 4, 94
  domestic policies 4, 85, 100
  and EMS 87–8, 145–6
  and ERM 2, 3–4, 12, 16, 84–102, 142, 143, 146–7, 151–2
  exchange rates 85–6, 87, 89–90, 91–2, 97
  general election (1979) 84–5
  and Germany 85, 87, 90–1, 94, 98
  inflation 4, 85–6, 89–90, 92–5, 97–8, 100, 229
  interest rates 6, 94, 146–7, 189, 198, 199, 201, 202, 214–15, 218, 221
  and Ireland 3, 39–41, 45, 46–7, 54–5
  labour costs 90–1

labour market 6
and Maastricht Treaty 95, 98–9
monetary policies 4, 86–8, 93, 97–100
opposition to ERM 84–8
pay policies 6–7, 93
public sector borrowing 100
recession 89, 92–5
return to ERM 97–100
suspended ERM membership 95–7
under Callaghan 84
under Major 89
under Thatcher 4, 84–8, 89, 93
unemployment 98

very short term financing facilities 96, 153
Visco equation for wages 67–8

wage negotiations *see* pay determination
wages *see* pay
Walters, Sir Alan 4, 85, 86, 87–8
Walters critique 87–8
welfare *see* social welfare
welfare economics 254
'wet' governments 176–7
Wicksell's theory 223
Williamson, John 91, 144–5, 163
working hours 7
  see also labour market

young people:
  unemployment 13